T0325275

A. CLEVELAND HARRISON

A Little Rock Boyhood:

GROWING UP IN
THE GREAT DEPRESSION

BUTLER
CENTER

BOOKS

Little Rock, Arkansas

BUTLER
CENTER **butlercenterbooks.org**

The Butler Center for Arkansas Studies
Central Arkansas Library System
100 Rock Street
Little Rock, AR 72201

BOOKS

First edition: April 2010

ISBN: 978-1-935106-18-0
      10-digit 1-935106-18-x

12 11 10 9 8 7 6 5 4 3 2 1

PROJECT MANAGER: Rod Lorenzen
COPYEDITOR: Ali Welky
BOOK DESIGN: Wendell E. Hall
PAGE COMPOSITION: Shelly Culbertson
PROOFREADER: Annie Stricklin

Funding for this book was provided, in part, by the Pulaski County Historical Society, P. O. Box 251903, Little Rock, AR 72225, www.pulaskicountyarkhistory.org.

All images contained in this book were provided from the personal collection of the author unless otherwise noted.

Library of Congress Cataloging-in-Publication Data

Harrison, A. Cleveland.
 A Little Rock boyhood : growing up in the Great Depression / A. Cleveland Harrison. -- 1st ed.
   p. cm.
 ISBN 978-1-935106-18-0 (hard cover : alk. paper)
 1. Harrison, A. Cleveland--Childhood and youth. 2. Little Rock (Ark.)--Biography. 3. Little Rock (Ark.)--Social life and customs--20th century. 4. City and town life--Arkansas--Little Rock--History--20th century. 5. Depressions--1929--Arkansas--Little Rock. 6. Little Rock (Ark.)--History--20th century. 7. Little Rock (Ark.)--Social conditions--20th century. I. Title.

F419.L7H38 2010
976.7'73053092--dc22
[B]

2010000459

Printed in the United States of America

This book is printed on archival-quality paper that meets requirements of the American National Standard for Information Sciences, Permanence of Paper, Printed Library Materials, ANSI Z39.48-1984.

TO THE LOVES OF MY LIFE

Tumpy, Kathleen, and Lee

IN REMEMBRANCE OF

my caring mother, Floy Estelle Harrison (née Honea)
1895-1981

forbearing father, Allie Harrison
1892-1958

incorrigible brother, James Franklin Harrison
1911-1968

The Harrison family before Cleveland's arrival.

Acknowledgments

MANY PEOPLE encouraged my writing: Martha Williamson Rimmer and Timothy Nutt, former editors of the *Pulaski County Historical Review*, who published my first reminiscences; Craig Gill and Stephen Yates of the University Press of Mississippi, who supported my first memoir; Jerome Klinkowitz, who first praised my professional writing; the late Don Harington, who gave impetus to the publication of this memoir; and Kathleen Gammill, Florence Adams Albright, and Linda Bell, dear friends, all of whom lent their expertise, encouragement, technical help, and advice. I am eternally grateful to Ali Welky, my friendly but meticulous editor, for her careful, imaginative edit. Also, I would like to thank the Pulaski County Historical Society for its assistance in publishing this book.

Portions of this book, in altered form, appeared in *The Pulaski County (Arkansas) Historical Review* and *Unsung Valor: A GI's Story of World War II*

Cleveland, his mother, and Grandpa Honea.

Contents

Deciding to remember, and what to remember,
is how we decide who we are.

ROBERT PINSKY
"Poetry and American Memory"

Those into whose lives you are born do not pass away.
You bear them with you, as you hope to be borne by
those who come after you.

J. M. COETZEE
"The Blow"

How they do live on, those giants of our childhood,
and how well they manage to take even death in their stride
because although death can put an end to them right enough,
it can never put an end to our relationship with them.
… They live still in us … The people we loved.
The people who loved us. The people who, for good
or ill, taught us things.

FREDERICK BUECHNER
The Sacred Journey

Preface

MY MEMORIES of growing up in Little Rock became more persistent after my retirement. Without provocation, vivid details emerged in my mind of our family's life during the Great Depression, before World War II halted the unbroken routines of the city and a massive tide of postwar change swept away long-remembered landmarks. I believe these unbidden recollections of our family's modest lives in six different neighborhoods in Little Rock and Warren, between 1927 and 1943, are an integral part of Arkansas's cultural history of the Great Depression.

So, based upon my personal experiences and those recounted by my parents and relatives, I have written of my childhood and youth, attempting to tell my story in the changing voice of the growing boy I was, avoiding as much as possible adult nostalgia, sentimentality, and the ironies of hindsight, and keeping the invented dialogues faithful to the personalities and circumstances involved. Only a few names have been changed, to protect certain people and their families from any possible embarrassment.

Even though the times, places, and families that blessed my life are gone, never to be known again, it would be a mistake to mourn their loss; there is no consolation for certain changes, separations, and endings in our lives. However, there is a measure of solace in resurrecting the all-but-forgotten, but fulfilling, period that I spent in Little Rock, Arkansas, before World War II, when our family was neither rich nor poor but Depression-shadowed, a period in my life I embrace and love. At least, that's my justification for recording these remembrances.

Time, Place, and Family

Because I know that time is always time
And place is always and only place
And what is actual is actual only for one time
And only for one place.

　　　　　　　　　— T. S. Eliot
　　　　　　　　　"Ash Wednesday"

THE TIME

When women and men of my generation speak of "the old times" or "the old days," we are gazing back across an expanse of time and landscape that includes the Great Depression and World War II, two of the major historical and political catastrophes of the twentieth century that affected every American family and broke many lives and hearts. Nevertheless, those disasters, as history proves, brought positive changes to our nation and its citizens.

But even before the Great Depression and World War II, the storied prosperity of the United States had bypassed Arkansas. In 1924, the year of my birth, most Arkansawyers lived out in the country. The majority lived on farms, with two-thirds of them working someone else's land, raising cotton on more than half the state's tillable acreage. The number of those in clerical and managerial white-collar jobs in cities and towns was small, and, even by 1930, less than one-tenth of Arkansas's population worked in wholesale and retail trades, like my father did. Fewer than five percent of the state's workforce were professionals.

Arkansas's economy depended upon King Cotton, its chief commodity. Though the price of cotton crested in 1919, its precipitous tumble began the same year. Even as the state produced impressive amounts of cotton, corn, rice, lumber, livestock, and fruits, Arkansas's overall economy declined. For before the crash on Wall Street, Arkansas had suffered floods, droughts, failing crops, tornadoes, race riots, and bankruptcies. The Great Depression merely worsened trends already underway across the state.

THE PLACE

Yet my youthful memories of Arkansas in those days don't seem as harsh as the historical facts suggest. Those of us growing up in Little Rock dwelled in a city blending small-town values with the culture and opportunities of the state's political, economic, and educational center. Our lives were not as circumscribed as those of Arkansawyers living in the narrow grooves and confined spaces of the state's smaller towns and villages.

Even though Little Rock's population was less than 100,000 throughout the 1920s and 1930s, the city equaled, in most respects, much larger cities of the United States, and it possessed every modern municipal convenience: electric power, natural gas, water works, a sanitation system, public transportation, telephone service, and contemporary public buildings. Many homes in the city's old and new subdivisions exemplified classic and contemporary architectural designs. The public school system, to the benefit of both white and black youth, absorbed the best in American educational trends, boasting up-to-date curricula administered and instructed by teachers holding college degrees. Graduates of Little Rock Senior High School and Dunbar Senior High School, no matter where they went or what they did thereafter, bore a strength of mind and character shaped in part by the Little Rock public schools during the scarcities of hard times.

The Great Depression, from 1929 until the late 1930s, appeared to be an endless economic crisis that the New Deal measures of President Franklin D. Roosevelt and the American Congress could not resolve. Only World War II, beginning in Europe in 1939, prompted the beginning of our economic recovery in the sixth year of the New Deal and nearly a decade into the Great Depression.

Less than three years after the war began in Europe, in December 1941, Japan attacked Pearl Harbor. A year later, my generation of adolescent males assumed adult responsibilities when Congress lowered the draft age to eighteen. Though not old enough to vote in local, state, and national elections, boys were old enough to serve in the military services, fighting the Japanese and Germans. Our service challenged our lives, changed our worlds, and altered our individual ambitions and hopes for the future.

THE FAMILY

My parents married in 1911 in Beebe, when Allie was nineteen and Floy sixteen; their son, James Franklin, was born ten months later. They remained in Beebe until the United States entered World War I, in April 1917, and men between twenty-one and thirty were required to register for the draft. Allie and two younger brothers had physical examinations in Little Rock; both his brothers were inducted, but Allie, whose right foot had been maimed in a logging accident, was rejected.

Quiet but patriotic, Allie chose to serve his country the best he could by applying for work at Camp Pike, the military cantonment being built by the War Department north of the Arkansas River. When he was not hired, he sought and won a job in Little Rock on a federal project constructing a picric acid plant for the manufacture of high explosives. Allie moved Floy and James Franklin from Beebe into a red-brick bungalow at Fourth and Sherman streets, near the plant. Floy kept house and worked part-time at Back's Department Store on Main Street, and James Franklin attended Kramer Elementary School at Ninth and Sherman.

When World War I and his job at the picric acid plant ended in November 1918, Allie looked for work among the furniture factories, woodworking and cottonseed oil plants, flour and feed mills, and ware-houses in the wholesale district, which was a maze of railroad spurs between East Markham and Rock Island Railroad shops on East Second Street. Outside a warehouse, Allie saw a driverless truck, its motor idling, at the loading dock. The driver had been fired by the warehouse supervisor, who then asked Allie to deliver the goods on the truck to Argenta, north of the Arkansas River. Even though he had never driven a truck, he assumed that accepting the temporary task might lead to a permanent job. With a black workman's help, he learned to shift the truck's gears and made the delivery without turning the motor off. When he returned to the American Wholesale Grocery warehouse, the manager hired him on the spot.

For the next three years, the family enjoyed a middle-class life in the city, until Dr. W. H. Abington, White County physician and state senator, reported Floy's mother was dying of cancer. Floy's father, Benjamin Honea, had hired a nurse-housekeeper, but she seemed more solicitous of his comforts than Floy's mother's. Floy persuaded Allie to move their family to tiny McRae, in White County, to care for Mrs. Honea. Allie found a job managing a drugstore-confectionary and distributing soft drinks to nearby towns. After work, he bred and trained pointer and setter birddogs, resumed hunting and fishing, and attended Beebe's Masonic Lodge 145. He and Floy's younger brother, Cleve, despite the uncertainties in commodity trading, formed a strawberry brokerage, hoping to profit from White County's abundance of strawberries and the growing popularity of fresh fruits as a source of dietary vitamins. But two years of bad weather, poor crops, and financial losses ended their partnership.

Floy, while caring for her mother and family, led the Girls' Auxiliary, a group similar to the Girl Scouts, and served as an officer in the Entre Nous Club, a women's social group. To please her parents, Floy taught Sunday School and played piano at the Baptist church and organ at the Methodist church. I was born in August 1924, a year and a half before my grandmother died in January 1926, and two and a half years before our family moved to Little Rock. As the second son of Allie and Floy Harrison, I was nearly thirteen years younger than my only brother, James Franklin Harrison, or "Buster."

Cleveland on tricycle with little friend at 313 East Thirteenth.

CHAPTER 1

Awakening in Little Rock

IN THE WINTER of 1927, when I was halfway to three years old and oblivious of my whereabouts, our family moved from the small Arkansas farm town of McRae to the capital city of Little Rock. Shortly after we moved, one of our new neighbors across the street made a toy airplane from wood scraps for me, and running home to show it to my mother, I heedlessly collided with a slow-moving truck in front of our house. That accident, like a doctor's slap on a newborn's bottom, awakened my conscious ego and memory.

My earliest memories remain my mother's warm arms, frequent soft kisses, round face, and smiling blue eyes. I recall, too, the soft wave she made in her bobbed blue-black hair with a hot curling iron I was never to touch. My tall, slender father, strong and quiet, treated me as if I were a little man; my short, muscular older brother, who resembled our mother, merely put up with me. In a photograph of me at the time—tousled black hair, pug nose, round eyes, and freckled cheeks—I didn't yet resemble anyone on either side of the family.

I was apparently too big for a baby's highchair. At meals, I sat in an ordinary chair on a book and pillow at the kitchen table beside my mother, across from my brother. We bowed our heads at every meal as my father, at the head of the table, prayed for God's blessing on our food and family:

Thank you, Lord, for this food.
Bless it to the nourishment of our bodies
and us to Thy service. Amen.

After our breakfast, my brother quietly disappeared as Mama cleared the table to wash the dishes, and Daddy remained seated, sipping coffee, smoking a cigarette, and reading aloud from the *Arkansas Gazette*. He and Mama often laughed at the sketches and captions of *Hambone's Meditations*, J. P. Alley's popular newspaper cartoon, repeating and relishing the rumpled little black man's philosophical remarks, like, "Everyone talking about heaven ain't gwine dere!"

Before Daddy left for work, in the midst of hugs and kisses, Mama reminded him to crank our Model T Ford carefully, because the motor's backfire could kick the handle and break his wrist. Daddy, smiling at her concern, pulled a wire protruding from the radiator, turned the ignition off, and spun the crank. Then he turned the ignition back on to spin the crank again, vigorously and without a shade of caution. The motor spit out scattered explosions, and he lithely leaped into the car's high front seat, waving goodbye, heading to the warehouse of the American Wholesale Grocery Company on Markham Street.

When Daddy departed for work, my only thought was of his return, of being picked up again in his strong arms, swooped high into the air, and dipped low through the open front door. Meanwhile, my big brother, mumbling goodbye, dodged Mama's kiss and departed for classes at East Side Junior High School.

I was confined to the house during the cold and rainy weather, and watched happenings on the street out front and in the alley beside our house from the doors, windows, and porch. Or I lay on my stomach in the living room, slowly turning pages, poring over black-and-white photographs in our thick, red *World Book Encyclopedia,* or I sat by the library table in my little oak rocking chair, listening to music and the voices on the radio.

Mama said I seldom protested at bedtime, always eager for her and Daddy to read stories. Gentle Mama chose pieces from *Mother Goose Rhymes, The Tales of Peter Rabbit,* and *Rebecca of Sunnybrook Farm,* her childhood favorites. Stalwart Daddy preferred books like *The Wonderful Wizard of Oz*—stories of self-reliance appealed to him as much as the colored pictures of Dorothy, Tin Woodman, Cowardly Lion, and Scarecrow did to me. Daddy read Joel Chandler Harris's stories in dialect as well as any actor I later heard, especially my favorite story, "Uncle Remus, or Mr. Fox, Mr. Rabbit, and Mr. Terrapin." Both Daddy and Mama diligently and patiently chugged through *The Little Blue Engine That Could*, puffing, "I think I can," as often as the tiny engine.

When their readings ended, I knelt beside the bed, clasped my hands palm to palm, and recited the child's bedtime prayer that Mama taught me:

Now I lay me down to sleep, I pray the Lord my soul to keep.
If I should die before I wake, I pray the Lord my soul to take.

Hugged, kissed, and tucked in bed by my parents, I recalled the day's sights, sounds, events, and faces, drifting off to sleep before my brother lay down beside me in the double bed we shared.

In March and April of 1927, the year of the Great Flood, rain fell ceaselessly on Little Rock, ominous dark clouds blossoming silently before the rain began pounding heavily upon our roof and the wind rattled our window panes. We frequently ate our breakfasts while sudden lightning flashes glared through the windows, and thunder rumbled overhead before my father and brother left for work and school in their shiny yellow rain slickers.

One morning, the ragged black sky sagged so low over our house, I felt like Chicken Little in the storybook: "Oh, my goodness, the sky is falling!" And when I saw the cascade of water filling the street, running in the gutters, and gushing over the curb, I ran to sit in Mama's protective arms on the rusty-brown sofa, even though its mohair cover usually rubbed a rash upon my arms and legs.

Every day, thunder clouds gathered, boomed, and dumped rain on our city. Daddy watched the river from his Markham Street warehouse as the swift brown waves, filled with debris, swept away the scrap and tarpaper huts squatters lived in along the river banks. One morning, he read in the *Arkansas Gazette* that a powerful surge of the flooded Arkansas River had pushed the big Baring Cross Bridge over into the water, like a broken tinker toy, even though the Missouri Pacific Railroad had parked boxcars loaded with coal on the track deck to steady it. In the afternoon, Mama showed me pictures in the *Arkansas Democrat* of flooded streets in downtown North Little Rock, expressing her fear that the raging waters would overflow the river banks and reach our neighborhood.

Near the end of April, Mama and I stood on the front porch singing,

Rain, rain, go away,
Come again another day;
Little "Cleveland" wants to play.

As we watched, the threatening black sky changed to pewter gray, and the misty arc of a rainbow spanned City Park. Mama, reassuring me as well as herself, told the biblical story of Noah and the Great Flood, how Adam and Eve's children grew so wicked that God flooded the world to punish them. How Noah, his family, and pairs of every beast on earth boarded his big boat, the Ark, and floated for forty days and forty nights, until God promised by a rainbow in the sky that He would never flood the earth again.

Even though floodwaters spread across the entire South, covering nearly one-fourth of Arkansas, which was the most severely affected state, Mama had faith that God would keep the promise He had made.

Every day, Daddy repeated, "Yes, sir-ree, bob, the whole state of Arkansas will never forget the flood of 1927."

After my "rude awakening" in Little Rock, I measured everyday life by the people I met and the parts of town I visited. On sunny days, I roamed freely within easy reach of Mama's voice in the back and front yards of our landlord's home and our modest house, side by side, with the other rent house beside him. Our white clapboard cottage in the middle of the block beside an alley, at 313 East Thirteenth, matched every detail of the other rent house—L-shaped front porch, back stoop, living room, two bedrooms, bathroom, and kitchen. In contrast, our landlord's home was an elaborate two-story, white clapboard with porches on both Thirteenth Street and Rock Street.

But the abode commanding my attention was an unpainted shack in the far corner of our backyard, where Mama said "knee-grows" lived. One day I was brave enough to walk toward it, intending to knock, when the squeaky roughhewn door abruptly swung open, and a short, dark-skinned woman in a bright calico dress, with an apron at her waist and bandanna on her head, stepped out. She was the first person of color I had ever seen, and she spoke in a manner I never heard before.

"Chile, I seen yo' afore when I cast my eye around. I 'spected yo' to come several times 'fore today, but duh weather been so bad, yo' momma kept yo' inside. Bless yo' li'l heart, I'se already met yo' sweet momma! Yo' see, I'se Mandy, the maid. Listen he-uh, y'all come over tomorry 'n strike up 'quaintance wit Jake, dat man of mine."

When we went to visit Mandy, she seated us in stiff upright mule-eared chairs beside a rickety, unvarnished wooden table. In the glowing but flickering yellow light of a kerosene lamp and the pulsating shadows it cast around the room, we saw the shack had no windows and the walls were covered with stained newspapers. In a faint mist of wood smoke, smelling of the fatback and turnip greens simmering in a pot on her cast-iron cook stove, she told how she and Jake cleaned and maintained the Adamsons' house, yards, and clothes in order to live rent free in their shack. But she said Mama could hire her to do housework, too.

The first day Mandy came to help Mama, she was accompanied by our landlord's daughters, two girls so opposite in appearance and manners they might have had different parents. Slender, wiry Dorothy Mae chattered like a mockingbird strutting and stretching its wings trying new songs. But big-bosomed Evelyn, in her Mother Hubbard dress, peering from eyes as round and blank as Orphan Annie's in the funny papers, dragged her words, clumped her feet, and preferred sitting. Outdoors, Dorothy Mae usually was bouncing a ball and picking up jacks, jumping a rope loop, hopping hopscotch chalk squares on the sidewalk, or making up plays for us to perform on the Adamsons' screened porch on Rock Street or their open front porch on Thirteenth, where I first acted like someone other than myself.

"The Adamson girls are mothering you," Mama said. "They've turned you into their living doll baby."

Besides her weekly bouts of washing and ironing with Mandy, Mama prepared three meals a day and shopped for groceries every day but Sunday at Baer and Son's Store on Commerce, at the dead end of Thirteenth Street beside the City Park. I accompanied her, and sometimes, on warm, sunny days, Mama took me to the park's new Foster Band Shell, which looked to me like half a giant white tennis ball split in two.

In the early morning, with hardly anyone else present, I mounted the stage and stood beneath the letters M-U-S-I-C on the arch above the apron, reciting captions I remembered from Hambone's cartoons, or acting like a flying monkey in the Land of Oz, or strutting like a drum major in front of a band. When hot nights of summer later smothered the city, our family strolled to the park and sat on quilts beside other families near the bandstand, cooling off while listening to musicians play military and popular pieces and politicians make campaign speeches.

But most mornings, Mama walked us directly to the grocery store, where I caught the scent of the kerosene pump out front before reaching the front door. Inside, under naked light bulbs at the ends of long electric cords, we shopped with aromas around us of raw pork and beef, and ham and sausage at the meat counter; dill and sweet pickles in the open crocks of brine and vinegar; and condiments, coffee beans, and bouquets of spices stacked on shelves of seasonings. We smelled the earthy smell of potatoes in bushel baskets and the fragrances of cucumbers, cabbages, tomatoes, and carrots in bins.

Mama filled the woven oak basket over her arm with canned goods, fruits, and vegetables and carried it to the front counter for Mr. Baer to add our bill with a stubby pencil on a square paper pad. At the checkout counter while he figured, we stood beside him enveloped in the sweet scents of sugar and vanilla in the cookies, candies, and chewing gum.

I stared into a hole on one side of a gaily wrapped cardboard box on the counter, waiting for Mr. Baer's usual question.

Totaling our bill, he would ask, "Has Cleveland been a good boy today, Mizriz Harrison?"

Mama's "Yes" would split his face into the smile of a pumpkin-head as he added a nickel to our bill. I reached into the hole and grabbed a small paper bag, untied a gaily colored ribbon at the top, and spread out on the counter a piece of candy, a stick of gum, and a trinket—a rubber ball and jacks, aggie with marbles, linked metal rings, paper parachute, tin whistle, or wooden soldier!

Mr. Baer always proudly reminded us, "A blind girl on Rock Street packs them little bags."

When he first mentioned the girl, I could hardly wait for Mama's permission to ride my tricycle around the corner to her house on Rock Street behind the Adamsons'. The blind girl greeted me, smiling with her eyes wide open, which was surprising. She told me about sorting and assembling items in the small bags, in good weather and bad, sitting on the porch behind three small tables separately piled with candy, gum, and prizes.

When I described the work the blind girl did on her own without seeing, Mama praised her for proving how productive disabled people can be.

Our neighborhood became my playhouse and schoolhouse. Dorothy Mae was the ringmaster for games and plays, and the black and white workers passing through the neighborhood served as my instructors in the small change of everyday life. I met all but the milkman personally. Yet without ever seeing him, I prepared for his stops, placing empty glass milk bottles on the front steps before he delivered the next day, sometimes sticking Mama's rolled-up note in the neck of an empty bottle to change her regular order. Then, as morning sunlight rimmed the borders of our olive green window shades, I heard the horse's clip-clop and the bottles' rattle in the milkman's caddy as he set the order down on our front steps.

Before sunrise, I also heard the dull thud of an *Arkansas Gazette* landing on our porch after a white boy on a bicycle tossed our daily paper. Though not much taller than me, the boy collected for the papers on Saturday afternoons and let me hold his big, skinny-wheeled bike, which had a dirty white canvas newspaper bag, emblazoned with ARKANSAS GAZETTE, hanging across the handle bars. The newsboy spoke to me like a grownup as almost everyone else did.

The iceman stopped at the curb, at what Mama called "a more reasonable hour," parking his horse-drawn wagon piled high with banks of ice steaming not from heat but cold. He came to stock our wooden Sears and Roebuck icebox, which didn't make ice like the landlord's big metal General Electric refrigerator that had a round white compressor coil on top. After the iceman checked the number to which the black arrow pointed on the white cardboard square in our front door window, he chipped a block of ice the proper size with a pick—a thin, pointed metal stick on a wooden handle.

Older neighborhood kids followed his wagon, scooping up the shiny silver slivers he sprayed across the wagon bed to melt in their mouths. Meanwhile, the iceman clamped the ice between steel tongs, carrying it across his back on his leather vest, to deposit in the top compartment of our icebox. The first chore I ever had was warning Mama when water from the melting ice filled the dishpan under the box, so it could be emptied before it spilled on the kitchen linoleum.

The next worker, the postman, came to our house twice every weekday and once on Saturday morning, rain or shine. If I saw the man in his dove-gray uniform, billed cap, and high-topped shoes coming up the street, with his sweat-stained leather mail bag over his shoulder, I ran and told Mama, who was always looking forward to replies from all our relatives and friends she wrote letters to.

One stormy day, after the postman placed letters in our mailbox on the porch post and then struggled to open his umbrella, I suggested waiting until the rain ended to resume deliveries.

He patted my head, struck a soldier's pose, and recited something he had obviously memorized, as I had my bedtime prayer or Daddy his blessing at mealtime: "Neither snow nor rain nor heat nor gloom of night stops these couriers from the swift completion of their appointed rounds."

"Are you a koo-ree-yur, Mr. Postman?"

Laughing, he said, "I certainly am, young fella."

Somehow I sensed that my parents, like the white and black men who worked in our neighborhood in all kinds of weather, were "couriers," too.

When trees and grass turned green, several other men came into our neighborhood. Sweet-voiced black farmers trolled the streets in rickety horse-drawn wagons, calling out a rhythmic singsong chant of vegetables and fruits they had to sell at the curb. Hearing their calls, I alerted Mama that produce fresher than at the grocery store was coming and held her small change purse to help her feel and weigh our family's favorites. The farmers proved their fruits ripe and sweet by giving us samples of berries, grapes, apples, and melons to taste.

The other black men, who came in horse-drawn wagons filled with battered, empty buckets, barrels, and lard cans, collected our neighborhood's kitchen leavings—cobs, hulls, peelings, seeds, rinds, and bones—from garbage cans lined up beside the alley. The "garbage men" either rented or owned farms outside the city limits and collected our discards to "slop their hogs." But the discarded paper trash—newspapers, letters, boxes, paper bags—we burned in wire baskets in the backyard. I begged to strike the "magic kitchen match" to set the rubbish ablaze, but my brother, who collected it, wouldn't let me.

When I finally noticed that other kids owned animals, I wanted one of my own. Dorothy Mae and Evelyn's gray tabby cat had tiny white feet like little boots; and Aunt Grace's poodle was as thin as the black squiggle of Maggie's dog in *Bringing Up Father*. Daddy told about training a liver-spotted pointer birddog to hunt quails, rabbits, and squirrels in Beebe and McRae. Though Mama never owned a pet, she tended the yellow canary Grandpa bought to brighten Grandma's final months. The pet I saw every day—an arrogant, orange and cream striped tabby, with copper eyes—was Buster's Ole Tom, roaming our house as if he owned it.

Buster's love and care for animals of all kinds began when a family friend gave him a rust-colored piglet on his eighth birthday. The pig, named Red, followed at Buster's heels like a dog and, as he grew bigger, carried my brother on his back. But Red's increasing size made him difficult to control; he tried to enter the house, rooted in flower beds, and tripped Mama when she fed him. To Daddy, Red eventually looked less like a pet and more like bacon, ham, and sausage hanging in the smokehouse. So early in the morning of the weather's first hard freeze, despite Buster's tearful protests, Daddy slaughtered big Red to cure him for eating. Mama described how Buster angrily refused to eat all bacon strips, ham steaks, or pork chops, even though they were never part of Red.

Yet, before I asked for a bow-wow or mee-ow of my own, no one had thought of giving me a pet. Red's sad end didn't temper my wanting a pet of my own. Everyone had an opinion about what kind of pet I should have. Daddy declared a dog wouldn't be right without a fenced yard—a yard that Dr. Adamson was not likely to approve. Mama firmly suggested that a canary wasn't a good choice, because she would have to feed and water it and clean its cage. And Buster claimed that Ole Tom simply wouldn't tolerate another cat. It was decided, considering my age, that goldfish were perfect.

Mama took me to Kress Five and Ten Cent Store on Main to choose from the jillions of colored fish swimming among the seaweed floating in the big glass tanks at the rear. As I watched so many fish swimming past, their colors and shapes changed for me like glass fragments in the tube of a kaleidoscope.

Mama finally urged, "We can't stay all day, Cleveland!"

The larger, more colorful fish were too expensive, so I chose two small goldfish. Mama bought a glass fishbowl and pink, purple, and green stones for the bottom and fish wafers for food. Since I loved *The Katzenjammer Kids* and their German accents in the dialogue balloons over their heads in the funny papers—though Mama had trouble saying "I vant evry-tink in evry-vay ta be niz und clean"—I named my fish for the Katzenjammer brothers, Hans and Fritz.

Every day, I spent time beside the bowl, watching the little luminescent Hans and Fritz squiggling in the shimmering water, their eyes unblinking, mouths pursing, fins waving, and gills oscillating. When I showed them to my Aunt Grace, she taught me an alphabet dialogue to recite:

A B C D goldfish.
M N O goldfish.
O S A R goldfish!
O G I C D goldfish!

Two of Mama and Daddy's schoolmates from Beebe, Aunt Ethel and Uncle Moss Means, lived a block from us on Rock Street. Though we were not related, I called them Aunt and Uncle, as children did with their parents' adult friends. Short, wide-hipped Uncle Moss, who wore his belt beneath his stomach, boasted having the same size waist since his teens. And Aunt Ethel, a slender, wide-eyed seamstress, had spectacles at the end of her nose and strands of strawberry-blond hair across her fair face. Childless, they wanted to entertain me with a collection of bobbins, thimbles, and empty spools on the floor while they exchanged stories with Mama and Daddy about folks in Beebe and White County. But I was more interested in their stories.

One of Daddy's favorite stories concerned Reba Fussell (he called her Reeby Fuzzle), who hated living in "a little bitty old country town like Beebe." So her father eventually satisfied her and her mother by finding a job in Little Rock. Reeby's boyfriend, Leland David, deeply disappointed by their separation, promised to visit her in Little Rock as soon as possible, but months passed before business took him to the capital city, where he phoned from the lobby of the Hotel Marion to invite Reeby to lunch.

When a woman's pretentious voice answered, Leland asked, "Who is this?"

The haughty voice replied, "This is Miss Ree-BEKA Fuss-SELL."

Daddy, acting as Leland David, said, "Well, REE-bee, this is LEE-Lawn Dah-Vahd from Bee-BEE! How about lunching with me at the Marion Hotel today?"

Uncle Moss nearly knocked me down leaping out of his chair, clapping his hands. "Goody, goody, oh, God! That's just how old Lee woulda said it!"

Excited by Uncle Moss's behavior, I pushed my pants below my waist like him, shouting, "Goody, goody, oh, God!"

Everybody laughed at what I did but Mama. Pulling up my pants, she pointed her finger in my face. "What do you mean repeating something like that?"

Uncle Moss said, "Don't fuss at him! Floy, who does the little rascal take after?"

"My brother Cleve, I guess … he talks as much or more than he does."

Later, Mama and I went to Pfeifer's Department Store, where Uncle Moss clerked in the basement. Dashing around the counter, he shouted, "Helen, here's that little corker I told you about. It's Floy Harrison and her boy. Do 'goody, oh God' for Mizriz Spriggs."

Mama smiled at him but nearly squeezed my hand in two. "You don't know the power of your own lungs, Moss Means. You mustn't make a fuss over something bad Cleveland's done."

"I just want Helen to hear the boy imitate me. How can I help you, Floy?"

"Allie needs a dress shirt and a pair of BVDs."

"Your wish, my dear girl, is my command." Hitching his trousers with his elbows, he led us to another counter.

Following him, I asked, "Uncle Moss, what's a BVD?"

"A company that makes men's underwear ... Bradley, Voorhees, and Day. Garments with a trap door in the back." Kneeling, he patted my bottom, singing softly in my ear:

An evening spent with Hannah on your knees
is like traveling through Alaska in your BVDs!

Mama said, "Moss! Don't! Cleveland never stops repeating things like that."

Even though Uncle Moss and Aunt Ethel were good friends of my parents, they were not as close to them as the Lloyds—Uncle Harold, a blond-headed, rosy-cheeked salesman, and Aunt Grace, an olive-complexioned, short-waisted brunette with thin bird's legs. They lived in a cottage at Fourteenth and Cumberland streets, cattycornered from East Side's auditorium, with their teenage son, Frankie. Their grownup son, Jimbo, was reputedly confined in an Illinois penitentiary for hauling illegal bootleg whiskey in milk bottles painted white to conceal the spirits inside.

Mama and Aunt Grace visited at each other's homes off and on all week. Uncle Harold came to our house on Friday evenings to tell Daddy jokes he heard on the road. When Mama objected to some of his stories, Daddy said, "Don't let them offend you, Floy. Fact is, Hal saves certain stories just to get a rise out of you for a laugh."

One Friday night, before Mama and Daddy left for their regular bridge game with the Lloyds, a car horn blared repeatedly in front of our house. Everyone left the supper table to determine why anyone was honking so persistently. The Lloyds, yoo-hooing and waving, were parked at the curb in a shiny red coupe.

Uncle Harold sprang out. "How about my new Reo, Al? It's called a 'Flying Cloud.'"

Daddy walked around the car before saying, "Pretty darned sassy for a travelin' salesman, Hal!"

"The latest model, Aloysius. This ole travelin' man deserves to ride in style!" Uncle Harold acted so free and easy compared to my father, but I liked Daddy the way he was.

The red two-seater was smaller and closer to the ground than our black, four-door Tin Flivver, and had a frame for a suitcase above its back bumper. Uncle Harold reached behind the coupe's rear window, turned a handle, and uncovered an upholstered leather seat inside the trunk.

"Well, I declare!" Mama said. "What'll automobile people think of next?"

"It's a rumble seat, y'all! Hop in! We'll take you on a spin around City Park before we split a deck of cards."

Daddy helped Mama slide into the rumble seat and squeezed in beside her. Uncle Harold hooked me under the arms and swung me up to sit on Mama's lap. The car slowly moved away from the curb but gathered speed careening around the curves in City Park, the tires squealing from Commerce to McGowan Street.

Mama squeezed the breath out of me, shouting, "Harold Lloyd! Stop this minute! I want out of this car!"

Laughing, Uncle Harold hit the accelerator, racing clear out to the airport.

Driving fast in the open rumble seat was far more exciting than driving slow in our old Model T on Sundays, even though our Ford could take off faster than the brand-new Reo. If Daddy shoved his left foot to the floorboard, the Tin Lizzie lunged ahead roaring and trembling, its hood fluttering. But usually Daddy drove deliberately, especially when passing the construction sites at the Albert Pike Hotel on Scott, and the nearly completed fourteen-story Donaghey Building on Main. At Fifth and Main, he extended his left arm and turned the car west going toward a shiny white pile that grew wider and taller as we approached it—the State Capitol building of Arkansas!

Daddy said, "The new state capitol is where the old state penitentiary was before the legislature decided to construct the capitol on the same ground. Governor Jeff Davis wanted to build somewhere else, and sneered, 'Them grounds is too poor for even two Irishmen to raise a row on.' But he lost that political battle, and the capitol is on that high site."

Mama seldom said a word against anyone but recalled that the board of deacons at Second Baptist Church had expelled Governor Davis for being a drunkard. I didn't know what that word meant, only that I loved going to the Capitol grounds to play at the foot of the tall statues of an angel and a Confederate soldier, and roll around on the green lawn, even though chiggers in the grass—itchy bugs too tiny to see—burrowed beneath my skin and raised hard red marks.

The best part of Sunday drives was near the end: crossing the Arkansas River to North Little Rock on the Broadway Bridge and returning to Little Rock on the Main Street Bridge. In the to and fro, I looked out the window across yellowish brown water swirling below us and saw toy cars and tiny people moving on the bridge opposite us. At least, what I saw were toys until Daddy explained their small appearance was the result of the four-block space between the bridges. I begged to stop on the bridge deck to see the miniature figures better, but Daddy said parking on the bridge was illegal, that policemen in blue uniforms with badges would put us behind iron bars in jail.

Crossing both bridges ended our Sunday drives until Charles Lindbergh returned to the United States after flying his airplane all alone across the Atlantic Ocean to Paris, France, on May 20–21, 1927. After his return, Mama read in the *Gazette* that the Daniel Guggenheim Fund was sponsoring a three-month nationwide flying tour by Lindbergh in the *Spirit of St. Louis* to all the forty-eight states. "Lucky Lindy" landed at Little Rock on October 1, 1927, and met local citizens who went to see his famous plane parked at the National Guard Airport, where they had their picture taken beside their hero and his plane before he flew to Memphis the next day. Thereafter, Daddy ended our Sunday drives at the airport on the eastern edge of town nearer our home.

When Mama and Daddy played contract bridge with the Lloyds and other friends on Saturday evenings, they left me with Buster. He was supposed to complete homework he had neglected while practicing with the track team, which included thirty boys, including his pals Homer Jones and Coy Adams. Mr. Jess Matthews coached the East Side team, who wore white shorts and blue tops with white diagonal stripes across the chest. When the team members visited at our house, they whispered, laughed, and exchanged jokes I didn't understand. I tried to tell my stories, but instead of listening, they threatened to pull my pants off or tossed me in the air between them.

Buster's best buddy, Homer Jones, usually came only when our parents were away. As tall as my brother, he had a long torso and short legs, which made him walk funny. And he talked louder and longer than all the other track boys together. Maybe that's why Mama thought he was a bad boy and called him "that Homer Jones." I asked Daddy why Mama spoke of him that way, and he ventured that Homer reminded her of Buster's bad companions in McRae.

Mama warned my brother, "You're known by the company you keep. There's no telling how boys like that Homer Jones affect your mind and habits."

But if Homer visited when Mama was home, she treated him just as she did all the other boys, as nice as could be.

If the boys ran out of something to say or do, Buster might entertain them by bending my arm at the elbow making the muscle bulge and rubbing his palm over it, winding the tiny hairs into little knots. When he straightened my arm, pulling the hairs apart, my arm stung. If I screwed up my face to keep from crying, the boys laughed, and I loved it. On the other hand, Buster's Dutch rub—planting his thumb at different points on my head and snapping my skull with his knuckles—hurt enough for real tears I couldn't contain. Homer thought pained expressions and tears were even funnier.

I actually wanted Buster to show his buddies one of his tricks with me: I squatted down, wrapped my arms around my thighs, and he placed his right arm between my chest and thighs, grasping my biceps and lifting me over his head. Even though I begged, he would rarely do it.

One Saturday morning, I found a large carp wedged inside my fish bowl on the table in the living room and ran to tell Mama.

Without hesitating, she went to our bedroom door. "Buster! Come out here this minute!"

Recognizing the impatience in her voice, he dragged out quickly in his underwear.

"Where did this big fish come from?"

"Oh, yeah, that. Well, uh, Mama, Homer and I..."

"I know you were with that Homer Jones Friday night, but don't mention him! What happened to Cleveland's pet fish?"

After admitting that he and Homer took two large carp from the fish pond in front of Franke's Cafeteria on Fifth Street, he said, "When I came home, I didn't know what to do with my big old carp. I couldn't fill the tub and put it there. That'd wake you and Dad. So I shoved it in Cleveland's bowl. Honest, Mama, I didn't know it'd eat the little fish."

"Take this giant fish back to Franke's and buy two goldfish to replace the ones it ate."

"No one knows we took 'em, Mama! And buying goldfish with my allowance isn't fair."

"How'd you like having Ole Tom stolen or run over? You killed those fish, and you'll replace them from your allowance. If you don't return the carp, that worsens what you did!"

Despite his fear of being caught by a policeman, Buster slipped the carp into the pool after Franke's closed late Saturday night. On Monday, he brought home a white carton, which I thought was a pint of ice cream until he dumped two goldfish in my bowl, proving he knew how to right a wrong. Yet, despite Buster's persistent teasing, I wanted to grow up like my big brother—strong, graceful, and good looking.

I was surprised one Friday morning at breakfast when Mama announced we were going to visit McRae, my birthplace. Slipping off the book and pillow I was sitting on, I jumped up and down with joy! It would be the first trip out of Little Rock I could remember, and my first chance to see the house where I was born.

We were going so that Mama could buy a crate of fresh strawberries to put up preserves, and she was afraid the best berries in the heart of strawberry country had already been shipped out of state in refrigerated boxcars. Strawberries were really popular across the country after newspapers and magazines reported that the vitamins in fruits and vegetables improved a person's health.

Daddy, chuckling over Mama's concern, told her, "Farmers in White County raise enough berries for you to have plenty of the best—the bigger farms plant scores of acres and the smaller ones seven to ten acres."

After we drove through the city of Little Rock to Highway 67 on the way to McRae, we passed Beebe, where Mama and Daddy first met at school and then married. The building I saw from the highway as we approached McRae was the railroad station and loading dock that Daddy said they shipped strawberries from in season. McRae, a "flag town" on the Missouri Pacific Railroad, was so small the station ticket agent waved a flag to signal engineers to stop and pick up passengers and freight. In 1910, when Grandpa first opened his store there, the town had no electric power, water works, sewer system, or even a bank. And the town still had less than a hundred "souls," until scores of men, women, and children came in dilapidated trucks and horse-drawn wagons to pick strawberries during the season.

When I saw the straggle of buildings of downtown McRae, partially hidden by the railroad embankment, Daddy abruptly twisted the car off the highway and drove slowly up a short gravel strip that he laughingly called "Grand Avenue," which crossed the tracks and intersected Railroad Avenue.

Mama pointed at a sign beside the tracks about a silent movie to be shown that night in the empty lot beside Herring's Store. "Allie, remember George Goodrich showing those silent pictures upstairs above Herring's store? Well, we're all going to see a movie there tonight, whatever it is, right after supper! Including Papa and Miss Green."

"That may take a little doing on your part, honey."

"Oh, Cleveland, look at that large sign on top of the building at the end of the street—Honea Mercantile Company—that's your Grandpa's store."

A big red-brick building stood at the end of a strip of unpainted, one-story fame buildings at the north end of Railroad Avenue, and it had a sign on the roof that Mama claimed had my grandfather's name. The store looked like the biggest one in town to me. Along the front of the one-story frame buildings leading to it was a rough-cut oak plank sidewalk covered by a steeply pitched corrugated metal roof, supported by upright posts with attached wooden benches between them.

Behind the building at the northeast corner of Grand Avenue stood a lopsided wooden shack; its one door, with vertical iron bars, hung loose and sagged from its top hinge, while the lower hinge, with bits of shattered wood, clung uselessly to the wooden upright. The shack, leaning over one side of a wide mud puddle, had only one window, without glass panes or a screen.

"What's that ugly old place for, Daddy?"

"The hoosegow, where the constable puts drunks to sober 'em up."

"What's a drunk, Daddy?"

"Allie! There's no need to tell about that. Please don't argue at Papa's."

"Uh oh ... That's hard to avoid, Floy. But take it easy, I'll behave."

Driving along unpaved Grand Avenue, we passed the town bank, livery stables, a grocery store, a seed-and-fertilizer store, and a drugstore, before turning onto a dusty lane.

We passed several widely separated houses before Mama pointed at Grandpa standing on his back porch beside "Miz" Alma Green, the woman he married after Grandma died (and who had been the nurse-housekeeper when Grandma was still alive). My mother always called her Miss Green, but she was Miz Alma to me. I was only a baby when we moved away from McRae, and this was the first time for me to really see them. Miz Alma, a bony, dark-skinned woman, had her mousey brown hair pulled taut as a swimming cap on her head. She had sharp features, black eyes, and tawny skin that made her resemble Indians I'd seen in pictures. But Grandpa was a chubby doll, with a round stomach and a shiny, round, pink head fringed with white hair. Neither of them said much greeting us, but Grandpa let Mama hug and kiss him.

After supper, Mama tried to persuade them to go to the picture show with us.

"Admission's only five or ten cents, Papa. And we won't walk. Allie will drive us."

"Aye gonnies, I'm ain't spendin' a thin dime watching shadows on a dirty bed sheet."

His attitude didn't prevent Mama, Daddy, and me from going, though. The canvas tent theater, covering half the vacant lot, had the wall flaps tied up to catch whatever breezes there might be had on such a sultry night. Daddy called the crowd "a full house," for the noisy berry pickers and their children had nearly filled all the wooden folding chairs.

But Mama spotted empty seats beside a long-legged table with the movie projector on top. With seats beside the projector, we heard the film passing through the projector gate clickity-clacking loudly and continuously, as the projector cast blinking images upon the screen. But no sounds could divert us from the mad spills and frantic races Buster Keaton undertook in his effort to tame a runaway train in *The General*, a silent comedy about a bumbling Civil War spy. It was the first time I watched Daddy watching movie comics, and his loud guffaws set the audience laughing even more, until we all nearly collapsed in tears and laughing-coughing fits.

Mama said, "Allie, they shoulda let you in free for boosting the laughs."

While the projectionist changed the movie reels, a chubby man in coveralls squeezed between the rows selling candy bars and popcorn, which added paper crinkling and lip smacking to the sounds of chairs scraping and tummies rumbling in the crowd.

Since Grandpa had dismissed the movie, I could hardly wait to tell him how much fun we had watching the "shadows on a dirty sheet." But he was already asleep when we got home.

The next morning after breakfast, Mama took me next door to the dark green house, trimmed in white, to see the bedroom where she bore me by the light of a kerosene lamp on a hot August morning.

But the movie the night before impressed me more, and my lifelong devotion to movies began.

After we returned to Little Rock, Mama rushed to Dr. Utley's hospital to check Uncle Cleve's condition, unable to forgive herself for being away two full days and nights. I wondered why she worried so much, because I heard his illness had something to do with "circus of the river." But it was really cirrhosis of the liver. Uncle Cleve was under the care of Dr. Thomas Utley, who had converted a two-story, red-brick residence on Fourteenth Street into a small hospital, so Mama was close enough to nurse him. Daddy's job and Buster's track practice prevented their helping much, and Cleve's wife, Aunt Naomi, was caring for their family back in McRae.

As Uncle Cleve's condition worsened, Mama spent more time with him, leaving me with Mandy, who talked to me in her special way while scrubbing our clothes on a washboard in a galvanized tub big enough for me to bathe in. She told me "bluing" keeps white clothes from yellowing and "starch" stiffens shirts and dresses to keep them looking neat for a longer time. When she went outside to hang clothes on a wire across the backyard, she let me carry the clothespin bag and hand her garments. And I held a big basket when she gathered the clothes off the line before sprinkling them for ironing. She had flatirons on the kitchen stove, heating them to press clothes on the flat board she had balanced between the breakfast table edge and the top rung of a chair.

The next year when spring cleaning time came, Mandy draped wool rugs over the clothes line in the yard like tents, beating the dust out of them with a broom. She let me beat a small throw rug. But when she and Mama canned vegetables and fruits in big, steaming vessels that might tip over and scald me, they wouldn't allow me near the kitchen.

Mandy's Jake let me drag his tools as he cut grass, dug flower beds, raked leaves, trimmed hedges, and made repairs at Dr. Adamson's three houses. Wearing old baggy pants, a wrinkled suit coat, and a rumpled felt hat, Jake resembled the drawings of Hambone in the *Gazette*. Watching and listening to him and Mandy, I had my earliest clues to how different humans may look, act, and speak. Their dialect fell deep inside my ears and took root in my own tongue, instilling in me an affection for them and their manner of speaking.

If no one could baby-sit me, Mama took me along to visit at the hospital. One day, after we climbed the steep, narrow steps to the hospital's shallow porch and entered the front door, a rotund man in morning trousers and frock coat came out of an office. Dr. Utley, the head of the hospital, spoke to Mama and led us down a narrow hall that had doors on both sides and a funny smell. Mama said the smell came from iodoform, a medicine.

We found Uncle Cleve propped up with pillows, reading a newspaper. He had a pale, freckled face, wavy auburn hair, and a rather long nose for a Honea. As Mama leaned over to kiss his cheek, he smiled at me, making me brave enough to speak to him.

"My name's the same as yours, Uncle Cleve!"

"Yep, sure is, hon. I'm proud of it. But giving you my name caused a fuss."

"Oh, Cleve, don't talk about that," said Mama. "He'll never stop telling it."

"Now, Floy, the boy deserves to know why he's not an *Allie*. Your folks held off naming you for a week after your birth, Cleveland. Maybe they didn't want to call you anything!"

"Cleve, don't tease him! You're such a mess."

"It's true in a way, Floy. Cleveland, you weren't the girl your momma expected, and she hadn't picked a boy's name. They'd given their fathers' names to your brother—James Franklin."

"That's not my brother's name, Uncle Cleve. He's Buster."

"Naw, that's his nickname, after a cartoon character. Your momma don't like it but uses it just the same. Allie called you Blizzard at first. To him, you resembled a funny-paper figure whose hair stood straight up. Floy, you need to keep the comics out of Allie's hands."

Mama said, "Thank goodness Cleveland's birth hair wore off before that old ugly name got set." She took my uncle's hand. "I really wanted to call him Willie Cleveland, after you."

"Your daddy was the trouble, Cleveland," my uncle laughed. "He doesn't like his own name. But he heard Floy was about to give you my name, and his own wasn't so bad, after all! So to satisfy everybody, they put Allie and Cleveland together."

Then Uncle Cleve said, "Pull up your shirt tail. Let me see your birthmark. Yep! Same as I thought, same shape and color as a real berry. It's a miracle, Floy, for a kid born in strawberry country to have a berry in the middle of his belly."

I liked Uncle Cleve's twinkling blue eyes and his claim that my birth-mark was a badge to be proud of rather than a blemish. Everybody has a navel, but I had a strawberry, too.

On very special days, Mama walked us to an ice cream parlor at Thirteenth and Main, passing handsome two- and three-story brick and frame houses that Mama said were the "homes of our wealthy neighbors." I clickity-clacked a stick against the black pickets of their hip-high wrought-iron fences, dodging broken bricks that big oak and elm tree roots had heaved up in the sidewalk.

One time, a large, brown praying mantis suddenly landed on my shoul-der, and Mama shouted, "It's a walking stick!" Flailing with her purse, she warned, "If a devil's walking stick bites you, your flesh falls off." Not wish-ing to lose the smallest particle of me, I flailed, too.

On another occasion, a large amphibian spurted from the high grass beside the walk, and Mama pulled me into the gutter "to escape the toad's poisonous bite that only boiling water will loosen." Imagining dangers on what had become a jungle trail, I began carrying my cap pistol.

Our safaris ended at the Terry Dairy Ice Cream Parlor, owned by Uncle Billy Terry, Mama's first cousin, who was a pioneer in the Arkansas dairy business. Inside the white tile walls behind a counter, two ladies, wearing starched white aprons and caps, waited on us. The chubby, rosy-faced lady lifted me up behind the counter to look down into the ice cream cylinders to pick a flavor, while the pale, thin lady held a cone wrapped in paper napkins and a silver scoop to fill the cone with ice cream. To keep cream from running down my fingers onto my rompers, I licked the mound of ice cream even with the cone's edge as Mama, scooping cream from a dish with a spoon, talked to the ladies.

After we finished, Mama wiped my face and hands with wet napkins, and we went next door into Uncle Billy's grocery store to check the latest special dairy products he was selling. I remember when Mama first found a pound of butter that was four separately wrapped quarter-pound sticks instead of a cake like hand-churned butter pressed in wooden molds on the farm. A pretty girl was demonstrating the new package's convenience, serving customers small, thin, square patties of butter on soda crackers. Mama left me with the girl while she continued shopping, and the girl con-tinued feeding me buttered soda cracker samples. When Mama returned, my stomach was churning with an excess of butter and crackers, and we left hurriedly, with her carrying a bag of groceries on one arm and me "hanging like the limp neck of a dying swan" on the other.

Another self-indulgent act of mine left a permanent scar on the middle finger of my left hand. The minor disaster occurred at Joe D. Back and Brother's Department Store, between Fourth and Fifth on Main, where Mama had worked part-time selling dresses during and after World War I. As we stepped off the elevator in the women's dress department on the second floor, I saw and wanted to examine a shiny brass tank standing upright beside the elevator door and look at the narrow, white, accordion-pleated folds in a glass case hanging on the wall.

But the sales lady who greeted Mama observed how much I'd grown and distracted me, leading me to a small electric merry-go-round to ride while Mama tried on dresses. So I climbed on the back of a little painted wooden horse and began circling, listening to the circus music, as Mama and the clerk pulled dresses from racks and entered a changing room. Circling round and round, I tried to catch Mama's eye when she reappeared in different dresses to look at herself in a three-sided mirror.

Continuously circling on the merry-go-round was boring, and I remembered the shiny cylindrical objects standing beside the elevator. So I dismounted my "horsey" and walked to the brass tanks. With every muscle tense, I turned one tank upside down to examine how it worked and dislodged the hose and nozzle attached to its side. Suddenly a stream of white foamy liquid spewed out and smeared the wall behind me. Trying to set the tank back upright to stop the flow, I grabbed the ring on top and nearly severed the tip of the middle finger of my left hand on a knife-sharp metal edge. The sales lady saw what happened and shouted for Mama while leading me to a first aid kit. The iodine she applied to my finger hurt worse than the cut, but I didn't cry, because I had left the merry-go-round without permission; it was my fault.

Several weeks later, Mama was hurting. She had a toothache and stuffed a cotton ball soaked in oil of cloves around the tooth without getting any relief. I sat on her lap and tried to soothe her by kissing and laying my warm hand upon her cheek, but nothing helped. The next day, we boarded a yellow trolley to the dentist's office. The window beside our seat was so high that I stood in the seat to look out, but Mama made me sit to prevent my falling if the car stopped suddenly. Facing the back of the yellow rattan seat in front of me, I listened to the grinding wheels, clanging bell, and brake sand swish on the tracks as we rode to Fifth and Main, which my father called "the crossroads of Arkansas."

We crossed Main and entered the white-brick Boyle Building, eleven stories high, the tallest edifice in Little Rock at the time. (Fourteen years later, it was the site of Draft Board B when I joined the army.) We boarded one of the three elevators in the lobby, and a small, dark man in a uniform jacket with brass buttons slid the doors together, turned a handle, and whisked us up to the dentist's waiting room, which smelled like the cloves Mama put on her tooth. The dentist and the lady receptionist in their white smocks who greeted us were Dr. Adamson, our landlord, and Miss Pearl, who lived at his house. He led Mama through a pale green glass door, frosted like winter, through which I saw their soft shadows.

Miss Pearl sat beside me on a bench leafing through pictures in *Ladies' Home Journal,* and I could hear a machine buzzing, on and off, in the room behind the green glass door. When I heard Mama's muted cry, I ran toward the door to keep the dentist from hurting her, but Miss Pearl stopped me. She insisted Dr. Adamson was installing a filling that would take Mama's pain away.

When Mama came back smiling, Dr. Adamson said, "Now, let's have a look at Master Cleveland's baby teeth."

The big dental chair I climbed up into resembled Uncle Papa's barber chair on the mezzanine at Blass's Department Store. (I called my cousin Uncle Papa because he bore such a close resemblance to Grandpa Honea.) The dentist's chair had a basin of running water by the left arm and a movable apparatus above the right arm. I looked through the window in front of me at building rooftops four stories below and felt an odd tingling between my legs, which Mama said was a fear of heights. But I didn't know I was afraid. Dr. Adamson had a small mirror on a white band around his head that flashed in my eyes as he poked inside my mouth with a metal stick, nearly gagging me.

Spraying red liquid in my mouth, he said, "Swish the Lavoris in your mouth and spit in the basin."

Calling me "a brave boy," he invited me to listen to the short-wave radio at his home.

Dr. Adamson's invitation and my visits only intensified the radio habit I had already established. We sat on a padded mahogany bench in front of his beautiful Atwater-Kent, a shiny rectangular wooden case, with AM and short-wave bands and big tuning knobs. The round speaker, covered in fabric and resembling a giant lollipop, stood separate from the radio on top of a table in one corner of the living room. The speaker of our little tabletop Crosley was inside the radio's bronze metal cabinet. Dr. Adamson scanned radio signals searching for the disembodied voices of foreign broadcasters, suggesting his preference for the Rice Krispies–sounds—snap, crackle, and pop—of short-wave foreign-language broadcasts. I preferred the steady signals and voices of Americans on WSM in Nashville or WLW in Cincinnati, America's clear-channel stations.

After listening to the garbled voices on a foreign station, I was bored, but he stared into space, musing, "Think of it, child. The people we are hearing are on the other side of the globe! Voices from the ether, out of space! Makes you believe in spirits and eternity, doesn't it?"

I didn't know what he meant. The voices and language sounded strange to me, not like the American entertainers on WOK in Arkadelphia and KTHS in Hot Springs.

Occasionally when Mama visited Uncle Cleve in the afternoon, leaving me with the Adamsons, the dentist was home. His presence at home in the afternoon confused me because my father came home from work only at noon and in the late afternoon. Dr. Adamson looked different, too, without his dental smock—shorter and rounder. In fact, he resembled the cartoon drawing of Mr. Herbert Hoover, a squashed figure holding a banner above his head with the slogan "Lower Taxes—Continued Prosperity!" in a frame on the wall of their foyer.

Dorothy Mae didn't say what the cartoon words meant, only that, "They're just for grown-ups. Little kids don't need to understand them." That disappointed me because I thought the words might be as funny as the squat figure of Mr. Hoover.

When I described the cartoon at supper, Daddy said, "By grabs, Doc Adamson's a Republican! That doesn't surprise me. What else would a well-to-do dentist be?"

Mama expressed for the first time surprise that Miss Pearl lived with the Adamsons. "Certainly beats anything I ever heard tell of. Married couples share homes with their parents, grandparents, and older relatives, but not with unmarried assistants who aren't even related."

I told my folks about finding Dorothy Mae reading a book in a bedroom upstairs that had five beds, side by side, practically touching. When I asked why so many beds were in one bedroom, she said they all slept in the same room to catch the breezes through the several windows. Later, after Mama told Aunt Ethel and Aunt Grace about the women and girls sleeping in their nightgowns in side-by-side beds in the same room with Dr. Adamson, their voices sank so low and their eyebrows rose so high, I wondered what was wrong with sleeping that way.

The Adamsons and Miss Pearl, who did almost everything together, took the girls and me swimming one Sunday. The adults carried their swimsuits in rolled-up towels, but the girls wore theirs. Since I'd never been swimming, Mama put a cotton romper on me and warned me to mind the girls and stay out of the water after we ate something to avoid having cramps. So I was already a little scared as we drove out Arch Street Pike to the Pine Bluff highway and the Shriners' Country Club, a natural-stone clubhouse beside a big lake.

The grown-ups went inside the clubhouse to put on their swimsuits, and we carried our inner tubes to a sandy beach beside the shallow section of water roped off for non-swimmers. Soon the adults came back, warned the girls to look after me, and then swam out to a raft in the lake. Both of the girls jumped into the water, but I was afraid; I couldn't see through the dark green water to the bottom. So Dorothy Mae led me in up to my waist to reassure me.

Meanwhile, Big Evelyn, paying no attention to us, flopped down into the water with a loud whomp and lay on her back, like a hilly island, floating out to the rope that separated our shallow section from deep water. I tried lying on my back as she did and sank to the sandy bottom and had to struggle to the surface, sputtering and gasping for breath. Frightened, even though Dorothy Mae would rescue me, I refused to dip my head under the water, so she folded heavy paper into a boat to float on the surface between us as we waded.

We played quietly along the waterfront until someone on the other side of the lake started shouting. We saw red, white, and brown arms of swimmers slicing through the green water coming toward us. The first swimmer to reach the shore stopped in shallow water until the others gathered around. He pointed at his leg. "I've been snake bit! These bloody holes are fang marks."

I added snakes to my fear of heights and dark water as the gang ran to the clubhouse. In the hubbub, our adults had swum to shore from the raft, and Mrs. Adamson declared we were leaving. Evelyn plopped down into water up to her neck, bawling. Dorothy Mae and her father grabbed her arms, trying to lift her out. She pushed them away, blubbering. Evelyn whimpered until the women returned from the clubhouse. Only the motherly voices of Mrs. Adamson and Miss Pearl lured her to the car, where they wrapped us in towels to keep us warm and the seat dry driving home.

Since my parents weren't members of a country club, we had no private lake to swim in. We entertained ourselves listening to our little Crosley radio, but their main entertainment, besides bridge games, was going to silent picture shows on Wednesdays in the red and gold auditorium of the Majestic Theater, between Eighth and Ninth on Main. Mama was always eager to see movies, especially like *The King of Kings*, the story of Jesus performing miracles and healing others before his agony and death on the cross. Our biggest surprise at movies was hearing the voice of Al Jolson singing in *The Jazz Singer*.

My favorite evening at the Majestic Theater involved live actors performing *The Torch-Bearers* on the stage. In order to see the play, I balanced on the front edge of my upturned seat to look over the heads of the adults in front of me. I remember before the curtain rose, the pit orchestra played so loudly that people shouted at each other. I wanted to shout: "Be still, while the music rises about us!"

But as the house lights dimmed, the music and voices faded and the front curtains parted, flooding the stage with colored lights. I was seeing and hearing for the very first time living people on stage rather than black, gray, and white shadows on a screen. They were doing and saying funny things. Daddy laughed at them just as he had at the silent movie in McRae. I felt the muscles in my face, arms, and legs moving in response to the actors on stage, sensing the rises and falls in the melodies and volumes of their voices. The play was about amateur actors rehearsing and performing, and, in some dominant way, it affected the rest of my life.

The next morning at the Adamsons' house, I repeated lines of dialogue and gestures that made the sisters laugh as the theater audience had the night before.

Mrs. Adamson said, "Cleveland's turned out to be a regular stage actor."

Later, I recited for the Lloyds, and they suggested letting me take elocution lessons from a teacher who lived across the street from them. Mama looked at Daddy, who said, "Money's too tight for elocution or expression lessons, whatever it is you call 'em."

For the first time in my memory, my father referred to hard times, scarce jobs, and low salaries. Fortunately, my parents scrimped to pay for my elocution lessons, a routine that was set from the very first day. I walked by myself to the Lloyds' cottage, and Aunt Grace led me across the street to Miss Millie Simmons. The slender, black-haired teacher lived with her parents in a two-story, red-brick house at the corner of Fourteenth and Cumberland, across from the East Side Junior High auditorium and gymnasium. I couldn't read it, but Mama said her framed diploma in Expression from Galloway College for Girls, in Searcy, was hanging on the wall over their fireplace.

Following her instructions, I stood at one end of her living room, opposite the balcony on the second floor by the bedrooms, where her parents peeked at me. I stood in "the best speaking posture," feet apart (one slightly ahead, with weight on the ball of the forward foot), back erect and flat, chest high, and chin up.

She insisted, "Good posture, Cleveland, is fundamental to your volume, appearance, and health, providing bodily poise and freedom for expressive movement."

I learned to recite, "with proper facial expression and gestures," "Wynken, Blynken, and Nod" and "The Duel," both by Eugene Field. After my first lessons, Miss Simmons sent Mama a note, saying I memorized easily, "thought the thought," and revealed meaning through my natural phrasing and emphasis. Mama especially liked the poem that defined her ambition for me:

> *Gran'ma says she hopes that when I get to be a man,*
> *I'll be a missionary like her oldest brother, Dan ...*

At the lesson's end, Miss Simmons escorted me to the Lloyds', where I repeated my lesson for Aunt Grace and Frankie. With Cokes, Frankie and I went to his room to listen to his crystal radio set, which had no cabinet or speaker like our Crosley and the Atwater-Kent. He attached a wire antenna to a window screen and passed another whisker-thin silver wire held between his fingertips across the surface of an irregularly shaped disk of gray lead crystal until the end lodged in a crevice and voices and music crackled in the earphones, surprising every time.

There were other surprises at Aunt Grace's. Even though our home was nice and clean and well lit, hers was a rainbow of colors from bright flowered drapes and white lace curtains at the windows. Her oddly decorated lampshades threw unusual shadows on the walls. And the incense she burned filled the rooms with rare aromas. She had more antimacassars on the arms and backs of her chairs than anyone else we knew, and her table tops were covered with tatted doilies, embroidered cloths, ceramic figures, ashtrays, and other odds and ends, which left hardly space enough to set anything down. I never sat in a chair without dislodging a pillow or something else, but Aunt Grace never fussed.

Even though Mama didn't do much home decoration with crafts like Aunt Grace did, she occasionally rearranged our furniture, "for variety's sake." Once, she placed our mohair sofa across one corner of the living room, creating a triangular space that I made my secret cave. But the Adamson sisters brought a strange girl with them when they baby-sat me, and she caused a ruckus. We played hide-and-seek, and Dorothy Mae favored the new girl, offending Evelyn by not complimenting her hiding place, or saying how hard she was to find. Evelyn whined until she and Dorothy Mae joined me in my cave behind the sofa.

When the new girl found us, she jumped off the back of the sofa, striking Evelyn with her foot. Evelyn was mad, and, crying in anger, pushed me at the girl. "Bite the mean ole girl!"

Instantly, I became "Maid" Evelyn's loyal knight, and rescued her by sinking my teeth through the girl's dress into her stomach until my jaw cramped. When I relaxed my bite, the girl ran out the front door screaming, "I'm telling my mother on you mean old kids."

Mama returned, the Adamson sisters went home, and I forgot about what had happened until the door bell rang. Mama opened the door and faced the injured girl and her mother.

The woman said, "Mrs. Harrison, I want to show you what your boy did to my little girl. Lift your skirt, honey, and show Mrs. Harrison."

The deep impression of my teeth on the girl's stomach resembled the tiny pink petals of a small flower.

Mama asked, "Did you do this?"

Struggling to speak over the knot in my throat, I tearfully promised not to bite anyone ever again and pressed my face into Mama's apron.

The lady, vowing her daughter would never play with us again, departed.

Mama pushed me away from her and looked into my eyes. "I'm so disappointed in you, Cleveland, for hurting another person, especially a girl."

"She's a lot older and bigger than me, Mama."

"Maybe so, but you've no right to punish or hurt anyone, whatever their age or size."

She put me in the pantry to ponder my future behavior. It was dark in there, and I wasn't tall enough to reach the light switch. The small window the sun shone through was too high for me to look out, so I sat on the floor and sang "When the Red, Red Robin Comes Bob, Bob, Bobbin' Along."

Mama tapped on the door. "Stop that singing, young man! Think about what you did."

I remembered my shame until I saw a bag of dried black-eyed peas on the shelf, which set me to wondering how many peas would fit inside my nose. I pushed so many peas up one nostril that I felt as if I were smothering, and ran out of the pantry clawing at my nose and screaming, "Mama, Mama, I can't breathe." She grabbed my shoulders, blocked the other nostril, and shouted, "Blow as hard as you can!"

When all the dried peas had popped out, I headed for the back door to escape being switched.

"Allie Cleveland Harrison! Stop where you are. Get back in that pantry, and don't touch another thing!" I knew that she knew the big bag of black-eyed peas still lay within easy reach.

Eventually, Mama let me out, took me on her lap, and told me, in a whispery other-world voice, about Buster as a baby in Beebe. "I left him dressed in his diaper playing with pots, pans, and a wooden spoon on the kitchen floor. As I did chores in the rest of the house, I could hear him beating pans on the floor. I didn't notice when he stopped. But I finally realized how quiet it was, and went back to the kitchen. Oh, my goodness! He wasn't there! I hurriedly checked the pantry, the dining room, and the back porch but didn't find him. But when I returned to the kitchen, I saw the bottom cabinet door half open and heard the oddest sound. Guess what? He was in the bottom of the cabinet smacking his lips while brown saliva dripped off his chin. The little rascal had managed to open and dip his hands into a can of sorghum molasses. When he spread his fingers apart, the film of molasses between his fingers looked like webbing in a tiny frog's feet. When I wagged my finger in Buster's face, saying 'Baad ... baaad boy!' he shook his head from side to side, mumbling, 'Uhnn, uhnnn talk!'"

Mama screwed up her face on "Uhnn, uhnnn talk," and I laughed and hugged her; she hugged and kissed me right back.

She said, "Buster's so much older that now you're my only child. He doesn't want to be corrected, but my little man minds what his momma says, doesn't he?"

Whether I did or not, I always paid close attention to both Mama and Daddy. On paydays, when Daddy handed her the rent money, Mama expressed how much she wanted us to have a home of our own instead of paying rent. I was with her when she placed rent money in Mrs. Adamson's hand, and I decided someone should put money in Mama's hand, too, so she could buy a house.

A few days later, our next door neighbor knocked. "Mrs. Harrison, we won't pay our rent for a few more days. Our check from the city's late this month."

Mama asked, "Why would you pay rent to us for Dr. Adamson's house?"

"Cleveland says Mr. Harrison bought the house, and we should pay our rent to you."

"Good gracious, we can't buy a house. We do well to pay rent. You musn't believe what Cleveland tells you. He's just 'putting on' and making up stories."

The neighbor lady laughed. "The little rascal certainly convinced me."

Perhaps her trifling remark stirred an awareness of a special ability within me. Mama didn't perceive it, though, and put me in the pantry again, promising to tell Daddy when he came home. In the meantime, I wondered if he would paddle me. He didn't; he simply sat down and stood me in front of him, boring his hazel eyes into my blue ones, as if trying to see inside my head.

Of course, when Buster heard what I had done, he had his say. "All kids imitate but they don't lie and show off like my baby brother."

I wasn't lying or fibbing, just telling stories like the grown-ups. How could I know the stories Daddy, Uncle Harold, and Uncle Moss told weren't always true? My stories convinced my parents that I'd become a preacher or a salesman, so they didn't punish me. But Buster, out of our parents' earshot, said my "foolish lies" embarrassed him with his friends.

"Just keep lying and pretending, and someday Dad will beat you the way Mama beats dust out of rugs."

The next time I was taken to see Uncle Cleve, he patted his mattress, and Daddy put me up beside him. The men steered away from his illness and talked about business in McRae before my birth, when they formed a strawberry brokerage, sure that crops in White County would be outstanding.

Daddy said, "Strawberries did so damned good in 1921, we thought we'd make a profit."

"What's a profit, Daddy?"

"In strawberries, little boy? Breaking even!" The men laughed.

Daddy said, "Two bad years in a row … too much rain splashed on 'em in '22, softening the berries. So little the next year, berries got no bigger than grapes."

After more talk about their mutual friends and relatives in White County, they were silent, until Uncle Cleve patted my shoulder. "How's my namesake doin', Allie?"

"He's a natural salesman, Cleve, got your gift of gab. If he don't sell 'em, he'll tell 'em a story."

On my last visit with Uncle Cleve, the carbolic disinfectant in the long corridor stung my nose, and before Mama opened my uncle's door, she pressed her finger to her lips to shush me. My uncle wasn't propped up as usual, but lying flat on the bed. He didn't seem to know we were there. I stood on tiptoes to see his face, which was white, his eyes closed. His appearance didn't scare me; perhaps the hours I spent beside Grandma as she lay dying had prepared me.

Before we left, Mama put my hand in Uncle Cleve's and held his other hand, praying with her eyes closed. My uncle stared into my eyes, as if attempting to infuse his spirit in me.

In the weeks that followed, Uncle Cleve's illness worsened, and Mama spent more hours at the hospital, leaving little time for her to prepare for Thanksgiving and Christmas at our house. But Daddy and Buster decorated, hanging a wreath on the front door and cutting a cedar tree in the woods near the airport, which they covered with angel hair, tinsel, tinfoil icicles, and glass ornaments.

Mrs. Adamson invited us over on Christmas Eve for a drink, called wassail, and a piece of fruitcake topped with hard sauce. But Dorothy Mae, Evelyn, and I drank fruit juice, and found the hard sauce lumpy and bitter tasting. What delighted me was Mama playing the piano when Dr. Adamson suggested singing Christmas carols.

She was unsure, but Daddy encouraged her. "Floy, just play the way you did at the Baptist and Methodist churches in McRae."

Mama said, "But it's been so long since I touched piano keys."

Sitting on the bench of the upright piano, she tentatively passed her hands across the keyboard, her rough fingers stumbling in a trembling effort to find the proper notes. Yet, to my untrained ear, I knew she carried the music, adding little rushes of grace and half-faltering surges of feeling. The other surprise that festive night was colored electric lights on the Adamsons' Christmas tree—green, blue, purple, ruby, and opal. Back home, when I compared their tree and ours, as I had with our Crosley radio and their Atwater-Kent, Daddy's mean eye flashed.

"Come here, young man. Let me tell you something! Though your mother's dear brother is dying, she decorated our tree, made fruitcake and date-nut loaf, and will prepare our dinner Christmas Day. If this house blew up or burned down, she'd see that you and Buster and I have a good Christmas. So don't let me hear you compare anything of ours with anybody else's."

Under our pretty little tree on Christmas morning were a scooter, a box of Tinker Toys, a big rubber clown doll, and a stocking full of fruits, nuts, and hard candies from "Sandy Claws." The rubber clown was as tall as I and bounced right back up when I knocked it down. Daddy was right. Everything didn't have to be big, shiny, and fancy for us to have a happy Christmas.

Two days after Christmas, one month shy of a year after my grandmother died, Uncle Cleve passed away. My folks didn't take me to his funeral or burial at the Beebe Cemetery, believing it would be too distressing. But Mama read aloud the long obituary Uncle Albert, her older brother, wrote for the *Baptist Advance*, which began:

*It becomes my sacred duty to chronicle the untimely
death of my only beloved brother, Willie Cleveland,
which occurred at a local hospital in Little Rock at
5:15 a.m. on December 27th after a lingering illness
of several months. His going was sad beyond expression
for he was in the noontime of life, just thirty-six on
October 2. He leaves a wife and four children, three
of which are small, one being a mere infant.*

Mama cried and cried, and my father and brother had the saddest faces ever. Even though the grownups acted sad about death, they talked about it happily: "Grandma and Uncle Cleve are better off now with God." And they confused me by saying, "Someday, we'll all be together in Heaven." If that's true, why put their bodies in the ground if they are going to rise up to Heaven?

My trust in Jesus was infinite because Mama and the Bible assured me. The first scripture I learned by heart was John 3:16: "For God so loved the world that He gave his own Begotten Son that whosoever believeth in Him shall have everlasting life." My mother's beliefs were the strongest religious commitment in our family, far stronger than my father's. Even though both joined the Second Baptist Church in Little Rock in 1917, Mama had been baptized as a girl in Cabot and Daddy only after they married in 1911.

On a few Sundays, Mama let Dorothy Mae and Evelyn take me to the red-brick Methodist Episcopal Church South, at Fourteenth and Scott, where the tall steeple so enthralled me that Dorothy Mae taught me to make a pretend-church by lacing my fingers together to make a steeple, and then revealing the "finger people" inside. I also first learned to sing the children's hymn "Jesus Loves Me" at the Methodist Sunday school class.

After Sunday school, I sat with the Adamsons in their pew in the quiet, dark sanctuary, listening to hymns and watching dust motes float in the beams of colored light streaming through the stained-glass windows. The window that especially held my attention pictured Jesus kneeling in prayer beside a gray boulder under a dark blue sky in the Garden of Gethsemane, the night of Judas's betrayal. Even though too young to grasp the meaning of worship, I sensed the wonder of honoring the One to whom we offered worship. But the church's claim on Sundays did not impress Christian principles upon me as did the daily cheer, compassion, and charity my parents displayed every day with friends and strangers, black and white alike.

Late one afternoon, a shiny black car pulled up in our narrow driveway, and I ran out the front door to see who was in it. My father in the driver's seat was smiling. He opened the passenger door. "Hop up here in our new chariot, sonny boy." He had traded our 1916 Model T Ford touring car, which sounded like a cement mixer with an ah-ooga horn, for a four-door, six-cylinder 1928 Chrysler sedan that purred as quietly as Buster's Ole Tom cat.

At supper, Daddy described his new job in Warren, a lumber town in southern Arkansas. The Ray-Glo Corporation of Cincinnati, Ohio, had hired him to sell natural-gas space heaters, with his headquarters in Warren. He had expected natural gas would replace wood, coal, and kerosene across the state when it was first offered to households in Little Rock, but seventeen years had passed before gas transmission lines reached southeast Arkansas.

So many men had lost their jobs that Daddy believed getting a new job was a miracle. Mama called it "God's blessing."

Even though Buster expressed no opinion about our moving, I didn't want to go and begged to stay in Little Rock playing with Dorothy Mae and Evelyn, listening to the wonderful Atwater-Kent radio, pulling grab bags from the box at Baer's grocery … and taking elocution lessons! When I didn't stop begging and crying, Mama lifted me up on her lap, speaking to me as if I were as old as my brother, for that's the way my parents would always treat me.

Smoothing hair back from my forehead, she said, "Cleveland, we all have to accept changes, big ones and little ones alike. That's the way life is going to be for you, too. So you have to face the changes without being sad or afraid, because something just as good, or sometimes even better, almost always comes along to replace what you lose. You wait and see, you'll make new friends in Warren, and we'll find another nice lady to teach you elocution."

Wanda Stovall and Cleveland with a turkey
at 332 Hermitage Highway, Warren.

CHAPTER 2

A Happy Year in Warren

ONCE MAMA CONVINCED me she would find an elocution teacher in Warren, I was as excited as my parents about moving—so eager that when the Terminal Van & Storage truck backed into our driveway, I carried my little oak rocking chair onto the front porch to load myself. But Mama warned me to stay out of the way, so I sat in the swing watching two burly moving men, huffing and puffing like the wolf in "The Three Little Pigs," carry our furniture onto their truck. As the men rested on the front steps, Mama had me carry them cold Cokes and ice water. Then, after wrapping our furniture in quilts as Mama did putting me to bed, they drove away to reach Warren before us the next day.

Even though Mama had kept bedclothes and quilts for us to sleep on pallets in the empty house overnight, Aunt Grace and Aunt Ethel "wouldn't put up with it!" Both insisted on our spending the night with them. So Daddy and Buster bunked at the Lloyds, who fed all of us supper, and Mama and I stayed with the Means, who prepared breakfast the next morning for everyone. When we returned home, Aunt Grace, Mrs. Adamson, Dorothy Mae, and Evelyn were on our front porch, waiting to say goodbye.

Aunt Grace, hugging and kissing Mama and me, claimed, "I don't know what Harold and I will do without you all."

While the women talked and the girls played hopscotch, Buster sat on the front steps brooding. Mama said he was upset about leaving his buddies, especially Homer Jones. I walked through the house beside Daddy looking for anything that might have been left behind before he strapped suitcases on both the running boards and laid one on the floor in back. Signaling it was time to go, he opened the car doors. Mama and Buster didn't move. I did though! I climbed in the car, eager to see the new town and our new house.

Daddy said, "Floy! Bus! Let's hit the road! Got a hundred miles to go before dark."

Mama touched Buster's arm. "Please, let the girls keep your cat, Buster. They've promised to take good care of him."

"Aw! Mama, I can't leave my buddies and Ole Tom, too." He gripped the loose skin on the cat's neck and plopped down in the back seat, making water spill through the lid holes in my goldfish jar.

As Daddy started the new Chrysler, without having to crank it, everybody but Buster waved goodbye. Daddy tooted farewell on the car horn and backed out of the driveway onto Thirteenth Street. He drove to South Main, and we coasted down the steep hill to Roosevelt Road with our car tires whirring on the bright red bricks like cardboard strips flapping against my tricycle spokes.

The suitcase Daddy put on the floor in back prevented my standing by the window, as I usually did, so Mama passed the bed pillows to Buster to raise me high enough to see out.

The hundred miles to Warren was the longest trip I had ever been conscious of taking. After getting on Arch Street Pike, we soon passed the Shriners' Country Club, where the Adamsons had taken Dorothy Mae, Evelyn, and me to play in the lake.

I shouted, "Daddy! There it is! There's that big lake where the snake bit a man swimming!"

Ducking his head to glance out Mama's window at the dark, shimmering water, he sniffed, "I've swum in ponds, creeks, rivers, and lakes without being snake bit. Maybe the man didn't see the reptile. Or toyed with it."

Farther out Highway 65, we passed two abandoned rock quarries on the left-hand side of the road, deep holes where engineers blasted gigantic granite boulders to make gravel to pave the road's surface.

"Daddy, the water in those holes is green."

"Yep, that water turned green from minerals and algae collected in it."

When we reached Woodson, a little wayside village occupied mostly by black people, Daddy drove under the canopy of an old natural-stone gasoline station by the road to fill our gas tank. But the big black man who came out to serve us said, "Lawsy me, mister, I only sells barbecue beef and pork." The aroma convinced Daddy to fill our stomachs instead of the gas tank.

Both my parents loved barbecue, even though the pepper-hot meat sauce disagreed with Mama and made my mouth sting. But she braved her upset stomach, just as I happily let tears roll down my cheeks.

Nearing Redfield, Daddy pointed off to the left of the highway at an old road half concealed by undergrowth. "There's the remains of the old Dollarway! That was the first hard-surface highway in Arkansas and first *concrete* rural road west of the Mississippi River. When it was completed in 1914, it was called "Dollarway" for the dollar per linear foot contractors got paid to pave it."

"Daddy, how do you know all kinds of stuff like that?"

"Well, sonny boy, I've lived in Arkansas all my live-long days and paid attention."

Past the Dollarway's ruins, we drove under a canopy of the entwined, tangled limbs of oak trees over the road to Pine Bluff. In the spring and summer, it would be a shadowy green tunnel of trees pierced by pinpoints of sunlight. When we entered the city of Pine Bluff, Daddy followed paved streets to State Highway 15, which turned out to be a gravel road. From there to Warren, the cars ahead or passing us stirred clouds of gritty dust, forcing us to raise the windows to only a crack at the top. Soon, the car's interior became so hot that Buster's tomcat started salivating and retching, threatening to throw up.

Mama warned, "Allie, you'd better stop the car before the cat vomits."

Daddy grumbled about losing time but stopped on the shoulder of the road. And Buster tied a thick piece of twine around Ole Tom's neck to prevent his escaping while walking him along the roadside.

Mama, glancing at them in the rearview mirror, said, "Ole Tom's suffering so. Buster shoulda let the girls keep the cat. But at our boy's age, he won't listen to anything I say."

My father sighed. "He's sad about leaving his pals, that's all, Floy. And he really loves the cat."

Once we were underway again, Daddy drove slowly, taking long looks at the thick groves of trees on both sides of us, finally declaring, "These pines and oaks are the tallest, broadest ones I've ever laid my eyes on." Farther down the road, he pointed at the thick hardwoods in the bottomlands and cypress sloughs, adding, "Trees like them truly make Bradley County a lumber center in this state."

I couldn't resist telling him, "I'm scared of those old dark woods, Daddy."

"Nothing to fear, little man. Only deer, wild turkey, and other small game in there." Since I wanted Daddy to be proud of me, I refrained from saying anything more about being afraid.

After stopping a second time to walk the cat and air the car, we arrived in Warren so late that Daddy sped on past the square in the middle of town to the pavement's end on the outskirts, where our car thumped off the pavement onto a gravel road.

Pointing at a one-story, white clapboard house on our left, Daddy said, "Floy, there's our new home—332 Hermitage Highway."

The Terminal moving van was parked in the driveway, and the crew was lounging on the front steps. When Daddy lowered his window to apologize for arriving late, Ole Tom leaped out, dragging the thick twine leash behind him. When Buster sprang after the cat's yellow streak, Daddy yelled, "Never mind that damned old alley cat! Let's help these men get our furniture in the house before it's too dark."

Daddy and Buster joined the moving men carrying and placing the furniture pieces where Mama wanted them. Trying to stay out of their way, I roamed the big lot; judging by the height of the house's roof and the depth of its eaves, it was much bigger than Dr. Adamson's rent house in Little Rock. And the driveway, instead of two narrow concrete strips, was a wide black cinder path from the highway to the one-car garage beside the house. The biggest surprise was a basement, with windows so narrow and dark I couldn't manage to see inside.

Giving up, I crossed to the front of the house and stood between two square wooden posts on the top step of the front porch, imagining I was a sentry pacing back and forth, guarding the parapet of an ancient fortress.

KA-BAM! An enemy shot rang out!

I nearly jumped out of my skin, as Mama always said. I turned to face the yellow, two-story frame house next to us where the door had slammed and saw a blond-headed boy, about my size, leap off the porch and run toward the picket fence separating our yards.

He stopped at the fence, swelled his chest like a pigeon, and shouted, "High-dee! I'm Joe Morris Wilson Junior! My daddy's a millwright!"

What an odd thing to say! But it was better than "my daddy's a *salesman*." What was that long word Aunt Grace said her older son was? That word that had more beats in it than *millwright*?

Oh, yeah. "I'm Cleveland Harrison. My daddy's ... a *bootlegger*!"

Joe Junior didn't act as though he cared one iota. Instead, he suggested playing cowboys-and-Indians, which lasted until dark when the moving van drove away.

Our family sat at a bare table in the empty kitchen, which smelled like old food, and shared the cold picnic supper Aunt Grace sent with us. Daddy said our new home was a "company house" that Bradley Lumber Company allowed him to rent because the Ray-Glo Corporation had leased space to display gas heaters at the commissary. Buster was eager to look for Ole Tom, but Daddy reminded him his first duty was enrolling at Warren High School the next morning.

Mama asked what I did while the men unloaded the furniture, and I told her about playing with Joe Junior and asked what a *millwright* was. But before anyone could answer, I asked, "When can I start taking my elocution lessons?"

Daddy frowned, the furrows on his high forehead as deep as the plowed fields we saw coming to Warren.

Mama quietly said, "We'll see about that after we've been here awhile."

After a quiet night of country sounds, a round of piercingly shrill shrieks awakened us before daylight. When I ran to my folks in their bedroom, Daddy said the steam whistles at the six sawmills in town were blowing at the same time, signaling the employees on the different shifts at the mills to start or quit work.

Mama said, "Well, I don't look forward to that racket every morning."

Since we had no food in the kitchen cabinets and no ice and no drinks in our Sears-Roebuck icebox, Mama sent Buster to Macy's, a little rinky-dink general store near the pavement's end, for bread, butter, cereal, milk, and coffee.

After breakfast, Daddy dropped Buster off to register at Warren High School, and we saw the two-story, red-brick Victorian building, which wasn't modern like East Side. Then we drove to the downtown square to shop for groceries. Warren, much smaller than Little Rock, wasn't divided into square blocks and seemed more spacious to me. Daddy said more than two thousand people lived there, considerably more than in little McRae.

The town's businesses were located on the square and the streets around it—hardware and variety stores, banks, savings and loans, groceries, and drugstores—and there were no tall buildings like in Little Rock. The tallest was the Bradley County Courthouse in the middle of the square, which had towers at each end, the taller one topped by a cupola with the face of a clock as round as a harvest moon. The clock bonged eight times as Daddy parked at an angle at the curb, the first time in my memory we hadn't parked parallel.

We walked inside the Bradley Store, the lumber company's commissary, where mill workers could buy groceries, meats, dry goods, clothing, and furniture on credit. I saw Daddy's Ray-Glo stove display and desk on the first floor, which convinced me he'd be home every night as he was in Little Rock. But only two days later, he packed the car with gas stove samples and left to call on furniture and hardware dealers in southeastern Arkansas.

Mama was disappointed that Daddy left town so soon, because the people in the house before us had left all the rooms dirty. With Daddy away, she had to persuade Buster to help her clean the sinks, tub, toilet, and stove. But for days, she swept the rugs, waxed floors, shopped for groceries, cooked meals, kept the books, and attended to Buster's and my health and conduct. Without Mandy, she also washed clothes, ironed shirts, mended socks, turned collars, and sewed on buttons.

We could hear the lonely whippoorwill calling in the deep woods behind our house, but Mama and I were seldom alone and lonely, even though Buster began hanging out with his new pals at school. Mrs. Stovall, our neighbor on the town side of us, paid Mama the first social call. She and her husband, Sam, had owned their home since before the birth of their daughter, Wanda, who was a year older than me. Mr. Stovall was employed by the Warren and Saline Railroad of the Bradley Lumber Company as a locomotive engineer. His wife said lumber companies in the South often owned railroads to transport their products, since many southern mills were too far from city markets for the major railroads to serve them.

When Wanda Stovall came home from school later that afternoon, she came over to play with me. She looked more like a boy, with her hair in a Dutch bob and wearing cutoff overalls, and played with the strength and energy of a boy.

Even though Joe Wilson Junior, the first person I met in Warren, lived right next door, two weeks had passed without his mother paying the obligatory courtesy call that Mama expected. She found a slight from a new neighbor difficult to understand; Southerners customarily welcomed new arrivals right away. Many other neighbors on Hermitage Road and members of the First Baptist Church on South Main had already called on us in the evenings.

The mystery wouldn't be solved until Mrs. Wilson saw Mama and me enter the Bradley Store. Mrs. Wilson was making a purchase when she saw us and, leaning close to the clerk waiting on her, she whispered, "See that black-headed woman and little boy. They moved into the mill house next door to us nearly two weeks ago, and I believe her husband's a bootlegger!"

"A *bootlegger*? Really, Mrs. Wilson! Where did you hear that?"

"The day they arrived in Warren. Their little boy told Joe Junior right off. Then I noticed her man packs his car before daylight and leaves on Mondays, and comes back late Fridays and unloads his car in the dark. That's proof to me!"

The clerk laughed. "Mrs. Wilson, he doesn't sell whiskey, he sells gas stoves. His desk and display are over there by the stairs. Your neighbors are Mr. and Mrs. Allie Harrison from Little Rock."

That afternoon, Mrs. Wilson called on Mama and apologized for her misunderstanding. After she left, Mama pointed out once again the trouble I caused using words I didn't understand and confined me in the kitchen pantry, which had no window or electric light like the one in Little Rock, to impress her lesson.

Later, I discovered Joe Junior had skewed his father's job, too. Mr. Wilson was a carpenter, not a millwright.

The first Saturday in our new home, Mama sent Buster to collect kindling for the wood cook stove, and he took me along to hunt for his cat, leading me into the woods deeper than I ever expected. Grabbing hold of me, he tried to drag me even farther into the underbrush, but I kicked him, twisting and pulling away so desperately that he began laughing, lost his grip, and let me break free. Straight as an arrow, I ran for home between the trees, over and around bushes, tripping and pushing everything aside, until I was in our backyard, breathless and triumphant. Buster's trick of hunting for Ole Tom hadn't worked!

When Buster came back with kindling, he threatened me. "Next time, buddy boy, I won't turn you loose. I'll take you so far in the woods, you'll never be seen again, just like Ole Tom."

"You don't scare me anymore, Buster. I found my way home but your old cat didn't."

In the week after I made my proud claim, Ole Tom meowed plaintively at our back screen door—thin and bedraggled. He smelled so gamy that

Mama wouldn't let him indoors until Buster came home and bathed him. Ole Tom resisted the soapy water, stretching out stiffly and scratching my brother's bare arms and hands bloody. Yet Buster finished bathing Ole Tom—as usual, more patient with the cat than he ever was with me, who never ever hurt him at all.

Nevertheless, my brother treated me better and took more time with me in Warren. Maybe he was busier and happier after making new friends with all the boys and girls at high school.

When I heard that the Warren high-school building had once been a Presbyterian training institute for GIRLS, I kidded Buster about going to a sissy school. I was proud, though, that he won a position on the Lumberjacks track team at spring practice running dashes and one leg of a relay. Mama bragged on him, calling him "fleet-of-foot." He brought his black and orange track suit home to wash, and when he wasn't looking, I tried it on to see what an "ath-uh-leet" felt like. Buster saw me and began laughing! With his shirt dragging the floor like an evening gown and his track shoes swallowing my feet, like those worn by cartoon characters, I resembled a clown. I tried to make him laugh some more waddling like a duck, but Mama called a halt, fearing the steel spikes on the toes of the track shoes would scar the hardwood floor.

She reminded us, "We take even better care of other people's property than we do our own."

In Warren, Buster began dating girls and dressing up. I don't know which came first, but he lingered longer in front of the dresser mirror, parting his black hair down the middle, and wearing ties knotted in what he called a Windsor knot. After he polished his shoes without being reminded, Daddy dubbed him "a mighty snappy dresser."

He suggested, "Boys, you'll always be respected if your hair's trimmed, your hands and nails clean, and your shoes shined."

Buster appeared to be dating a different girl every afternoon or night, going places for Cokes, ice cream, or something. Even though Mama often asked, he wouldn't tell her much about the girls he dated. But when a girl at church claimed "he's the best ballroom dancer at Warren High School," Mama persuaded him to take lessons from one of the two dance teachers in town: Miss Evelyn Deroux, who commuted from Pine Bluff, or Mrs. John Hemphill, the wife of the county agriculture agent. Buster picked Mrs. Hemphill, whose fee was smaller because she didn't commute. I asked why my folks could pay for his dance lessons but not my elocution lessons.

Daddy straightened me out in a sentence. "Listen, young fellow, you're free to take elocution lessons when you have a job and can pay like your brother does."

That's when I heard Buster had been hired part-time as a *soda jerk* at Glasgow's Confectionery, "The Place Where They All Meet," which featured soft drinks, candies, cigars, and billiards. I told him he was "a full-time jerk!" and he chased me in and out of the house, threatening to jerk a knot in me.

Only a few days after he started working there, Mama took me to Glasgow's to watch him mix and serve refreshments. I wanted to sit on a tall stool at the high front counter where he was working, but Mama preferred to stay out of sight and avoid embarrassing Buster. Remaining out of sight was almost impossible at Glasgow's, for the mirrors on all the walls reflected images of everybody at the marble-top counter and tables in the shop. So Mama picked a table in a distant corner and placed an order with another waiter for what were reputed to be "the best chocolate malts anyone ever tasted." So many kids waited at the counter for cherry and lime Cokes, phosphates, strawberry fizzes, chocolate malts, and sundaes that Mama didn't need to worry about Buster spotting us.

Later, he started working at night as a *car hop*, which seemed as funny to me as *soda jerk*. I imagined him hopping like a bunny rabbit while balancing a loaded tray to serve people in the cars parked at the curb beside Glasgow's.

What Buster didn't tell my parents about was playing pool and bowling in the back room at Glasgow's after work. Even though he competed in pool with the best players in town, including even the Reverend Bruce C. Boney, the town's revered Presbyterian minister, he didn't tell Mama and Daddy, who wouldn't approve.

My father and Mr. Stovall had both grown up in the country and quickly became friends, sharing stories out in the driveway on weekends about farming, fishing, and hunting. One Saturday, Mr. Stovall suggested going fishing together the next weekend on the Saline River and taking Buster along. All the rest of that day, Daddy and Buster bored Mama and me with old fishing and hunting stories. The next week, when not at school or work, Buster prepared their fishing equipment—lines, hooks, poles, and bait. I wanted to go with them, but Mama asked me to keep her company while the fishermen were away.

Before sunrise the next Saturday, the fishing party loaded their gear and Buster into the bed of a beat-up truck, and Mr. Stovall drove them out the rutted, dusty old Hermitage Road to a landing on the Saline River. Joe Junior and I sat on our front steps watching them leave and griping, until Joe thought of taking a fishing trip of our own in the woods behind our houses. I didn't hesitate, because after playing in Joe's favorite hideouts and escaping Buster, I no longer feared the deep woods.

We dug up worms and put them in a can, tied strings and hooks on bamboo poles, and put the lunches our mothers prepared in a cardboard box. After their warnings to be careful and be back before dark, we took off. Joe Junior led me through the thick stands of trees and deep underbrush until we came upon a shallow but fast-running creek. We tossed our baited fishing hooks and lines into the clear water and sat side by side on the shady bank, whispering to avoid disturbing the fish. Our quiet mumbles weren't necessary, though, for nothing in the water nibbled at our bait; there were no real fish of any size in the creek. Finally, "bored to Kingdom come," as Joe Junior said, we removed our shoes and socks and waded into the creek, watching the sunfish, minnows, tadpoles, and crawfish squirm around our bare toes on the muddy bottom.

Abruptly, Joe leaped on the bank. "I know whut! If we cain't ketch fish, we'll trap birds."

"How can *we* trap birds? They're so skittish, they'll just fly away."

"I'll show ya. Git that box that has our lunches in it and follow me." We gathered the box and our shoes, and I followed him to a small clearing. "Here's a good place to set a trap after we eat the sandwiches."

We stuffed our mouths with sandwiches as Joe studied the trees and bushes looking for the right limb to cut off. Eventually spotting a branch with a Y-notch at one end, he cut it off and fitted one edge of the lunch box into the stick's cleft, propping it up. Then Joe Junior attached his fishing line to the bottom end of the stick and laid the string along the ground between the cardboard box and some bushes. I thought of placing bread crusts left from our sandwiches under the box as bait.

"Now," Joe Junior said, "we'll git behind these here bushes and wait till some old bird lands and hops under the box for the crumbs. I'll pull the string, and the box will drop over him."

For what seemed like hours, we sat in the bushes telling stories, waiting for a bird to light and hop under the box to eat crumbs. A few flew over, chirping loudly, but not one alighted near our trap. Our only fun was watching squirrels leaping about, chattering, and digging up morsels they had buried earlier. Sitting beside Joe Junior, I realized that although he was older, I was slightly taller, which made matters between us more equal.

As the dapples of sunlight faded in the deep woods, we wiped our muddy feet, put on our socks and shoes, and headed home, hoping the fishermen had returned with their catches and stories. No such luck. They hadn't come back! And Mama was fidgeting because Daddy didn't take her to buy groceries for Sunday dinner. Joe Junior said Mama could drive our car to the store, though she never had.

I urged, "Mama, let's drive to the store and get the groceries!"

"Oh, Cleveland, I could never drive the car."

"I bet you'd drive as good as Daddy if you tried."

"Well, truth is, I used to drive our old Model T in McRae till I nearly pulled the barn door off backing out. Your daddy grew so angry and made so many rules for me, I was afraid to drive anymore."

Joe Junior and I fiddled around some more in the yard, and the fishing party finally dragged in just before sunset and began dividing strings of crappie, catfish, and bass among them. But Daddy kept his very special catch, a snakelike black eel. Mr. Stovall said he couldn't recall when someone last hooked an eel in the Saline River, and Joe Junior ran home to fetch his dad for a looksee.

Pulling the eel from the fish bucket, Daddy struggled to catch hold of the slimy-looking body; its only resemblance to a fish were small fins near the end of its tail. He tried to measure its length as the eel writhed every-which-a-way, wrapping around Daddy's wrist and arm.

Daddy laughed. "Just 'cause an eel's out of water, he don't give up!"

"What are you gonna to do with it, Daddy?"

"Skin it and eat it, boy. Gotta cook it tonight, though. You only eat eel when it's fresh."

A few men in the yard who had eaten eel couldn't say what the flesh tasted like. One man said, "Maybe it tastes like chicken. Every other food in the world seems to."

Daddy began preparing the eel for Mama to fry, driving a nail through one of its eyes to pin its head to a backyard fence post. With his fishing knife, he made a shallow cut at the base of the neck and pulled back the skin around the eel's head. Then, gripping the cut ends with pliers, he tugged until the tough black skin slipped off in one piece.

Watching Daddy cut the full length of the eel and scrape the guts and kidneys out, Mama said, "Oh, Allie, that's sickening."

The men laughed.

She asked, "You're not suggesting we really eat that ugly snake, are you?"

"It's not gonna taste good, Daddy!"

"It's a fish … considered a delicacy by some. That's good enough for me."

Mama was so reluctant about preparing the eel that Daddy fixed supper, frying strips or filets of eel along with a few crappie and catfish.

Sampling the eel at the table, Daddy declared, "It's sweet and savory, Floy. Better try it."

But Mama and I wouldn't eat eel. We couldn't get the picture of a black snake out of our minds.

After moving to Warren, Daddy took our car to the Chrysler dealer for regular checkups, and he met the manager, Mr. Russell Hendon, and his wife, Liz, the secretary at the dealership. Shortly after he met the Hendons, who were younger and had no children, they had us over for supper and became fast friends with my parents.

When the couples began playing contract bridge on weekends, Buster's job at Glasgow's prevented his baby-sitting me, so my folks took me with them on bridge nights. At first, they put me in the kitchen at the table to draw and color with crayons and listen to the radio. But when other couples joined the bridge parties, their games grew more competitive and lasted well past my bedtime.

So, when my bedtime came, Mama put me down to sleep beside the jumble of guests' coats on the bed in the host's bedroom. Lying on their bed behind the closed door, I could barely hear the adults in the other room talking about *rubbers, tricks,* and *passing,* which made no sense to me. Bored but unable to fall asleep, I started trying on the different coats and jackets and parading in front of the dresser mirror. The shapes, materials, and textures of coats reminded me of various human and animal characters that I pretended to be. In a lady's short fur jacket, I became a mole burrowing beneath the hillock formed by the overcoats. With the thick fur trim of a lady's tan coat around my neck, I roared like a lion. When I pulled a woman's gray coat sideways, with one sleeve hanging down loosely from my head, I became an elephant. Different types of coats created endless possibilities.

When bridge games ended, Daddy bundled me, still half-awake and pretending to be asleep, inside his warm coat jacket and carried me to the car. Going home, I listened to my father laughing and teasing Mama about her good luck at cards, how she could bid and win while talking about everything under the sun but the game. From the driveway, I floated aloft in Daddy's arms to my and Buster's bedroom, where I changed into my jammies and slid limply into bed. Mama later came to the bedroom in her gown and robe, her face smeared with cold cream, heard my prayers, tucked me in, and bestowed an icky kiss on my cheek.

Mama's new friends invited her to many activities besides bridge. One morning, Mrs. Hendon, the car dealer's wife, honked out front to take us to a "quilting bee" on a farm farther out Hermitage Road. I was eager to go, assuming, without knowing what a "quilting bee" was, that we'd eat hot buttered biscuits with honey. An overnight rain, after filling the ditches on both sides of the road, had slacked but was still falling. Under an umbrella, we hurried to the car, with Mama carrying our lunches and a sewing kit in her basket, and me clutching my favorite car in my fist.

Two church ladies and their bags already filled the back seat, forcing me to sit up front on Mama's lap, as Mrs. Hendon steered the car slowly and cautiously along the muddy road, dodging potholes and letting faster cars pass that splashed us with mud. Neither of the ladies in back talked. The only sound in the anxious silence was wipers slashing the mud spattering across the windshield. Yet, creeping along at turtle speed, I felt the muscles in Mama's legs tense as our car's wheels slid in and out of the muddy ruts.

When we arrived at the farmhouse, a few women were already sitting on four sides of a square frame suspended from the ceiling in the center of a room. Standing beside the frame, my eyes level with its surface, I decided *quilting* might be a game like bridge. Mama and Mrs. Hendon put our lunch baskets in the kitchen and returned to sit alongside the other women, tucking their knees under the multicolored sheet that covered the frame.

Mrs. Andrews, the hostess, explained to Mama, "The quilt we're making has three fabric layers—thin top and bottom layers and softer material in between."

I pushed my little car on the floor along the walls trying to hear what the women were talking about. Finally, I slid past Mama's legs under the frame. No one objected, I guess because the country women's skirts covered most of their legs, which were encased in heavy cotton stockings. Lying on my back, I saw the bottom sheet of the quilt was muslin sacks, imprinted with sugar and flour company labels, sewed together. The women were spreading an even layer of raw cotton on top of this bottom sheet for the lining, called *bats*, and stitching the bats at intervals to prevent the cotton from wadding up.

While their thimbles and needles clicked, they took turns repeating Bible verses. In one of their longer pauses, I crawled out from under the frame and stood beside it, announcing, "I know Bible verses, too: *For God so loved the world that he gave his only Son, that whosoever believes in Him should not perish but have eternal life.*"

"That verse is the heart of the New Testament, Cleveland," said Mrs. Andrews.

"And I know a poem by Robert Louis Stevenson I learned in elocution."

The ladies smiled and mumbled to each other, which I assumed meant they wanted me to recite.

A child should always say what's true
And speak when he is spoken to,
And behave mannerly at table;
At least as far as he is able.

Mama said, "That'll do, Cleveland."

Mrs. Andrews said, "Oh, he's not a bother, Mrs. Harrison. He speaks so clearly for such a little boy, he definitely had elocution?"

"Yes, in Little Rock. We're looking for a teacher here for lessons."

After lunch, the women went back to the frame, and Mrs. Andrews brought out a paper grocery bag full of quilt blocks she had sewn together from calico and gingham scraps left from her dressmaking. I watched the women begin sewing the squares together, forming an overall pattern they called *Grandmother's Flower Garden*.

Earlier, Mrs. Andrews had named and demonstrated different quilt stitches for Mama, the names of which stirred pictures in my mind: *featherstitch, brier, lazy daisy, ocean wave, snail trail*, and *dot-and-dash*. The women's sewing movements, in-and-out, up-and-down with their hands, joining squares together for the top layer, looked like naughty children picking at the food on their plates without eating. The women bragged about the patterns of their quilts at home, mentioning Shoo-Fly, Sunbonnet

Sue, Sherman's March, Churn Dash, and Dresden Plate.

I was pushing my toy car across the unfinished pine floors when my right knee unexpectedly stopped moving, hung on something. I checked and saw a narrow sliver of soap-bleached raw pine in the floor had pierced the skin of my kneecap so deeply it wasn't bleeding or hurting much. Since we were in company, I didn't tell and worry Mama. Good thing, too, because not long afterward, the women started to put away their sewing kits and gather their belongings to leave.

Outside, the rain had stopped, but the sky was still cloudy and dark. In the fading light, Mrs. Hendon driving away from the farmhouse turned on the headlights to see the road better and avoid deep ruts in the mud and gravel going back to Warren. Even though the drive was slow, Mama didn't seem to be in a hurry; I guess she was relaxed, knowing only our two suppers had to be prepared before we listened to our favorite radio shows.

A few days later, I awoke and found my knee hot and throbbing. I forgot about the pine splinter and now it was embedded in pus and hurting. Lucky for me, Daddy was home, because Mama would have been so afraid of hurting me trying to remove it that she would have. But he pulled the sliver out in one piece with eyebrow tweezers, causing no pain at all. While soaking my knee in alcohol, he warned me about cleaning deep puncture wounds, using iodine, and keeping gauze under tape over it. He said a farm boy in Beebe who ignored a wound like mine died of lockjaw.

There was a fun part to any scrape or wound, though: I could wear the bandage like a soldier's medal and impress Joe Junior and Wanda Stovall.

One weekend, Daddy drove us to McRae without Buster, who was working at Glasgow's and dating girls. But Daddy didn't understand why Mama felt responsible for Grandpa Honea and wasn't eager to go.

"Floy, your dad may be overweight, but he's strong as an ox. Alma waits on him hand and foot, morn to night, with or without you there."

"He may have treated my sister Iona and me strictly and harshly, but he was protecting us. He's my Papa, and I want to help care for him in his old age."

I never knew what mean things Grandpa did to Mama and her sister. Nor did I know why Daddy and Grandpa didn't get along. I never knew when we were going to visit him, for my folks seldom discussed their plans in front of me. I just knew a trip was likely when Mama laid out the crinkled-leather Gladstone bag, and Daddy took the Chrysler to the Red Rose Garage and Filling Station to have our tires, oil, and gasoline checked.

Once we passed through Little Rock and North Little Rock headed into White County, we had a surprise. The lanes on each side of Highway 67 had different surfaces—the westbound lane was gravel and the eastbound concrete. Daddy claimed the state hadn't collected sufficient taxes to pave both sides at the same time. To avoid the gravel surface, the cars going west drove as far as they dared on our side. When Mama saw cars coming toward us in the same lane, she cringed and gasped, fearing they wouldn't cross back to the proper side.

Daddy said, "Floy, taking deep breaths when you see a car coming our way won't change a thing. They're at a good distance and will get on their side, whether you expect it or not."

So he continued driving along the menacing concrete lane without a worry in the world about colliding. Mama distracted herself by telling me about the family of Benjamin Franklin Honea and Elizabeth Ann McCuin and their three boys and three girls. Their first daughter was stillborn and their eldest, Iona, died bearing her first child. Their youngest boy died of croup after playing in a wet sandbox on a cold autumn day. The three who grew to adulthood were Albert Lafayette, Willie Cleveland, and Floy Estelle. Mama was born in Hazen, Arkansas, where Grandpa owned a livery stable before his first grocery store in Beebe. Fifteen years later, in 1910, he and Uncle Cleve founded Honea Mercantile Company in McRae, but Mama stayed in Beebe with Grandma to finish public school.

Mama said, "Your Grandpa had a picture of all us Honea kids put on the one-pound can of ground coffee sold at Honea Mercantile."

"Oh, Mama, can I see the tin can and how you all looked as kids?"

"Well, I can't promise. Papa may still have one of those old coffee cans."

Daddy said, "If Cleveland sees the Honea kids, he'll see how beautiful you were, Floy."

"Oh, now, Allie!"

"Well, it's true! Cleveland, your momma, though innocent and awed by the world, was really popular in Beebe."

Daddy dropped us in McRae at the store to visit Grandpa first without Miz Alma and drove back to spend the night in Beebe with Big Daddy and Grandma Harrison. Grandpa saw that Buster wasn't with us and didn't hide his disappointment. That didn't surprise me, because Mama said Buster and Uncle Cleve's son, Charles, were Grandpa's favorites. Except for Buster's black hair, he and Charles looked like Honeas, short and muscular, with pale complexions, very much like the photographs of Grandpa when he was young.

Even though my grandfather rarely spoke to me, or chatted with anyone else for that matter, Mama urged me to talk to him. So to please her, I tried to find something to say to him.

"I know a poem, Grandpa."

"Your grandma would've liked that."

"I know all the lines of Eugene Field's 'Seein' Things' by heart."

"Well, good for you."

"I'll say it for you, Grandpa."

I ain't afeard uv snakes, or toads, or bugs, or worms, or mice,
an' things 'at girls are skeered uv I think are awful nice!

When I finished all the verses, Grandpa said, "Well, it's sure long enough," confirming he thought me too talkative and assertive for a child.

While Mama talked with her *Papa*, I wandered around with his clerk, Andy, inside the big seed-feed-and-dry-goods store. It was extremely dark, because the wide canopy at the front of the store shaded the smeared show windows, and the narrow horizontal windows above the wall shelves admitted mere slits of lights. The bare electric bulbs hanging at the ends of long wires beneath the embossed tin ceiling tiles shed very little light in the corners or between the tables in the middle of the store piled with coveralls, overalls, blue jeans, and flannel shirts. The darkness overhead partially concealed the coils of flypaper lumpy with the carcasses of dead blue-green flies.

"How do you reach stuff on those high shelves, Andy?"

"I climb this here ladder that moves on rollers and ketch aholt of 'em with this *grabber*." He showed me a long pole with a clamp on one end that he used to snare out-of-reach items.

Andy pointed at a stain on the floor by the back wall where he said a World War I veteran fell asleep one day running a half gallon of molasses into a jug. Leaning against the back wall, the hundred-pound burlap bags of feed and seed and forty-five-pound flour sacks were taller than me. The cans of fruits and vegetables I saw on the shelves were as big as nail kegs. Andy offered me saltine crackers from an open barrel and a slice of Kraft cheese cut off a big wheel on the back counter before leading me to a long glass display case near the front door.

He pointed out the different tobacco products Grandpa carried: small cloth bags of Bull Durham for roll-your-own cigarettes; hip-flask tin cans of Prince Albert and Sir Walter Raleigh tobacco for pipes; ornate wooden boxes of Havana cigars; small urn-shaped jars of Garrett's snuff; Horseshoe tobacco plugs wrapped in heavy lead foil, and Brown Mule chewing tobacco in twists. Grandpa smoked a corncob pipe himself and sold tobacco items to the old men who sat on benches in front of stores, smoking, dipping, and chewing. I had to be careful about stepping off the boardwalk into tobacco spit, discarded chews, and cigar and cigarette butts.

Even though very few customers shopped that Saturday afternoon, Grandpa waited until nearly sundown before closing. On our way to his house, we walked two "country blocks" (no corners or intersecting streets) along Grand Avenue until the street branched off into a narrow dirt lane, passing private homes on wide lots separated by picket and barbed wire fences.

"Why are there so many fences, Grandpa?"

"Arkansas has no range laws. We gotta erect fences to keep other people's cows, horses, and pigs off our property."

Grandpa's weathered old gray clapboard house and the dark green cottage next door, where our family lived while taking care of Grandma, came into view. Miz Alma greeted us at the back door without a smile but with a stick stuck in the corner of her mouth.

"Miz Alma, what's that sticking out of your mouth?"

"My dip stick. A sweet hickory twig to smear snuff on my gums."

"Whatta you wanta do that for, Miz Alma?"

"Because snuff tastes sweet and gives me a lift."

"Can I taste your snuff, Miz Alma?"

"Nope. Tobacco powder's not for little boys. It'll make you sick."

Before we had supper, Grandpa proudly led Mama and me on a tour of his barn, fenced cow lot, woodshed, chicken coops, and vegetable garden. "I can handle all my own needs, daughter. Got a garden for vegetables, hens for eggs and pullets, and cows for milk and butter."

With daylight nearly gone and the house dark, Miz Alma lit coal oil lamps in the living room, dining room, and kitchen. Ever since McRae's early days, when a generator furnished electricity only from ten in the morning until four in the afternoon, Grandpa had coal oil lamps for light, his fireplace for heat, and wood stoves for cooking. But Miz Alma proudly showed us Grandpa's anniversary gift to her in the kitchen—a cream and green enameled kerosene cook stove with a glass-paneled oven door through which I could see biscuits baking.

Like everyone in McRae, Grandpa had a fresh-water well, but unlike others, his well-head was under the back porch roof. Before washing up for supper, he let me draw water from the well by lowering a galvanized-steel tube attached to a hemp rope over a pulley. The full tube of water was too heavy for me, so we pulled it up together. When I released the lever at the top of the tube, water gushed into the cedar bucket at my feet.

Lathering our hands with soap from a dish beside the bucket, we washed in a ceramic bowl, and dried on a common towel hanging from a wooden dowel.

"I bet it's hard drawing enough water to take a bath, Grandpa."

He harrumphed, "Mighty foolish using well water for bathing. For that, I collect rain water in barrels under the drain pipes from the roof."

I plunged the big dipper, as Grandpa and Miz Alma did, into the water bucket on the counter and drank the cold well water that had the bright metallic taste of tin. Later, as we prepared to sleep on the screened porch, Mama told me to use a drinking glass instead, in order to avoid the germs others left when drinking from the common dipper.

Our routine at Grandpa's changed a little bit with each season. In winter, everyone sat in front of the fireplace after supper, Grandpa in his overstuffed leather chair, Miz Alma in a straight-backed wooden rocker, and Mama and me on the squeaky leather sofa. The adults talked mostly about Honea and McCuin relatives I had never met, Grandpa recalling old times when he owned a livery stable at Hazen, where Mama was born, and a grocery store at Cabot and Beebe before starting his general mercantile store in McRae. Miz Alma listened, stoic as an Indian, sucking on her snuff stick, and I chewed a piece of Juicy Fruit gum, quiet as a mouse.

I fixed my eyes on the yellow-red-and-bluish streaks of flames in the crackling fire in the fireplace, watching ghostly figures flare up, flicker, and evaporate as quickly as they appeared. When I looked away from the fire's glare into the room's gray gloom, I saw the linked shadow-figures of our family dancing on the living room walls. Finally, to relieve my burning eyes and my face that was slightly numbed and swollen by the heat, I faced away from the fire and saw the firelight reflecting on the adults' faces, altering their features.

Eventually weary of fantasy visions and adult talk, I searched the room's dark corners for Grandma Honea's coral-pink conch shell, a souvenir from her childhood. Pressing the shell to my ear, I could hear what Mama called "the slow, sad murmur of a distant sea," a line she remembered from a poem, and imagined the sea waves rolling over Jonah and the whale and Jesus and the fishermen in the storm.

Usually, not long after supper in any season, Grandpa asked Miz Alma to fetch enormous Red or Golden Delicious apples from a crate kept in the kitchen. Slipping off the pale yellow or pink tissue wrappings, he leaned forward, pulled a knife from his rear pocket, and opened its long, sharp blade. With a newspaper spread across his lap, he pared skin off the apples as if shaving whiskers from a man's cheek, preserving as much juicy flesh as possible. He divided the crisp apple wedges among us and tossed the coils of peel into the fire to sweeten the air in the room.

After supper on summer visits, we sat out on the front porch, the grown-ups in rockers and the swing, with me on the front steps. The adults rocked gently, talking quietly and gazing across the yard as moonlight silvered the picket fence and whitened the empty unpaved street out front. In the thick, hot darkness, I smelled night odors drifting from the woods and nearby gardens, and listened to crickets churring, katydids and tree frogs peeping, and owls hooting. Buzzing mosquitoes discovered us soon after and began crash-diving into our tasty flesh, before Miz Alma placed lighted citronella candles at the edge of the porch and sprayed bug repellent, pulling and pushing the plunger of a pump spray can of Flit.

As she did this, I repeated, "Quick, Henry, the FLIT!" the radio slogan of the manufacturer, which annoyed Grandpa, who had no radio and had never heard the commercial.

As darkness deepened, the rows of four-o'clocks along the edge of the front porch slowly closed their petals, like pursed lips, and fireflies began flashing their lemon tail lights. They floated so lazily across the yard that I easily scooped them from the humid air into my sweating palms to put in my "glow jar." In bed on the sleeping porch, I stared at the fireflies blinking in the Mason jar, a magic lantern on the bedside table that stirred my fantasies and guarded me in the night.

Grandpa's house had only one bedroom, so summer and winter Mama and I slept on the screened porch, going to bed and getting up earlier than at home, whether weekdays or weekends. In summer, with the canvas curtains raised to relieve the heat, if we didn't get up with the sun, we lay in full view of neighbors and passersby. In winter, with the curtains down, the view of outsiders was blocked but not the drafts of frigid air. I had to snuggle down into the warm valley of the sagging goose-down mattress beside Mama, hoping I wouldn't have to use the slop jar, Grandpa's "thunder mug."

By far the worst possibility was having to walk outside at night along a narrow path of wooden planks, slippery with damp moss protected by the droopy trees, to the toilet. The privy had two holes, one large for adults and one small for women and children, with no partition in between. Balancing myself over the smaller hole, I dreaded someone coming in to sit beside me (though they never did), or being stung by flies, spiders, and wasps hovering in the miasma below me. Holding white-knuckled to the sides, I drew short, shallow breaths to avoid the stench and germs in the fetid air.

The only wipes were paper wrappings off apples and oranges, or pages torn from Sears-Roebuck catalogs and old *Arkansas Democrat*s, none of which met Mama's sanitary standards. Once back in Warren, I appreciated for evermore the proximity, privacy, lights, soft tissue, and easy flush of a commode.

During our visits in McRae, Mama called on friends she had made while nursing Grandma, and Daddy visited former customers and business-men he knew when managing a drugstore-confectionary and delivering soft drinks to Beebe, Garner, and Griffithville. Mama's best and oldest friends in McRae were Mrs. Maymie Herring and her husband, Homer, who owned Herring's Variety Store in the old red-brick building beside the First Country Bank, at the corner of Grand Avenue and Railroad. When the Herrings first moved to McRae from Cabot, in 1915, they worked for Grandpa and Uncle Cleve until starting their own business.

After reminiscing with the Herrings, Mama left me at their store and went to call on her other friends. Mrs. Herring led me through the store, choosing odds and ends of merchandise for me to arrange in her front window. Upon Mama's return, Mrs. Herring showed my display, bragging about fabrics, colors, and prints I chose.

She asked, "He's just a lil' ole boy, Floy. Where'd he learn to do some-thing like that?"

"Maymie, your guess is as good as mine. He always *notices* things like that."

"He recited poems for me and customers, remembering every word, as far as I could tell."

"Oh, Maymie, I hope he didn't show off too much."

"Not at all. I just love what he does."

Daddy picked us up after Sunday dinner at Grandpa's for the drive back through Beebe, Ward, Cabot, and Jacksonville to Little Rock, a trip that seemed longer traveling on the dusty, unpaved side of the road.

Passing through the little towns between Little Rock, Pine Bluff, and Warren was tedious, especially in winter, when the sun sank before we reached the gravel road to Warren. One evening just beyond Pine Bluff, Daddy broke the boring twilight spell by slamming on the car brakes, pitching Mama toward the dashboard and me into the back of the front seat.

Mama gasped, "What's the matter, Allie?"

He leaped from the car without answering, and Mama shouted, "Allie! Don't leave us in the middle of the road! We'll be hit by another car!"

Instead of heeding her, Daddy crouched in the headlights' glare, slipping down as low as two bright red dots gleaming just above the road bed. Then, whipping off his wide-brimmed felt hat, he made a swooping leap and clamped his hat over a small animal.

"A possum!" he said, thrusting it into the toolbox on the running board.

"I declare, Allie, I don't know what you want with an ole possum!"

Without answering, he started the car and resumed driving.

After a moment, Mama said, "I don't understand you 'n' Buster 'n' animals."

Finally home, Daddy stopped in the driveway and opened the toolbox, exposing the snarling varmint baring its yellow teeth and hissing. He wrapped his hat around it again and carried the possum to our woodshed.

In the middle of the night, I heard squawking chickens at the Wilsons' next door, creating an awful ruckus that lasted for a long time before quieting down.

The next morning, Mrs. Wilson, hanging out wash on the other side of the backyard fence, told Mama, "A possum killed a hen in our chicken house last night before Joe scared it off."

Mama, certain it was the possum Daddy caught, offered to pay for the hen, but Mrs. Wilson refused. "Any ole possum or raccoon can get in that beat-up henhouse any time."

A few days later, I found my goldfish floating on the surface of the water, their shiny orange-gold scales bleached dull white. Brokenhearted, I ran to Mama, who made me eat breakfast before taking me on her lap to suggest having a funeral for Hans and Fritz in our backyard. Since I didn't know what a funeral ceremony was, she explained what I had to do. For their caskets, I filled two narrow pencil boxes with crinkly tissue paper, and dug small rectangular holes at the edge of the woods for the graves. Then Mama and I each carried a little casket, singing "Shall We Gather at the River," which seemed right to me for a fish's funeral. As my last gesture, I placed small cardboard headstones at the foot of each tiny grave.

At breakfast on Saturday, after I described our burial ceremony to Daddy, Buster busted out laughing. "Whatta waste of time with dead fish. They're only fish, for gosh sakes! When Dad and I clean fish, we don't bury guts and scales in a ceremony. We toss 'em in the garbage can."

Mama scolded, "That's a terrible thing to say, Buster. It's not the same at all. Cleveland loved and cared for the little goldfish for months. It's heartless to make fun of him."

"Well, I'll tell you one thing, Mama, I'm not buying any new goldfish. I didn't kill 'em."

Before the goldfish were replaced, Daddy brought home a short-haired, black guinea pig given to him by a customer in Monticello. He had a small white saddle across its stout back, short black ears, beady black eyes, a twitchy nose, and almost no tail. He was so curious about things I named him Nosey. The first night and day, Mama let him run loose in the house, tunneling under things and walking on the hearth bricks, which Buster claimed cooled his tiny feet. But his free run ended when Mama found pellets on the living room carpet and kitchen linoleum.

The next night, Buster brought home a cardboard box from Glasgow's filled with hay for the guinea pig's toilet and bed, and I cut doors and windows in the box for Nosey to crawl in and out. Buster insisted guinea pigs needed raw vegetables as roughage to gnaw and grind on to stay healthy, so Mama began saving spinach leaves, carrot shavings, celery stalks, and cabbage cores. Daddy even suggested I might find clover and dandelions in the backyard and woods to feed him.

Nosey's different sounds let me know he liked to be held and petted. When I rubbed his soft coat, he murmured, gurgled, and cooed, but if I did something that frightened him, he hissed and his little sharp teeth chattered. Even though Buster warned me that the scared guinea pig might bite me, Nosey never did.

I spent weeks tending the guinea pig, but it was far more difficult caring for him than feeding goldfish and cleaning their bowl. I had to trim Nosey's claws regularly, being careful not to strike the quick and hurt him, and since his tiny footpads and toenails were as black as his coat, trimming them safely was hard to do. In the long run, the guinea pig required so much attention that I had to give him away when I started school. Still, Mama insisted that having pets like Hans and Fritz and Nosey taught me to care for someone besides myself and to tend a creature smaller and weaker than me.

As I grew older in Warren, I improved at imitating the ways people stood, walked, and talked—enough to make Buster laugh at my impressions. I learned to imitate voices listening to more radio programs than anyone else in our family. But in the evenings, Mama joined me, sitting in Daddy's armchair as I sat on the floor beside her, absorbing music, comedy, and drama broadcasts on the Philco radio console that replaced our small tabletop Crosley.

Since I was seldom in the presence of African-American people in Warren, *Amos and Andy* became a favorite of mine because it reminded me of Mandy and Jake's voices and speech and my imitations of them. Even though the actors were white men, they captured the simple, trusting, high-pitched whiskey voice of Amos and the domineering, deeply pitched bass resonance of Andy. And each actor did a dozen other voices, like Lightnin' and Kingfish. Even though I couldn't match their pitches, I could deal with their rhythms, pronunciations, accents, and phrasing.

Mama and Daddy thought *Amos and Andy* had problems similar to the ones real people were facing, like when the stock market crashed and the old swindler Kingfish Stevens claimed he lost lots of money.

"Andy, dey wipe me out. Yo' see, a week ago Thursday, de big crash started. De bulls 'n' de bears was fightin' it out, and de bulls chased de bears."

I didn't know what Kingfish referred to, but his manner of speaking was funny. When I fell into the habit of repeating Amos and Andy's favorite phrases—"check and double check" and "ain't dat sumpin'," Mama didn't wait long to say she had had enough of that!

Four nights a week, we also tuned in to *Lum and Abner,* two country characters and their friends living in the hills of western Arkansas. Calm Lum Edwards and excitable Abner Peabody owned and managed a store similar to Grandpa's, called the Jot 'Em Down General Store in Pine Ridge, Arkansas. Chester Lauck, who had a deep, resonant voice, played patient, dense Lum, Grandpappy Spears, and Cedric Wehunt. And Norris Goff, who had a lighter, higher-pitched voice, played Abner, Grumpy Doc Miller, and the old skinflint Squire Skimp. I imitated Abner's high-pitched voice best, especially using his byword "Aye, doggies," which matched Grandpa's "Aye, gonnies."

Of all the radio performers we listened to, my folks preferred Will Rogers speaking in his Oklahoma twang for thirty minutes every Sunday night. Even though he was the most popular commentator on American radio, he claimed, "All I know is just what I read in the newspapers." His use of chuckles and extra long pauses after his own jokes and witty remarks puzzled me until Daddy explained they were devices that let the audience know when to laugh and helped him avoid stepping on laughs. Sometimes, in mid-sentence, Mr. Rogers would suddenly change from a serious to a lighter tone setting up the remarks to follow, and he used words like "kinder," "sorter," "woulda," and "coulda" to appear folksy and conversational to his audience.

While we lived in Warren, Daddy also tuned to Lowell Thomas and his nightly radio programs on both NBC and CBS, listening to the news about the evolving Depression, increasing unemployment, and the falling national income. Mr. Thomas reported that President Hoover was trying to persuade Congress to pass public-works bills to get more men employed, and that poor people were marching on and petitioning the White House for help in relieving their hunger.

The news on the radio worried Daddy so much that any time professional baseball with the St. Louis Cardinals was on the station KOMX, he tuned to the game.

After a girl at high school complimented his dancing, Buster took both ballroom and tap from Mrs. Hemphill. I wanted to know how to tap dance like the men and boys in the movies, but he refused to teach me. Impatient with him, Mama forced him to show me a few basic tap steps: the *brush*, kicking one foot backward and then forward, before slapping the ball of my foot on the floor to make a single soft tap; and the *shuffle*, sliding my foot forward, then brushing backward on the floor. And the transition, or *ball change*, shifting my weight from the ball of one foot to the other.

After mastering those steps and a few others, I asked Mama for metal taps on my shoes to *hear* my steps as I danced with the music on the radio. A cobbler downtown attached loose taps to the toes and heels of my oldest shoes, so that my foot's tiniest movement clicked taps. On my own, I discovered that by tensing my leg muscles extra hard, I made my shoe toe quiver, trilling taps lightly passing my foot across the surface of the floor.

One morning at breakfast, Buster told us his dance class would be performing in a charity pageant sponsored by Warren's civic clubs at the Pastime Theater on Cedar Street, where their slogan was "In Business for Your Pleasure." Mama, Daddy, and I were pleased to have a chance to see him dance for the first time, but he didn't want to participate. He loved ballroom dancing but hated solo tap, even in front of our family. I couldn't understand not wanting a chance to perform in front of everyone.

Buster always made fun of my wish to perform. "Doing what? Humming on a comb, telling a fat lie, or imitating a monkey?"

Any chance to be in the pageant seemed unlikely for me until our Sunday school teacher, Miss Ginny Perkins, volunteered to read a children's story and sing a medley of bedtime songs in the pageant, *if* our mothers would let us be the chorus for her songs. Of course, all the mothers were flattered for us to perform and volunteered to sew light blue pajamas for boys and pale pink nightgowns for girls. For once, Mama sewed my costume without Aunt Ethel's help, proving to be a good seamstress.

Mama usually trimmed my hair every few weeks to save money but decided a professional hair cut was in order for the pageant. So the Saturday before the pageant, Daddy took me to his favorite barber, singing and whistling on the way to the tune of "Shave and a Haircut, Two Bits." Since I had heard that phrase on the radio and had attempted to tap its rhythm at the end of my homemade dances, I asked what the phrase meant.

He said, "*Two bits* are Spanish silver pieces worth about a quarter."

When we arrived at Shorty's Barber Shop, Mr. Earl McGuire, who usually shampooed and trimmed my father's hair, was busy. So we sat on a long bench listening to stories about hunting, fishing, and the doings around town. Daddy left the bench and mounted a chair on top of a little platform, placing his feet on two iron footrests, shaped like the soles of his shoes, to get a shoeshine.

A small black man named Eddie polished Daddy's shoes, twirling and slapping a cloth across them, almost breaking into a dance. When he slapped the shoes one last time, Daddy stepped off the footrests, flipping a coin in the air to the shoeshine man, who smiled and said, "Thank ya', Mr. Harris."

By then, the barber had placed a board across the arms of his chair for me to sit on. "Hop up here, young man. Let's see what we can do with that thick head of hair." Spreading a cutting cape over me, he fastened it tight around my neck with a clip.

Daddy said, "Just give him a regular cut, Earl. Get rid of some of that mop."

I asked about the leather strap hanging by a clip and chrome buckle from the chair.

"That's a horsehide *strop*, son, for sharpening the blades of straight razors."

"How do you do that, Mr. McGuire?"

"Well, I *strop* by laying the back of the razor on the strop at a flat angle. Then I draw the razor away from me before turning it over and drawing it back towards my body."

"That boy's mighty *in*quisitive, Earl," said an old man. "Ya think he's got *ancestors*?"

"Oh, looks like it to me."

"Well, he's sure nuff got *garments* all over him."

"No, I don't! I had a bath before we came down here." Everybody laughed.

Another man said, "Well, it's a cinch that boy's got *scruples*."

"Daddy, I don't have any old scruples, do I?"

My father smiled. "Well, if anybody in this shop has 'em, *you* do, boy."

The men murmured agreement, and I knew, from their smiles, they were kidding me.

After cutting my hair, the barber rolled a wet brush inside a soap mug, which had a picture of a farmer and his wife on its side, and lathered the back of my neck and shaved it with a straight razor. He wiped the soap off with a warm, wet towel, and sprinkled talcum on a long, hairy brush, which he whisked across my neck and face, nearly smothering me in a cloud of powder. Rubbing a drop of Wildroot hair tonic on my hair, the barber tried, without success, to slick my cowlick down.

Mr. McGuire said, "Allie, you can bring this boy back any time. He's a quiet, steady fella."

Rehearsing our scene at church, we alternated boys and girls, going on stage in line holding hands, and sitting on the floor in a semicircle, with Miss Perkins sitting on a stool in the center. She told her story and sang "Pretty Baby," "Sleepy Time, Gal," and "Japanese Sandman," words and tunes I already knew from listening to the radio.

The night of our performance, I saw the Pastime Theater for the first time. The odd-shaped three-story building, about the width of seven cars parked at an angle, had a shallow canopy out front over the main entrance.

The theater's façade was three flat stucco profiles of tower walls, one partially covered in ivy. Inside, although the stage held a movie screen, it was wide and deep enough for live performances.

Our group gathered in a messy room at the back of the theater for our teacher and a few mothers to apply lipstick and rouge on our faces to emphasize our features under the bright stage lights. Before guiding us on stage, Miss Perkins put her finger to her lips, shushing any urge we had to talk while a comedy act performed in front of the curtain on the deep apron. From behind the curtain, hearing the audience shuffling, coughing, laughing, and talking excited me so much that I hugged girls on either side of me, which I never did in rehearsals at church. Waiting for our act to start, my heart was beating faster and I needed to pee!

As applause for the act ahead of us died, the front curtains parted, and we saw hundreds of expectant faces staring at us. Even though instructed to look only at our teacher, I couldn't resist searching for my parents' faces in the crowd. Some in the audience talked loudly before Miss Perkins began her bedtime story, and I wanted to say "shush" just as she had to us.

We had heard her tell her story often enough to repeat it ourselves and were eager to hear our cue to begin singing. The pianist vamped "Pretty Baby," leading up to the first song in Miss Perkins's medley: "Everybody loves a baby, pretty baby," and we sang the refrain. For some reason, I hugged and nuzzled the cheeks of the little girls beside me as we sang "pretty baby," and members of the audience laughed. While Miss Perkins was singing "Japanese Sandman," I gave in to a mysterious urge, rose, and walked behind the line, kissing each little girl on her cheek. When I reached the end of the line, the audience was laughing and applauding.

Daddy, coming backstage to pick me up after the show, said, "You're a crackerjack! That was a humdinger of a stunt you put on in that last song, boy. You're plumb loco about those sweet little girls, aren't you?"

Mama asked, "Were you supposed to kiss those little girls? Did you practice that?"

I admitted doing it on the spur of the moment but couldn't explain why. Mama reminded me I needed to contain myself, that Miss Perkins was the focus.

The next morning at breakfast, Buster had his usual say. "Upstaging the lead and stealing that scene's not right, buddy boy. Your smart-aleck stunt embarrassed me with my friends."

On my fifth birthday in August, my parents gave me *Hurlbut's Story of the Bible for Young and Old*, a thick, green book of stories from the Holy Bible, illustrated with hundreds of black-and-white and colored pictures. When Mama read a story at bedtime, I concentrated on the illustrations, imagining the actions of the figures in the drawings. Daniel sitting between two lions in the Den of Lions, as a third roared over his shoulder, was real enough to me to hold my breath, hoping he'd be safe. Mama assured me as usual, "Daniel was always safe because he trusted God."

One picture showed the black figure of Satan, pointed horns protruding from his forehead and giant bat wings sprouting from his back, standing face to face with Jesus, challenging the son of God. In the theater of my mind, I watched Satan flaring his enormous wings and thrusting a stone in Jesus's face, challenging, "If you're really the son of God, turn these stones into bread!" The scene reminded me of the face-offs between movie heroes and wicked villains.

One night, so impatient waiting for Mama to come read the usual Bible story, I said the words on the page out loud to myself. When Mama came, I went on reading to her. She was amazed even though she coached me in the alphabet and to look at the letters on pages while listening to her daily readings, unconsciously mastering the basic elements of reading. What I couldn't "read" I remembered from all the previous repetitions. When I finished the story, I told Mama I wanted to go to school like Joe Junior and Wanda.

The next day, she asked Mrs. Stovall about my being admitted and learned that Warren schools accepted children before they were six years old if the first-grade teacher, after an interview, judged them "ready."

So Mama took me to East Elementary School for the first-grade teacher, Mrs. Pierce, to evaluate me. She asked me to describe our neighborhood, our house, my room, and our family's friends.

At the interview's end, she asked, "Is Cleveland your only child, Mrs. Harrison?"

"No, he has a brother, nearly thirteen years older. Why do you ask?"

"Well, his vocabulary at his age is more common with an only child. He also has better consecutive memory than many five-year-olds. He told me a story in sequence with details."

With the teacher's permission, I started first grade, walking to school with Joe Junior, Wanda, and other children from South Main and Hermitage Road. Every day, I entered the front door of the old two-story, white clapboard building with the gently curved front, square bell tower, and peaked roof to climb the wide steps to my classroom on the second floor. Mrs. Pierce taught reading, writing, and simple arithmetic to the first half of the first grade from eight until noon every weekday.

We sat in tiny kindergarten chairs at a low table reading our textbook, part of an illustrated series titled *The Child's World*, featuring the characters Baby Ray, Baby May, and their pets.

One little dog he had to keep, keep, keep.
Two cunning little kitty cats creep, creep, creep.
Three white rabbits with a leap, leap, leap;
All saw that Baby Ray was asleep, sleep, sleep.

Mrs. Pierce drilled us each day in the letters and sounds of the alphabet, teaching us to spell simple words, divide them into syllables, and repeat them in sight reading.

On our way home at noon, Wanda and I competed telling Little Audrey stories. I would say, "Little Audrey's younger brother asked, 'Why do you always sleep on your stomach every night, Little Audrey?'" When she couldn't answer, I gave it: "Little Audrey laughed and laughed, because Uncle Sam was looking for a new naval base." Then Wanda challenged, "Do you know why Little Audrey jumps from an airplane without a parachute?" Her answer: "Because she's wearing her new spring coat." We laughed at our own answers, thinking our puns the best.

Wanda was so proud of the hunting and fishing exploits of her father and brother that she ran over to our house to tell us about fish they caught and brag about bigger ones that got away. One day, she was boasting about small animal skins her brother tacked on the wall of their back porch, and I let her know, "Those little animal skins are nothing to be proud of. Before we moved to Warren, my father and brother hunted black bears all over the place. They came face to face with a big bear standing on its hind legs, growling and showing long yellow teeth, but they didn't run. They raised their rifles and killed him. Later, they had a man who stuffs animals make a rug out of the bear hide with its head attached. It hangs in my brother's room."

A few days later, at the end of a visit with Mama, Mrs. Stovall said, "I can't leave here till I see the bear rug on the wall in Jimmy's bedroom."

Mama replied, "We don't have a bear rug on a wall or anyplace in this house."

"Cleveland told Wanda your men killed a bear and made a rug from the hide."

Mama, looking hard at me, shook her head. "Mrs. Stovall, you mustn't pay attention to what Cleveland's likely to tell you. He keeps making up stories."

Even though Mama dealt with some pretense of mine almost daily, she never punished me. My Daddy came back home off the road one Friday night with a true story far more exciting than any I made up. He told us at the supper table, speaking as if it were happening right then.

"On my way to Lake Village, I saw an old country woman standing by the road asking for a ride. It was extremely cold, and she had on a long overcoat, a dress reaching to her shoe tops, and a bonnet and gloves. I figured the covered basket on her arm held her lunch. So I pull up to the old lady, leaned across the front seat, and asked where she's going. She says in a husky voice, probably from a bad cold, 'I'm headin' to Collins, beyond Monticello. My daughter's sick.'

"As a rule, I don't pick up hitchhikers. Too many robberies on Arkansas highways to take a chance with a stranger, even a woman. But the woman's emergency and long way she had to go led me to give her a lift. I pass through Collins on my way to Lake Village, so I said, 'Well, climb in.'

"When the old lady opened the back door to get in, I pointed at the stove samples filling the seat and asked her to sit up front with me. She got in carefully, arranging her skirt and sitting as far away from me as she could. I couldn't get a conversation going on the road, but thought her long silence and short answers showed her concern about her sick daughter. While driving, I saw from the corner of my eye the woman's large, gloved hands and the covered basket on her lap, and how her bonnet hid her face. Farther down the road, when she adjusted her seat position, I saw the cuff of a man's trousers below her skirt.

"To test her, I asked, 'Did you hear the car thump just now? Hear that sound? I better stop and see if one of my tires is flat.'

"Pulling off the road, I asked her, 'Would you look at my rear tires? Don't want to ruin a tire riding on a flat.'

"She hesitated putting her basket down, but got out and crossed to the rear of the car. I lifted the cloth off her basket and there was a big old horse pistol! Let me tell you, I hit the gas pedal so fast and hard my acceleration slammed the front door shut. That old woman was left standing in my dusty tracks. After driving a mile or so, I stopped and looked again at the .32-caliber Colt Single Action Army pistol. That's a frontier cowboy's weapon, Floy. I don't know whether he planned to rob me or steal the car, or both. I found the police station in Monticello and reported the incident to police officers and left the basket and pistol with them."

Frightened by Daddy's story, Mama quickly left the table, and just as suddenly came back to make him promise never to pick up another hitchhiker.

Before we moved away from Little Rock, the politicians were campaigning for president of the United States, and my parents and their friends, Democrats all, were talking against Herbert Hoover, the Republican candidate, the man I saw in the cartoon on Dr. Adamson's foyer wall, and his vice-presidential running mate, Charles Curtis, from Kansas. The Democratic candidates were Alfred E. Smith, from New York, and Arkansas's own Senator Joe T. Robinson. Daddy favored Mr. Smith, even though my parents worried about a "Yankee Catholic" president. I heard Mr. Smith speaking on the radio in a funny accent I tried to imitate.

Daddy was voting for Mr. Smith because he was a Democrat and opposed Prohibition. You see, my father was making "home brew" in our basement, despite Mama's opposition to liquor of any kind. She was worried about Daddy breaking the federal law and being arrested. He had two big earthenware crocks in one corner of our basement filled with an odd-smelling mix he called mash. The fermenting mash, releasing gas through a small red rubber tube into a water-filled fruit jar, made bubbles that fascinated me. Daddy knew just how long the mash needed to ferment before he sucked on the tube, drawing liquid to his lips, and inserted it in the neck of a brown glass bottle. After a bottle filled, he pinched the tube and inserted the end in the next bottle. He used a capper that looked like a small car jack, sealing the bottles by pressing hard enough on the metal tab to fold its edges around the bottle's lip.

Sometimes, in the middle of the night, I heard bottles exploding and my parents rushing to the basement to clean up. Yet, no matter how thoroughly they cleaned, the odor seeped through the house. Mama feared the neighbors knew Daddy made home brew and would report him.

I was excited about Christmas coming, but my belief in "Sandy Claws" was shaky. I couldn't figure out how a jolly fat man could fly in the air in a sled pulled by reindeer or how he could land on our roof and be thin enough to come down our narrow chimney carrying a huge bag of toys. The only chimney and fireplace big enough for Santa was Grandpa Honea's, and Santa couldn't even come down his chimney if a fire was burning. My faith was first shaken on Christmas Eve in Little Rock, when I heard Mama and Daddy talking while placing gifts under our tree. Still there might be another explanation since so many people believed in St. Nicholas, Santa's other name. Why would stores be covered with wreathes, trees, and strings of colored lights if there was no Santa?

Mama hadn't yet put up our tree and decorations, so when I saw a man-sized colored cutout of Santa Claus advertising Coca-Cola at the A. T. Davis Drugstore on Main Street, I was enthralled. I began talking to the cardboard Santa at the store's entry before and after school, asking him if his stomach really was a bowl of jelly and how he managed to come down tiny chimneys with fires in the fireplace. I invented Santa's answers, speaking in as deep a voice as I could. I wanted to take Santa home with me but was afraid to ask the druggist.

However, one day Mr. Aubrey Davis, the straight-laced, cold-natured drugstore owner, was standing by the front door beside the Santa when I stopped and without thinking I asked, "Can I have that Santa Claus?"

His eyebrows raised and, looking straight into my eyes, he shook his head. "Nope!"

Just before Christmas Eve, I was talking to the cardboard Santa at the drugstore when Mr. Davis and his pharmacist, Mr. I. E. Pirtle, walked out the door. Again, I blurted out how much Santa meant to me.

Mr. Pirtle said, "Aubrey, give the figure to the boy! Christmas is just around the corner. We'll just throw it away later."

The kids beside me looked away or down at their feet, embarrassed, expecting Mr. Davis to refuse. Instead, the old man huffed, "Take it, if you want."

Since the figure was too wide and long to carry by myself, a bigger kid helped me tote Santa to my house.

Mama asked, "Where in the world did that big old thing come from?" And I told her what happened. Flabbergasted, she said, "What a nerve you have for a little boy, Cleveland." She let me keep Santa on our porch long after the holidays.

Just before Christmas, Daddy drove us to visit the Hendons at their automobile sales and repair shop in a fancy new building in Fordyce. Daddy parked our car at an angle in front of the showroom window that had a cardboard cutout of a boy in footed pajamas standing beside a General automobile tire, holding a lighted candle in his hand. Standing beside the cardboard boy, who was my height, I wanted to take him home to Santa. But I didn't ask Mr. Hendon.

I truly helped prepare for our Christmas celebration for the first time in Warren. Buster and I cut a cedar tree in the woods behind our house, the freshly cut trunk smelling like the inside of the old cedar chest in my parents' bedroom. As Buster dragged the tree on the ground to the side porch, I ran ahead, begging him not to break a limb or get the tree dirty. As usual, he paid no attention. Then we went to the scrap pile at the nearest mill for two-by-fours, and he made a stand for the Christmas tree that filled our house with its resinous scent.

On Wednesday morning, which was Christmas Day, I was up at dawn rummaging among the gifts, looking for ones with my name. Santa Claus left a few clothes but mostly toys: a baseball bat and glove, a Tinker Toy set, and a Lionel train with a locomotive powered by a wind-up spring, which pulled boxcars, Pullman cars, and a red caboose on metal tracks in the living room. The locomotive spring was so stiff Daddy had to wind it and ended up playing with the train more than I did. Driving a little lead automobile beside the tracks, trying to beat it to the crossing on the figure-eight tracks, was endlessly exciting.

The best gift, though, was a complete cowboy outfit: leopard-skin chaps, plaid flannel shirt (with Hoot Gibson's head embroidered on the breast pocket), patterned red bandana, wide-brimmed felt hat, and a six-shooter in a holster on a cartridge belt. I had seen Hoot Gibson that autumn in *Flaming Frontier* and *The Silent Rider*; he was my favorite movie cowboy. Wearing my new outfit, I galloped around the yards with Joe Junior and Wanda, slapping my buttocks (the flank of my horse) pursuing whichever was the cowboy or Indian villain. I upset Wanda by calling her a squaw; she claimed to be a brave but looked like a villain with her short haircut and cutoff coveralls.

My other movie heroes, Buddy Rogers and Richard Arlen, played aviators in *Wings*, wearing jodhpurs and boots, leather jackets, and aviator caps. One of my Christmas gifts was an authentic leather aviator cap that had ear flaps that snapped under my chin and helped me impersonate the aviators. The goggles that protected my eyes from the searing wind in the open cockpit up in the sky could be pushed on top of the cap after I landed. Mama gave me an old scarf so the loose ends could flap in the slipstream as I ran with my arms outstretched like airplane wings. Whether riding a horse or flying a plane, I wore my new leather boots, which had a knife in a scabbard on the side of one boot.

My lack of interest in the hard ball, bat, and baseball glove disappointed Daddy, a devoted fan of the St. Louis Cardinals ever since Dizzy Dean from Lucas, Arkansas, joined the team. He read newspaper stories from the sports pages to me about the Gashouse Gang, trying to encourage me to listen to the games with him. But baseball was too slow to hold my attention.

After Mr. Hoover became president, Daddy claimed, "Hoover's prosperity is an empty promise. Business is no better, no matter how good it was under Coolidge."

Since my father didn't own stock or invest in the stock market, like some of his customers, the big bull market on Wall Street didn't make an immediate difference to him. But his interest changed in October when he read about the "crash" on Wall Street. Back home off the road, he read the *Gazette* and listened intently to the radio news. One evening when the Hendons visited, the men had fun singing a ditty about President Hoover:

> *Rockabye, Hoover, on the treetop,*
> *When the wind blows, the market will drop.*
> *When the boom breaks, the prices will fall,*
> *Down will come Hoover, Curtis and all.*

In the spring of 1931, after the long, hard winter, times grew tougher when the stock market fell all to pieces and banks busted right and left. I didn't know we were neither rich nor poor but Depression-shadowed. Like many families in town struggling to do the best they could, my father received a telegram from Ray-Glo Corporation headquarters, transferring him to Little Rock. Since so many men in Arkansas had lost their jobs,

Mama concluded that Ray-Glo was taking its first step before firing him, so that uncertainty ended our stress-free life in Warren. But remembering what Mama told me before leaving Little Rock, I faced the change without being sad or afraid. I was going back to elocution lessons with Miss Simmons and games with the Adamson sisters again.

While Mama and Buster packed our personal belongings and hired a moving van, Daddy drove across his sales territory thanking his customers and asking them to keep in touch.

PHOTO OPPOSITE PAGE:
Cleveland at Parham School.

CHAPTER 3

In and Out
of Arkansas

WE SETTLED IN Little Rock again in the winter of 1930. My parents, unable to find a suitable house before leaving Warren, rented a furnished apartment on Scott Street, between Tenth and Eleventh, and stored our furniture until another place could be found. We were only two blocks away from the Second Baptist Church, closer than ever before to our religious home. But even with that rare advantage, Mama, who seldom faulted anyone or anything, complained about the shabby house that she and Daddy had chosen much too quickly.

Since I was not yet in school and had no other children for playmates nearby, the somber-gray winter weeks seemed unending while my parents sought another place to live. Playing alone on our tiny front porch, I had only happy memories of sunnier days romping with Joe Junior and Wanda in Warren to cheer me. Even my brother, who was a senior at the new high school on the west side of town, wasn't teasing me or having old friends over for fun anymore.

Mama's and my visit with Mrs. Adamson in the old neighborhood was disappointing; Dorothy Mae was in class at East Side, Evelyn in a special school, and another family in our house at 313 East Thirteenth. Mama's assumption that Ray-Glo transferred Daddy to Little Rock prior to firing him was a concern that certainly put elocution lessons on hold. Yet Daddy, at supper each evening, claimed he was selling more gas stoves to furniture and hardware dealers on Seventh Street, Little Rock's Furniture Row, than he had in southeast Arkansas.

Mama faced her worries with fierce bouts of scrubbing, sweeping, and dusting everything in sight. I seldom entered a room without her running me out so she could clean it. On Mondays, she washed clothes, boiling the sheets, towels, and bedclothes in a big pot on the stove. Tuesdays, she pressed the clean clothes, using her new electric iron. Wednesdays, she took me to the store, shopping for groceries. By Thursdays and Fridays, she had swept and mopped every room, and dusted every table and chair in the house.

But she finally set aside her bucket, broom, dust rag, and mop, and we set out on foot searching for an unfurnished house that suited her taste and "our family's pocketbook."

That accounts for my parents being so busy after our return to Little Rock that they didn't notice until late one rainy afternoon that my big brother was on the skids. Daddy was already home, and I was standing by the front window, watching rain dripping off the roof and dead leaves floating in the gutter, when a black police car stopped at the curb. A uniformed policeman and *Buster* got out! Hollering to my parents, I opened the front door before the bell rang, assuming my brother had a new friend who was a policeman. Daddy invited them in, but nobody sat down. I tried to catch my brother's eye, but he wouldn't look at any of us.

The policeman said he picked Buster up after a pool hall manager, on Louisiana Street, reported an underage boy shooting pool for money. The manager had warned Buster he would call the police if he came again, yet my brother sneaked back in.

The officer said, "Mr. Harrison, Jimmy claims he wasn't gambling, but every pool or snooker game I know of involves a bet of some kind, if only the price of a game. If he shows up in a pool hall again before he's twenty-one, I'll take him directly to jail."

After the officer left, Daddy said, "Buster, I don't want a son of mine hanging out at a billiard parlor. It's not a good place for a grown man, much less a boy—the cussing, drinking, smoking, and gambling. With money so scarce, don't ever let me hear you're gambling."

"I'm no kid, Dad. I'm old enough to take care of myself. Besides, nothing's *wrong* with pool. I played pool at Glasgow's with the most important men in Warren . One was a preacher."

"Did you lay bets on games with the preacher, too?"

Without answering Daddy's question, Buster said, "The first few days after we came back, I felt out of place at high school. So I skipped classes looking for a job."

Mama said, "Oh, Buster, you don't need a job. You need your education."

"I'm out of place at high school, Mom. Homer and other guys I knew at East Side aren't there, either. Homer's not old enough for the navy but his momma let him join anyway ... Besides, I need to find a job if Dad's going to lose his."

Daddy said, "What a helluva thing to say! I'll be damned if a son of mine has to help me make a living."

"Buster, please stay in high school. Allie and I regret not finishing."

I spoke up, "I won't quit high school when I'm big like Buster!" But I was too little for anyone to pay attention.

It was natural for Buster to feel grown up and want to help our family. Our parents were so young when he was born, he grew up as their little equal. For the first time, I realized that silent and short as Bus might be, he was thoughtful and strong. He could probably knock a bigger man down or drink a glass of home brew more readily and neatly than he could talk openly to anyone, even our father. A few weeks later, Buster was tending produce at a grocery store on the far east side of town and had officially dropped out of school. Nothing more was said in my presence about his returning to high school. How the issue was settled, I never heard.

I wasn't eager to attend a new school where I didn't know anyone, either. Even though Mama wasn't sure where they'd rent a house, she planned to enroll me at either Fred Kramer Elementary School, at Ninth and Sherman, or Parham Elementary, at Fifteenth and Vance, each an equal distance from our temporary home. Several ladies Mama met in the neighborhood insisted the best teachers were at Parham, so she took me there to register. On the way, I realized we were passing the clinic on Fourteenth Street where my dear Uncle Cleve had died.

Parham School, a two-story, red-brick building on a whole city block, was larger and newer than East Elementary School in Warren. Miss Bullitt, the sharp-featured principal, greeted Mama and me with a frown in her office, before peering at my school record through the rimless pince-nez glasses pinching the bridge of her nose. When Mama informed her that I was only five but had completed the first half of the first grade in Warren, the principal told her I entered school too soon and my half-day classes were inadequate. Mama asked her to let me read and do an arithmetic problem for her, but Miss Bullitt refused.

The next morning, I entered school for the first time in Little Rock and the first grade for the second time. My new teacher, Mrs. Shipp, not much taller than us first graders, had brightly rouged cheeks and frizzy white hair. Slightly clownish in appearance, the jolly little woman satisfied my every wish in class—leading us in painting pictures, sculpting clay, singing songs (solo and in chorus), reciting memorized poems, and acting in short plays. Her class was perfect, since elocution with Miss Simmons didn't seem likely anymore.

After enrolling me at Parham, our family moved a few blocks south on Scott Street to a pale yellow frame duplex in a neighborhood dominated by the East Side Junior High School campus and a mix of businesses, boarding houses, private homes, and apartments, many plastered with "For Rent" signs. Even though Mama preferred to pay a lower rent at the Cozy Apartments, she chose the apartment in a duplex at 1500 Scott for more privacy and quiet. The apartment on the other side of our duplex faced a two-story house with a man's name, Augustus Hill Garland, and wraparound galleries on two floors on the other side of Fifteenth. Another house with the name of a woman stood at the corner of Fourteenth, one block north of us—the Villa Marre. Its mansard roof sloped down the sides of the second story, looking as if builders tried to save money buying fewer bricks. Cattycornered from us, the four-story, red-brick East Side Junior High School building, standing on ground covering a city block, dominated the neighborhood like a castle.

Before the Terminal Van and Storage Company men had finished moving our furniture into the apartment, the other family in the duplex appeared on our doorstep. Mrs. Helen Elliott, taller and thinner than Mama, welcomed us with coffee and Cokes and introduced her husband, Mr. James Elliott, a railroad conductor for the Rock Island Lines, and their son, Jimmy, a ninth grader at East Side. Mr. Elliott, a short, muscular man with a slightly smashed nose and heavy brow, had the appearance of a friendly boxer.

Their wiry fifteen-year-old son, whose straight brown hair partially hid his forehead and lean face, shook my hand as if I were a grown up. Instantly I heard a buzzing and felt a vibration in the palm of my hand that made me think a bee had stung me. I jerked my hand back and the boy began laughing.

Mrs. Elliott said, "Tsk, tsk! Shame on you, Jimmy! Forgive his trick, Cleveland. I'm sure it's the first of many coming your way."

Mama discovered she had one acquaintance in our new neighborhood, my great-aunt Betsy Terry, Grandpa Honea's sister, who lived two blocks away at 1719 Scott Street. Her one-story, painted-white brick house was across from the City Curb Market and cattycornered from a fine white two-story clapboard at 1600 Scott, owned by Dr. Jefferson G. Ish, the principal of Union School, a combined elementary school/high school for black students, and his wife, Marietta. Mama expressed her surprise that blacks lived in our white neighborhood, but Aunt Betsy said blacks and whites had lived as neighbors in the 1500 and 1700 blocks of Scott, Cumberland, and Main streets as long as she could remember. Ever since first seeing Jake and Mandy's shanty, I was aware, without knowing why, that black people didn't live in the same neighborhoods as whites and had separate cafes, schools, and churches.

After Mama heard about Dr. Ish's education and reputation, Daddy told a story about a proud, elderly black man who proved equal or superior to a few prejudiced whites in McRae in the early 1900s. Like small country towns all over Arkansas, the whites didn't permit black people inside the town limits after sundown and posted warning signs on the outskirts: "Negro, don't let the sun go down on you in McRae."

The Aroma Hotel (named after a type of strawberry, Daddy said) was near McRae's town limits and a favorite rooming house for white boarders because it had rocking chairs on the gallery to relax in after meals and before bedtime. Near sunset one evening, the white male boarders who had gathered on the porch watched an elderly black man hurrying as fast as his old legs would carry him, trying to reach the town limit before sunset. He was so intent on departing that he failed to speak to the white men on the porch, who always expected black people to acknowledge their presence.

One white boarder leaned across the gallery rail and proclaimed like an ancient prophet, "He who passeth by and speaketh not is in danger of hellfire!"

The old black man, without breaking his stride, replied in the voice of an evangelical preacher, "He who addeth to and taketh from is a liar, and the truth's not in him!"

The elderly black man, perhaps better schooled in the scriptures, was by that time safely across the town's limits.

On my route to Parham School each day, I walked with Marcele Roberts and Herbert Reamey, two other pupils in Mrs. Shipp's class. Herbie, shorter and more athletically inclined than me, usually carried a baseball glove with his satchel. Marcele, younger and taller than both of us, tolerated our kidding. I didn't know they would eventually also be my classmates in junior and senior high school.

Since my half days at Warren hadn't included playing on the grounds at recess, I enjoyed cowboys-and-Indians and cops-and-robbers for the first time at school. For some reason, other kids depended upon me to invent different reasons for battles between cowboys-and-Indians, and different kinds of criminals for cops to pursue.

Playing on the swings, seesaws, and roundabouts, I quickly identified the most dangerous equipment. Standing in the swing seat, pumping my legs hard, I tried to rise as high as the chains allowed, determined to conquer my fear of heights. I soon found that a trustworthy companion is needed at the opposite end of a seesaw after a boy elevated me to one's full height before leaping off and watching me crash. But after lunch, I was my own worst enemy, testing my digestion on the roundabout by circling just short of being sick at my stomach, determined to conquer all the rides like other kids. Even in games and make-believe, there were hazards.

In class, I soon disproved Miss Bullitt's assumption that my half days at school in Warren weren't sufficient by completing my lessons so quickly that I unintentionally distracted other pupils. Mrs. Shipp simply gave me more stories to read and poems, whose end rhymes and matching sounds within lines entranced me, to memorize.

In the short time I spent at Parham, I had the most fun performing in a pageant on George Washington's birthday. Class members played "the Father of Our Country" at different chronological ages, giving me my first formal opportunity to act. After hearing Mrs. Shipp read Parson Weems's story about Washington, I wanted to play him as a little boy chopping down his father's cherry tree and refusing to lie about it. That role offered a chance to carry a hatchet and wear knee britches, a short white tie-wig, side-curls, and a pigtail that matched the picture in the story book. But Mrs. Shipp liked my soprano voice and cast me as Baby George to sing the opening song.

I wasn't very happy about her choice, because it meant wearing an ankle-length white muslin nightgown and a nightcap with a gathered ruffle, laced with baby-blue ribbon, which Aunt Ethel helped Mama cut and sew. Even though some boys in class called me a sissy for wearing a nightgown, that didn't bother me. I was Baby George, an actor in a costume in a play.

On performance day, the pupils, teachers, and mothers at Parham gathered after lunch in the auditorium for the program, narrated by Mrs. Shipp. I sang my solo opening the play.

> *February twenty-second, seventeen thirty two,*
> *Little Georgie Washington first said, "Boohoo, boohoo."*
> *Rock baby, rock baby, rock baby, rock.*
> *In Westmoreland County in the old Virginia state,*
> *There was born this hero who became so good and great.*
> *Rock baby, rock baby, rock baby, rock.*

On stage again, for the first time since the Pastime Theater in Warren, I savored performing and hated to leave the stage as the audience applauded.

Mrs. Shipp began her narrative:

When George was about six years old, he was given a hatchet by his father, and like most little boys his age, he went about chopping anything that came in his way. In the garden, he tried the edge of his hatchet on a beautiful young English cherry tree.

Herbie, as Parson Weems's George, entered holding a cardboard hatchet and began chopping at the base of a small cardboard tree, which toppled over as the hatchet blade fell off. Herbie ran offstage.

Tall Marcele Roberts, as George Washington's father, entered and saw the fallen tree: *I would not have taken five guineas for my tree. Who has destroyed my tree?*

Mrs. Shipp: *Nobody on the plantation would tell George's father who chopped the tree down until little George appeared with his hatchet.*

Herbie walked on stage with a hatchet, the blade again secured to the handle.

Mr. Washington: *George, do you know who killed that beautiful little cherry tree yonder in the garden?*

George (backing away from his father but still looking into his eyes): *Pa, you know I can't tell a lie. I cut it with my little hatchet.*

Mr. Washington: *Run to my arms, you dearest boy, you have paid me for the tree a thousand fold. Such an heroic act by my son is of more worth than a thousand trees.*

Embarrassed, Herbie ran into Marcele's arms.

Those of us in the chorus sang "Oh, Dear, What Can the Matter Be?" As we ended the song, a taller boy came on stage, as Washington the gentleman-farmer, and described the plantation of Mount Vernon on the banks of the Potomac River, and the crops he raised.

The chorus sang one verse of "Drink to Me Only with Your Eyes," and Martha Custis Washington, the president's wife, entered. Then George and Martha and two other couples bowed and curtsied to the audience, and repeated their gestures to their partners. Facing the audience, the ladies laid their left hands upon the gentlemen's right hands, took small steps with their right and left feet, and pointed their toes, tapping three times on the floor before commencing a minuet.

When the dance ended, a phonograph recording of "The Girl I Left Behind Me" played, and four Minutemen in ragged Revolutionary War army uniforms and bloody bandages marched on stage carrying an American flag, two of the boys pretending to play toy fifes and tin drums.

Finally, our entire class stood and sang a salute to the first president of the United States of America:

He comes, he comes; the hero comes.
Sound on your trumpet, beat on your drums.
His ranks abound in great array, the hero of Ameri-cay.
Welcome, welcome, hero of Ameri-cay!

To everyone's relief, there were no major hitches in our pageant, except for the cardboard hatchet blade breaking, cotton wigs falling over faces, leg hose sliding to shoe tops, and lines forgotten or misspoken when cast members searched for their mothers' faces in the audience.

Serious music enveloped our home daily, for our landlord, music professor Joseph Rosenberg, had a studio of the same architectural style behind our duplex. It was at the rear of the north end of the sprawling one-story, white-brick Imperial Laundry building that faced Main Street. As a concert pianist, the professor practiced and instructed students every day, their music wafting through our open or closed windows and doors. The professor, founder of the Little Rock Choral Society, rehearsed choral groups and individuals as well as piano students throughout every day, informally educating our musical ears by playing Chopin, Liszt, Mozart, Schubert, and Rachmaninoff.

After school, looking into his studio window, I saw Professor Rosenberg playing the grand piano, his long dark hair, usually combed straight back, rising and falling over his eyes as his hands sprang in the air, then crashed onto the keyboard. Perhaps the bunches of firecracker notes he struck playing Rachmaninoff explains my preference for piano as a solo instrument.

But another kind of music fell upon our family's ears before and after classes at East Side—the shouts and laughter of kids playing on the school grounds and passing our house on their way to the major trolley stop at the corner of Fifteenth and Main. But the shrill steam whistles at the Imperial Laundry, like the whistling shrieks of lumber mills in Warren, sometimes at intervals overwhelmed their exuberant shouts and loud noises. Clouds of steam from dozens of ironing boards and washing vats poured out the pipes on the white building's roof, reminding me of water spewing from a great white whale's blowhole. But the African-American laundry workers dressed in their all-white garb, chatting and laughing, presented a show during breaks behind the building on Fifteenth—fanning and swabbing their foreheads, faces, necks, and forearms with towels, while sharing talk, songs, and jokes.

To Mama's surprise and relief, the Ray-Glo Corporation didn't fire my father, after all. Instead, they sent him out West to sell gas stoves. After school was dismissed for the summer, Daddy invited Mama and me to accompany him on the trip. Mama begged Buster to go, too, because he had never been out of Arkansas, for only my father had ever traveled outside the state. But my brother feared he'd lose his job if he took a break and would be unable to find work upon our return. Mama wanted him to go with us, but her real concern was Buster's behavior when left on his own. Daddy insisted he was old enough to care for himself, and she gave in.

The morning we departed for Denver, Colorado, Daddy told Mama and me that neither sunrise, sunset, his pocket watch, or the miles covered on the Esso road map would determine how long we drove each day; he would! We dressed for travel as if going downtown: I wore a camp shirt, shorts, stockings, and high-top shoes; Mama, a dress and hat; and Daddy, a business suit, dress shirt, tie, and hat. In the early-morning darkness, my father strapped suitcases and a stove sample wrapped in canvas on the Chrysler's running boards, and Mama put a basket with our lunch and supper beside me on the back seat. I pretended to be a pioneer on the way to the prairies of the Western frontier, though riding in a Chrysler rather than a Conestoga wagon.

We crossed the Arkansas River on the Main Street Bridge, drove through North Little Rock, and headed north to Fort Smith on U.S. Highway 65. As the golden sun arose, I saw the highway ahead along the floor of a valley. Daddy said Indians and hunters going West had first traced the same path in the wilderness before Arkansas was a state in the Union. As we came nearer to Russellville, I saw looming on our right a smoky blue haze that later turned out to be a mountain range. On higher ground near Clarksville, we passed several flimsy fruit and vegetable stands beside the road before Mama could persuade Daddy to stop for baskets of apples and peaches to eat on the trip.

Near sunset, we were in the outskirts of a big town, and Daddy pulled into a tourist camp. Unpainted, screened-in cabins were arranged around an open space in the middle of a tree-shaded lot.

"Are we in Colorado already, Daddy?"

"Not by a long shot, boy. We're in Fort Smith, near the northwest corner of Arkansas."

I followed my father into a little office in the middle of the weedy lot. He signed the register, and the manager gave us towels, sheets, pillowcases, and thin blankets for our beds. Daddy drove the car up beside one of the cabins and Mama got out. The only light in our cabin was a single bulb hanging on a wire nailed to a ceiling joist, barely providing enough light to see the iron cots and thin mattresses that Mama had to make up for us to sleep on. Since our cabin had no bathroom, we walked nearly half a block to the toilet and cold showers.

Back in the cabin after washing up, Mama said, "Allie, I had no idea it was so primitive on the road. Paying a dollar for this place was too much."

After a restless night trying to sleep on the cots, we drove away in a mist early the next morning. Standing behind the front seat looking over my parents' shoulders, I strained to see through eddies of morning mist the state line between Arkansas and Oklahoma.

Daddy said, "State lines are easily seen on a map but less apparent on the ground, son. Like some other dividing lines in our lives."

When a sign at Oklahoma's border finally came in sight, Daddy surprised me by revealing that my Great-grandfather Billy Watt Nation, a Baptist minister, was a *Boomer* who entered Oklahoma Territory in 1893 to start his own church. Daddy promised to tell me more about Grandma Harrison's father, my Scots relative, later.

Entering the town of Muskogee, our car sank to the hubcaps in a muddy bog on Main Street, forcing Daddy to drive a slow, even rate to avoid getting stuck and paying one of the men with a mule team beside the street to tow us. Mama spread her fear from one end of town to the other, expecting our car to stall and us to have to walk through the muck. But the car slogged on, out the other side of town, without stopping.

Finally, in the outskirts of Oklahoma City, Daddy left the main highway searching for the state capitol building. We drove on city streets in neighborhoods, passing vacant lots with derricks pumping oil. When we reached the Oklahoma state capitol building, it had no dome! But it otherwise resembled Arkansas's capitol.

Disgusted at finding no dome on the capitol building, Daddy claimed, "If Oklahoma just collected taxes for the oil pumped inside the city limits, the state could pay for a dome, even in these hard times."

Throughout the trip, Daddy stopped only for gasoline, meals, toilets, and tourist camps. Even though we were trying to reach Denver on a date set by Ray-Glo, Mama insisted on three meals a day at decent-looking cafes, frequently requiring us to leave the highway and find town centers. The farther west we traveled on the flat plains, the more the towns in the far distance tended to resemble ant hills. Smaller villages looked like mere bumps on the horizon, the homes and businesses so close together there were no outskirts. Approaching a small town, the first building—a filling station, garage, grocery or dry goods store—changed the highway into Main Street from that point until past the last store. Tourist camps, camping sites, hot dog stands, chicken-dinner restaurants, and tea rooms cozied up to each other on deeply rutted, muddy, or dusty streets in most small towns.

Crossing Oklahoma, I sat by a rear window beside a sample heater, blanket, pillow, and ceramic water jug, sometimes passing the time counting the mailboxes on posts at the edge of the road, the telegraph poles beside railroad tracks, and the crisscrossed railroad signs where side roads, with washboard surfaces, crossed the railroad tracks.

Each day we encountered small signs standing short distances apart beside the highway, with rhymed verses advertising a shaving cream.

Mama said the rhymes built expectation, making travelers notice them and encouraging sales:

Take a tip—for your trip—no wet brush—to soak—your grip—
BURMA-SHAVE.

Mama and I (Daddy only a few times) repeated the lines and rhymes out loud just for fun.

Dinah doesn't—treat him right—but if—he'd shave—Dinah-mite—
BURMA-SHAVE.

When my eyes glazed over from gazing at shimmering waves of heat rising from the surfaces of fields and highways, I lay down on my back on the car's floor with my eyes closed, feeling the car's motion on the smooth and rough road surfaces with my whole body, just as a blind man feels Braille with his fingers reading a book. By the time we crossed the state line into Colorado, my eyes, nose, and back had absorbed the look, smell, and feel of Oklahoma from east to west.

Entertaining myself on the long days, I sang almost every song I had learned at school and over the radio. Drawing nearer to Denver, I began singing "Springtime in the Rockies":

When it's springtime in the Rockies, I'll be coming back to you.
My little sweetheart of the mountains, With your bonnie eyes so blue.

Patting Mama's shoulder, "Mama, you've got bonnie blue eyes, and you're *my* sweetheart!"

"That's the sweetest thing to say, Cleveland. I hope you'll always say nice things to others. Your brother never does. Allie, I hope Buster's working and taking good care of the house as you predicted."

Daddy smiled. "You can depend on it, Floy."

Looking at the flat fields and the empty road ahead, my vocal needle got stuck, as steel needles sometimes did in the grooves of records I played on Aunt Grace's Victrola. The sights outside the windows brought to mind how lonely the countryside makes you feel:

Look down, look down that lonesome road,
before you travel on.
Look up, look up, and seek your maker,
before Gabriel blows his horn.
Weary totin' such a load,
trudging down that lonesome road.
Look down, look down that lonesome road
before you travel on.

The next morning before we got on the road, Daddy said, "Cleveland, you sang or hummed one blasted song all day long yesterday. I don't want to know how lonesome the road is anymore, you hear me!"

Mama agreed, even though she was repeating a refrain of her own: "I wonder what Buster's doing while we're gone ..." "I wonder if he's keeping decent hours and eating right ..." "I hope he locks both the front and back doors when he leaves home." Daddy shook his head after she mentioned each of her worries.

Daddy said, "Floy, you don't give Bus an iota of credit. He's practically a grown man."

Since my parents discouraged my singing, I had to do something else to fill my mind, so I asked about their families. To my surprise, everyone on both sides of our family, except Grandpa Honea, was born and raised in Arkansas. He had moved from Georgia when only a boy. And both the Honea and Harrison families had lived in the same three central Arkansas counties before settling in Beebe. Mama, though born in Hazen, lived in Cabot and Ward before moving to Beebe.

Daddy said, "Your momma was mighty popular when we first met at school in Beebe. She had lots of friends and never turned down their invitations to parties. Uncle Ben demanded she devote herself to the Baptist church and had too many rules to protect her."

Mama said, "Allie, that's enough about Papa's rules and protecting me."

"He wanted her to marry a preacher. Maybe that'd get him into heaven."

Mama gasped, "Allie! What a thing to say, especially before Cleveland."

"He asked Baptist ministers to Sunday dinner. Afterwards taking his nap, leaving your momma with 'his men of God,' who made improper advances."

"Now, Allie. You've no need to mock ministers and religion."

"What are *advances*, Daddy?"

Mama raised her voice, "Allie Harrison, stop talking to him about Papa and me."

Daddy added, "They tried to hug and kiss her. I don't blame 'em for that. But when your momma told Uncle Ben about their behavior, he didn't believe her."

"All right, I'll tell my own story. One of the worst times, Papa refused to let me go to an ice-cream social even though I had Mama's permission. I went anyway. That's when Papa marched into Miriam Abington's house, called me down in front of my friends, and, after nearly dragging me home, switched my bare shoulders so bad, I had to wear a winter dress to cover the welts."

To me, it sounded like a picture show about a good girl and mean old father.

"That's why your momma dated me a few times before Uncle Ben knew about it. When I proposed, she accepted me without his permission, digging a real gulf between us."

"He's too little to hear and understand things like that, Allie."

"Aw, Mama, I want to know all about you. How old were you when you all married, Mama?"

"Sixteen. Three years younger than your daddy."

Daddy chuckled. "Miss Lizanne approved of our marrying, but Uncle Ben thought us too young. Truth is, Floy, it wasn't unusual to marry at our ages back then."

"Maybe not, Allie. But I'd have a fit if Buster got married at the age he is now! My only regret is our not finishing high school."

"At the time, we had more education than most. But I wanted to work."

I asked, "What kind of work did you do, Daddy?"

"Well, hon, lots of different kinds of jobs—ran an icehouse and meat market, butchered hogs and cows, traded horses. Worked on a crew cutting timber with a crosscut saw, clearing woods for the railroad."

Mama frowned. "When your daddy hewed logs for cross ties with a seven-pound broad axe, he struck a knot in a trunk and the blade bounced back and sank into his right foot between his big and middle toes. When the cut got so infected, Dr. Abington thought Allie might lose his foot."

"You and Doc saved my foot, that's for sure, Floy."

As Daddy slowed down in the next town to buy gasoline, Mama saw a cafe neat and clean enough on the outside for us to have lunch inside. After filling our stomachs and gas tank, we hit the road again. Mama suggested a nap for me, but I wanted Daddy to tell me about the jobs he had.

Daddy said, "While my foot healed, the Missouri Pacific and Iron Mountain Railroad put me in charge of black crews loading cross ties and supplies on freight trains. I can still see those muscular black men bouncing up a flexible plank onto the flatbed railcars with the cross ties on their bare shoulders. I can still hear steel gangs chanting in cadence, laying tracks, a deep bass booming, 'Little Rock!' And crew members stroking sledge hammers, grunting, 'MEM-phis … MEM-phis.'"

Mama said, "Supervising black work crews didn't pay your daddy enough to support a family. And I wouldn't let him skin trees anymore, that was too dangerous. So he cruised timber with a compass in one hand to keep a straight course walking tracts of virgin timber in White County, measuring tree girths and estimating the number of cross ties in each one."

"But I'm telling you! Walking pained my old foot so much, I had to quit."

Drawing near Denver just before sunset, we saw a sign warning of a turnpike tollbooth ahead. Daddy said, "Dadgummit, I hope they're not gonna charge for each one of us in the car."

Hearing the concern in his voice, I lay down on the floor and pulled the backseat blanket over me. At the lighted tollbooth, the officer charged Daddy for our car but not the passengers. After passing the turnpike barrier, I remained hidden, out of sight for so long Mama grew alarmed.

"For goodness sake, Allie! Where's Cleveland? Did he get out at the tollbooth?"

Laughing, I burst out from under the blanket, proud to have saved Daddy money by hiding. But Mama made me crawl up beside her to hear about "honesty and paying one's fair share."

We drove into the city's outskirts after dark, in the midst of Denver's Fourth of July celebration. Fireworks exploded all around us, pinwheels spinning on tree trunks leaving afterimages of red, white, and blue circles in the air and flooding the streets with sparkling lights. Daddy stopped at a filling station for directions to the boarding house where my parents had rented a room by mail. We found the two-story rooming house perched high on a hillside beside an empty, overgrown lot, so Daddy parked at the curb on the street at the bottom of the hill.

We lugged the Gladstone and other bags up steep steps to the front porch, where the landlady, a large woman with gray hair piled high on her head, greeted us at the front door. Mrs. Hardcastle helped carry our bags to our second-floor room, which overlooked the front porch roof and the street below. My fear of heights prevented me from looking out the upstairs window, but downstairs, sitting far back from the porch's edge, I gazed at the dark mountains in the distance.

For the next few days, before his sales trips to surrounding states, Daddy called on dealers at hardware and department stores in Denver. After his departure, Mrs. Hardcastle suggested places for Mama and me to visit, explaining how to get there. With her directions, we took a streetcar to the Museum of Natural History, the first museum I had ever visited.

Many exhibits were realistically mounted, especially the stuffed animals and birds, including a bald eagle clutching a snake in its claws and beak. But my favorite exhibit was of butterflies, a brilliant display of multi-colored, iridescent butterfly wings spread apart and held in place by pins. The attendant explained that dying butterflies fold their wings, so curators used a chemical to relax and spread their wings before mounting them. The custodian saw I was too short to view the displays from above and brought a stool for me to stand on and look down into the cases. Bidding us goodbye, he suggested visiting the Colorado State Capitol on the other side of the city park.

On our way to the capitol, we came upon the first fountain I'd ever seen, spraying water high into the air. After standing so long at the museum, we sat on the fountain's edge, watching sunlight strike the cool mist spouting above our heads, forming tiny rainbows in the air. The glistening Colorado State Capitol's gold-plated dome reminded me of the absent dome in Oklahoma City.

We had supper after our forays downtown, and later sat on the boarding house's wide front porch, listening to elderly boarders repeat what they had read in the daily paper or heard on the radio. A few asked us about our sightseeing adventures and our lives in Arkansas. I told a friendly old lady about my elocution lessons and was asked to recite something. With Mrs. Hardcastle's encouragement, I repeated Eugene Field's poems and sang "Springtime in the Rockies" and "My Blue Heaven" to applause and compliments.

Within days, our stout, friendly landlady was hovering over us and calling me "her little hillbilly." I tired of being called what I considered a "hick," and told her, "We aren't hillbillies! Nobody's barefooted in overalls in Little Rock." Little did I know.

She laughed, "Mrs. Harrison, I like this spunky little rascal of a boy!"

Mrs. Hardcastle served us only bacon, eggs, and biscuits for breakfast until I asked for cinnamon toast. Claiming to be ignorant of the ingredients and how to make the special toast, she led me into the boarding house kitchen to mix cinnamon and sugar on buttered bread. She laughed following my instructions, and then offered cinnamon toast every morning for the remainder of our stay.

Two weeks later, Daddy returned to Denver and drove us into parts of town we hadn't reached on the streetcar. When he planned to take us to Boulder, Mrs. Hardcastle voluntarily prepared us a picnic lunch in a big wicker basket. In the outskirts of Boulder, he parked in a thickly wooded park for us to eat lunch off a wooden picnic table beside a natural-rock oven with an iron grill. While we ate, little auburn-haired chipmunks, their short tails uplifted like spatulas, kept darting cautiously about us, pausing only long enough to beg for tidbits.

The next week, Daddy took us to Colorado Springs. Before I knew he planned on taking a trip, I was in the tall grass in the vacant lot next to the boarding house catching grasshoppers and placing them in a glass fruit jar that Mrs. Hardcastle provided. I took the jar with us and studied the grasshoppers until we began climbing Pike's Peak. Daddy promised himself to drive the entire twelve-mile toll road up the side of the mountain, beginning at the heavily forested base and ending at the thin tree line near the mountain's crest. On our climb to the top, I counted more than a hundred curves, with Daddy's help, while Mama looked down the steep precipices from the front passenger seat, gasping in fear at each turn.

According to her, "Your Daddy drives too fast or too near the road's edge."

Each deep breath she took, Daddy smiled and mumbled, "Oh, now, Floy."

Before we started to Pike's Peak, Mama complained she was hot. So she certainly didn't expect such a sharp drop in temperature at the mountaintop and hadn't brought wraps for us. In our summer clothes, we walked through the thick beds of snow piled high on the road's shoulders and slopes near the peak and braved the cold wind gazing at the distant valleys below and beyond Pike's Peak. Even though I was shivering in the brisk wind blowing across the peak, chills running up and down my spine, I couldn't resist scooping up handfuls of snow to roll a snowball. I'd hardly finished it when Mama hurried us back to the car.

Without thinking of my grasshoppers' lives as we began our slow descent, I dropped my snowball into the jar and then watched the green grasshoppers attempt to escape, squirting brown "tobacco juice" in the snow until they froze. Mama, like the grasshoppers, sat still and relaxed going down the mountain, making no further observations to Daddy.

The last site we visited in Colorado was the Royal Gorge, where the Arkansas River had gouged its way through the Rocky Mountains thousands of years before. Standing beside the highest suspension bridge in the world, Mama declared her knees felt too weak and her lungs too breathless to walk on the bridge deck above the gorge. But Daddy, insisting we'd both regret not making the effort, put his arms around both of us and pushed a "united" threesome onto the bridge—one stalwart and two reluctant—to look as much as we dared over the rail into the frightening abyss.

After one night in Denver, Daddy embarked on his last sales trips in Nebraska and South Dakota, where the friendly furniture and hardware dealers insisted his name meant "son of Harry" and his coloration (black hair, olive skin, and hazel eyes) proved he was a *black Norwegian*. But cordial as the Scandinavian dealers were, they didn't reach into their pocketbooks for money to buy gas stoves.

They told Daddy, "Times is too hard to move stoves, even with a good supply of natural gas."

As our six weeks at her boarding house ended, Mrs. Hardcastle gave us a dark maroon leatherette album of beautiful colored photographs of Colorado: Pike's Peak, the Royal Gorge Bridge, and a few places we hadn't visited. Its maroon pages were held in place by a thick gold cord with tassels. Mama kept the gift on the open leaf of her secretary in our living room.

I realized on our way back to Arkansas that my mother had been as blithe and unknowing on the trip as I, just another kid. And that I had traveled more in one summer than she had in all her thirty-six years. Like me, she had never been out of Arkansas or laid eyes upon a road map before— so the turns and twists, rises and falls of the landscapes, the sights of big and little towns surprised and informed her as much as me. Going home, with my eyes glued on the passing land, I noticed that fields and roads seen from the opposite direction didn't appear the same at all, and that the trip home seemed twice as long. I guess my excited expectations traveling out West made the trip seem faster and briefer.

We arrived in Little Rock after dark, and Buster wasn't home. Our apartment's appearance partially explained Mama's concern about leaving my big brother alone. Beer bottles, smudged glasses, and cigarette butts littered the living room, and every dish in the kitchen was stacked in the kitchen sink, unwashed. In our room, the bed had never been made, and his unwashed clothes lay piled in a corner.

My folks put me to bed and sat up waiting for him. I fell asleep so quickly that I never knew what happened when he came home.

Following our Colorado trip, Mama and Mrs. Elliott in the other apartment became really good friends, visiting every day, exchanging recipes, borrowing ingredients, and sharing dishes when their husbands were out of town. The Elliotts' family pet, a small Boston bull terrier named Jiggs, tagged after Jimmy and me when we played in the yard or sat on the vestibule steps talking, as we often did. Jimmy, unlike Buster, treated me as his equal, not a baby *bother*. For me, Jimmy repeated jokes from the *East Junior Journal*, the weekly student newspaper:

Question: Do you know why I'm always tired on the first day of April?
Answer: Who wouldn't be after a March of thirty-one days?

Question: Who was Atlas?
Answer: The world's biggest gangster.
Question: Where did you get that idea?
Answer: Our history book says he held up the world.

Jimmy told me, "Arkansas's the only state mentioned in the Bible."
"Oh, Jimmy, that's not so. You're making that up."
"It says, 'Noah looked out of his *Ark and saw* the waters had subsided from the earth.'"

Jimmy played practical jokes on anyone he judged a likely victim. One special trick of his from the magic store downtown was a full pack of Juicy Fruit gum with a concealed spring that snapped your finger as you withdrew a stick. He had a set of false teeth that chattered when set on a flat surface and a finger ring that buzzed your palm when shaking hands.

I especially enjoyed watching Jimmy play tricks on my naive mother. One day when we were visiting Mrs. Elliott after school, he came home from East Side, greeted us hurriedly, and ran upstairs. Returning almost instantly, he carried a beautiful box, its cover printed in Old English script: *Fruit Flavored Creams of the Highest Quality, Dipped in the Purest of*

Chocolate. Since Mrs. Elliott and I had already fallen victims to his trick, we knew what was coming. He carefully removed the glittering foil and colored ribbon, and offered each of us chocolate creams and then waited for Mama to bite into hers. When she tried and couldn't sink her teeth into the candy, she just held the piece of candy in her hand, talking with Mrs. Elliott.

Jimmy urged her, pleading, "Mrs. Harrison, isn't this special candy?"

Mama tried to bite her candy again, with the same result. Then she saw we were not eating, only smiling at her. Pressing the piece with her fingers, she realized it was rubber.

We laughed, of course, but Jimmy, holding his sides, rolled on the floor.

Another afternoon, Jimmy and I were sitting on the front steps outside our apartment talking when a neighborhood woman passed by. Her stomach was so large, she walked with a rolling gait. I watched her closely until she walked past us before asking Jimmy, "Did you see how big that woman's stomach is?"

"Yeah, what about it?"

"Her arms and legs aren't fat, but she's gotta lotta fat on her stomach."

"Naw, that's not fat. She's gotta baby in there!"

"A baby?"

"You bet, kiddo."

"How'd a baby get in her stomach?"

"Not inside her stomach, kid, in her womb."

"Her wound?"

"Nooo! W-O-M-B, womb."

"What's that?"

"An organ inside 'er to hold eggs and babies."

"She's got eggs inside her?"

"Yep, the baby came from an egg."

"How'd anyone put an egg inside her?"

"Nobody put an egg in her. Her body made it, and her husband fertilized it."

"He put fertilizer in her, like Mama does with plants?"

"It's not the same, you little dope! … Well, it is in a way."

"I don't understand, Jimmy."

"You're too little to understand, Cleveland. Anyway, that lady's gotta baby."

When Jimmy went home, I ran to Mama in the kitchen. "Mama, the lady down the street with the big stomach has gotta baby inside her."

Whirling to face me, Mama demanded, "Cleveland! Who told you such a thing?"

"Jimmy Elliott, just now."

"Well … yes … he's right, she *is* going to have a baby."

So Jimmy was right, that's where babies come from … not the cabbage patch or a big diaper hanging from the beak of a skinny, long-legged stork. But I didn't ask how the baby got inside her, something Jimmy didn't volunteer and Mama didn't seem to think I needed to know.

With Halloween approaching, I could hardly wait for that night to put on my costume, ring doorbells, and soap car windows. Jimmy promised to let me help move porch furniture from one house to another in the neighborhood. When I told Daddy our plan, he described how on Halloween he and his Beebe buddies took a neighbor's buggy apart and reassembled it on the roof of a farmer's barn. And how the next Halloween, they topped that trick by hoisting a milk cow in a sling with a pulley to the loft of another farmer's barn. After telling me exciting stories, Daddy claimed I was too small to ring doorbells and move furniture in the dark. It didn't seem fair to me.

Buster told me that people in costumes would be parading on Main Street on Halloween night, and I assumed he meant to take me. But he laughed, "I can't do that! Me and my buddies don't do kid stuff like that."

I begged him so often that Daddy and Mama agreed to walk me as far as the Blass Department Store, at Fourth and Main. Excited, I asked my folks to wear costumes like me, but they laughed at my suggestion and dressed as they always did. I donned my Hoot Gibson cowboy suit.

Daddy said, "That outfit might be just right for riding herd on the stampede of crazy people downtown."

Our trek on Main began in total darkness at Fifteenth Street. Very few cars or pedestrians traveled at our end of Main at night, which left the sidewalks and street much darker and quieter than expected. I didn't act or say anything to suggest to Daddy I was a scaredy-cat; I just got between him and Mama, holding their hands real tight. At Fourteenth, a single yellow electric bulb under a tin shade barely threw a tiny circle of light on the sidewalk and street below, just enough to sculpt the curb and make dark shadows. The sparkling white artificial icicles dripped off the roof at the Frozen Custard drive-in across the street, and the Wonder Bakery's walls were painted with red, blue, and green balloons, with the air smelling of baking bread.

Between Eighth and Ninth streets, I saw through the display windows the partially lighted bottling machines at the Orange Crush Bottling Company throwing grotesque shadows across the windows and showroom floor. Across the street, only a single strand of colored bulbs encircled the dark Hob Nob Drive-in parking lot. At Ninth, we emerged from darkness into the glare from the tall billboard spotlights on the southeast corner, which lit the whole intersection like the middle of day. We were close enough to hear the shrill noisemakers three blocks away and see the brilliant lights reflecting off the Boyle Building's white brick surface onto buildings beside and opposite it.

At Seventh, the parade of Halloweeners coming across from the Donaghey and Wallace buildings pushed us toward the Capitol Theater, where people in masks and costumes engulfed us. There were more figures from there to Fifth Street than I'd ever seen in Hollywood movies. Some were dressed like funny-paper characters—the Captain and Katzenjammer Kids, Felix the Cat, Moon Mullins, Tillie the Toiler, Maggie and Jiggs. Clowns of all sizes had white faces, bulbous red noses, and yellow wigs. A few hillbillies clad in denim overalls had giant rubber feet. Country girls in calico dresses had mop wigs with plaited pig tails on their heads. A couple of gypsies with earrings and head scarves carried crystal balls, and pirates with black eye patches and high boots shook their swords at us. The gorillas and bears growling through the open mouths of their fake heads lunged at us. There were big and little people, their ghost eyes shining through jagged holes in the bed sheets draped over them, and Charlie Chaplain doing the camel walk, twirling a Malacca cane.

Suddenly, big boys in ordinary street clothes darted around us, snatching off masks and hats, and grabbing noisemakers. I released Mama's hand and held my cowboy hat real tight. A policeman chased the big boys across the intersection at Fifth and Main to the Exchange Bank Building, where they escaped.

Even though the traffic lights changed from red to green, the cars stuck at the intersection didn't move. A motorman inside a streetcar stalled at Fifth clanged his bell relentlessly, urging car drivers to clear the tracks, when the big boys appeared again. Crossing behind the streetcar, they pulled the overhead trolley wheel off the power line, clicking the lights off and on repeatedly and showering sparks on the roof and pavement. Then the boys put fingers in their mouths, whistling through their teeth, and jumped up and down at the rear of the streetcar. When another cop chased them, they disappeared among the other merrymakers as slickly as the chipmunks did in the Colorado park.

Daddy said, "Boys like them greased the streetcar tracks on the hills in Pulaski Heights and the trolleys slid on the rails."

The sounds of the clackers, kazoos, cowbells, castanets, tambourines, and whistles hurt my ears, so I held my hands over them. From Fifth and Main, I saw the state capitol glowing in white light in the distant west, like the Taj Mahal. The display windows at the United Cigar Store, Kempner's, and Kress Five and Ten Cent Store glistened with coats of glycerin, which Daddy claimed prevented soap from sticking to the glass. So the boys and girls with big tan bars of OK laundry soap were marking the windows of cars parked at the curb, filled with occupants gawking at the passersby.

When we reached Kress Five and Ten Cent Store, Mama was tired and wanted to go home. But Daddy led us to Hegarty's Drugstore, across from Blass, to sit down for a treat. The short young soda jerk, observing the passing crowd from the front door, nearly disappeared behind the tall marble counter drawing our Cokes. We sat in bent-wire chairs at tables with marble tops, like those at Glasgow's in Warren. When the boy delivered our drinks, I blew my straw wrapper at him, and he dodged, laughing. Encouraged by his response, I sucked my straw and rattled my ice so noisily Mama called me down, embarrassed by my behavior.

We headed home, passing Worthen Bank, the Royal Theater, Haverty's Furniture Store, and the Exchange National Bank at Capitol and Main, where we caught a streetcar home.

The year 1931 brought several unexpected changes to our family. At the beginning of the year, Daddy had to stay in bed for several weeks. Since he wasn't contagious, I could visit him after school any time I wanted.

"I'm sorry you're sick, Daddy."

"I'm not really sick, hon. Just bulges through my stomach muscles. Some men get them."

He had developed hernias on both sides of his lower abdomen, an inherited weakness that allowed his intestine to push through the stomach wall.

Daddy reckoned his hernias broke through while he was carrying stove samples to and from stores on our western trip. Dr. Silas Fulmer, our family physician in the Donaghey Building, wanted to repair them, but Daddy didn't trust surgical operations. So the doctor prescribed bed rest and fitted him with Palmer trusses, oval rubber pads on web belts that supported the walls of his abdomen and kept the intestine from pushing past the groin muscles.

Even though Daddy hated staying in bed, it gave me a chance to learn more about his life.

"Why aren't you tall like Big Daddy, Uncle Earl, and your other brothers, Daddy?"

"Well, boy, I don't know … seems to me five feet ten and a half's pretty good. Every family has a runt like me, I 'spect."

"What's a *runt*, Daddy?"

"Someone who should have grown bigger and didn't, I guess. I had pneumonia and diphtheria at your age. Maybe that stunted my growth."

"Daddy, our Colorado trip was long. What was the longest trip you took as a little boy?"

"Riding on a train from Beebe to St. Louis, Missouri, when I was ten. Your great-grandpa Billy Watt Nation and I spent a week at the Louisiana Purchase Exposition in 1904."

"What do you do at an *exposition*?"

"Well, for one thing, we watched the Olympic Games on the grounds of the exposition."

"What kind of games are those, Daddy?"

"They're competitions. Athletes from foreign countries competing to see who can run fastest, throw farthest, jump highest, and leap longest."

"What did you like best at the fair?"

"Well, I'd say riding the biggest Ferris wheel ever built. They brought the big wheel from Chicago where it had been part of the 1893 Columbian Exposition. It was a little frightening. For food, I liked my first hamburger best, a fried chopped-beef sandwich on a bun."

"Did you eat desserts at the fair like Mama makes?"

"Yeah, but they were different in those days. I licked ice cream off a rolled-up wafer shaped like a cone by an Italian. The first iced tea I ever drank was made by an Englishman when people stopped drinking hot tea in sweltering weather."

"Someday, I'll go to an exposition and take rides and eat ice cream cones."

"Well, I wouldn't be surprised if you do things nobody's thought of yet."

One afternoon, Mama brought the family photo album into Daddy's room, and we sat on opposite sides of him looking at photos taken before and after their marriage. In one, Mama was dressed like a Gibson girl, with her hair puffed out and tied with a wide taffeta bow. The long skirt of her shirtwaist dress, cinched at the waist, emphasized her curved hips but slender figure. So small and dainty, she had pale skin, black hair, and blue eyes. I saw why my father fell in love with her.

Daddy wasn't as handsome as she was pretty, but he was tall, slender, and wide shouldered. Mama thought he was built like William S. Hart, the famous silent-picture cowboy. I laughed at the snapshot of Buster at six months, lying on his stomach on a cushion naked, his wide, round eyes looking back over his shoulder. A much later picture showed him looking self-important standing by Daddy beside his birddog pup on the fender of a muddy Model T. My father, in a canvas cartridge vest and wide-brimmed felt hat, held a pump-action shotgun, and my brother, in a shawl-collar sweater with his canvas hunting cap pulled down over his eyes, gripped a .22 rifle. I looked at them and wanted to be as close to them as they were to each other, but it was a wish never to be fulfilled.

When he turned to the largest photograph in the album, which was me at six months of age, Daddy said, "A professional colored photo like that cost a pretty penny in McRae in 1925."

I didn't let Mama turn the page until I had a really good look at that fat, round baby boy sitting sideways in the brown wicker chair, a blue taffeta pillow at his back, his chubby legs in white stockings under the chair arm which his plump forearm rested on.

Mama said, "Your round happy eyes are so inquisitive. I guess it's true that 'a child born on the Sabbath day is fair and wise and good and gay.'"

Daddy tut-tutted. "Floy, that's an old wives' tale … but maybe true."

Mama took all the snapshots in the album herself with a Brownie Kodak box camera, recording how family members looked before my birth—Daddy tall and slender, his black hair combed straight back without a part; Mama short and plump, her bobbed black hair parted in the middle; Buster not much taller at twelve than me at six. His freckled arms, legs, and face and unruly hair reminded me of Huckleberry Finn, but in another photo about the same time, he was as neat, clean, and proper as a wet-combed Tom Sawyer cleaned up for church. Grandpa Honea held me on his knee beside Buster, looking stout but not fat; and Grandma, a gaunt invalid in a dressing gown, sat in an easy chair on the front porch, cautiously clasping me in her frail arms.

During Daddy's confinement, relatives and friends visited us often, especially Aunt Ora and Uncle Roy Bunch, who lived in a big house in Sylvan Hills in North Little Rock. Aunt Ora, Mama's first cousin, was the daughter of Walker and Oma Honea, Grandpa Honea's brother and his wife. The Bunches, our cousins, were so much older I called them Aunt and Uncle. Aunt Ora was a neat version of Marie Dressler in the movie *Min and Bill*, but Uncle Roy, a locomotive engineer on the Rock Island Line, was bigger and rounder than Wallace Beery. With permanent work and no financial problems, he and Aunt Ora, a jolly jack-of-all-trades, brought food and drinks, as well as jokes and stories they laughed at as if hearing them for the first time.

One of Aunt Ora's stories was about her parents. "My father, Walker, practiced law, and my mother, Oma (the family called her *Oh-mee*), was a housewife. Workmen did the farming on their farm near Lonoke. Momma cooked a midday meal on a big wood stove every day for all the hands and expected Papa to cut kindling and collect cord wood before going into town to lawyer. But with Papa's mind on legal cases, he forgot his one chore so frequently that Momma finally lost patience when he failed once too often. Papa arrived for the dinner meal at noon and found the farmhands gathered at the table but no food in sight—only Papa's axe lying across his plate."

Uncle Roy and Aunt Ora doubled over, as far as roly-poly people are able, laughing.

On another visit, when Aunt Ora arrived carrying a gallon jug filled with a dark purple liquid, I asked, "What's in that jug, Aunt Ora?"

"Rheumatism medicine for your daddy, honey."

"Daddy has hernias. He's never mentioned having rheumatism."

Aunt Ora laughed, "Oh, he suffers from it something awful, sweetheart."

Pouring homemade blackberry wine for everyone but me, she said, "Floy, have a glass."

"Ora, you know I don't drink alcohol. Cleve's sickness means I'm too susceptible."

"That's nonsense, Floy! Come on, be sociable. Have a little wine."

Mama, finally sipping from her glass, said, "Wine makes me feel so warm behind my knees."

Aunt Ora started to tell another joke, but Mama stopped her. "If this is one of your risqué stories, Ora, don't repeat it. Cleveland's such a parrot, he'll tell everyone we know."

"Don't worry, Floy, he won't understand this one."

Aunt Ora said, "Allie, you'll love this story. A little boy about Cleveland's age was standing at a candy counter trying to choose which flavor lollipop to buy. As he pondered, a Catholic priest, wanting to make a purchase, came up and grew impatient waiting for the boy to make up his mind. Finally, the priest said, 'Young man, if it's so hard to make a choice, give your money to the orphans instead!'

The little boy faced the priest and said, 'Listen, mister, if you wore your pants the way you do your collar, there wouldn't be so damned many little orphans.'"

Mama said, "Ora, that's disgraceful. I'm ashamed to hear such prejudice on your lips!"

But Aunt Ora was right—I didn't understand the joke, only the laughter that resulted. I couldn't wait to tell Jimmy Elliott to get a laugh of my own.

Sadly, soon after their last visit with us, Uncle Roy died of a heart attack in the cab of his locomotive, and Aunt Ora moved in with her daughter and son-in-law, Dorothy and Hubert Bolton, who was a salesman at Haverty's Furniture Store between Fourth and Fifth on Main, next to the Royal Theater.

When Aunt Ora next came to our house, she told us about visiting Hubert in the hospital after his appendectomy. She suggested, "Hubert, lift your gown and let me see the scar from your operation."

He frowned. "Ora, I can't show you that. It wouldn't be decent."

"Don't be silly, Hubert. I changed your diapers when you were a baby."

"Well, Ora, that's true. But, believe me, you wouldn't recognize the old place today."

Aunt Ora could hardly catch her breath from laughing.

She was not only big, rawboned, and funny but could do almost anything—cook and bake, brew wine and beer, and sew her daughter's clothes and her own. Mama said Ora was too big to be stylish but was an excellent seamstress like Aunt Ethel. Only a few days after Mama mentioned to her that I'd outgrown my Sunday-go-to-meeting suit, Aunt Ora arrived at our house with a lightweight, tan wool jacket and skirt she had outgrown and a pattern for a boy's suit. Through many cups of coffee and lots of talk, she removed the stitches from the skirt, laid the material on the dining table, pinned the pattern sheets on it, and cut the parts.

Most of that day, I stood on a dining room chair while she fitted, pinned, and stitched the suit to fit me. It would have been boring if she hadn't teased Mama about happenings in Beebe and McRae. One story included Roland Shelton, who courted Mama before she married Daddy. Maybe my aunt only kidded her about being stuck on Mr. Shelton, because Mama pooh-poohed her story.

The two-piece tan suit Aunt Ora made had a pullover jumper with the collar, chest pocket, and sleeve cuffs trimmed in dark brown.

After my aunt left, I told Mama how itchy the wool was, and she said, "Don't you ever let on to your Aunt Ora."

Late one afternoon, a boy in a light brown uniform, a visored cap, and leather leggings rode up on his bicycle and handed Mama a yellow envelope. Her hands shook opening the envelope.

I asked, "What's the matter, Mama? What's that?"

"A telegram! I can't imagine anyone sending us a telegram. It's bound to be bad news."

After reading it, she handed the yellow sheet, with strips of square black letters pasted on it, to Daddy, saying, "I knew it when they sent us back to Little Rock." They took turns reading it, their facial expressions growing as pained as when Uncle Cleve died. But they didn't cry. Then they sent me to my room to draw pictures and read, and the house fell silent, except for the murmur of voices in their room.

At supper, Daddy told Buster and me he had lost his job, speaking with a break in his voice. "I'll just have to start over again as if my earlier years meant nothing."

Whether Daddy lost his job because of his physical disability or bad business, my parents didn't know. What I knew was how somber everyone was and how short Daddy's temper became. Even though Mr. Elliott, in the other apartment, continued as a conductor for the Rock Island Railroad, other men in our neighborhood were out of work, too. A man across the street started making chili in his garage to sell from home and at grocery stores for income. Daddy loved chili enough to send me to buy several brick-size blocks covered in orange fat, which he scraped off before heating it.

Once Daddy was back on his feet, he left after breakfast every weekday to look for a job selling some kind of product or butchering cows and pigs. But there were no openings. Luckily, Buster's salary as produce man at Piggly Wiggly and my folks' savings account paid for the rent and groceries. Mama asked Grandpa to send fresh eggs for me to sell from house to house in the neighborhood. And the Wonder Bakery truck driver, who stocked Grandpa's store in White County with bread and pastries, agreed to deliver crates of the eggs to our house for nothing. While this was going on, our meals were the same and I never felt deprived of anything.

My biggest egg customer was Dawson's Drugstore at Fifteenth and Main, which bought a supply of eggs each week. I liked delivering the eggs to Mr. DeShields, the druggist, who called me his "little butter and egg man," listened to my stories and jokes, and tipped me with a stick of candy when I delivered. My affection for Mr. DeShields helped Mama fool me one day.

Mama was concerned about my health and kept track of my bowel movements, convinced a daily habit was essential to good health. "Have you done your job today?" she would ask. Or if she had me open my mouth and decided my tongue was coated, or looked at my face and found my complexion pasty, she assumed I was constipated and resorted to her favorite treatment for all family illnesses—laxatives. Mama wasn't alone in the practice, for many people who grew up in rural areas clung to medical cures from the past. She relentlessly dispensed purgatives of noxious-tasting, strong-acting laxatives, like Epsom salts, cod liver oil, calomel, the crushed herbal leaves of Black Draught, and a yellow liquid in a bottle labeled 666. Mama's mere mention of her favorite laxative—a tablespoon-ful of castor oil—clogged my throat and made my stomach quiver.

Seeing a castor oil bottle in her hand, I backed away like a crawfish, stopping only when she shouted, "Allie Cleveland Harrison!"

On the particular day that involved Mr. DeShields, she had earlier decided a laxative was in order, and I had retreated as usual. Then she went to the phone without pursuing me; her acceptance of my refusal was a surprise! A little later in the morning, she sent me with the usual basket of eggs to Dawson's Drugstore. Mr. DeShields paid for the eggs but offered a glass of root beer as a tip instead of the usual stick of candy. A true devotee of root beer, I eagerly stood at the marble counter watching him punch the fountain pump, squirting syrup into the cup, and pulling the phosphate lever to spike it with fizz.

Pushing the glass across the counter, like bartenders in Western saloons in movies, he said, "Bottoms up, cowboy!"

I sipped slowly to make the drink last, but I finally tilted the glass as cowboys do gulping shots of whiskey. My mouth filled with root beer thickly laced with castor oil! Shuddering, I spit the repulsive mix back into the cup!

I had been betrayed! My faith in Mama and Mr. DeShields was gone, at least temporarily. Mama almost had her way with the castor oil by enlisting my friend.

Besides crates of fresh eggs, Grandpa also sent canned goods, wheels of cheese, and even fresh vegetables from time to time. One shipment included a twelve-inch string of glistening red peppers, each two to four inches long. Mama hung the string of scarlet peppers on a hook on the screened-in back porch and gave me orders not to touch them. I heard her order but paid little heed.

Left alone with Buster one day, I tootled on tissue paper folded over the teeth of a comb, jauntily high-stepping through the hall to the bedrooms and the kitchen, where I shoved a kitchen chair out on the porch to climb and take the string of peppers off the hook. As I lowered the dried peppers, they rubbed against each other, rustling or rasping like a Mexican musical instrument. So I began shaking them in rhythm, singing "Say 'Si, Si'" and dancing through the house. When I tired of the song and dance, I laid the peppers down to play another game. Later, I carelessly rubbed my eyes, getting the pepper oil on my fingers into my eyes, searing my eyeballs; the more I rubbed away tears from my eyes, the worse they burned. I didn't tell Buster, hoping it would stop and Mama wouldn't learn what I'd done.

Finally, I begged for his help, and he said, "That's what you get for not minding Mama."

Once back home, Mama saw my flushed face and eyes swollen shut from the toxicity of the pepper oil. "Oh, dear! What's wrong with your face?"

My brother said, "He's been crying after getting a little pepper in his eyes."

"Buster, you're old enough to keep him out of mischief and take care of his hurts. Why haven't you rinsed his eyes with water or something? Cleveland, come into the bathroom."

Mama washed my face with soap and placed a cloth soaked in ice water over my eyes, a hot and cold lesson in relief of your misery.

But my most serious illness had nothing to do with laxatives or chili peppers. Until we moved back to Little Rock, I was seldom sick with anything other than a sore throat or common cold. So the day my nose ran and I sneezed and coughed repeatedly, Mama assumed I had another cold. A couple of nights later, I itched all over but didn't tell her, not wanting her to check my skin and worry. A day later at breakfast, Buster complained about my moving too much in bed and kicking him in the night.

After looking at me, Mama exclaimed, "Gracious, Cleveland, you have spots on your face. Take off your pajama top."

There were pinkish dots topped by white blisters on my chest.

She said, "My goodness, I think you've got the chicken pox."

Kept home from school, I watched the rash spread to other parts of my body. When I scratched, Mama warned me about having scars if the skin was torn. To avoid that possibility, she trimmed my fingernails and put white cotton work gloves on my hands, and bathed me in a tub of warm water and oatmeal to ease the itch. Talk about oozy! But the slimy flakes of oatmeal made the rash less annoying. On the third day, another wave of blisters spread as the pox of the first wave reached my ears and mouth and crusted over.

Buster raised more cane than usual about sleeping with a restless bed mate. "Mama, I put up with him kicking even when he's well, but I can't put up with him putting on a show in bed."

"A show? What do you mean? What's he doing?"

"I wake up in the middle of the night, and his hands in those white gloves are flapping like Al Jolson as he mouths "Swanee" under his breath."

Mama asked, "Cleveland, why on earth would you do that in the middle of the night?"

"I wasn't sleepy. Buster was asleep, so he didn't say anything. I didn't mean to wake him."

"Well, you did, you little sap. *Swanee, how I love ya* wouldn't soothe anyone to sleep. With his scabs, Mama, it's like sleeping with a leper. I'm moving out to the living room couch."

Grandpa Honea's unexpected arrival in the truck with the Wonder Bread driver never disturbed Buster but bothered me. Grandpa usually arrived about sundown, after the salesman drove from White County. With his little black satchel in hand, he knocked at the front door.

Greeting him, Mama asked, "Oh, Papa, why didn't you let me know you were coming?"

"Notion just struck me this morning."

"You could've called on the phone to let me know."

"Aye, gonnies, I ain't spendin' extry money on no long-distance phone call."

"I hope we'll have something you like at supper, Papa."

"Whatever you serve'll suit me."

Mama knew better, and Grandpa did, too, but he never accepted that his surprise visits were trouble for her. And since there weren't separate bedrooms for each of us in our apartment, Buster and I gave up our bed; Bus slept on the living room couch, and I lay on a pallet under the dining room table, my favorite spot. Grandpa's hours also prevailed during his visits; we went to bed earlier and got up earlier. Even Daddy observed Grandpa's schedule without complaining, which was Mama's doing.

At five in the morning, I joined Buster in the living room, so Grandpa could eat the full breakfast Mama prepared for him—two eggs sunny side up, bacon, biscuits, and milk gravy. He drank several cups of his brand of coffee, "saucering" the coffee by pouring some into his saucer at intervals to cool. After his early supper each evening, Mama mixed him a hot toddy from a bottle of whiskey kept just for his visits—quite a concession for someone so opposed to liquor of any kind.

Grandpa usually called on his sister, great-aunt Elizabeth Terry, beside the Terry Dairy Company plant on Scott. Even though it was only a short distance from us, he complained about the walk. Aunt Betsy's "colored" maid, no bigger than her tiny mistress, ushered Grandpa, Mama, and me into the sitting room, where my aunt, dressed in her Sunday best, sat in a graceful occasional chair. Oftentimes, her sister, great-aunt Jane, was there, too. Both had the snow white hair common to the Honea sisters and brothers, except for Grandpa's white fringe. Sometimes Aunt Jane's husband, Uncle Lafayette, a carpenter and painter at the dairy, joined us.

The object of my affection at Aunt Betsy's house was the silver gumdrop tree on the table beside the loveseat in her formal sitting room. Someone's Christmas gift many years before, the small tree was merely the top of a thorn bush mounted upright on a heavy wooden base. The maid impaled on each thorn tip a flavored gumdrop for guests—cherry, orange, lemon, licorice, and grape. Since Aunt Betsy nearly always asked me to recite or sing, I knew my reward afterward would be all the gumdrops I could eat. And the maid would, as usual, foil Mama's effort to limit the number by replacing them as fast I consumed them. That's probably why "Goody, goody, gumdrop" was such a favorite expression of mine.

Soon after reciting, eating, and then growing weary of grown-up talk, I escaped to the front porch to sit on the painted white cast-iron bench or in the creaking, low-slung wooden swing. Aunt Betsy's porch, whatever the season or time of day, was dark and cold, for the dairy's brick warehouse wall threw a gigantic shadow across her front yard, keeping it cool even on the hottest summer days. Two magnolia trees covered in brittle, glossy leaves also shaded the porch, and carpeted the lawn in dry leaves changing slowly from green to golden brown.

Aunt Betsy knew how much her brother Ben loved ice cream and had her maid call me inside. I stood beside my aunt as she fished in the drawer of her delicate kneehole desk for a small wooden chit I could exchange for ice cream in the dairy's white-tiled sales room next door. Even though Grandpa preferred plain vanilla, I wanted flavors with color, so the clerk allowed me to stand behind the counter on tiptoes peering into all the ice cream drums to choose. Then she packed two shiny white cardboard cartons, one with vanilla for Grandpa and one with chocolate or strawberry ice cream for me and the others. I took them back to the maid, who piled heaping scoops in fragile china bowls for us to eat in the sitting room. Grandpa's visits with his sister usually ended too soon for me, and, sadly, shortly after our last visit, dear Aunt Betsy died at the ripe old age of eighty.

But a happier event followed soon after our family's sad loss. Mama and I came home from town one afternoon and found Daddy sitting in the middle of the sofa with his arms spread across the back, smiling broadly. Before Mama uttered a word, he jumped up to hug and kiss her, something I rarely saw him do.

Daddy had found a job!

Cleveland at 1301½ Gaines Street.

CHAPTER 4

Good Neighbors, White and Black

OUR FAMILY CELEBRATED Daddy's new job with the Metropolitan Life Insurance Company by eating slices of Mama's lemon meringue pie at the kitchen table. What Daddy would sell wasn't clear to me; I knew a little something about groceries and gas heaters, but insurance was a complete mystery.

"What *is* insurance, Daddy?"

"Well, sonny boy, someone buys a policy by paying money on a regular basis to a company that promises to pay the policy holder a specified sum of money if a certain person dies."

"Do you have life insurance on us if we die, Daddy?"

"I sure do. I own policies for you, your mother, Buster, and me."

"I'll bet you'll make lots of money selling policies to other people, Daddy."

"Not likely, sonny boy. But it's better than no job at all."

My father didn't write a single contract his entire first month at Metropolitan. Maybe that's why my parents broke their rule of not talking about finances in my presence. I heard Daddy say, "Floy, even sharing Buster's salary, we won't be able to pay rent and buy groceries, too."

Mama replied, "One thing we *can do* is find a cheaper place to live."

The next morning, she telephoned her friends asking about low-rent houses near them. Myrna Westmoreland, at the Fairview Apartments on Gaines Street, mentioned a place one block north of her. Within a week's time, my parents rented an apartment on the west side of town and pre-pared to transfer me to another elementary school. Mama salved my reluctance to change again so soon by promising to have me advanced to the second grade.

My last day at Parham, when the Arkansas Transfer Company moved our furniture to our new home, Daddy picked me up after school and drove us to a blood-red brick-veneer duplex at 1301 ½ Gaines. Climbing short flights of stairs to three separate small landings in the apartment foyer, I realized "½" in our new address meant upstairs. Now I could watch people from a window without their knowing and without Mama telling me not to stare. The mahogany newel posts on the stairs reminded me of the wooden pulpit and lectern at Second Baptist Church, and would be good places for me to perform.

Inside the apartment, immediately left of the front door, was another door, composed of glass panes, that opened onto the front porch, where our swing already hung from the low ceiling. The living and dining rooms had ivory-colored plaster walls shining brightly and blond hardwood floors glistening like new. I walked out on the screened back porch, which was twice as big as Scott Street's, and looked down the back stairs at the yard. The steep stairs took my breath away.

Again, there were only two bedrooms, with a tiny bathroom in between them. Even though Buster had expected to have a room of his own, he didn't fuss. Maybe teasing me made up for his lack of privacy. Even though our room was large enough to get in and out of bed on both sides, we would have to share the small closet. I just wondered how the nice apartment could cost Daddy less money.

After my quick survey of our apartment, I ran outside and checked our new neighbors. I saw not one white boy or girl on the block, only bands of black kids, older and younger than me. At supper, I revealed there were more blacks than whites in our immediate vicinity.

Daddy, looking at me, asked, "Why do you think I can afford this place?"

The nearest whites lived in the apartment below us. Mrs. Flowers, a widow, welcomed us with a yellow pound cake and apologized for her son's old jalopy in the front yard. Her daughter, Dorothy, and younger son, Weldon, were a senior and sophomore at Little Rock Senior High School, and her older son was an auto mechanic in Fort Smith. Mrs. Flowers identified our other white neighbors: two elderly, unmarried Catholic sisters, Misses Margaret and Martha McKinney, in the white bungalow next door; and Edward and Lydia Richter, native-born Germans but naturalized Americans, in the pale green cottage beside the McKinneys'. The last house on our side of the block—a three-story boarding house next to a Standard Oil service station, on the northeast corner at Fourteenth and Gaines—was occupied by black people.

On the block across the street, four small, unpainted shotgun houses were wedged so close together that Mama believed the black families in each house heard every word spoken in all the others. Opposite us, on the southwest corner of Thirteenth, Springfield's Grocery occupied a small red-brick building. North of us on Gaines, the blocks across from Mount Holly Cemetery to Ninth Street's black business district had more ramshackle houses, overflowing with black families.

Mrs. Westmoreland, Mama's friend in the Fairview apartments in the 1400 block, insisted, "The best people live only on south Gaines."

Claiming to be a graduate of Blue Mountain College in Mississippi, she always bragged to Mama about her son, Teddy, an airplane pilot. I don't know why Mama had a friend so determined to prove superior to her, for Mama's face revealed that Mrs. Westmoreland succeeded. Fortunately, Mama could claim her wealthy first cousin, Will Terry, and his wife were two of the "best people" on south Gaines, and owned a beautiful home across the street from ex-governor George W. Donaghey, who was instrumental in the completion of the Arkansas State Capitol building. Uncle Billy not only owned Terry Dairy but was president of the Little Rock Public School Board. I doubt, though, that Mama ever mentioned her relation to Mrs. Westmoreland. (The Terrys' son, Seymour, the same age as Buster, later won a posthumous Congressional Medal of Honor for valor on Okinawa in World War II.)

Our first Sunday afternoon on Gaines, Daddy drove eight blocks south on the street for a visit with the Terrys. Going back home, Mama talked an awful lot about the handsome homes and beautifully landscaped lots at that end of Gaines.

Daddy finally said, "Those fine places are for highfalutin people, Floy. But we live next door to the noblest persons in Little Rock's and Arkansas's history."

What a happy prospect, I thought! "Really, Daddy? The McKinney sisters?"

"Nope, the generals, governors, judges, mayors, and senators slumbering beneath the loam at Mount Holly Cemetery—men and women who developed this city and state."

Ignorant but curious about cemeteries and historical figures, I walked on the sidewalk between unpaved Thirteenth Street and Mount Holly's natural-stone retaining wall, turned left at Broadway, and went north to the cemetery's entrance. The natural-rock pillars supporting the black cast-iron gate had concrete orbs as big as basketballs on top. The arch over the opening had a heart-shaped outline in the center of which MOUNT HOLLY was inscribed.

I knew nothing about dead people, above or below ground, so entering cautiously, I stood in the protective shadow of a tall marble angel whose open eyes stared in the direction of the ranks of old, stained tombstones. Realizing dead bodies in caskets were beneath my feet, I wandered respect-fully among the lopsided obelisks, crypts, headstones, angels, hooded figures, and empty urns, attempting to avoid stepping on a body I could not see. The names and dates on many cracked slabs and crumbling headstones had dimmed with age, dead grass and weeds growing along the edges of almost every grave. Marble columns, large and small, over different graves across the cemetery were obelisks like Frank Smythe Jr.'s souvenir of the Washington Monument. (He was two classes ahead of me.) What puzzled me most were the letters *RIP* and *IHS* marked upon many tombstones.

Fearless, since no one was around, I walked to a small, white frame hut in the middle of the cemetery, which had two windows, an oversized door, and a brick chimney.

I was circling the hut when a low voice growled, "Whadda ya want in here, boy?"

Turning to the voice, I faced a thick-bodied man with a reddish brown face, shaggy black hair, and clay-stained pants, shirt, shoes, and bare ankles. He carried a shovel caked with red clay in his hands.

To conceal my anxiety, I asked, "What's this little building for, mister?"

"The receiving house ... more of a tool shed now. I think ya better go somewhere's else to *look*, kid."

Even though he made no physical or verbal threats, I ran back to the entrance. On Broadway heading home, I realized the man merely worked as a gravedigger.

Nearing Thirteenth and Broadway, I smelled sugar and vanilla in the air. Tracking the direction of the scent, like a birddog, I saw a sign in the yard of a shotgun house on the other side of the street that said DAD'S OATMEAL COOKIES. But I had no money to buy a cookie. At home, I asked Mama for a nickel, but she wouldn't let me go back, because I'd have to cross Broadway, probably the widest, busiest street in Little Rock. But she satisfied my curiosity about the mysterious initials on the tombstones in Mount Holly, which represented "rest in peace" and the name of Jesus Christ.

I waited patiently, knowing Mama's sweet tooth would prevail. Shortly after, she joined me crossing Broadway at the Fourteenth Street traffic signal to buy cookies in Dad's front room.

School was already in session in the spring semester of 1931 when Mama walked me to Rightsell Elementary School, pointing out the traffic dangers at street corners, driveways, filling stations, and trolley crossings. When we reached Rightsell, the plain, buff-brick building had none of the decorative columns, arches, or bay windows of Parham. We reported to the principal, Mr. Victor L. Webb, a tall, big-boned man, his face framed by silver gray hair and the smile on his lips half-hidden by a thick white mustache. Even though his gentle eyes and deep resonant voice were reassuring, he had a contradictory and threatening thick leather strap on his desk.

Mama's explanation of why I repeated the first half of the first grade at Parham, even though my reading and arithmetic were stronger than average first graders', persuaded Mr. Webb to let me prove my abilities. He seemed pleased to take me to the classroom next to his office, which was the first half of the second grade. At recess, a little girl classmate told me that our teacher was Mayor Horace A. Knowlton's wife. And friendly boys took me after school to a giant chinaberry tree to collect berries for slingshot pellets in the Knowltons' front yard on Izard Street.

I left home early the next morning to walk the nine blocks to school by myself and arrive on time. Our class began with us standing beside our desks facing a big American flag on the wall above the blackboard, its forty-eight white stars on a blue field on the same side as our hearts. We put our right hands over our hearts and raised our left hands, repeating in unison: "I pledge allegiance to the Flag of the United States of America and to the Republic for which it stands, one Nation indivisible, with liberty and justice for all." ("Under God" wasn't added until 1954.) Then a classmate stood and read a short verse from the King James version of the Holy Bible.

A week later, Mr. Webb sent a note to Mama, acknowledging that my skills in reading, arithmetic, singing, and performing convinced Mrs. Knowlton I belonged in second grade. But I was disappointed that we didn't perform the same artistic activities as we had in Mrs. Shipp's class. Even though we made up and performed skits at Halloween, Thanksgiving, Christmas, Valentine's, and Easter, we seldom invented stories, recited poems, or sang as we had at Parham. And our art work was mostly cutting out silhouettes of hearts, flowers, leaves, ghosts, turkeys, and wreaths from colored paper to paste on our monthly calendars.

At recess, we played outside on the graveled grounds unless it was rainy or too cold, when we stayed in the large basement playroom. In good weather, I tried to explore all the grounds, but a sixth-grade boy with a monitor's orange and white badge pinned on his chest stopped me, explaining that the first three grades played "at the sides of the building under a teacher's watchful eyes." Only the upper grades played in the open, gravel-covered grounds at the back of the building.

Luckily, our part of the grounds had seesaws, swings, the Great Circle—a circular sit-down bench that turned in circles—and the Great Stride, an iron Maypole set in concrete with chains attached to a rotating disc on top that swung around. The first time I grabbed a ladder-like hand-hold, I took long strides, pushing out as high as I could without caution, and swung free. Suddenly, the boy ahead of me let go and his loose chain smashed into my head, leaving my ears ringing, and a knot on my forehead rising, like those on Jiggs when Maggie struck him with a rolling pin in the funny papers.

In bad weather, despite the older boy's warning, I gradually toured the entire building at recess, at lunch, and on errands, walking from the basement cafeteria, playroom, toilets, and furnace room to the two upper floors of classrooms, past the teachers' lounge on the second floor. A new auditorium had been built at the rear of the first floor the year before I came. I volunteered to fill our class's paste pot in order to see the custodian's room in the basement. But crossing down the faintly lighted stairs to a windowless supply room, my shadow on the wall spooked me.

The friendly janitor, a thin, cocoa-colored wisp of a man with a white mustache like Mr. Webb's, greeted me with a smile. Neatly dressed in a starched white shirt, with sleeve garters, a shiny black bow tie, dark trousers, and suspenders, he had on high-topped leather Romeos like Grandpa Honea's. Surrounded by shelves of chalk boxes, erasers, paper towels, toilet tissue, and floor sweep, he introduced himself as Uncle Henry.

While removing a damp cloth from a large ceramic crock in one corner of the basement, he asked my name and class room. As he dipped a thick ceramic coffee cup into a white jelly—a mix of resin, starch, and water—and dumped globs of it into our pot, I saw he had more wrinkles in his dark skin than my parents did. But I couldn't guess how old he was.

Throughout the next four years, Uncle Henry, sweeping and dusting the building, remained a sympathetic friend to us white children, but I wondered what black men like him really thought and felt about us.

One afternoon, before the school bell released us, Mrs. Knowlton asked each of us to find out and report in class the next day what kind of sandwich our mother could prepare for a PTA meeting. The next morning, she asked our mothers' choices. The other kids had remembered and named peanut butter and jelly, pimento cheese, tuna fish, and other sandwiches. But I forgot to ask Mama and attempted to hide my failure by naming bacon-lettuce-and-tomato, my favorite.

Mrs. Knowlton seemed unconvinced. "Are you sure, Cleveland?"

After school, Mama read the note pinned to my coat, exclaiming, "You named bacon-lettuce-and-tomato? What on earth were you thinking of?"

Nothing really! I tried to cover my irresponsibility without knowing how much the ingredients cost or the difficulties of making and serving a BLT at a public meeting. In Mama's note of apology to Mrs. Knowlton, she offered egg-and-olive sandwiches, for which we always had plenty ingredients since Grandpa Honea kept us well supplied.

Food rarely entered my mind until I sat at the table at mealtimes. At lunch, I either ate a sack lunch from home or bought a meal in the cafeteria. No matter how strapped for cash anyone's families might be in those hard times, the city offered no free breakfasts or lunches. Mama was convinced the lunches served at school were probably the best meals many poor kids had every day.

Two short, ample-figured dietitians, Miss Dempsey and her sister, Mrs. Kaiser, selected the menus and supervised the black women who prepared, cooked, and served the hot meals every school day. As we passed the steam table choosing our dishes, the dietitians checked our trays to be sure our choices were sufficiently balanced and nutritious foods. I would have eaten chili or chili-macaroni and drunk chocolate milk every day if the meat and vegetables were not "forced" upon me.

During my early weeks at Rightsell, I could hardly wait for the final class bell, watching for the minute hand of the electric clock to jerk at 3:20 and RING so I could run home. But gradually, I heard there were exciting things to do after school on the way home—stopping for gum or candy at the grocery store at Nineteenth and State, despite the school rule against it; strolling home beside Jeanette Adair and lingering in her yard telling a story or joke; dodging the snarling black chow on Gaines Street when he was loose; loitering on Jim MacFarlane's porch or in Catherine Rightsell's gazebo across the street from him; visiting my Uncle Poppa in his barbershop beside Bullion's Grocery on Gaines; leafing through magazines at King's Drugstore; spelunking in a tunnel of cardboard boxes in a boy's empty garage—these were fun activities I could choose from every day.

When walking home, I didn't like being with kids who argued and with bullies picking on someone. A few boys who teased girls also picked on Frederick Cloud, a tall, strong, blond-headed boy one grade ahead of me, so good natured that bullies assumed he was a sissy. I walked part of the way home every afternoon with Frederick and two other pals. Arthur Stranz always dropped off first, at 1855 Gaines, where he lived with his father, mother, and little sister. Jim MacFarlane, a half grade ahead of me, stopped next at his home, at 1610 Gaines, where he and his widowed mother, Eleanor, lived with his maternal grandmother, Mrs. Miles. Big Frederick parted last at Fifteenth and Gaines without my ever knowing his home address.

Sometimes Frank Smythe Jr. walked as far as Piggly Wiggly before turning away to his home, between Arch and Gaines on Fourteenth. For a brief period, I visited and joined him in his hobby, molding toy lead soldiers using melting pots, ladles, a hot plate, and lead slag. His father was a friend of a linotype operator at the *Arkansas Democrat*, who provided the lead slag.

Clamping metal plates of opposing concavities together, we filled them with lead that formed three-dimensional soldiers in various standing, kneeling, or prone positions, holding either rifles or swords. Wearing heavy gloves, I held the mold and Frank poured the hot lead through a hole at the top of the mold. After the lead cooled and hardened, we removed the blanks of soldier figures and sandpapered and smoothed their raw edges. I enjoyed most the tedious but fulfilling job of painting uniforms on figures, matching the colored pictures in books of military uniforms from different countries with sable brushes and banana-oil paints.

We duplicated in the Smythes' attic library military formations from famous battles, spreading the brightly colored soldier formations on the floor, shelves, desks, and chairs, Frank commanding the English army and I the French. He based his maneuvers on European battles of the eighteenth century. Since he actually controlled both armies, he was always victorious. But I didn't mind, for Frank was a melancholy reminder of the bedridden boy in Robert Louis Stevenson's *The Land of Counterpane*:

> *And sometimes for an hour or so*
> *I watch my leaden soldiers go,*
> *with different uniforms and drills*
> *Among the bed-clothes, through the hills.*

I hadn't yet heard about retirement, since my grandfathers in Beebe and McRae still worked, so I found it hard to believe Frank's grandfather, who was a widower, didn't have a job. One Saturday, Frank, without revealing what he had in mind, took me next door to his grandfather's house. From the dark silence in the house, I assumed no one was home, that we were alone. Frank led me upstairs and through his grandfather's bedroom into the bathroom, opened a cabinet door, removed an object I didn't recognize, and plugged its electric cord into a wall socket. Then, before I realized what he was doing, he had pulled his pants off and invited me to do the same.

I asked why, and he said, "You'll see."

I had never been even partially naked with another boy, nor seen anyone but my brother without clothes, so I hesitated. Only after Frank kept insisting did I remove my pants but not my underwear. He was playing with himself by pressing the electric machine against his "pea pod." Watching him made me extremely uneasy, and from the ache in my throat, I knew what he was doing and wanted me to do was wrong. So I pulled my pants up and said I had to go home.

With few friends his age, Frank continued asking me to spend Saturdays with him, but I pulled away. Except for seeing him on my way home from school, I rarely went near his house.

The girls in my class appealed to me far more than Frank—not as lovey-dovey girlfriends but in their personal qualities, such as Mary Jane Moriarty's poise, which I wished to possess. Slender as a reed, her hips narrow as her shoulders, she moved with the angular grace of a long-legged water bird. Taller than most boys in our class, she talked to strangers and adults with absolute ease. I also wanted to be as attractive and likable as my second cousin, Mary Vincent Terry, who had shiny black hair, blue eyes, and a peaches-and-cream complexion, like my mother's.

My secret choice of a real girlfriend, Jeanette Adair, lived across the street from Arthur Stranz on Gaines. The willowy blonde with aquiline features was the girl I singled out for special interest, a circumstance involving practically nothing on her part; it simply meant she was under my constant surveillance. Suffering embarrassment, fright, and knowledge of being in enchanted territory when I was with her, I wanted her to like me better than the other boys. But she never revealed her feelings, only smiled and laughed at my impressions and stories. I wondered what made girls act so differently from boys if they liked someone.

In the fall term, after passing second grade, I climbed two flights upstairs to the third-grade class taught by sprightly little Miss Bradley. (When I reached high school, Miss Bradley was rooming at the home of Aunt Lodie, Uncle Albert Honea's widow, on South Broadway.) Miss Bradley, an older woman, dressed in somber-colored dresses rather than the bright prints favored by young teachers.

Stressing social sciences, arithmetic, and Bible history, she required us to gather and organize information on subjects in notebooks that we illustrated with pictures cut from magazines or drew by hand. There were no more art lessons with paint and clay, or seasonal skits. She held Arthur Stranz's notebooks up as examples for us to emulate. Of course, the kids whose work was poor claimed Arthur's mother prepared his booklets, which wasn't true. Arthur's writing, printing, and drawing during class proved it was his own work. My written reports never equaled Arthur's in appearance, but Miss Bradley praised my oral reports and Bible readings.

I never expected Bible study of any kind in public school, but Mr. Webb, our principal, instructed us one hour each week in Bible history and the geography of the Holy Land. He had written, with two other authors, *The Old World, Past and Present: A Unified Course in the History and*

Geography of Europe, Asia, and Africa, for Elementary Schools. Daddy called his Bible lessons unusual in a public school but didn't object. Mr. Webb's thin textbook did not dwell on biblical figures in the Old or New Testaments as our Sunday school teachers did. He concentrated instead on historical and geographical elements in the Bible. Pulling his brightly colored maps of the Ancient World down over the blackboard, he showed us the probable settlements of Noah's descendants; the garden of Eden between the Tigris and Euphrates rivers in Mesopotamia; the division of Canaan among Israel's Twelve Tribes; and the historical sites in Jerusalem and Bethlehem.

More appealing to me than the maps were his pictures of biblical clothing. The Hebrews and their neighbors wore woven shawls and tunics, with enveloping robes and drapery protecting heads and necks from sun and wind. The patterns and colors of cloth—wide perpendicular stripes of white, ecru, brown, ochre, blue, rust, and dull green in Joseph's coat and garments worn by Joseph, Mary, and the Wise Men—fascinated me.

The bathrobe and house slippers I wore as a wise man's costume never seemed quite right in Christmas plays at Second Baptist Church after Mr. Webb's lessons.

My early interest in clothing as costume explained why a pair of corduroy knickers together with Calumet Baking Powder remain in my memory. Continuing to wear my usual clothing in third grade—a camp shirt, shorts, and long cotton stockings supported by elastic garters—I felt like a baby. Since many of my classmates wore knickers, knee-length britches banded at the knees, I begged until Mama was persuaded to buy me a pair at Gus Blass Department Store. Her practical aim to keep me warm led her to wool knickers that buttoned below the knees, but since wool rubbed a rash on my legs and buttons let the pant legs droop when running and wrestling, I protested. Converted by the points I made, she bought corduroy knickers with only wool in the knee bands.

Ironically, she wiped out a good purchase for daily wear by insisting that the knickers be for dress-up occasions.

But Mama still treated me with a sweet after our shopping excursions. Even though we could afford only one pair of knickers, she allowed me a penny for a treat at Springfield's Grocery across the street. The first time I visited the store, Mr. Sam, the owner, rushed to the counter to wait on me.

And "wait" he did. It took me so long to choose a single piece of candy that when I returned the next time, he didn't move from his chair.

Without him impatient behind the counter, I stood with my mouth watering, staring at chocolate bonbons, peanut brittle, lemon drops, licorice lollipops, praline patties, salt-water taffies, Turkish delights, tutti-frutti, jaw breakers, jelly beans, candy cigarettes with red tips, chocolate cigars with gold bands, twists of black and red licorice, and wax bottles filled with colored liquids. Tempted as I was by each of Mr. Sam's crystallized sugars, my hypnotic trance ended by choosing quantity over allure—two-for-a-penny, individually wrapped Tootsie Rolls, peanut butter logs, and banana caramels.

Mama, like many of our other neighbors, bought only emergency items at Springfield's, such as kitchen matches, toilet paper, or laundry soap, because other items cost too much. Sadly, as the Depression deepened, Mr. Sam was slowly going broke, unable to compete with one of the original Piggly Wiggly chain stores of Mr. Clarence Saunders of Memphis, Tennessee, at the corner of Fourteenth and Gaines.

In time, Mr. Sam would be forced to sell his stock and store fixtures. Near his closing, he asked, "Cleveland, do you want the Calumet sign on this building?"

"Sure do, Mr. Sam. It's so slick on the front side, I'll make a sled out of it."

"I don't see how you can do that without snow. But it's yours if you'll take it down."

I wanted to slide down the grassy slope of our side yard on Thirteenth on the shiny enamel sign that curved around an outside corner of the store and appeared to be three-dimensional, shaped like a three-foot-tall, two-foot-wide, red and white baking-powder can. Decorated with an Indian head in a feather bonnet, it featured the slogan *Baker's Best Always Pleases.*

Borrowing a screwdriver from Daddy's toolbox, without his permission, I removed the sign from the corner of the building and dragged it to our garage. But the screws in metal straps attaching the sign to the wall were rusty and couldn't be removed. While I pondered my next move, Mama called me inside to dress to go to town. After changing into a clean shirt and my new corduroy knickers, I dragged the baking powder sign from the garage to the top of the grassy slope, sat carefully between the two rusty metal straps still protruding from the back, and pushed off.

Whoopee!

The sliding sign jerked to an abrupt stop. One corner snagged a weed and threw me forward. One metal strap had ripped a three-cornered tear in the leg of my knickers! Gee whiz, only my first ride on the sign …

Running upstairs, I begged Mama to mend my pants, but she only said, "Oh, dear! Not your new corduroys! Well, I can't do anything about them right now. Wear 'em as they are or take 'em off and put on your school clothes."

"Mama, I can't wear shorts and stockings *or* torn pants downtown. I'll just stay home."

But she took me in shorts and drooping stockings. What appeared to be disaster proved a blessing—when Mama patched my knickers, she let me wear them any time I wanted.

Anyway, that's how the Indian pipe of peace met the cloth of the king— when (you have to say it out loud), "Cal-u-met cord-u-roy."

Taking my bath one Sunday night, I gingerly rubbed a sore spot on my stomach with my washcloth. I didn't tell Mama because her "doctoring" would probably hurt more than the swelling. I secretly watched the red spot swell more, altering in color. In the bathroom, I peeked under my shirt to check the purplish red rings, big as a half dollar, encircling a yellow core. By mid-week, the lightest brush of my shirt against the spot's surface brought excruciating pain. Yet the pain and appearance weren't frightening enough to tell my mother.

By Friday morning, I was slouching to prevent my clothes from touching the boil. As I headed toward the front door leaving for school, Mama asked, "Why are you holding yourself oddly?"

Straightening up, I continued walking, eager to escape. Following me, she repeated, "Why are you walking such a strange way in such a hurry?"

"I don't know what you mean, Mama. I guess my stomach hurts a little."

"If you're sick at your stomach, maybe you need a glass of soda water?"

"No, ma'am. It's not *inside* my stomach, it's just a sore spot on the outside."

"Young man, stop where you are. Take off your jacket. Let me see that spot."

"Aw, Momm … maa, it won't do any good. You'll make me late for school."

"Never mind school, young man. I want to see your stomach this minute."

So I pulled up my undershirt. Mama gasped and led me into the bathroom. With my stomach bare, I saw a livid aureole of multicolored rings around the core of the festering boil. When Mama was set to squeeze the boil, I couldn't keep from crying. Luckily, her lightest pressure released the core, bringing swift relief. After draining and cleansing the site, Mama wrote a note explaining why I was late coming to school. But I ran all the way and arrived breathlessly on time. At recess, I had fun telling everyone how fast I ran the nine blocks.

Daddy called my massive boil a "carbuncle," the first of my several skin eruptions that year. I might have avoided some illnesses by asking kids after they recovered about their symptoms, but I didn't. So the day I felt tired, sleepy, itchy, and too hot to eat my lunch, I didn't worry Miss Bradley about it. I just asked to be excused repeatedly for a drink of water.

Miss Bradley finally said, "Cleveland, your face is flushed, let me feel your forehead." Laying her cool hand on my forehead, she exclaimed, "Oh, my, I'm afraid you've caught the measles that are going around. I'm sending you straight home to your mother."

When I showed up, Mama couldn't believe her eyes. "Why was school dismissed so early?"

"It wasn't. Miss Bradley says I have the measles."

She felt my forehead, took my temperature, and called Dr. Fulmer. Following his instructions, she put me to bed and pulled down the shades. By the next morning, a red, blotchy rash had bloomed on my face and ears, and during the day it spread slowly across my torso, arms, and legs. Even though Buster had measles growing up and was immune, he slept on the sofa in the living room until my rash faded, unhappy his bed partner was susceptible to childhood diseases.

Before school dismissed for the summer, I fell ill again, but this time no one had trouble identifying my malady because a friend already had a severe case of mumps. Hearing that Jimmy Moncure's testicles were painfully swollen, I had no idea what or where testicles were until Jim said "nuts." The only swollen glands I had were between my ears and in my jaws, making chewing and swallowing painful.

After my recovery and return to school, a brown-skinned young man was standing by the flagpole surrounded by a circle of boys when I arrived before first bell. Not much taller than the oldest boy, he was too old to be a new pupil and spoke with a foreign accent. He tossed a small double disk of wood attached to a string in front of him as he talked, and the disk returned to his hand like magic. At first, I was too far away from him to see the string attached to the spinning disk in the demonstration. He called it a *yo-yo*, a toy with two wooden discs connected in the center by a wooden axle, which had a string looped around the axle so the disk could spin.

After the yo-yo man's spiel, an older boy said, "You don't talk like us. Where you from?"

The smiling yo-yo man, his glistening teeth whiter than the stripes and stars of the flag fluttering over our heads, said "I live in the Philippine Islands across the Pacific Ocean."

The young Filipino, a professional salesman for the Duncan Company, toured all forty-eight states demonstrating and selling yo-yos. Part of his sales scheme in cities the size of Little Rock was teaching kids how to perform tricks with a yo-yo and to compete in championship contests to popularize yo-yos. He remained on the school grounds most of the day, demonstrating "the hesitation," "walking the dog," "around the world," and "loop the loop." After his demonstrations, he sold colored yo-yos and supplies to kids willing to spend their lunch money on *junior* yo-yos for a nickel, *beginners* for a dime, two strings for a nickel, and a rule book for a dime.

I just watched what he did and tried to master his Filipino accent. I would never have spent my lunch money on a toy.

Even though teachers at school taught me a lot, I was learning more about people in everyday life outside the classroom, especially accompanying my father when he collected insurance fees on Saturdays.

He said, "I work on Saturdays because weekends are the only times I can find certain breadwinners at home."

Early Saturday morning, Daddy drove us to the Boyle Building at Fifth and Main, where we rode an elevator to the tenth floor and entered a big room shared by all the Metropolitan insurance agents.

One smiling agent in the room greeted Daddy, "Hey, Al, you planning on getting your boy into the business, too?

"Charley, Metropolitan couldn't do better."

"It's Saturday, man. Don't you ever take a day off?"

"Not if there's a chance I'll find someone home and collect."

After he and other agents smoked and exchanged stories, Daddy drove us to what he called his *debit* in Pulaski Heights, to follow up on sales leads and collect from policy holders unreachable on weekdays. Daddy told me he took the debit in Pulaski Heights assuming the city's well-to-do, well-known men in business and politics would pay their bills regularly and on time. But after a few months at Metropolitan, he realized that wasn't true.

As we drove along the curved, undulating streets to the crests of many forested foothills, I had an opportunity to look at houses of many different sizes and styles on odd-shaped lots. Daddy pointed out and named Tudor manors, Cape Cod cottages, French chateaux, New England farmhouses, and Spanish haciendas.

He said, "Son, some of the owners of these elegant houses either don't pay bills or pay them late. That's not a proper way of doing business. And if they don't pay their insurance premiums, it hurts our family."

He described how a few people wouldn't answer their doors or phones and let their insurance policies lapse. A few others, to avoid losing the money they had invested, asked him "to carry them," promising to pay their premiums the next month. Daddy tried to be sympathetic and covered for those men he trusted.

We usually ended collecting on Saturdays in the Heights at the Arkansas State Asylum for Nervous Diseases. In our Chrysler, we climbed the steep curve of the asylum road to a cluster of red-brick buildings at the top of the hill. I knew we'd park by the central tower of the five-story building. One Saturday, getting out of the car, we saw a woman reaching through the bars in a tower window, flailing her arms.

Daddy and I reached the front steps and started up when she shouted, "At last you're here, honey! I knew you'd come get me. Bless your heart. I knew you wouldn't leave me in this goddamn place. I'll get my things right now to go home. You're the sweetest man God ever made. Thank you, baby, for coming for me."

My father stopped, looked up, smiled, and waved at her.

"Who does that lady think you are, Daddy? Why's she talking that way?"

"She's sick, hon. Wants outta this place. And I don't blame her."

Daddy had to collect from policy holders in different buildings, and he left me with nurses who made over me as I accompanied them on their rounds. Walking down the halls and into the ward lounges, we encountered patients sitting in chairs in odd postures, leaning on the walls or staring at them, and pacing back and forth as lions do at the zoo. A few patients stood in frozen positions like department store mannequins. If patients talked or stared in my direction, I mistakenly thought they were speaking to me or wanted to, and I waved at them. A few older women reached out to grab me, and the nurses hurriedly stepped between us and pushed me away from them. On one of the floors, a group of small black people, called pinheads by the nurses, surrounded us. Their heads were no bigger than a doll's but their bodies, though equally small, were well proportioned. They reached out to hug and kiss me, like little children, but I shrank from them without understanding why. All through the hospital, I wondered what was going on in the minds of the persons confined there.

Daddy finished collecting insurance payments and took me to another red-brick building on the asylum grounds to visit my grandparents in their private apartment. My grandfather, James David Harrison, who had been a leading businessman in Beebe before his retirement, was superintendent of the ward for the criminally insane, a political appointment for his service to the Democratic Party in White County.

Even though the men imprisoned in my grandfather's ward had been judged insane by the courts, Big Daddy wasn't sure the men were really sane or insane when they committed their crimes.

He said, "Many of these men pled insanity for shorter sentences and better living conditions in this ward."

Whether sane or insane, if an inmate defied a guard's authority or acted violently toward a guard or another prisoner, he was locked in the *cool-down room* in a zinc-lined tub filled with ice water. Big Daddy said guards sometimes held an inmate's head under water until he behaved, and that seemed similar to an act of cruelty in a medieval torture chamber to me.

On one of our Saturday visits, Big Daddy had an inmate brought to his apartment to play his guitar and sing for us. The scrawny, snaggletoothed little prisoner sang jail-house blues, a kind of three- or four-note rhythmic chant, ending with the short refrain "Poor boy."

Lice in the jail big as a quail,
When you turn over they tickle your tail.
Poor boy!

The other verses he sang named the peculiarities of fellow prisoners, ridiculed keepers, and complained about ward conditions. Big Daddy laughed at the song and told the prisoner he was searching for ways to improve the conditions he sang about in his song. My grandfather's stern manner and steely eyes concealed his sense of humor and delight in fun, even though I was sometimes the butt of his jokes.

After our visit, on our way back to the car, the disturbed woman still stood in the window and screamed, "Leaving, are you? You son of a bitch! Just showed up to torture me. I should've known. Dumped me in this filthy hole to get rid of me! You bastard! I hope you burn in hell!" Whining in a shrill voice, she thrust her bare arms through window bars, shaking her fists at us.

When we got back home, I impersonated the deranged woman, showing Mama how she acted without using her curse words. Then I sang the little prisoner's song for her. Buster said, "Mama, don't let him sing that song to anyone else. It's about sex in jail between men."

I didn't know what he meant; nor did Mama, I suspect.

It didn't take long for Buster to get acquainted with Dorothy, Mrs. Flowers's pretty, slender daughter, who had bounteous brown hair and dark eyes. He wanted to take her to the movies on weekends but worked too late on Saturday nights to do it, and Mrs. Flowers didn't approve of going to movies on Sundays. After he got off from work during the week, Buster and Dorothy sat out on the downstairs porch if it wasn't too cold. Buster's infatuation with her reinforced his and my only mutual interest; we enjoyed the movie magazines that Dorothy shared with us. Buster read the stories, and I cut out the pinup pictures of our favorite movie stars to hang on the wall over the head of our bed. Each time she gave us a new magazine, I changed the pictures on the wall, always including my favorites: cowboys Hoot Gibson, Buck Jones, and Tom Mix, and actors Clark Gable, Harry Carey, Janet Gaynor, Jean Harlow, Joan Crawford, Charlie Chaplin, Joe E. Brown, Harold Lloyd, and Laurel and Hardy. A few of Buster's actor preferences— George Raft, Jack LaRue, and Paul Guilfoyle—baffled me. He wouldn't or couldn't tell me why their acting personalities appealed to him. Maybe because all were short and slight with dark hair, like him.

I paid only one thin dime for admission to a movie, but my folks paid a quarter or thirty-five cents. Consequently, free radio was our family's chief entertainment. My parents never set a rigid bedtime for me, which permitted me to hear the best radio shows on the air, including Fred Allen on *The Linit Bath Club Revue* on CBS, Sunday nights at 9:00. Mr. Allen's dry, unhappy, singsong drawl and nasal twang, and Portland Hoffa's high-pitched falsetto, were relatively easy for me to imitate. Even though the political satire in their clever sketches escaped me, Mr. Allen's characterizations of a judge, hotel manager, or circus barker and Portland's different scatterbrained roles appealed to me. Also appealing was Allen's cast of oddball stooges—a pompous floorwalker, cheap Scotsman, and stuttering professor—whose voices I added to my vocal repertoire. Even though his program changed networks and titles, from *Salad Bowl Revue* to *Sal Hepatica Revue* on NBC, Allen's type of comedy never changed.

Another comedian practiced a type of comedy better suited to the sense of humor of most grammar-school kids. I first heard Joe Penner on Rudy Vallee's *Fleischmann Yeast Hour*, saying stuff like:

> Penner: Hello, Rudy, wanna buy a duck?
> Vallee: No, I don't want to buy a duck!
> Penner: Oh, you nah-ah-stee man!

Later, he appeared on *The Baker's Broadcast*, with Ozzie Nelson, his orchestra, and singer Harriet Hilliard. The comedian depended on silly, simple lines that kids would repeat until he invented another expression: "Iz zat so?" "Don't ever dooo that!" and his silly laugh, "Nyuk, nyuk, nyuk!" which led my classmate Jimmy Wirtz to impersonate Penner in costume on every Rightsell school program.

While we lived on Gaines Street, I heard another NBC comic greet the radio audience with "Jell-O again." But Jack Benny didn't become a favorite of mine until his Chevrolet Series, when I was older and more "sophisticated." Mary Livingston, his real wife, played the girlfriend bursting his bubble of braggadocio, and Don Wilson, his large, robust announcer, added girth and a jovial laugh.

My other comic favorites, George Burns and Gracie Allen, appeared on CBS's *Robert Burns Panatella Program*, with Guy Lombardo and his orchestra. I hung on to giddy Gracie's every scatterbrained word. If George observed, "Gracie, you ought to live in a house of the feeble-minded," she had the positive reply, "Oh, George, I'd love to be your houseguest sometime."

I doted on her naive comebacks and mixed-up vocabulary:

> George: Gracie, you know what a wizard is?
> Gracie: Yes, a snowstorm.
> George: Then, what's a blizzard?
> Gracie: A blizzard is inside a chicken. Anybody knows that!

We heard another form of "absurd comedy" every Sunday night listening to Walter Winchell, the radio commentator. Sitting beside Daddy in the living room, I heard Winchell discuss famous and infamous *names* in the news, what Mama called "useless, nasty celebrity secrets." Winchell's telegraphic style, including the latest slang and incomplete sentences, and his breathless New York accent held my attention because no other radio voice matched it. He spouted words and phrases I had never heard before in a kind of verbal shorthand, like *scram, pushover,* and *belly laughs.* While delivering stories in his staccato style, he spoke at a rate noticeably faster than anyone I ever heard talk in Little Rock.

Mama didn't understand why Daddy listened to Winchell, because ordinarily my father ignored similar items about persons and events that Winchell mentioned in his newspaper column. Really, my father was most excited by baseball games over the radio, especially when his beloved St. Louis Cardinals beat the Philadelphia Athletics, winning the 1931 World Series.

If I was at loose ends on weekday afternoons and Saturdays, I visited Mr. and Mrs. Richter, two houses south of us, oldsters who were as absorbed in each other as youngsters like Buster and Dorothy were. The old German-American couple lived such orderly lives, doing nothing more than necessary and everything without haste. They made me feel welcome and comfortable as I sat in their kitchen, listening to their Bavarian clock tick away, awaiting the moments when the cuckoo bird popped out to sing his song. Even though Mrs. Richter urged me to call them *Tante* Lydia and *Onkle* Ed, in the German manner, I resisted because my parents had never met them.

In warm weather, we sat in their backyard under an arbor of grape vines that Mr. Richter tended for fruit to brew wine. Under the shady arbor, I listened carefully to their speech, trying to capture by ear their rhythm and accent, because foreign dialects fascinated me. To get Mr. Richter to talk, I asked about the propellers and frames of airplane wings that hung on the walls in his backyard workshop, and the tail section hanging above our heads. He described his work as an aviation mechanic at Command-Aire Aircraft Company in Little Rock, in 1928, helping build the *Little Rocket,* which won the All-American Flying Derby the year before we moved to Gaines Street.

My other older friend was Weldon Flowers. I hung out in our own front yard with him, watching as he tinkered with his stripped-down Model T Ford, a whomperjawed steel frame with four wheels and an engine, with a front seat attached. Even without the car's body, he regularly spun his old flivver around the neighborhood with me beside him, until Buster told Mama that Weldon wasn't legally old enough to drive. She didn't apply the brakes to my riding with him until I told her about looking through the car's partial floorboards at the street below.

Mama gasped, "Why, if you slipped, you'd be killed instantly!"

Weldon himself stopped driving after breaking his leg playing tackle football on the practice field beside Little Rock Junior College, which occupied the old U. M. Rose Elementary School, at Thirteenth and State Street. When Weldon's high-school classmates signed their names on the plaster of Paris cast encasing his leg, he invited me to add mine, which suggested he considered me an equal. After a few days, all the smudged names and slogans on the cast began fading, like my brother's relationship with Weldon's sister.

Buster liked Dorothy Flowers a lot, dressing up and spending part of his salary taking her to dances at high school and sneaking her into the Rainbow Room over the 555 Service Station, at Third and Broadway, even though she was underage. When she signed her graduation picture, "With all my love to Jimmy," those six words led Mama to think they might get married when she graduated. But Mama didn't need to be concerned. After Buster attended Dorothy's graduation and accompanied her to the senior preview at the Capitol and prom at high school, nothing happened between them. Soon after, when Dorothy's older brother in Fort Smith lost his job, she and her family moved away.

I continued going to see the big boys play football on the field beside the Junior College building after Weldon left, and I discovered that the college's front porch was perfect for my imaginary adventures. Jim and I, inspired by movies like *The Seas Beneath* and *One Way Passage*, played a game of *ship* standing on the low walls and square pedestals of the porch on Saturdays, pretending to be sea rovers facing gales, belaying pirates, running athwart ships, and watching for storms or enemies from the foredeck.

Yet in the midst of one voyage, it wasn't imaginary wind I heard in the rigging but raucous human voices a short distance away. I faced Izard Street, and boys in odd bits of colorful clothing were turning the corner, one in a clown suit crawling on his hands and knees licking the sidewalk.

Close behind, the other boy, in ordinary clothes, carried a wooden paddle with a painted insignia on the blade. On second glance, I saw the crawler wasn't licking the walk but pushing a peanut with his nose. The second clown who rounded the corner, with a grapefruit suspended from his neck by heavy twine, was rolling a car tire. He, too, was followed by another boy with a paddle. This second clown alternated between sucking the grapefruit and chewing a cud of tobacco, and then spitting in the gutter. As the foursome passed, I asked what was happening. The boys with the paddles stopped and said, "We're initiating these clowns into our fraternity."

Even though I didn't know what a *fraternity* was, I was wise enough, even at my callow age, to disapprove of a group that punished prospective members.

That summer, with no white children in or near our neighborhood, I played with three black boys whose last name was White. Though ignorant of *irony*, I nevertheless recognized the opposition between their last name and their color. The Whites lived in an unpainted house on Thirteenth Street, behind Springfield's Grocery. One boy was older than me, the second my age, and the third much younger. Even though I met Mrs. White, they never mentioned their father.

Soon after we began playing together, Mama asked, "Who are your new playmates, Cleveland?"

"The Whites."

"Now, don't joke, Cleveland. I've seen the boys, hon. What's their name?"

"They're colored, Mama, but White is their last name."

Mama didn't object to my playing with them or visiting them in their three-room house, the walls of which, like Mandy and Jake's, were covered with old newspapers and the small windows hidden by burlap curtains. With no electric lights, gas heaters, or running water, Mrs. White burned kerosene lamps, cooked on a wood stove, and drew water from a faucet in the middle of their backyard.

I never saw her sons help with household chores, which may explain why they couldn't understand my wanting to watch their mother make laundry soap. She mixed white wood ashes with animal fat, salt, and water in a wooden keg that had an open spigot at the bottom. Then she poured a half bucket of boiling rain water into the keg and closed the spigot until water dripped from it, before adding more ashes and water and leaving the mix overnight.

The next morning, she said if an Irish potato floated in the lye water, the mixture was strong enough for her to add more melted fat, ashes, and water and boil the mix in a black cast-iron pot in her backyard until white bubbles appeared on the surface, proving the soap was ready.

She washed clothes in the back yard bent over a scrub board and a big Number 3 galvanized zinc tub. She shifted the soggy clothes to a big iron pot full of boiling lye water in the middle of the yard, and punched and swirled them around like the agitator of a washing machine or a witch stirring a cauldron. Finally, she lifted the dripping, soggy clothes out of the pot on the end of the broomstick into another tub to rinse and add bluing. After she wrung the clothes out, she hung them on the fence and bushes to dry.

Later, I watched her ironing the clothes using several heated flatirons that must have weighed about six pounds a piece. Having to heat the irons on the wood stove and press the clothes on the padded kitchen table in the summer heat was almost unbearable. The only step my mother shared with Mrs. White was boiling our clothes to make them germ free.

I played with the White boys almost every day that summer, especially hide-and-seek in the evenings, because of the White boys' special way of counting and efforts hiding me when Jim, Arthur, and other white boys came over.

The middle brother would say, "Hide behine me, Cleven. Turn yo' face down, he only see yo' black hair."

Their hide-and-seek count was a rhythmic chant that told a simple story:

Last night and the night before,
twenty-four robbers at my door.
I got up and let them in,
hit 'em in the head with a rolling pin.
Bee bowl, bee bowl, I can see you all
hiding behind that tree.
Ain't gonna count but one more time
before that evenin' sun go down. All hid?

One morning, I went with the White boys on errands for their mother to Ninth Street, the heart of what blacks called "the Line." They took me to the multistoried Mosaic Templars of America building, on the southwest corner of Broadway, and the Bethel A.M.E. Church, cattycornered from it, proudly claiming both were built by and belonged to blacks. Then we walked west on Ninth Street past a few businesses—a beauty parlor, liquor store, pawn shop, pool room, rental rooms, and clothing store. At the Chat and Chew cafe, a sign out front advertised "chittlins," which the boys identified for me as hog intestines specially prepared for "mighty good eatin'." The thought of putting animal guts in my mouth might have sickened me if I hadn't already witnessed the baloney mush stuffed into animal intestines at Finkbiners Meat Company on a class trip at Rightsell.

Outside the Gem Theater I studied the photographs advertising black films—*Daughter of the Congo* on the marquee and *The Darktown Revue* photos displayed on lobby billboards for coming attractions. I studied the actors' faces closely in the stills, because movies with African-American casts were never shown at downtown theaters. My laughing at some of the poses and facial expressions made the boys nervous and we quickly left. On the way home, we passed the Graystone Hotel, which was for blacks only.

One Sunday evening, the White boys introduced me to a small black boy called Lige, who lived in the shotgun house beside Springfield's Grocery. Even though he was my age, he knew great swaths of holy scripture compared to my sparse memory. When prompted, he would cut loose with a whirlwind of a sermon. He seemed to need to ask his mother's permission to preach, though.

"Mammy, the Holy Ghost done lay His hand on me."

"You go right on, little Elijah! Tell what in your heart."

From nowhere, as if responding to a mysterious signal, other blacks from down the block gathered in front of little Elijah who was standing on his porch.

"Brothers and Sisters, the Lord require a lot of you." A few "amens" greeted his opening remark.

Elijah continued, "He ask ya to 'fess up to your sins and do good. Yeah! That's what He say, 'fess your sins and do good." Raising his volume and pitch, he began preaching, "You cant just go on sinning the ways you do. No, suh! You in danger of hellfire! The Lord see what you doing. He know what in your heart. He know ever thing, don't you forget it, brothers and sisters. God's watching and speaking to you now. I've got the word in me. The Lord have mercy on you, if you don't change your ways."

His voice—bending, scooping, and wavering in pitch—captured everyone's attention. Heads nodded their assent, moaning and laying on the "amens" in cadence with Lige's points.

"The Lord don't 'prove of drinking and lying, stealing and messing round. The Lord want you sober, speaking true. He don't want you taking nothing from your neighbor, or fooling round with his woman."

Little Elijah, raising his eyes, pleaded, "Come on down, Jesus, see 'bout your children!"

His musical voice matched the ivory smile on his sweet, beatific face. For when he finished his piece, the little preacher sang without accompaniment "Little Black Train." We joined in the chorus:

> *Little black train is a-comin',*
> *Get all yo business right;*
> *Go set yo house in or-duh,*
> *For the train may be here tonight.*

Afterward, his momma held out a battered felt hat, and a few grown-ups, black and white, dropped in a few cents, one way his mother helped feed herself and her son.

At home, I did an impression of little Elijah for my family. But on the occasions when I preached to neighborhood kids or to my visiting cousins and friends in our apartment stairwell, I did it sedately and less emotionally, imitating the manner of Dr. Calvin B. Waller of the Second Baptist Church. Praying from behind the second newel post (my pulpit) on the middle landing, I thanked the Lord for weather conditions (part of every Baptist Sunday school prayer) and repeated Bible verses learned at church, most often singing a chorus of "I Shall Not Be Moved."

At the song's end, I extended my open arms with the invitation to join by confession of faith or transfer of membership. Pronouncing the benediction, I released the restive congregation.

When public school was back in session, I joined my white friends again at Jim's home, where we played in the shadow of the huge water tank inside the five-foot-high chain link fence around former governor Samuel Brough's backyard. Why a painted silver water tank remained after the city installed the municipal water system, we didn't know and no one could guess. One day, playing cops-and-robbers, Jim tried to escape a "cop" climbing the Broughs' fence, and a kid not yet in our gang shot him with an air rifle, the BB shot lodging so deep in Jim's bare leg that a doctor had to remove it.

The shooter, Sanford Hooper, didn't apologize; I suppose he didn't care. A regular member of our gang would have regretted the mistake enough to ask forgiveness. Before we invited Sanford to join our games, he stood on his front porch hollering nasty remarks at us for no apparent reason. Then, after we took him in, he almost always complained about the way games were conducted, or else bullied and hit someone for inconsequential reasons. Maybe he resented his mother's divorce from his father, or perhaps his stepfather abused him. Even though we didn't know his family situation or why he acted as he did, we still didn't abandon him as a playmate.

A sweet-spirited, calm girl, whose presence in the neighborhood I enjoyed, was Betty Romick, Jim's friend. Her father, Major Romick, a member of the 154th Observation Squadron of the Arkansas National Guard out at the airport, flew his biplane low over the neighborhood, dipping and waggling his airplane wings over their home on Izard Street. All of us kids stood in Betty's front yard, waving and shouting, as he circled overhead repeatedly, seeing but not hearing us. Flying with him in the airplane, as Betty and Jim wished to do, however, never entered my mind. (At the end of World War II, the major welcomed Jim and me home from the service and served us highballs.)

Big, heroic Ken Kavanaugh lived next door to Betty. If he was home on Saturdays, or after school, the tall, rangy Little Rock Senior High School football star sometimes played catch with us across the yards and in the street. Our group of elementary-school kids and Ken produced the neighborhood version of Jonathan Swift's *Gulliver's Travels*, for he, as Lemuel Gulliver, was over six feet tall, and we were six-inch-tall Lilliputians beside him. After he left Little Rock and became an All-American at Louisiana State University and an all-star end with the Chicago Bears professional team, we bragged about playing with Ken before he was famous.

Another playmate on the fringe of our gang was a girl across from Jim's and Governor Brough's houses. Catherine Rightsell lived in a spacious white-brick home at the back of a lot half the size of a city block, which was screened from the street by the thick stand of trees surrounding it—a great space for hide-and-seek and capture the flag. Catherine had an illness of some kind and spent a lot of time in a hexagonal gazebo at the center of the lot, playing quiet games with a maid.

But a noisy threat prowled next door to the Rightsells. Outside a beautiful Tudor-style house inside a fenced yard, a nasty-tempered chow dog seemed determined to guard his master's house, and he became our unintended playmate some afternoons. Even though the owner kept the beast inside the house or fenced yard most of the time, the black dog occasionally escaped. Of course, free of any restraints, he surged in our direction barking viciously, baring his purple-black gums and long yellow fangs. Our only escape as a gang was our running in so many different directions the dog was confused, not knowing which way to turn before his owner retrieved him.

However, the biggest, most threatening neighborhood dog in appearance was Nebo, a tall, thick-coated black Airedale, owned by the Terry Fields family, on the corner of Fifteenth and State. Nebo loped about as if he were owner of everyone's property, particularly in the blocks around Governor Brough's home. One day, I brandished my new-found biblical scholarship, suggesting to buddies that maybe the dog viewed our neighborhood as Moses did the Promised Land from atop Mount Nebo, that some member of the Fields family even had that event in mind when choosing Nebo for the dog's name. Even though the Terrys kept Nebo corralled with a rope, the powerful dog broke loose regularly, always heading in the direction of our voices.

The first to see Nebo, his ears drawn back and short tail upstanding, shouted, "Nebo's loose! Nebo's loose!"

Then our gang took off in the directions of the four winds, hiding on porches and climbing fences and trees—all that silly activity to escape Nebo, who had not yet harmed any person. I guess we just expected a dog his size to be vicious enough to bite. Our response to Nebo revealed how often negative attitudes toward persons and animals are based only upon their appearances.

At times, though, we were in harm's way at odd moments in unexpected places. One Saturday, Jim and I left for a Bob Steele movie at the Roxy Theater, with Mama warning us to come directly home and not loiter downtown. But after the show, it seemed innocent enough to visit the Western Auto Store, at Third and Louisiana, and check out the latest models of boys' bicycles. Heading back to Main Street, I couldn't resist looking at the men's clothes in the Bauman Clothing Store's display in the side window of the Stein building on Third Street. But I was so intent looking at the clothes I didn't notice a broken bar in the iron sidewalk grate over the basement ventilator. My right foot stepped through the break and the broken end of an iron rod penetrated my leg. As Jim helped me pull my leg out, I saw a big, bloody hole beneath my right knee.

Jim frowned and took a deep breath. "We better get you to Hegarty's Drugstore. Mr. Hegarty will know what to do about the gouge in your leg."

With blood running down my leg, puddling in my shoe, I felt no pain, but I was scared, trying to keep from crying to avoid others noticing me on our way to Fourth and Main.

The fountain clerk saw us enter the drugstore with me limping, and shouted, "Mr. Hegarty, you're needed up front!"

The pharmacist came instantly and led us behind the latticed pharmacy partition at the back of the store. He seated me on a brown, wood-slatted chaise lounge, wiped the dried blood off my leg and foot and around the puncture wound before giving me a shot. Applying antiseptic and a padded bandage to the wound, he asked me how the accident happened.

He said, "That puncture's pretty bad, young fellow. That's why I gave you a free tetanus shot. But you keep it clean and apply this medicine. It'll heal in no time. Now, boys, you go straight home and tell his mother."

When I worried on the streetcar about being spanked for going to Western Auto after the show, Jim said, "Your momma will be so concerned about your wounded leg, she's not gonna think about spanking you."

We got off the streetcar at Fifteenth and Gaines, and I walked home alone. Mama wasn't home and our front door was locked. I sat on our front steps, sniffing and feeling sorry for myself, until Miss Margaret McKinney came over and asked me what was the matter. After holding my tears back for so long, the dam broke, and she led me to her house where she and her sister hovered, listening to my story, while stuffing me with cookies and milk until Mama came home.

That night, Mama baked an egg custard pie, and we took it over to the McKinneys the next day as a token of thanks for their care. Recalling Daddy's warning about lockjaw, I carefully tended what I thought was my "battle wound," which steadily attracted gnats and itched something awful while healing. Even though Mama insisted I keep it covered, I regularly lifted the bandage to see the gash that left a scar on my leg for life.

During the winter, Mama often sent me to buy hot tamales, a family favorite, even though she had trouble digesting them. The black man who sold them parked a two-wheeled, wooden cart inside a piano crate beside

Piggly Wiggly every day but Sunday. He and his wife made the fresh tamales at their home on Eighth and State every day, and he pushed his cartful on foot from there. To keep the hot tamales hot, he heated clay bricks in the oven of his wood stove and stacked the bricks around the large tin lard buckets in which he stored tamales inside the wooden cart. To insulate the cart and later wrap tamales for customers, he filled the space between the bricks and cart walls with newspapers. With only space enough for him to sit inside the crate, I stood outside to talk with him. He was an out-of-work carpenter who learned to cook tamales from his momma, combining ground beef and peppers rolled in corn meal, wrapping them in corn husks, and steaming them. (How such simple ingredients could upset Mama's stomach was beyond me.) His cooking skill and his momma's tamale recipe were helping him and his wife survive in the Depression.

One night during that hard winter, a cold rain fell that formed layers of ice on every outdoor surface. Even though we kids still had to attend school, almost all other foot and car traffic had stopped. When the hot tamale man arrived at his usual time in his regular place, his spot beside the curb on Fourteenth was dangerous, for cars and trucks were sliding on the ice-slick streets, skidding into curbs and onto the sidewalks. Older pedestrians dared not walk outside risking a fall. Mama locked our apartment's back door to keep us from falling down the steep back steps.

But Mr. Richter—plump, rosy, and smiling—ventured outside into the winter wonderland intent upon taking a few turns on icy Gaines wearing a pair of ice skates he had brought from Germany. Since temperatures seldom fell low enough to freeze water solid on large surfaces in Little Rock, there was no outdoor ice-skating rink. But Mr. Richter found a short stretch of ice on the street thick enough for a few strides, which delighted all us black and white kids in that block of Gaines. Inspired by his short, dramatic display, I went to the garage and tried to whittle skate blades from a piece of wood lathe to nail to a pair of old high-top shoes. While I struggled, the little surface of ice melted. I had no chance, like Hans Brinker, to compete for silver skates.

The rain that came again overnight slowly turned to sleet, piling snow on streets and sidewalks so thick that school was dismissed. The next morning, I skidded to Jim's and Arthur's homes to play, but in the afternoon, they planned to sled down the hillside streets of Izard and Chester on either side of Rightsell.

At noon, I hurried home to ask Mama to let me join them. She agreed reluctantly but wouldn't let me go until she filled me with hot soup and improvised an outfit to keep me warm and dry enough outside: two shirts, two pairs of pants, Daddy's hunting boots and boot socks, my mackinaw, a wool toboggan cap, and a scarf. But I had no gloves. Hardly able to move, I slogged through nine blocks of snow and ice to take turns on Jim's sled and scooting down, in between turns on the sled, on a heavy piece of cardboard. But, as usually happens when one is having fun, the hours passed too rapidly and darkness fell too soon. Walking home in the fading light, the sharp wind chapped my face and my ungloved hands turned blue. Of one thing I was certain: I preferred games without snow and ice.

Even though Christmas approached at a hard time, I still asked for a bicycle like Jim's. I warned my parents long before the holiday, feeling real grownup thinking that far ahead. Jim's thin, steel-frame bike had skinny tires on wide-diameter wheels and was tall enough for a grown man. To keep it upright standing still, Jim tilted the bike sideways, one leg over the center bar with his foot on the ground. Even though my parents didn't say yes to giving me a bike, they didn't say no.

On Christmas morning, instead of finding a tall, big-wheeled bike, I saw a smaller, 26-inch bicycle standing against the wall beside the tree. Where my parents found money enough to buy it, I didn't know, but there it was—a beautiful blue bike, with *Great Northern* emblazoned in bronze letters on the neck of the frame. Even though secondhand, the bike appeared to be in excellent condition.

But the frame of the bike had no center bar. For gosh sakes, a girl's bicycle! I couldn't ride a girl's bike! Every guy who saw me would make fun of me. Yet, knowing how much trouble my parents must have had finding a bicycle they could afford, I could and did ride the bike that very day and many thereafter. My other present, besides fruit and candy, was a Daisy air rifle, for Daddy believed every boy should learn to handle a weapon for hunting, if only a BB gun to begin with.

Christmas afternoon, my parents visited the Westmorelands, leaving me with Buster, who was napping on the sofa. When he awoke, he grabbed my air rifle from under the tree and loaded it with BBs. I pleaded for him to give it back, even tried twisting it out of his hands, but he held me away from the rifle with one arm. Then, inspired by a scene with William Powell in *The Thin Man*, Buster lay back on the sofa and took aim at glass ornaments on the tree, shattering them one by one. He knew what Mama's reaction would be to what he had done and the mess he made, so he forced me to sweep up the glass shards and threatened me if I told. I planned to tell on him anyway.

Mr. Westmoreland gave Mama a surprise Christmas gift. A real craftsman with wood, he had designed and built a beautiful walnut table with a cloverleaf top for her. Perhaps he was making up for his wife's pretentious treatment of my mother.

Before the Christmas holidays, Grandpa informed Mama that her first cousin, the son of Uncle Mark McCuin, Grandma Honea's brother, lived at the Savoy Apartments, two blocks away from us. We called on Gilbert McCuin and met his sister and her son, Quentin, visiting from Cincinnati, Ohio. Quentin, two years older than me, had curly blond hair, a ruddy complexion, and chapped hands and cheeks. He was the first Midwesterner I ever met and he spoke in a different dialect: short vowels, sharp consonants, and pronunciations like *boosh* for "bush." We played outside the apartment until I complained about the cold and we crossed to King's Drugstore to sit inside. He described winters in Cincinnati when snow piled up in the streets and on the lake shore, and the ponds froze hard enough to sled and skate on the ice.

Quentin bore little resemblance to Uncle Mark, who had sharp features and dark olive complexion; it was hard to believe they were related. I seldom saw my uncle from Lonoke, where Grandma Honea was born and married Grandpa. I remembered Uncle Mark because I saw him scratch his nose with his little finger, and thought he had stuck his finger up his nostril. Aghast that an adult violated Mama's rule against picking one's nose, I said, "Uncle Mark, you're not supposed to put your finger in your nose!"

"Who says so?"

"Mama."

"Why not?"

"She says it's dirty and nasty."

"I'm not dirty or nasty. You're the most outspoken kid I know. Besides, I didn't put my finger in my nose."

"But I saw you do it, Uncle Mark."

"You only think you did, Allie Cleveland."

He held his right hand in front of my eyes and spread his fingers; the little finger of his right hand was missing from the first knuckle. Embarrassed by my mistake, I was ashamed to ask about the knot the size

of a small rubber ball on his forehead. Later he told me the bantam egg–
sized bump was a cyst.

One afternoon in early spring, I came home from school and found
Buster already there. The owner of the grocery store where he worked
claimed business was bad and let him go. A few days later, we were in the
swing on the front porch after school, and he said, "If I didn't know better,
I'd bet that guy coming this way is Homer Jones."

A sailor in dress blues, with a long torso, short legs, and his cap over his
eyebrows, was ambling along the sidewalk toward our house.

Buster got up and hung over the porch rail, shouting, "Hey, sailor!
Where's your ship?"

"In San Diego, old buddy!" That guy in the sailor suit was Homer, all
right!

Greeting Homer in the foyer, Buster slapped him on the shoulder, and
I said, "Homer, you look like a real sailor."

"Well, if I ain't, I ain't damned sure what I am, kid!"

Watching him climb the steps to our apartment, I saw how tight his
uniform fit around his hips and how the legs flared out at his ankles. His
jumper collar, wide as his shoulders, flapped down to the middle of his
back, and the black kerchief at his neck was tied in a square knot. A sailor's
uniform was a great costume and even Homer looked good in his!

Sitting down with Buster in the swing, Homer said, "I see little brother's
grown a bit but still hangs around."

"Yep, not much has changed here. Except I lost my job a week ago."

"I thought you'd be in high school, Jimmy? Listen, if you ain't, you
oughta join the navy."

Whispering and snickering in Buster's ear, he touched his own crotch.
"Boy, I've had some great times. I'll tell you more when there ain't no big
ears around."

I asked, "Why are all those buttons on the front of your pants,
Homer?"

"To keep the broad fall front of my pants up, junior."

Turning to Buster, he said, "Jimmy, let me tell you … about San Diego…"
Dropping his voice to almost a whisper.

"Can I try on your cap, Homer?"

"Sure, kid!" He whipped it off and handed it to me. "Seat the Dixie cup on your head parallel with the floor, half an inch above your eyebrows. That's right."

The cap did seem like a giant Dixie cup, the kind King's Drugstore served ice cream in. Adjusting the cap, I asked, "Homer, have you really sailed on a ship in the ocean?"

"You bet, two ships. Went to the Philippine Islands on one and came back on a different one."

"A man from the Philippine Islands came to school one day selling yo-yos."

"Yeah, yeah! … Jimmy, when I was in San Diego …"

"What's it like being on a great big ship, Homer?"

Buster pushed me toward the door. "Get lost! Mama, come get Cleveland!"

My mother came to the porch door. "Why, lo and behold, it's Homer Jones! Welcome home, Homer. I'll bet your mother's glad you're back."

"He's got stories, Mama, and I wanna hear 'em without Cleveland butting in."

"You come with me, honey. Let them talk. I'm glad you're back safe and sound, Homer."

"Thank ya, Mrs. Harrison."

I sat on the sofa in the living room listening to the radio while the men shared old times. After casually examining the soiled brim of Homer's cotton cap, I could see but not hear through the porch-door panes. Homer was gesturing and changing facial expressions, widening his eyes and narrowing them to a sneaky look, and Buster was smiling, nodding, and speaking animatedly. Gee, I wanted to hear what they were saying! Watching Homer, I understood why Buster liked him so much—he was my brother's absolute opposite, aggressive and blustery, full of life, with no family loyalty to restrain his adventurous spirit. They stayed on the porch until nearly dark when Mama invited Homer to stay for supper, but he refused.

In the middle of supper, Buster mumbled, "I'm joining the navy. Homer's happy and earning enough to send a few bucks home."

Mama looked at Daddy. "You're doing nothing of the kind. We need you here at home."

"Why? I don't have a job. And can't find one. What do you say, Dad?"

"Well, I wouldn't be too hasty, son. The navy's right for Homer but may not be for you. Give yourself more time to find a job here."

In the spring of 1932, after the hardest winter our family ever had, times were harder on our family than the weather. With the stock market in a shambles and banks in trouble, Daddy lost his job with Metropolitan! My father and brother were both looking for work every day unsuccessfully. While trying to find a job, Daddy talked with some other unemployed men who said they were going back home to the farm, or renting houses with land attached to raise crops to feed their families—natural choices for men in Arkansas who grew up in the country doing chores on farms.

After more weeks passed without finding work, Daddy announced at supper one night, "When a man's really down, the best place for him to go is home. The crash may hit farmers hardest, but they can still feed themselves." And Buster wanted to join him on Big Daddy's farm near Beebe rather than go to the navy.

Mama said, "Allie, this is your home. You don't belong at your dad's place. Besides, how can the two of you be in the country and help us in town?"

"Floy, we'll go to work on the farm and send vegetables and meat as often as we can."

"Oh, Allie, I don't want you leaving Cleveland and me here by ourselves. But you've obviously made up your mind. I hope and pray it helps. We'll be lost and lonesome without you two."

To me, living on Big Daddy's farm seemed exciting. I wanted to go with them to live in the big two-story, six-room frame house in the country, with screened-in front and back porches, surrounded by a picket fence. Grandma always made fruit juice from the big, ripe cherries from their trees in season. And my grandparents always had a place for us because there were beds in every room but the dining room and kitchen. But Mama reminded me I had to stay in school, and she wasn't convinced my father and brother on Big Daddy's farm outside Beebe would help us in Little Rock.

My father and brother drove the Chrysler to the farm in White County, leaving Mama and me with no transportation. So she decided we would walk to services at First Baptist Church, at Twelfth and Louisiana, which was closer than Second Baptist. Uncle John Terry (Uncle Poppa), a member of First Baptist and admirer of their pastor, the Reverend Arden B. Blaylock, urged Mama to transfer her letter to First Church, but she only agreed to attend there as long as my father and brother were away.

About the time we started going to First Baptist, the Reverend Aimee Semple McPherson, founder of the International Church of the Foursquare Gospel, was touring the United States in a revival. She, or a female evangelist like her, had posted slogans on billboards around Little Rock, proclaiming, JESUS IS COMING SOON! GET READY! and WHERE WILL YOU SPEND ETERNITY? Rev. Blaylock and the other clergymen in Protestant churches in the city, supporting her belief that "Jesus is the healer, baptizer, savior, and returning king of the world," invited her to fill their pulpits.

With Sister Aimee's belief that the fine arts belonged to God, she brought music and drama into the sanctuary to illuminate the Bible stories in her sermons. As I heard someone say, "She was my cup of tea." The one night Mama and I went to her revival, Sister Aimee dramatized the final choice humans must make in living their lives before Eternity. Two actors on opposite sides of the chancel posed as St. Peter at Heaven's Gate and the Devil at Hell's Gate.

The sanctuary had filled and buzzed with excitement when the organ sounded trumpets, and Sister Aimee emerged from the rear of the chancel, gliding swiftly and gracefully down the platform toward the congregation. She stopped between the gates of Heaven and Hell, and I saw her hair was rolled in tight curls on both sides of her head and her white satin gown, of a Byzantine or Early Gothic design, had a brilliant red cross appliquéd to the breast. The gown's sleeves fitting close at her shoulders flowed loosely from the elbow almost to the floor. So when she lifted her arms, the sleeves unfurled like white angel's wings, causing women in the audience to gasp and the crowd to applaud.

Straight away, she began singing the opening hymn, motioning for the congregation to join her. After leading us in several more hymns, Sister Aimee delivered the prologue. As she ended, costumed figures began running down the aisles onto the platform, followed by the beams of spotlights. From that moment until the end of the play, each character sought to enter Heaven's Gate. Those St. Peter admitted for eternity shouted with joy, while those denied entry cried out in despair and the Devil, laughing in triumph, pulled them through Hell's Gate, condemned to eternal damnation.

The service certainly clarified where I wanted to spend eternity after I died.

While my father and brother were away on the farm, Grandpa Honea visited us more often, especially after Honea Mercantile Store burned down along with the rest of a whole city block in McRae's big fire on Railroad Avenue—including McCaleb's Hardware, Ford's Cafe, Evans Meat Market, and Springer's Bakery Shop.

When the Wonder Bread man dropped Grandpa off in late afternoon, Mama changed our sleeping arrangements: Grandpa took my bed and I joined her. With his new grocery store on Grand Avenue doing so well, he kept pointing out how Daddy failed to provide properly for his family and insisted on giving Mama money. Why would he say such a thing? Daddy wasn't responsible for the hard times, and Grandpa only added to Mama's unhappiness about my father being away. You see, I heard her tell Aunt Ora how bitterly disappointed she was that Daddy had gotten drunk and wrecked our Chrysler. But Aunt Ora said she ought to be happy Daddy wasn't injured.

After Daddy and Buster were gone a couple of weeks, Mama developed a dry, hacking cough and complained about her chest hurting. One night, her high fever and shivering chill frightened her so much that the next day she kept me home from school to go with her to Dr. Silas C. Fulmer in the Donaghey Building. After he examined Mama, his nurse, Miss Leona Glover, drove us home in her car. Even though it was daytime, the nurse put Mama to bed and called Aunt Ora.

I thought Mama had "ammonia" until my aunt talking on the phone to Daddy in Beebe said she had "double pneumonia." The next day Daddy and Buster took a bus to Little Rock because the Chrysler still hadn't been repaired.

The evening of the day Dr. Fulmer examined Mama in his office downtown, he came to our apartment. When she fell into a paroxysm of coughing, he told Aunt Ora Mama had bacterial pneumonia in both lobes of her lungs, the worst kind, and warned that airborne droplets from Mama's coughs might make us sick, so I was not to enter her room.

I asked Dr. Fulmer, "Why don't you give Mama some medicine and make her well?"

"If you'll be real quiet around the house, Cleveland, and let your mother rest, that's the best medicine for her. In time, her chest will clear, and she'll be well again."

"It's true," Aunt Ora said. After the doctor left, she told me, "We'll depend on prayer and the doctor's promise."

Even though my aunt pooh-poohed her own chances of contracting pneumonia, she followed the doctor's orders where I was concerned and wouldn't allow me near Mama.

Both Daddy and Buster arrived home soon after, carrying fresh and home-canned vegetables and meats from Big Daddy's farm. While he prepared all our meals, Daddy told me how to butcher hogs and render lard in processing meat—cutting bacon, ham, shoulders, spareribs, side meat, backbone, and pork chops. Every part of a hog was saved, with some parts mixed with spices in a congealed mush or *souse loaf* to slice. He cooked the next day's meals in the evening, and we had roasts with baked and fried potatoes, pork chops, beef stew, and cornbread. Then, during the day, he and Buster alternated caring for Mama and searching for jobs. My brother found a part-time job first at King's Drugstore as a soda jerk, which didn't seem to be a joke anymore.

Mama didn't appear to be recovering, though. Since I couldn't hug and kiss her before leaving for school each day, I stood outside her room to hear her weak "goodbye" through the door. Lonely and afraid, I told Aunt Ora how much I longed to see my mother. Hugging me, Aunt Ora said, "Cleveland, your momma longs to see you, too. But Dr. Fulmer says you have to be separated until his medicine and our prayers make her better."

When Aunt Ora told Mama how much I wanted to see her, my mother sent permission for me to look inside Grandma Honea's small black trunk, which I had often begged to do. It held Grandma's odd items, like doilies, antimacassars, quilts, a hairbrush, a lady's flannelette wrapper. Holding and seeing Grandma's black, high-topped, lace-up shoes for some reason made me feel closer to my mother.

I didn't know that pneumonia followed a pattern, warning if someone was likely to live or die, and that the crisis in the illness came on an odd-numbered day after the diagnosis. One day, Mama's fever rose so high that Aunt Ora called me home from school and phoned to ask Dr. Waller and Rev. Blaylock to pray for Mama. Finally, after seven days, Mama's temperature fell to normal, and I was allowed a short visit before school and again in the evening.

My mother's recovery reinforced my belief in the power of prayer.

So many incidents occurred with my father and brother home and my mother recovering from pneumonia, the events remain unconnected in my mind and difficult to sort out.

When Franklin D. Roosevelt was inaugurated as president in March of 1933, we heard him declare that "the only thing we have to fear is fear itself." From then on, my father seemed more confident, and we heard about a new part of the New Deal over the radio every day. Daddy read items from the *Gazette* to Mama after breakfast about the National Recovery Administration, a mammoth federal agency, nicknamed the NRA, which was supposed to govern prices and wages to help the country get out of the Depression. Then, I began seeing the blue NRA signs displayed in the windows of businesses all over Little Rock—a blue pot-metal eagle with wings outstretched, a lightning bolt in the left claw and gear wheel in the right, with the slogan WE DO OUR PART underneath.

The Four-Minute Men, along with other speakers sponsored by the government, publicized the NRA, speaking in theaters and at churches, over the radio and in movie shorts, and in full-page ads in newspapers and magazines.

One morning in June, Mama and I took a streetcar to watch a big parade march down Main Street in support of the National Recovery Act of 1933. There were crowds of people downtown as big as those on Halloween night in 1930, but this time, they were waving American flags and blue banners with NRA eagles on them as floats followed the bands marching along Main. Even though I didn't really know what we were celebrating, I enjoyed the parade and the little American flag I was given to wave.

Free for the rest of the day, I was eager to ride the streetcar back home to play with Arthur, Jim, and Johnny Spraggins, Jim's next door neighbor who was Arthur's cousin. It was always great playing in the soft dirt under the big oak trees in front of Jim's house, making tunnels and mountains for cars around the roots. Looking out the streetcar window going home, Mama and I saw small oblong bundles, covered in bright specks of color, lying at doors on porches of houses. The one at our front door had the same yellow, blue, and red balloons on the wrapper. Mama said the miniature loaf of Wonder Bread was the best way she knew to advertise in hard times—an edible gift.

Not long after we found our small loaf on our doorstep, I was riding on my bike past Piggly Wiggly when a young woman, costumed as Robin Hood, carried a heavy bag out of the store and got into a green coupe with "Peter Pan Peanut Butter" painted on the doors. I watched her drive away and followed her bright green car south on Gaines to Wright Avenue and Lee Weber Grocery at the corner of Chester Street. Inside, she started handing out samples to customers and gave me a jar of the free peanut butter to spread on the free loaf of bread we received from Wonder Bread.

After months of waiting, Grandpa's insurance company paid for the loss of his big mercantile store in McRae's big fire. Grandpa Honea offered to loan my parents money until Daddy found a job, perhaps at Mama's suggestion. Whatever the case, my father refused to accept money from Grandpa, claiming, "It's another damned effort by him to bribe his way into our personal lives. I don't want a loan from him or to be beholden to Uncle Ben Honea in any way."

But Mama quietly and persuasively convinced Daddy that his and Buster's experience selling groceries, produce, and meats prepared them to manage a grocery store successfully, if only he would accept Grandpa's loan.

In autumn, as I entered fourth grade, my folks leased a grocery store at 2327 Wright Avenue, at the foot of the Rice Street intersection. They bought the store's equipment and stock of canned goods, meats, and poultry from Mr. William Goode, a red-faced, overweight older man, who owned the block of buildings between Rice and Dennison on the south side of Wright Avenue, including a barbershop, two empty buildings, and a dry-cleaning plant above a cafe. Mr. Goode was retired and lived separately from his wife in the back room of the empty store next to the barbershop. Mrs. Goode still lived in their home at the foot of Rice Street.

In our family's new business, my brother handled groceries and produce, and my father managed the store and meat market. They hired a strong young black man to sweep and mop, stock shelves, kill and pluck chickens, and deliver groceries on his bicycle. The most impressive day for me was when Mr. Earl Vaughter applied gold-leaf letters on the front windows and recessed door at the store's entrance: HARRISON and SON, GROCERIES and MEATS. I was so proud of that sign.

The store's handsome oak counter, parallel with the front windows near the entrance, had a cash register and adding machine on top. To the right of the counter, the refrigerated display counter, separating the grocery section from the meat market, had Toledo scales on top. Behind the meat counter, two widely spaced butcher block tables sat on a linoleum floor covering, sprinkled with sawdust for easy cleaning. At the back of the meat market, a small room contained two wire chicken coops, a hot water heater, and a galvanized metal sink for cleaning poultry.

The kaleidoscope of cans and cardboard containers on the shelves and the stacks of bread, graham and animal crackers, and cereals made me think I was in a wonderland playhouse. The candies, in paper wrappings different from those at Springfield's Grocery, were wonderful, too. Until Mama and Daddy bought the grocery store, I considered the Chrysler our proudest possession. But the handsome buff-brick store and its splendid contents surpassed any automobile.

The first Saturday I spent at the store, Colonel, the black handyman, proudly showed me how he prepared a chicken to sell in the meat market. Grabbing a vicious-looking knife and a chicken from the coop, he led me out the back door. He told me to stand back and then clamped the chicken's head and beak between the fingers of one hand and without warning whacked the chicken's head off! When he dropped the headless chicken, with its ragged neck spouting blood, I had to dodge the dying, flapping body on the ground. When I jumped around escaping the flouncing chicken, Colonel slapped his thighs, laughing at my gyrations.

Finally, the chicken lay a bloody, dusty corpse, and Colonel took the carcass into the little back market room to dip in scalding water in the metal sink to help pull the feathers off more easily. To remove the hair-like feathers remaining on the skin, he lit a blowtorch and lightly ran the flame over the bird, singeing off the little hair feathers. After that, he pulled out the bird's pin feathers with pliers and took the bird to Daddy to be eviscerated, and then washed the bird, inside and out.

Once Buster realized his good-humored new companion was illiterate, he started playing tricks on him. At noon one day, my brother pretended to be eating snakes from an oblong can of fish filets, labeled SNAKS. Opening the can, Buster forked and held a fish filet in the air before popping it into his mouth, chewing and smacking loudly. "Hmm, hmm! This snake's mighty good meat."

"Folks don't eat no snakes, Mr. Busta! Is you sure dat's snake meat?"

My brother pointed at the label, calling the letters one at a time—S-N-A-K-S—to prove they spelled *snakes*. Colonel was convinced and gulped a filet. He liked the fish so much, he begged to open a can every day, but SNAKS were too expensive to continue the joke. So he and my brother graduated to sardines and crackers at lunch.

What started as simple teasing, Buster soon took to larger, meaner turns. One morning, he soaked Colonel's bicycle seat with a bottle of oil of wintergreen. Colonel bagged telephone orders for women in the neighborhood and loaded the first deliveries in the bike's front and rear wire baskets and pedaled up the Rice Street hill in front of the store. Before he had biked half a block up Rice, which could be seen from the store's front window, Colonel got off to inspect the seat. He didn't remount the seat but rolled the bike loaded with groceries up the hill, and was gone for a long time, because rolling the bike was slower than riding.

When Colonel finally returned, he said, "Mister Busta, that cycle seat like hot coal on my butt. I couldn't stay on for no length of time fore I got off 'n fan my be-hine. But fannin' don't do no good. So I jes walk that ole bike to Miz Glover's. She say, 'Colonel you smells like cough drops,' and ask if I got a cold. You think I been haunted?"

Colonel's naive response to this trick and others egged my brother on. Mr. Lokey, the barber next door, after hearing the wintergreen story, joined Buster in teasing Colonel. The barber had woven raw copper wires through the wooden slats of a chair and connected them to a rheostat on a shelf behind his barber chair to tease customers. He could shock a victim regulating the electric charge received without being seen. So Mr. Lokey suggested Buster send Colonel to his shop for a free haircut.

Buster, smoking a cigarette in front of the store and shop with Mr. Lokey one slow morning, decided the day had come. When Colonel returned from a delivery, he told the handyman that customers complained that he needed a haircut, and he should go next door to the barbershop.

Colonel protested, "Mister Busta, I ain't got no money for no haircut. Besides, ain't no white barber gonna cut my nappy hair."

"Don't worry. Mr. Lokey said he'll cut your hair for nothing."

At supper, Buster reported the scene when Colonel sat in the electric chair waiting for his free haircut and white customers diverted him as Mr. Lokey slowly strengthened the electrical charge to a painful level.

Colonel leaped up, shouting, "Lawsy me, that old chair done caught me on fire!"

His reaction was what Mr. Lokey, Buster, and the white hangers-on waited for. Their cruel laughter left me feeling close enough to Colonel to be his brother.

A few days later, I went to get a haircut and waited while Mr. Lokey finished cutting someone else's hair. The usual men in the shop were killing time. After a bit, a young guy stood up, signaling everyone to be quiet, and approached an older man slumped over napping in a chair. The young man pulled a small box of matches from his pocket, carefully fitting a single match head between the sole and upper part of the old man's shoe, and then lit the match. Everyone stared at the old man's foot waiting for the match head to ignite. When it flared, the old man leaped up with a startled expression on his wrinkled face, stomping his foot. All the men had a high old time laughing as he removed his scorched shoe and cooled his seared foot. I didn't laugh at the first "hot foot" I'd seen; it was no joke. Minutes later, when the electric pulse raced across my bottom, tingling and growing hotter, I knew the source and scooted forward on the chair.

Defeated, an old codger said, "You didn't give the young'un the full charge, John."

In those days, grown men teased the young and elderly, the white and black, without conscience, just for a laugh.

Back home on Gaines Street, the Springfield store remained empty. One afternoon as I skated in front of our apartment, a truck parked out front. Several men and women carrying metal-topped tables and huge aluminum pans and racks went inside, and I crossed the street to see what was happening. I met Mr. and Mrs. Thomas L. Pitts and their sons, Baron and Tom, who lived just south of us on Gaines at the Windsor Apartments. The Pitts family was opening a glazed-doughnut shop; their recipe, different from that of all the other bakeries in town, was based on potato instead of wheat flour.

The family received me as if I were a family member when the shop opened. I loved doughnuts, a goodie I seldom had, so I wanted to know how they were made. The Pitts allowed me to stand beside family members one after another, watching each step in doughnut-making.

During this long process, the Pitts family allowed me to go anywhere in the kitchen except near the deep-fat fryers.

Baron, the older son, liked to kid me and answered all my questions. Every day but Sunday, he parked his two-door sports sedan in front of the bakery and gave me permission to pretend I was driving, primarily by turning the steering wheel. He told me not to shift gears, step on the starter, or apply pressure to the brake pedals. Most afternoons, I ate free doughnut "holes" before going outside to sit behind the steering wheel in Baron's sedan, pantomiming every move I saw him make starting the car before driving away—turning the ignition key, stepping on the starter, shifting gears, and applying brakes.

"Hud-nnn, hud-nnn, hud-nn!" I hummed, revving the motor.

One afternoon I could no longer resist the urge and jammed my foot down on the starter pedal. The ignition growled and the car jumped! I was so scared, I whirled out the door, promising to give up pretend driving. A few days later, when Baron asked why I wasn't driving anymore, I confessed what I had done and apologized. He laughed and patted my head, okaying my continuing the game.

But "driving" was never the same after that.

In the middle of the night, I awoke to see red flames lapping at our windows and walls. Certain our house was on fire, I shook Buster and ran to tell our parents. Red flames were flickering on their walls, too. All of us were alarmed until we saw the red reflections were on the underside of the clouds from a house fire down the street. I ran outside and discovered the black boarding house was spouting scarlet flames and billowing black smoke from all its windows and doors. The boarders, who usually sat out on the porches, day and night, were standing in the street, watching everything they owned burn up.

As the flames flared higher and great smoke clouds rose over our block, the sirens of fire trucks wailed in the distance, coming from the fire station at Twenty-third and Arch. Daddy had us dress for fear the fire trucks and crews might arrive too late to prevent gasoline pumps at the Standard Oil Station, by the boarding house, and the Magnolia Petroleum Station, on the opposite corner, from exploding and setting the whole block on fire. But the firemen arrived and attached hoses to the hydrants on Fourteenth, aiming them at the filling stations and Richter house. By then, the slowly collapsing rooming house was scattering fiery embers in every direction.

After breakfast, I ran to see the still-smoldering hulk and found that the black walnut trees in the yard survived the flames and matched the color of the ruins. Months before, the landlord had given me permission to gather black walnuts in his side yard, and, removing the oily black outer shells, I stained my hands as brown as those of the boarders.

Mr. Richter saw me surveying the lot and came outside to point out the paint blisters the fire raised on the walls of his house.

He said, "Id vas a close call."

Later, the weather warmed, and men came to knock down the remains of the walls and chimneys and haul them away.

But we were about to be knocked down and hauled away, too. Our scrappy family had kept our grocery store going despite losses selling groceries and meat on credit. My folks continued treating all customers— those who paid and those who didn't pay their bills—as they wished to be treated themselves, sensing that the hard times had struck almost everyone we knew equally.

I told my parents about seeing our credit customers paying cash at Black and White and an independent grocery store east of us on Wright Avenue.

Daddy said, "Everything's gonna get better. They'll pay as soon as they're able."

I asked, "But if they've got money, why don't they buy from us?"

Mama excused debtors who paid cash at other stores, claiming they were ashamed to face her and Daddy.

Nevertheless, every night at supper, my parents and brother discussed how to find ways to cope with the loss of customers and keep the business afloat. Some of their proposals were renting a less expensive building in the neighborhood from Mr. Goode, doing away with charge accounts, and selling the store's equipment and stock to go out of business.

PHOTO OPPOSITE PAGE:
Cleveland with the cast from a play he wrote while at Rightsell School.

CHAPTER 5

Wrong on Wright Avenue

IN THE SPRING of 1934, my parents rented an empty store, with an apartment at the rear, at 2315 Wright Avenue. That meant only one rent to pay. Moving the store one block east was less important than the changes in our living conditions and the store's policies: from credit to cash-and-carry, earlier openings and later closings, and only family members as employees. My mother would work out front if either my father or brother was absent, and I would replace Colonel, delivering groceries on my bike after school and on Saturdays.

Our new home was in another school district, which required me to transfer to Centennial Elementary School on Battery Street. Even though I begged to remain at Rightsell, Mama wanted to abide by school-board rules this time and insisted good teachers and new friends would be found at Centennial. But only a week later, for reasons she never shared, she told me I'd continue at Rightsell by riding the streetcar. That was okay with me, because for as long as I remembered, I loved riding a trolley.

On the day Daddy, Buster, and Colonel finally moved the store's stock and fixtures to the new site, Mama picked me up after school to show me the trolley route I would take to and from school. We rode from

Rightsell to the drugstore across from the senior high school at Sixteenth and Park, and walked south from there to Wright Avenue, where Mama pointed at our "new store," a dirty white building with sun-blistered clapboard siding, beside a weed-strewn vacant lot. It was hard to conceal my disappointment.

The store front had four barred, double-hung house windows rather than store display windows, and the front-door screen, bulging from too many pushing hands over years of use, had a small painted enamel Wonder Bread logo on it—a cluster of red, yellow, and blue balloons—the only sign a business occupied the building. Mama opened the screen door, and a tiny bell hanging in the top corner rang ding-a-ling, the only bright note in an otherwise dreary place. The narrow windows admitted hardly enough sunlight to see our golden-grained oak counter that sat parallel with the front door and had an old silver-metal cash register in the middle and rectangular glass cases on top at opposite ends.

Behind the counter, the wire racks and wall shelves were already stacked with bakery and canned goods. The refrigerator counter separating the meat market from the groceries had Toledo scales and a butcher-paper roller on top, and two butcher block tables on the sawdust-covered linoleum behind it.

Mama led me through a door at the end of the meat counter into a big open space, not an apartment room, for only the kitchen and bathroom had walls and doors. Our porch swing was hanging in what Mama called "the living room space." The rear door, beside Buster's and my bed, opened into a long hall, with storage closets on both sides, that led to the screened-in back porch and fenced back yard. From the porch, Mama pointed at the vacant, weed-covered lot beside the store that was included in the lease and that Daddy planned to rent to people with house trailers.

"Mama, this place is so old and ugly."

"It is, but our move will reduce overhead and keep us near our debtors."

What a comedown from a beautiful apartment on Gaines and handsome store at the foot of Rice Street to this tumbledown shack.

My life at Rightsell School underwent big changes, too. My fourth-grade teacher, whose booming voice matched her ample bosom, was impatient with everyone in our class. She insisted we talked too much, too little, or out of turn. Mrs. Marty scolded everyone and exiled the "guilty"

to the cloakroom, often forgetting she had sent them there. For readmission to class, we had to stand at the front of the room, name the mistakes she accused us of, and apologize to her and our classmates, an act we soon performed with more assurance and skill than our lessons.

One day, Mrs. Marty angrily put a note in my hand and sent me to Mr. Webb, where I saw the leather strap lying on his desk again. Without knowing what I had been charged with, I expected him to whip me, something my father had never done. But as Mr. Webb read Mrs. Marty's note, his cheeks and mustache began bulging and trembling. Though he appeared to be smiling, he said in a very serious voice, "Silence is a virtue you need to cultivate, Cleveland," before sending me, unpunished, back to class.

Mrs. Marty couldn't be denied punishing me, though, and confined me in the cloakroom. Before I left for home that afternoon, she pinned a note to Mama on my jacket. My parents read her accusations of my "cutting up, teasing neighbors, and talking out of turn." Without lecturing me, they repeated Mr. Webb's advice in different words.

Some other mothers told Mama that Mrs. Marty and her husband, a building contractor, were at odds with each other and that their personal troubles affected her behavior at school. After Mama went to school and conferred with Mrs. Marty, she decided my problem was being insufficiently challenged in class, so she signed me up for the free violin lessons offered once a week at school.

When I met the teacher, Miss Katherine Lincoln of Hendrix College, the slender young woman's hair and skin color reminded me of President Lincoln's in the big sepia photograph on the wall behind Mr. Webb's desk. At my first lesson, Miss Lincoln placed my left hand around the scroll of her own violin and my chin over the end of the sound board, measuring me for a violin of the proper size. Her hands smelled of lavender perfume as she checked to see if my right arm properly bent at the elbow.

"Obviously, you'll need a smaller instrument in order to play."

Uh, oh! That means violin lessons are off; my folks can't afford a violin!

Mama took me downtown to Tate's Loan Shop, between Fourth and Fifth on Center Street, which had decals of three golden balls above the doors and on the windows, the mark of a pawn shop. Even though not a music store, its front show windows were cluttered with different musical instruments—bass horns propped against the wall; violins in open cases; and an array of saxophones, trumpets, and clarinets standing, leaning, and lying about—plus framed pictures, metal and chalk statuettes, sports trophies, rings, and mugs in a jumble. To Mama's and my surprise, she could rent a smaller violin, which was an *unredeemed pledge.*

At the next lesson, Miss Lincoln, placing my hands in the proper left- and right-hand positions on the smaller fiddle, found my elbow bent properly. After being shown how to use the bow and the sound box, I simply mimicked violinists I saw in movies, assuming the proper posture and bowing positions with ease. Perhaps impressed by my potential, Miss Lincoln introduced the musical scale and notation in her next lessons.

After several weeks, she assumed I was ready to rehearse and perform "Twinkle, Twinkle, Little Star." Even though I regularly practiced the piece at home (to Buster's distress and Mama's delight), I spent more time randomly twanging strings than struggling to master the simple melody on the strings. Propping the sheet music against a tall vase on the dining room buffet, I happily scraped away, as the friction on the strings stirred a dusty cloud filled with the piney odor of rosin.

On the day I performed for Miss Lincoln, I sang the song under my breath, searching with the bow for the right notes, because I couldn't follow the notations on the sheet music. Stroking the bow hesitantly, searching for a melody I hoped was lurking in the strings, I slid to the precipitous bottom of Miss Lincoln's scale of potential violin players.

With my final notes fading in her ears, she smiled, patting my small, sweaty hand. "Cleveland, you're a charming little boy with a sweet singing voice, but the violin's not the instrument for you."

When I informed Mama, she was relieved to have only rented the fiddle but disappointed my lessons had ended. Buster's words capped my lone episode as an instrumentalist.

"Mama, he'll only master humming through a comb wrapped in tissue paper."

My natural "artistic instruments" were my voice and body, singing and acting in auditorium classes. Misses Betty Brown and Margaret Whaley, two young women teaching fifth- and sixth-grade dramatics, music, and oral reading, apparently believed mimicry, joking, and public speaking (which annoyed Mrs. Marty so much) were talents. Miss Whaley, the prettiest teacher I ever saw, had a sweet face and disposition, soft curves, and shiny brown hair. But slender, wiry Miss Brown was the liveliest. Her kinky, copper-red hair and freckles bespoke a directness, energy, and quick temper that no other teacher before her had displayed.

The directness she showed during our silent reading period after lunch was one instance. I noticed Miss Brown behaving slightly off center about something, circling around the square arrangement of our desks in the middle of the large auditorium. Sneaking a peek, because she didn't permit looking up and daydreaming during reading, I saw her nose held high, nostrils flared, and her searching eyes wide, like those of an animal stalking prey. Not satisfied about something, she changed her circular pattern and strolled down one aisle and up another, until stopping abruptly beside Clifton Smith.

She asked, "Clifton, do you need to leave the room?"

He protested, but she had identified the source of the silent seepage and sent him to the restroom.

Once a month, Miss Annie G. Griffey, the Supervisor of Elementary Education in Little Rock schools, interrupted our class. It wasn't clear whether she was checking on us or our teachers. The short, stout, elderly lady was always dressed like England's Queen Victoria in an old-fashioned, ankle-length, black bombazine skirt, pleated black shirtwaist, high net collar of rigid stays and purple velvet ribbon, and a small black hat with veil. Tapping the floor with her ebony cane, she walked regally across the auditorium to sit at our teacher's desk. She seemed always to arrive unexpectedly, interrupting our class and turning the fun of singing into a stiff formality.

To develop our creativity and self-confidence, Misses Whaley and Brown had special days for us to perform on the small stage at the front of the auditorium, reading aloud, reciting poems, singing songs, and performing skits. The teachers had a printed slogan hung on the auditorium's rear wall—SPEAK LOUDLY, SLOWLY, and DISTINCTLY—which remained before our eyes as we faced the audience.

On Free Spirit Day, on Wednesdays, I was always eager to improvise. In one skit, I pretended to be stung by a swarm of bees, instinctively tensing the large muscles in my back, legs, and arms, making my body tremble and jerk, which spurred laughing fits among my classmates. To keep them laughing, I prolonged the spastic throes. In my naive experience, I was learning a fundamental lesson of theater: the physical messages of an actor's body and face are primary, coming before and during the speech. Once I established my belief in my actions, my classmates cast me more often than other pupils in their plays, in which I played villains, old men, wild animals, and well-known movie actors.

I borrowed many plots from folk songs. For example, I staged *A Frog He Would A-wooing Go* with simple props and drapes, and played the Frog, with my close friends acting the roles of Miss Mousie, Uncle Rat, Bumble Bee, Crawley Bug, and Captain Flea.

My most ambitious play was based on the song "Soldier, Soldier, Will You Marry Me?" in which a love-stricken girl falls for a soldier and tries to lure him into marriage by giving him gifts.

> Girl: *Soldier, soldier, will you marry me,*
>   *With your knapsack, fife and drum?*
>
> Soldier: *Oh, how can I marry*
>   *Such a pretty girl as you*
>   *When I've got no coat to put on?*

So the girl ran to the tailor's shop and bought the soldier a coat. When that didn't work, she fulfilled each of his other requests, giving him shoes, hat, and gloves, only to learn he was married. After reading the lyrics, Mama insisted on my casting kids who could furnish their own props.

My best buddies acted the roles of my black friends on Gaines Street in one play—Conway Carrigan, Junior Bell, Johnny Spraggins, Jim MacFarlane, Bert Gaster, Clifton Smith, Frederick Cloud, and Jamie Jamison. The plot escapes me, but I remember we used the hide-and-go-seek count as part of the action. We blacked our faces and hands with burnt cork, and the guys smeared their make-up badly, letting their white skin show through. Applying my makeup, I worked carefully, spreading burnt cork and cold cream so smoothly and evenly that I could have walked down Ninth Street without being taken for a fake black person. I didn't think I was making fun of black people by coloring my face and speaking in dialect. I just wanted to be as lifelike as possible. Still, duplicating their outside did not bring me any closer to knowing how they thought and felt inside.

Most characters in my plays were boys; for some reason, I couldn't create believable girls. That was odd, considering how much I liked girls and girls liked me. On Valentine's Day, they filled my mailbox with cards of sweet sentiments rather than comic valentines with nasty comments and ugly pictures like boys sent. At the class post office, I mailed special cards to girls and boys I considered different: Billy Jean Staub ran faster than most boys; tall Mary Jane Moriarty was sophisticated, as was Conway Carrigan; willowy Jeanette Adair made me feel protective; blond Benson Weir was handsome; and perky Dorothy Koepple had the biggest smile. I wanted to offer her an Indian beads-on-wire ring but wasn't courageous enough.

During the semester, Misses Whaley and Brown combined fun and art education arranging us in *living pictures*, imitations of famous paintings. Catherine Rightsell loaned me a two-piece blue satin uniform to pose as *The Blue Boy* in Gainsborough's portrait. Mama, attempting to match the costume in the painting, hemmed the long legs inside the pants up to the knees, pulled long white hose over my legs, and tied white bows at my knees and on the insteps of my shoes. She reproduced the Blue Boy's hat—a soft, wide-brimmed cavalier hat with an ostrich-feather plume—by painting a soft, broad-brimmed straw hat with black paint and sticking a cardboard plume in a wide ribbon around the crown. When I later tried to return the costume, Catherine made it a present.

In the winter term, there was a city-wide play competition for Fire Prevention Week. I wrote a play centering on a villainous fire bug named Flame, who waited behind doors and in hidden corners to catch people using matches, electric cords, candles, coal oil lamps, and fireplace screens carelessly. I had no knowledge of irony or the difference between representational and presentational theater when instinctively placing Flame on the apron of the stage in direct contact with the audience, laughing, sneering, and commenting sarcastically as characters committed careless acts igniting fires.

To help me build a proper costume for Flame, Mama gave me money to buy sheets of different colored crepe paper at King's Drugstore to cut and paste together for flames. Before I left for school on performance day, she covered my legs and body in red, orange, yellow, and blue crepe paper that had been cut with ragged edges to suggest flames rising. The crepe paper had not been treated with flame retardant in those days, so a lit match could have made a giant Bunsen burner of me on my way to school. In the play, I circled as the fluttery flare of a blaze, shaking my body, legs, and arms violently.

After winning first place at Rightsell, I joined the winners from other elementary schools at the Main Fire Station, on Markham at the foot of the Broadway Bridge, next to City Hall. We were made "honorary firemen for a day," and rode beside uniformed firemen in the high beds of the city's red fire trucks. The parade route was east on Markham to Main Street, south on Main to Ninth, then north on Broadway back to the fire station. As the big, red, roaring trucks, after stopping at each traffic signal, shifted many gears numerous times, we were standing proudly beside real firemen. People along the route stopped to look at us, smiling and waving without knowing who we were or what we had done. Under our borrowed, wide-brimmed leather firemen's helmets, we must have looked like small leatherback turtles with heads retracted beneath their shells.

I was disappointed only once in auditorium class, when teachers cast another boy in a part in a PTA play. Before the audition, I read and memorized the leading character's lines, an instantaneous process for me from the first. But the teachers cast frail little James Moon, who rarely spoke in class and never played active games outside on the grounds, in the lead. His fine black hair hanging in bangs over his pale forehead and spidery thin arms and legs hardly seemed right to me for a hero. Even though James understood the part, he added no emotion or emphasis when speaking the dialogue.

"Why did teachers choose James Moon instead of me for that part, Mama?"

"He has as much right to perform as you do, Cleveland. Teachers are helping him gain confidence."

But it didn't seem right to cast a boy who couldn't do justice to the part. Yet the play, even with James in the lead, impressed PTA officers, who asked radio station KARK to broadcast the play so families could hear their children on the radio. The day before the broadcast, however, James came down with the croup, and Miss Whaley asked me to substitute for him on the broadcast at suppertime the next day. Mama couldn't take me, so I rode the streetcar and found KARK on the mezzanine floor of the Albert Pike Hotel by myself. Acting in a play before a microphone was as easy as riding to and from the studio and finding the station alone.

When I returned home, Mama said, "You see, Cleveland, nothing's permanent. You should have been happy, not scornful, of James Moon's good fortune."

All of us in the fifth and sixth grades took drawing and handwriting lessons. Miss Wherry, a large-framed, big-featured woman with dark hair cut in a mannish style, taught us in the big art room on the second floor. She towered over us, even having to kneel beside our desks to look at our work. The first day, she made clear in a deep, resonant voice that she wouldn't put up with talking, writing notes, or dawdling.

Following the Palmer cursive handwriting system required us to face our desks squarely and move our whole forearm advancing the pencil point across the surface of the writing paper. I looked around to see what others were doing, and despite Miss Wherry's instructions, everyone was sitting in whomperjawed ways to write; few of us took the proper position at our desks or held our pencils correctly. Boys were grasping the wooden tubes in their palms, like the handles of mallets, while girls pinched pencils in their finger tips, as if holding a tiny bird's neck. Half of us held pencils straight up while others held them on a slant. Some rested their hands below the lines on which they wrote, and left-handers bent their arms around the paper sheet like contortionists. And almost all of us applied our pencils to paper with different pressures, leaving spaces of various lengths between the letters and words.

In one exercise, we wrote a full page of only one word, *Summertime.* I capitalized the letter *S* exactly as the Palmer system required, using a swirling configuration of my whole arm and repeating the movement with each lower-case letter, too, inscribing the best word I ever put on paper! Miss Wherry patted my head, satisfied with my work, but I bragged out loud to a neighbor, and Miss Wherry sent me to the cloakroom.

I was already facing the cloakroom wall when Scott Riggin, who sassed Miss Wherry, joined me. From my first day at Rightsell, Scott picked on me for a reason I never knew or understood. Maybe he didn't like my face. It was true that I once accidentally gave him a comeuppance when he cornered me at the edge of the upper playground wall. He leaped at me, I ducked, and he flew over my back, like a movie stuntman, and hit the ground four feet below. With breath knocked out of him, he lost any immediate interest in me.

But now, facing in opposite directions at opposite ends of the cloakroom, we stood like dueling opponents before turning to fire their pistols. Scott hissed over his shoulder, "Cleveland, you're a silly little squirt and a fool."

I whirled and faced him. "If I'm a squirt and fool, Scott Riggin, you're a big *damned* fool!"

Unfortunately, my curse and Miss Wherry's entrance coincided. Harrumphing like a gorgon, she grabbed my ear and pulled me across the hall to the teachers' lounge.

Closing the door, she said, "Now, young man, I'm washing those nasty words out of your mouth with soap!"

Yanking a towel from the dispenser and dampening it with soapy water, she stuffed it in my mouth. I gagged, and my jaw flew open, and I nearly threw up. With bubbly saliva dripping off my chin onto my clothes, she allowed me to spit the towel out and rinse soap from my mouth. While drying off, I "cased the joint," as Jimmy Cagney did in gangster movies: the teachers' inner sanctum had curtains over the tall double windows and brown wicker furniture, its cushions covered in green baize. With my mouth tasting like Lifebuoy soap, I absorbed the soap's aroma and the wisdom never to curse in the presence of a teacher.

Later, my descriptions of the interior of the teachers' lounge seemed far more interesting to my girl classmates than to the boys.

Of all the kids in my class that day, I must have had the cleanest mouth. But teachers encouraged us to practice good personal hygiene for the whole body and taught us how to bathe, comb hair, cut nails, and brush teeth properly. To reinforce their lessons, they showed black-and-white dental hygiene cartoons similar to Walt Disney's, in which tiny, animated black decay germs, their eyes mere slits and mouths lipless, attacked gums and teeth inside an open mouth. The hero who rescued the orifice was a jolly toothbrush with a rotating head, swirling inside the mouth, its white, elfin bristles scouring teeth in clouds of foaming toothpaste that wiped out germs, as our class cheered its victory.

In addition, a medical doctor, approved by the Little Rock public school system, examined our bodies and gave us shots for contagious diseases. The physician at Rightsell arrived wearing a khaki British military uniform—wide-bottomed shorts, knee-length tan hose, a stiffly starched safari shirt with epaulets, and a pith helmet. A faint slant of his eyes and an ivory-colored complexion lent a slightly Asian cast to Dr. Corydon Wassell, who had just returned to Little Rock after twelve years on a mission in China. (During World War II, he became a hero fighting the Japanese in Java, and he was immortalized in James Hilton's *The Story of Doctor Wassell*, with Gary Cooper starring in the movie.) He led the teachers in examining our eyes, ears, and teeth, and assigning health ratings—gold for excellent, blue for good, white for average—for the citywide school health parade in late spring.

On a bright, cloudless morning, we loaded on busses for the health parade at the track meet for elementary schools at old Kavanaugh Field, behind Little Rock Senior High School. For the biggest citywide health event of the year, we wore our colored cardboard crowns (mine was brilliant blue, my favorite color) and marched around the cinder track. At parade's end, we filed into the rickety old gray wooden grandstands to watch Rightsell's best boy and girl athletes compete against pupils from other schools in relays, sprints, potato races, and basketball over-and-under. My classmates Billy Jean Staub and Clifton Smith won the fifty-yard dash for girls and boys.

My earlier failure to play the violin didn't worry me, for I already knew that oral reading and acting were my special abilities. My fifth-grade teacher, Mrs. Dell Park, a short, chubby, soft-spoken, white-haired lady who tried especially hard to develop good oral readers, praised my readings. As a top reader, I was careful to pronounce correctly, break in logical places, and pause at commas and stop at periods. I also looked into my listeners' eyes and faces to see how they responded, letting my voice rise and fall without settling on one note, unlike kids who glued their eyes to the page and read looking down.

Mrs. Park said, "Someday, Cleveland, you'll study with my daughter."

"Who's she, Mrs. Park?"

"Dell Park McDermott, a graduate of Galloway College in Searcy. She teaches at Junior College."

My worst habit at reading sessions was whispering to neighbors, especially to girls, when others read out loud. One day, while Junior Bell was reading, I complimented Marmay Booker—a tiny, pink girl with bountiful auburn hair and a charming smile—for being pretty. She smiled and thanked me loudly enough for our teacher to hear. Mrs. Park confined us behind the upright piano in one corner of the room as punishment. Checking us later, she looked around the piano just as I kissed Marmay on the cheek. Mrs. Park removed temptation by sending Marmay to her desk, and punished me by slapping my hands with a ruler and leaving me behind the piano.

Her slaps weren't impressive after the serious hand slapping I suffered on the playground playing Paper Rock Scissors, in which the winner would clamp his extended index and middle fingers together and strike the loser's wrist as hard as possible.

Girls, who didn't wish to be slapped, preferred less punishing verbal games like Knock-knock, which I played at school and at home. *Knock, knock. Who's there? Major! Major who? Major answer the door, didn't I!* The best knock-knocks were music titles: *Chester song at twilight, Cecil have music wherever she goes, Greta long little doggie, Arthur any more at home like you,* and *Domino thing if you ain't got that swing.*

Buster, totally exasperated by Knock-knock, demanded, "Mama, make him shut up!"

The financial difficulties my parents suffered at our grocery store seldom entered my mind. My mind was on school lessons, outdoor games, and play acting. I also read lots of books and magazines in the school library about children in other parts of the world, which created fantasies in my mind based on facts. I satisfied my curiosity about human anatomy by looking at pictures of naked African native men and women in *National Geographic* magazine, feeling guilty knowing Mama wouldn't approve.

After reading a story in *National Geographic* about physical arrangements inside Jewish synagogues, I decided to become a Jew. My justifications were my bluish-black hair similar to that of many Jews, and my wish to be like Jesus.

Jim heard me talking about my "adopted" religion and took me aside. He said, "You go to Second Baptist Church, don't you? You've never been in a synagogue or a cathedral in your life. You're no more a Jew than you're a Catholic like me."

Of course, he was right. I went to the Second Baptist Church and had been promoted just the year before from the Primary to the Junior Department for four years. Every Sunday, Mama and I rode the streetcar to Eighth and Main, then walked one block to our church on the northeast corner of Eighth and Scott. The intersection held an example of Western architecture on each corner—a buff-brick Gothic Presbyterian church, a pink Georgian Boys' Club, a gray Roman Masonic temple, and a white Greek neo-classical Baptist church. The church was impressive, but my Sunday School class met in an unpainted clapboard building—too cold in winter and too hot in summer—between the church and the white frame New England meeting house where Daddy attended the Brooks Hays Bible Class, at the corner of Eighth and Cumberland.

Between our Sunday School class and the main service, Bob Halley, Marshall Measel, and I hung out together, Sunday pals only, because they lived in Pulaski Heights. We waited in the shadows of the nineteen massive columns of the Albert Pike Memorial Temple for a little old lady—dressed formally with hat, veil, and gloves—to park her small black electric car in front of the temple. Once she crossed to church, we inspected the vehicle thoroughly, even touching it.

The car was the same shape and size at both ends, with its motor—a set of batteries—behind the passenger compartment. We looked through its pristine windows at an immaculate interior—the driver's high-backed bench seat covered in plush gray upholstery, a large tiller instead of a wheel for steering, slender silver vases of fresh roses beside the two side doors, and tieback curtains at the side windows to shade the driver and passenger. The name of the vehicle's manufacturer was on the hood's metal plate— *Detroit Electric Car.* Daddy claimed it was for town driving only, because the electric charge lasted a hundred miles.

But some mornings, our "sweet tooth" demanded more attention than the car, and we hurried west on Eighth Street to Schmand's Pal-o-Mine Candies, a narrow building beside the alley between Main and Louisiana. Looking in the front display window, we inspected the specials with lower prices among the sweets. Inside, left of the front door, a marble soda fountain counter seduced you, but the candy was to the rear in candy counters, some open but most glass-enclosed and full of delicious sweets. I gazed longingly at the fancy chocolate creams covered in colored filigree, knowing I'd buy the smaller candies that cost less and took longer to consume. One favorite, "candy perfume drops," were small, hollow sugar beads filled with colored water flavored like root beer, grape, and strawberry.

At the end of car inspections or candy purchases, with barely minutes before the main service began, we hurried to the church and climbed the steep marble steps to the narthex, tromping up the wooden stairs to take our balcony seats above the congregation and minister.

Dr. Calvin B. Waller, in his chair on the platform, was dressed in the clothes of an eminently respectable Protestant minister—stiff white shirt, with wing-tipped collar and dark cravat, black broadcloth frock coat, pearl gray vest, and gray striped trousers. His sermons were as formal as his clothing, reasonable in tempo and tone, modulated in voice, with no emotional display at all. Visiting revivalists in summer provided the fiery delivery some in the congregation preferred. Even though I was too young to understand all of Dr. Waller's words and ideas, nothing about his appearance and delivery escaped my notice.

If he confused or bored me, I focused on the events in the life of Christ illustrated on all sides by the stained-glass windows that burnished the sanctuary in softly lit pastels on sunny days. During the final hymn, Dr. Waller stood beside the pulpit, spreading his arms wide, inviting potential members to come down front to meet him, the deacons, and the congregation.

After his benediction and the congregation's mass exit, many older members stopped outside in the narthex or on the steep front steps above the sidewalk to talk. With fingers crossed, I watched fearfully their nonchalance on the precipitous steps—feeble and poorly balanced, the old people were ready to fall backward or trip. Until Mama, who wasn't very old, carefully tiptoed down to the sidewalk, I feared she might fall.

On Sunday afternoons, I met with the Royal Ambassadors. As a regular member, I advanced through every rank from Page to Ambassador Plenipotentiary in three years, memorizing and reciting Bible verses. Our group supported the Lottie Moon Christmas Offering for the Chinese with our allowances and prayers each year. Miss Moon was a Southern Baptist who had tended the physical and spiritual needs of the Chinese in Shantung Province since 1918. As Royal Ambassadors, we also contributed by performing skits and arranging parties at Thanksgiving and Easter for younger children of the church. At Christmas, I played Santa Claus in a rented costume stuffed with pillows, laughing "ho-ho-ho" as deep as I was able, handing out gifts to the primary classes. At Christmas, growing older and taller playing a Wise Man, I felt my bathrobe shrinking on me to the size of a holiday jacket.

My really dramatic role at church wasn't in a play but making a real-life protest. When our class was promoted from Mrs. Franklin Langston to Mr. William Riley, we wanted to follow the same lesson plan we'd observed for three years with her—a round-robin prayer of a single sentence each, praising or appealing to God; recitation of one Bible verse; and presentation of a brief view of the Bible lesson. If we had forgotten to prepare a Bible verse, we competed to be first reciting the briefest, simplest verses in the New Testament. The favorite choice, above all the rest, was "Jesus wept."

Mrs. Langston grew impatient with our competition, and said, "I believe we are all now thoroughly familiar with John 11:35. It will no longer be acceptable."

But that problem didn't exist with Mr. Riley, for he alone read Bible verses aloud, delivered the lesson, and prayed. Paul Barnard (whose father was an attorney and secretary to Representative Brooks Hays), Charles Meltabarger, John Delamore, Marshall Measel, Bob Halley, Jimmy Koch, and I joined in asking Mr. Lindsey, the superintendent, to replace Mr. Riley or transfer us to another teacher. Our protest may have been the first time in church history that intermediate pupils stormed the administrative Bastille of Second Baptist; maybe, behind the scenes, we were a sensation among the adults, for they returned us to Mrs. Langston, fulfilling the prophesy that "Little children shall lead the way."

While studying American history at school, we read about Benjamin Franklin's "discovery" of electricity when lightning struck his knuckles as the key attached to the string of his kite attracted lightning in a thunderstorm. After reading the story, I wanted to fly a kite but without being shocked. When March winds finally blew, I had saved enough pennies to buy a kite kit and thick ball of twine at Neel's Drugstore. Daddy helped me assemble the diamond-shaped kite, fitting the string in the outer seams of the paper into notches at the stick's ends for strength. I was ready to go, but Daddy insisted a kite needs a tail for stability in the wind. Mama supplied thin cloth strips from her sewing basket, which we tied together for a long tail.

The deep vacant lot beside our store, with only one trailer, had space enough to fly a kite. Holding the ball of twine in one hand and the kite on a short leash in the other, I ran up and down the length of the lot trying to elevate the kite in the breeze stirred by running, but without success. With business so slow, Buster came out to watch and offer instructions. He advised holding the bridle with my back to the wind to elevate the kite. I lifted it above my head and pulled the line and the kite rose slightly only to sink to the ground tail first. Buster advised waiting until the next day for a stiffer breeze, and I remembered Mrs. Langston quoting Ecclesiastes, "all is vanity and a striving after wind."

The next day, wind was strong and gusty after school. I held the kite up high again, and ran until the wind caught it, tugging it higher. I quickly released the twine from the spindle as the bright paper diamond soared higher than the store's roof and over the tall trees on the lot across the street. Windy gusts blew increasingly strong, lifting the kite higher and higher, until it pulled at my hands as if alive.

I walked my way to the store's front door and hollered to my folks, "Come out and see my kite flying over the corner of Park Street."

Since everyone was busy, I settled for the solitary delight of the kite soaring without my effort, until it hovered in the sky more than a block away. Suddenly, though, the wind slacked, the kite stalling erratically before dipping toward the ground. Even though I pulled and wound string on the spindle rapidly, I couldn't keep sufficient tension in the line. The kite sank into the treetops across the street in the Leiths' yard, leaving the kite string suspended about three feet above the street's surface. A car roaring past on Wright Avenue caught the string on its radiator ornament. Without thinking, I held the string tighter, clinching my fingers instead of releasing them. The burning sensation as the string seared the flesh nearly to the bones in my fingers snapped me awake.

Trying not to cry, I hid my right hand in my pocket to avoid my brother's comments, and sneaked through the store into the bathroom to bathe my hand in alcohol, an excruciating choice. For days thereafter, washing my hands slowed the healing and made cuts burn like fury.

In a physical way, I learned to let go of a lost cause without doing further damage.

One Saturday, Jim and I met in front of the United Cigar Store, at Fifth and Main, on our way to the Royal Theater to see *Charlie Chan in London*, starring Warner Oland, the Asian detective. My choice was the new murder mystery, *The Thin Man*, with William Powell and Myrna Loy, but Jim preferred the polite Asian detective whose wisdom helped capture a murderer in three days to prevent an innocent man from hanging.

Even though I went to picture shows almost every Saturday afternoon, only one movie ever made me afraid and sad at the same time. Completely engrossed in *All Quiet on the Western Front*, I identified with Lew Ayres, the boyish, sweet-faced actor playing Paul Bäumer, a German soldier. Near the end of the movie, Paul leaned over a pile of sandbags in front of a trench to touch the wings of a butterfly that reminded him of his childhood hobby. The camera focus shifted instantly to a French soldier aiming a rifle and pulling the trigger. The sharp crack of the rifle and the picture of Paul's fingers tensing were simultaneous. In a close-up, his still hands showed his young life snuffed out. The final montage of the movie was a ghost-images parade of Paul and his comrades floating over rows of crosses in a military cemetery. I cried, for the boys who lost their lives were like real friends.

Perhaps real veterans of the Great War like Herman Wilburn, in his caravan beside our store, also helped stir my tears. After his wife, Emma, invited me into their trailer for cookies and cocoa, he showed me Army Signal Corps photographs of the war in France. Even though horrified by his stories, I couldn't resist poring over pictures of dead, wounded, and crippled men on battlefields; the disfigured faces and bodies at hospitals; and the rubble of French villages and the ruined countryside. After fighting in the war, Herman became a pacifist, distributing copies of *War Against War*, a book so full of gruesome pictures I hid it from Mama.

Another World War I veteran lived across from our store in a pale yellow, two-story house, at 2304 Wright Avenue. Mrs. Leith, wife of John Leith, a printer, had been a nurse in the American Medical Department in France and England in 1917–18. The couple had three kids: Marion, a vigorous tomboy, a year older than me; Cecile, daintier than her sister and my age; and Herbert, a slight but muscularly energetic boy. At their house on rainy days, I questioned Mrs. Leith and she described nursing wounded men in temporary hospitals—churches, cellars, and caves—as shells exploded around them. Her frightening stories hypnotized me.

A third veteran came to our store once a month, displaying war's horrors even more concretely. Charley Potter, a cutler, arrived at our store sitting in the high driver's seat of a miniature green wagon pulled by goats in a leather harness jingling with shiny brass bells. He appeared normal until he lowered himself to the ground with his muscular arms and you saw he had no legs, only stumps covered by a padded leather apron. His hands in heavy leather mittens became his feet as he pulled himself around his wagon to unload the grindstone and sharpen the knives, cleavers, and saws in Daddy's meat market. As he worked, he told me about fighting in the trenches and losing his legs under heavy artillery fire.

I realized how lucky my father had been to escape fighting in the war and hoped my brother and I would be equally fortunate if another came, a thought that wouldn't have occurred to me if the pacifist and the cutler hadn't spoken of a man named Hitler and possible war with Germany.

—⟋⟋⟋⟋—

I discovered the boundaries of our neighborhood and made friends with boys my age delivering groceries on my bike: Park to Rice Street from east to west, and Wright Avenue to Sixteenth from south to north. Many of the families living in big old Victorian houses near our store had children, and all the boys but one fought rubber-gun battles with ammunition cut from inner tubes for car tires.

Buster drew a crude sketch of a pistol on a one-by-four piece of wood that I cut out with Daddy's saw. For ammo, I cut rubber bands from an old rubber inner tube, the replaceable lining holding air in car tires in those days. You loaded the pistol by stretching one-inch-wide rubber bands from the barrel tip to notches at the back of the hand grip. To fire it, you lifted the end of a single band off the grip with your thumb. Some guys hooked rubber bands over the barrel tip, securing the other ends with a clothes pin attached to the butt. Really inventive "gunsmiths" made barrels with longer pieces of wood and cut half a dozen notches to fire all the rubber bands in rapid succession, like a machine gun.

We fought our rubber-gun battles from yard to yard over whole blocks trying to capture a wooden fort constructed in the lower branches of a large oak tree on an older boy's property. Each day, the first boy to arrive in the yard held the fort until outflanked or outnumbered by latecomers. I tried to persuade chubby Charles Reed, who lived next door to the tree house, to occupy the fort until I arrived, but he feared being hit by rubber bands and ran away when a fight started. His reluctance was understandable; well-placed shots really stung, especially on the face.

Though Charles was a bit older than me, he had a girlish manner; yet he was a fun playmate, especially when producing shows, like those in *Our Gang* comedies, on a shallow stage in his garage. He invited me to see *The Scarlet Empress*, starring Marlene Dietrich as Catherine the Great of Russia, at the Pulaski Theater. At the candy counter, he bought licorice drops, thick dime-size plugs of black candy. Neither the flavor nor the texture of licorice appealed to me, but I ate a few drops to be polite. While sitting on the balcony watching the movie, I softened and pressed a single drop flat across my front teeth, tapped Charles on the arm, and smiled. When he saw my "missing" teeth, his shrill, girlish laugh made people turn to stare at us. Escaping their stares, we slumped down in our seats out of sight.

The Scarlet Empress was made before the Hays Office censored movies, and Charles made fun of the erotic story and what characters said and did in the love scenes. But the Empress's affair with the sneering Count who brought her to the Russian court didn't interest me as much as the scenery and lighting, the statuary of deformed gargoyles and slaughtered humans, and the gigantic palace doors that required six or eight actors to open. Every costume was elaborate, but Dietrich's frequent changes, veils, and jewels exceeded all the others.

Later, we went again to the Pulaski to see the mystery-musical *Murder at the Vanities*, starring comedian Jack Oakie and the Danish singer Carl Brisson. We stayed all afternoon in order to learn the song "Live and Love Tonight" which Brisson sang to Kitty Carlisle beneath a palm tree on a desert island, while chorus girls of Earl Carroll's *Vanities* waved giant ostrich-feather fans simulating waves lapping the seashore. We could hardly wait to recreate the movie's biggest production number in Charles's garage theater.

We nailed a big tree limb to a wooden base we painted green and tan to represent the beach and attached cardboard palm-tree leaves. For ocean waves, we suspended a blue bedspread loosely above the floor and aimed an oscillating fan beneath it to blow undulating waves. Bare-chested in ragged shorts, with a sash around my waist and a crepe-paper lei around my neck, I sang "Live and Love Tonight" standing beside the tree without Kitty Carlisle or any other pretty maid. Half a dozen kids, including a few our age who were baby-sitting little brothers and sisters, applauded the number. But all the kids acted as though laying their dirty little hands on the trembling bedspread was more entertaining.

Mama eventually drew me away from Charles by foisting a new play-mate on me. Doing her usual good turns, she suggested to a widow in her Sunday School class that I'd be happy to play with her son. Despite my reluctance, Mama sent me to play with Mrs. Steiner's son, Lamar, at their house on Park Street. Older and bigger than me, Lamar and his manner and clothes seemed all right for Sunday school but not for outdoor games. He tried to be friendly, yet that didn't include playing outside. Fearing he would break his thick glasses, he preferred examining coins and stamps, lifting each stamp with tweezers as if human hands might harm them, and insisting that I study them too, by pointing out colors, designs, and cancellation marks. He was nice and smiled a lot but being with someone so nakedly eager to be friendly was uncomfortable.

The Saturday Lamar led me up to his attic, I recalled Frank Smythe taking me to his grandfather's bathroom and suspected his motive. Lamar, though, opened a dusty trunk instead of his trousers' fly and pulled out a metal helmet, khaki jacket, and a pair of canvas leggings, parts of a World War I army uniform that I assumed was his dead father's. For a change, he suggested going outside to parade on Park Street in the army jacket and helmet. My costume was a musty American flag he wrapped around my shoulders, calling me "Mr. Liberty." Then, he led our march to Harrison Groceries, where Mama praised our get-ups, particularly Lamar's, and Buster teased me for being the female icon of Columbia Pictures.

Herman Wilburn, whose caravan was on the lot beside the store, called me aside and said, "Using our flag as a costume, you desecrate it. Learn the rules for handling the flag to show proper respect."

Even though I learned to cover my heart pledging allegiance to the American flag, I knew nothing of the protocol surrounding its display.

A closer friend than Lamar was Maynard Ferguson at the Pines Tourist Camp and Service Station on our side of Wright Avenue. He and his mother, a waitress at Mrs. Jeanne Burke's Cafe, lived in a tourist-court unit alongside other women and children who seemed to have no husband or father. The women, going in and out of the units most of the day, apparently had no jobs, and in the evenings sat in lawn chairs talking and drinking what I thought might be whiskey. Sometimes I saw women go inside units with men and close the door for a long time. Maynard and I played Lemonade with their daughters, a game involving one team challenging another: "Lemonade, what's your trade? Get to work and show us something!" The challenge team named the initials in the pantomime's title to help the opponents guess. That was right up my alley—W W W W—"Washing Washington's White Waistcoat"—always won the first bout with any group.

One night, Maynard and I sat opposite two girls in the tourist-court swing—two bench seats facing each other inside a suspended frame. We were rocking back and forth, like a clock pendulum, telling stories, as one girl in the swing drew on a piece of cardboard with a long lead pencil. Suddenly, Maynard leaped up and began pumping vigorously with his legs, widening the arc of the swing. But his movements jerked the whole frame off balance, and the girl with the cardboard, attempting to keep her balance, jabbed the point of her pencil deep into my kneecap, embedding the lead point in the flesh beneath the skin.

I wondered why I was so often a target for knee and elbow skins, splinters, and pencil points. Apologizing in tears, she tried to remove the sliver of lead from my knee, but it remained there like a tattoo for years to come.

That puncture pain did not equal what Maynard and Bobby Button voluntarily imposed on each other for fun! They favored an arm-skin twist, grabbing another boy's forearm, gripping it tightly with both fists close together, and twisting in opposite directions until the victim, thinking his skin would split, yelled "uncle," or cursed the twister. Their other torture was the "pump knot," or "forearm lump," when a boy rapped another's forearm with his knuckles and raised a lump. In the exchange, the victim attempted to raise a bigger lump on the first boy's forearm. I didn't comprehend why anyone willingly sought to torture or be tortured.

Maynard, older and tougher than me, was in the sixth grade at Centennial School and hung out with Bobby, who was older, taller, and heavier than either of us. One afternoon, Maynard and Bobby came back from seeing *Gargantua*, a cheap rip-off of *King Kong*, at the Crescent Theater on Second Street. They sat on the concrete wall of the vacant lot beside our store and described for me their excitement when the giant gorilla looked as if he wanted to make love to a partially clad woman. I didn't recognize "that look" or understand "making love," but I acted as if I did. They repeated the forbidden f-word I saw on walls but never thought or said out loud, even to myself. Maynard probably was learning about sex from the men who hung around the tourist court.

Bobby lived two blocks west of our store on Thayer Street, near the viaduct that crossed the Missouri Pacific Railroad tracks. Rawboned and big as a man, his aggressive but good nature held sway over all us smaller kids. He thought and talked a lot about sex, often reciting verses that aroused my curiosity but not my nascent libido. Mama, whose antennae could detect a nasty boy blocks away, met Bobby when he came to the store. When she told me not to play with him, I asked why, and she said, "I just know he's not a nice boy."

She was right, as usual. Bobby, revealing the sexual anxieties of younger boys, recited nasty doggerel something like this:

Bribing a girl with just a few cents,
I got her down behind the fence;

And made her promise not to holler,
As I laid on her for half a dollar.
Then I scrounged another two bits,
to get her to let me feel her big tits.
Then for just another tiny nickel,
She grabbed and held my sweet pickle.

If Mama knew I thought, heard, or spoke such words, she'd sew my lips together, stuff cotton in my ears, and lock me in the kitchen pantry ... if we had had one at the store.

Despite Mama's warning about the mental and physical dangers of big Bobby and the railroad tracks, I hiked to his forbidden territory across from Roselawn Cemetery to play beside the tracks under the viaduct. Bobby had found and gathered scrap lumber along the tracks and was building a flat-bottomed boat to float in a deep ditch that filled during the heavy rains. He set me pulling and straightening nails as he assembled the frame, sides, and bottom of the boat.

Waterproofing the vessel had been unlikely until Bobby found a broken keg of tar near the tracks, built a fire, and melted big chunks in a can. He and I spread tar with sticks on the seams of the boat's bottom, applying almost as much tar to our clothes, hands, arms, and faces. Leaving the boat to dry overnight, I removed tar flecks from my hands and arms before going home. But the brown blotches embedded in my pores and the stains on my shirt and pants didn't come off.

At home, I closed and locked the bathroom door (the only lockable door in our apartment) and used Mama's favorite cleanser, but Old Dutch merely wiped the natural oils from my skin. The continuously running water alerted Mama, who knocked.

"What's going on in there?"

I opened the door, hesitantly telling her how we tarred the bottom of the boat. She asked my playmate's name, and I named him. Without criticizing Bobby or me, she suggested removing my clothes for her to wash and that I avoid playing with tar again. Eventually, I wiped away tar from my skin with rags soaked in turpentine, but Rinso White didn't phase the polka dots of tar on my clothes.

The next morning, I ran to the railroad tracks to help launch our boat in the ditch. But big Bobby, a fat-lipped, goofy smile on his face, was sitting in the boat, sinking in shallow water.

Mama's warnings about the dangers near the railroad tracks beneath the viaduct proved stronger than Bobby's schemes. I heard that more than forty passenger trains approached and left Union Station each day, passing under the viaduct, slowing down coming from the south and speeding up going north. I had often stood beside the steel behemoths passing on the railroad tracks until a speeding train created a vacuum beneath the cars that pulled me toward the tracks. I was waving as usual to the engineer of an accelerating train when the train's draft tugged me toward the tracks. I saved myself by dropping flat on the ground. Thereafter, I avoided being under the viaduct when a train approached.

Living near the railroad tracks, though, had its advantages. The rumbling and whistling in the far distance of express locomotives under a new moon was poetry and music to my ears. Visions of tunnels, mountains, and plains in faraway places stirred in my mind while I lay under the breeze of an oscillating fan on humid summer nights, or snuggled under downy covers on frosty winter nights, when ponderous freights with lonesome wails and express trains with short whistle blasts drew closer to the ravine by Roselawn Cemetery and our store.

When the Leith kids across the street invited me to White City swimming pool in Pulaski Heights, I pleaded with Mama, who was afraid I'd catch infantile paralysis from the crowd in the water. I didn't know anyone who was sick, and she had not stopped me going to movies. Apparently, nothing could prevent the disease and its crippling effects on thousands of kids each summer, leaving them partially paralyzed or unable to breathe on their own. Many kids were kept alive in iron lungs, a cylindrical chamber fitted around the body from the neck down that breathed for them, forcing air in and out of their lungs.

I had been swimming only once since the Shriners' Country Club with the Adamsons. At Spring Lake, I refused to get in the water because I couldn't see the sandy bottom. But I wanted to go to the Mayor's Annual July Picnic at White City in Forest Park. Since the picnic was held during the day at the big municipal swimming pool, I was convinced that bright sunlight would let me see the bottom and help me conquer my fear of water. I pleaded without any success until Mama, seeing pictures in the *Gazette* of two lifeguards at each section of the pool, relented. With her strict rules of what to do and what to avoid, I agreed.

For the long trip, Herbert and I had our suits rolled in towels and Marion and Cecile carried theirs in satchels. We rode the streetcar from Sixteenth and Park and transferred at Third and Victory to another trolley that climbed Kavanaugh Boulevard around wide curves and steep hills to Forest Park.

We got off just before the trolley reached the turnaround at the end of the line at what was truly a White City! Everything in sight glistened white—the new bathhouse–concession building; the rims of the rectangular pool, twice as long as it was wide; the big open shed over a portion of the pool; the two diving towers with springboards; and the high-roofed open pavilion at the west end of the pool. Why kids pushed and shoved getting off the trolley, trying to reach the concession or changing-room counter first, I didn't understand.

At the counter, a bronzed attendant in swim trunks issued numbered wire baskets to store our clothes and matching numbered medallions attached to elastic garters. I took the compulsory shower before entering the pool facing the wall to prevent Herbert from seeing the birthmark on my stomach. I was eager to wear my new two-piece swimsuit, but he wore only black wool swim trunks. I wore a white singlet top with my black wool trunks to cover my strawberry. Worried about keeping my refreshment and carfare money safe, I wrapped it in a handkerchief and pinned it inside my pants pocket in the basket, hoping no one would think of searching there.

The water nearest the bathhouse was only a foot or two deep, so I bravely crossed beyond the second divider, marked FIVE FEET, because I could still see the bottom through the crystal-clear water. Marion and Cecile leaped in immediately, but I sat on the edge of the divider watching them wallow and dip underwater and burst to the surface, laughing and spewing water from their mouths and noses. With envy and increasing courage, I walked into water above my waist but didn't go near deeper water under the diving boards. Marion and Cecile cavorted only with each other, but some older girls flirted with the divers at the base of the platform.

Heeding our parents' warnings not to stay in the water and sun too long, we got out after an hour and bought hot dogs and Cokes; then we waited fifteen minutes by the clock to avoid the cramps before jumping back into the water for another hour. All of us emerged from the pool to take our showers, tomato red, smelling of chlorine, our hair soggy wet.

The streetcar home descended the hills whipping up a breeze as swift and powerful as those on carnival rides, but our hair and clothes dried slowly. Wonderfully relaxed on a bench seat all by myself, I remembered that Daddy would ask and be disappointed that my fear of water persisted. Big Daddy Harrison once threw Daddy into a creek and let him thrash about until he swam.

I wondered if I'd be brave enough to manage to rescue myself that way.

When our family gathered in front of the radio after supper to listen to our favorite variety and comedy shows, I felt the strongest bond with them and the world of entertainment. One new show was *Major Bowes Original Amateur Hour*, which assured me that even boys from small cities like Little Rock could perform on national radio shows. The program opened to the sound of a clanging gong, followed by the announcer naming the sponsors and Major Bowes, an older man, who spoke through his nose in a singsong voice:

"The wheel of fortune spins. Round and round she goes. Where she stops nobody knows."

Few of the contestants sounded Southern, judging from their New York, New Jersey, and Pennsylvania accents, and most were mouth organists, bell ringers, jug players, musical sawyers, garden-hose players, Swiss and country yodelers, tap dancers, and men impersonating famous people. Even though Daddy judged almost all of them "mediocre," Major Bowes seldom struck his gong, even for the worst acts.

When I expressed an eagerness to sing and recite on the show, Buster laughed. "If anyone would make old Major Bowes kick the gong around as never before, you'd do it."

I remained discouraged until Bob Buice, who sang bass in the Second Baptist Church choir, won first place singing "Wagon Wheels" on the Amateur Hour, and toured with the road show before becoming an announcer at KLRA in Little Rock. But if I won, I would have to stay in school and couldn't tour.

Baseball also figured in family listening. Benny Craig, the Colonial Bread Man, broadcast Little Rock Traveler baseball games on KLRA. But Mr. Craig wasn't watching games at a baseball field in Little Rock or on the road; he was sitting in front of a microphone in the picture window at the Colonial Bakery offices at 201 North Cross Street. Wearing a Colonial Bakery uniform and goofy hat similar to a police officer's, except for a Colonial Bread logo badge, Benny Craig read a transcript of baseball plays off the telegraph ticker that clacked in the background, and he rang a flat-toned bell when a player hit the ball.

He ended the Colonial program with, "This is Benny Craig, the old bread man, signing off. Remember, no one ever stood as straight as the one who stoops to help a child."

During the baseball season, my father devotedly followed the Gashouse Gang of the St. Louis Cardinals, rarely missing a broadcast after Dizzy Dean, an Arkansas native, joined the team in 1930. Dean's four consecutive strikeout titles impressed Daddy so much, he couldn't stop talking about Dizzy and his brother Daffy, especially after they won two games each in St. Louis's triumph in the 1934 World Series.

Daddy quoted old Dizzy: "It's doggone nice for an old cotton picker from Arkansas to be up there with them fellers." He was especially fond of Dizzy's remark, "It ain't braggin' if you can do it."

One Saturday morning, Daddy gave me the rent check to take to our landlord, Mr. Goode, who lived by himself in the back of the empty store next to Mr. Lokey's barber shop. I ran to the store in the middle of the block and knocked on the double door at the front. When Mr. Goode didn't answer, I tried the door and found it unlocked, cracked it, and looked into the unlighted empty space at the front.

I called out, "Mr. Goode! Mr. Goode! It's Cleveland. I've got Daddy's rent check."

When he still didn't answer, I stepped inside and crossed to the door in the rear partition and called his name again. "Mr. Goode?"

I didn't want to surprise him. Starting past a short hallway at the end of the partition between the front and back rooms, I saw a man's bare ankle and foot in a house slipper at the bottom of the sill of an open door.

I hesitated about approaching the door, assuming Mr. Goode might be in the toilet. "Mr. Goode?"

He didn't answer, and the foot didn't move.

Crossing and looking in the door, I saw Mr. Goode sitting on the commode with his pants on, slumped against the side of the sink.

"Mr. Goode, are you all right? Mr. Goode?"

Crouching down, I looked at the old man's face and saw his slack jaw and gray skin. He looked so bad sick, I ran to the barber shop next door to tell Mr. Lokey, and he sent me to get my father.

When Daddy and I reached Mr. Goode's place, Mr. Lokey had called a doctor and was waiting for his arrival. The barber declared the grand old man was already dead, and the customers in the barber shop stood looking into the bathroom at Mr. Goode's body. When the doctor arrived, he confirmed the old man probably died of a heart attack earlier that morning. Daddy and the doctor left to tell Mrs. Goode on Rice Street, and I remained studying the face and body of the first dead person I had seen.

After Mr. Goode's death, Mama sent me to visit Grandpa Honea and Miz Alma in McRae. Daddy drove to the old store building on Grand Avenue where Grandpa moved after the insurance company paid the claim on his store that burned the year before. When we arrived, Grandpa was sitting in his wooden armchair beside his Allsopp desk, in his usual gray pants with suspenders, long-sleeved dress shirt buttoned at the neck, and sleeve garters above his elbows. He greeted us by moving his corncob pipe from one side of his mouth to the other, without getting up, and pointed at the window ledge for us to sit. Daddy set my suitcase down and told Grandpa the day he'd be back to pick me up.

Grandpa said, "Any day you want."

After Daddy left, Grandpa didn't say much, so I explored his new store, a smaller, frame building cattycornered from the hoosegow with a stock reduced to fewer canned goods, fresh fruits, wheels of cheese, bags of seed and feed, and tobacco products. His desk at a right angle to the front window and double front doors allowed him to see customers come and go. The store shelves on one wall behind a counter were filled with selected canned goods, with crates of apples and oranges and two wheels of cheese on the counter top. The round sharp-cheddar-cheese container, covered by a window screen lid, sat beside a barrel of saltine crackers.

Even though a few women came and went, the store was a man's world, where men who purchased almost nothing freely sampled cheese and crackers without asking. I thought only potential paying customers deserved samples. The hungry loungers gathered every day at the back of the store and sat in chairs and on crates with their feet propped on the cold potbellied stove's fenders. Their main activity, besides smoking and snacking, was spitting into wooden Kraft cheese boxes half-filled with sand, Grandpa's cuspidors for chewers, dippers, smokers, and spitters. Grandpa introduced me as "Floy's boy," and the old men, curious about an unfamiliar city specimen, automatically called me Allie Cleveland, because most were acquainted with Mama and Daddy. At sundown, Grandpa walked us home past the cottage where I was born, and Miz Alma greeted us on the front porch.

During the following week, I learned that she, not Grandpa, had asked Mama to send me for a visit. For the first and only time, Miz Alma shared personal information with me. Born Alma Honneycut, she had married Mr. Green, and had two sons, Eli and Thilbert, and a daughter, Thelma. After Mr. Green died, she worked as a housekeeper until my grandfather hired her to tend Grandma Honea during her lengthy illness. With well water for cooking and bathing, wood and kerosene for fuel and lights, and an outdoor toilet, she catered to Grandpa's needs. Besides sweeping, mopping, and dusting every day except Sunday, she also prepared three meals a day, washed and ironed clothes, and canned fruits and vegetables—living within Grandpa's rigid time schedule for rising, eating, working, and sleeping. I wondered in the long silences we had after supper whether they talked to each other when alone, for Grandpa had no radio and took no newspaper, so there was certainly time enough for their conversations.

Miz Alma didn't treat me like a guest; she allowed me into their daily lives. If she picked a hen to cook for dinner the next day, she let me capture the bird in the barnyard, after warning me to hold it under my arm to prevent its beating wings from striking my eyes and sharp toenails from scratching my hands. Miz Green then grabbed the chicken, wrapping her hand around its neck, and whirled the creature until the head wrung off, the body dropping to the ground. After the headless chicken, with blood running from its neck, flapped in circles until it stopped moving, Miz Green put the chicken in a dishpan and poured boiling water over it to loosen the feathers. I picked off the feathers, which stank from the hot water, removing even the tiniest down until the naked, headless bird was thoroughly cleaned. Miz Green split the carcass's belly with a long, slender knife and removed the intestines with her long, skinny fingers, carefully saving the liver, heart, and gizzard for giblet gravy, one of Grandpa's favorites.

The next morning at the store, Grandpa opened the set of double doors at the front and back and sat at his desk checking accounts. A scrawny man, appearing too weak to lift a hammer, arrived at the back platform of the store in a dray wagon loaded with bags of seed. The heavy wooden wagon had detachable sides and rode low, its front jacked up and its rear sloping down like an African hyena's rear. Watching the drayman unload bags of seed and feed on a dolly (a platform on wheels), I understood the reason for the wagon's detachable sides and low-slung rear, which made it possible for a small drayman like him to drag objects off the wagon into storerooms.

While the drayman worked, some old-timers walked in past Grandpa at his desk. Wilborn Barnes spoke first. "Mornin', Ben, how you feelin'?"

"Fair to middlin'," Grandpa answered without looking up from invoices and bills on his desk.

"How bout this heat?"

"It'll do for the dog days."

A procession of middle-aged and older men in overalls and coveralls, in beat-up straw and felt hats and caps, slowly dragged to the back of the store, taking their regular places around the potbellied stove. Not one saw the irony of sitting around a stove in late July or early August, hoping a gusty breeze would sweep through the back doors to cool them. Following their *grand seating*, there was a quiet period preparing for the gab session to follow—stuffing pipes, lighting cigarettes, cutting chewing-tobacco plugs, filling lower lips with snuff—the regular preludes to complaints, gossip, and reminiscences.

An old man said, "I swear I been plain tuckered out the last few days."

"Cain't reckon why, Charley!" said Odie Forrest. "You ain't done nothing more than pry your body loose from one chair to squat in another."

"Well, jeer if you want. Ya jes ain't never had arthur-ritis actin' up on ya."

Edgar Menton joined, "Speakin' of actin' up, I seen ole Merlin by the station the other day. He acted plum bum fuddled."

"I wuz tole he has old timer's disease."

"Well, his wife Maude creeled her ankle, slipping off the porch trying to help him."

"What does 'creel' mean, Mr. Winfield?" I asked.

"Sprained it, boy! I didn' know you wuz payin' no 'tention to us old country hicks."

"It don't help for Maude to have them very close veins, either."

"Edgar Mason's fretful after losin' his job. Never seen him so down in the dumps."

"Speakin' of dumps, I declare my garden's just about withered away with rain so scarce."

"Ticks and chiggers is reviving in my fields like they got religion."

"Flies is all over my cows. One of 'em has pink eye. I blame it on the dog days."

"Allie Cleveland, listen here. Don't you bother with no stray dogs while you're in town. You're a city boy, and dog days is most likely the time for dogs to go mad."

When a woman wearing a bonnet that practically covered her face came in, their talk dwindled watching her collect cans from the shelves, sugar and flour from barrels, and carry her basket of goods to Grandpa, who obviously believed in self-service. Similarly, male customers came through the rear doors and purchased sacks of seed or feed, carried and weighed the bags on the platform scale, and loaded them on a dolly to cart to their wagons. While tending all his customers, Grandpa exercised only his thumb and index fingers, listing and adding charges with the stub of a pencil. Understandable, I guess, for an obese man in his eighties.

On our way home for lunch, Grandpa, who talked as seldom as Buster, stunned me by looking across the vacant fields and pronouncing, "You know, meadowlarks and bobwhites just fall silent in the daytime when it's hot like this." Grandpa had always seemed stuck in such a rut and so quiet, I assumed he paid no attention to anything but meals and customer payments.

One morning near the end of my visit, the grizzled old geezers at the back of the store had nothing better to do than tease me.

"Why, I bet this boy has a bunch of ancestors, don't you?"

"He's probably got cooties in his clothes. And that's not good visiting yore grandpa."

"Do you think he's too young to scrutinize girls?"

Smiling, I expressed pride in my dead relatives, denied body lice, and admitted looking at girls.

"By grabs, Ben Honea, this lad's smarter than you are."

"Allie Cleveland, wonder if you'd fetch me some cheese and crackers from the counter near you?"

"Elmo, what makes you think Ben's boy is your servant? Don't do it, Allie Cleveland. Let him keer for hisself. Wants you to treat him like his old woman does."

Everybody laughed. Then the old men, slouching around the stove, resumed their discussions of crops they hadn't raised; cows, horses, and mules they didn't own; and young girls and widows they admired from afar. Exchanging sly looks, they punched their conclusions by spitting, "patooie," into the wooden cuspidors.

The extended talk at the back of the store and infrequent shopping at the front persisted every day until noon, when Grandpa pulled his big, old, gold railroad watch, with the silver Lookout Mountain fob attached, from his vest pocket to check the time. With both the big and little hands on twelve, he cleared the old codgers from the premises, locking the back doors first.

After he locked the front doors, we walked home for lunch, which was already on the table when we arrived. Exactly sixty minutes later, Grandpa checked his watch again, to avoid opening too early, I guess, and turned the key, and we entered the store. Why he stuck to such a rigid schedule in the face of lackadaisical business mystified me. At five o'clock, we closed and walked home for supper, which Miz Alma served as soon as we washed up on the back porch.

When my parents picked me up, I couldn't wait to describe the state of ennui at Grandpa's store.

Days before my birthday in August, my mouth watered in anticipation of the cake Mama promised to bake for my present, since we had no money for another gift. Her dark chocolate cake, covered in seven-minute white icing, could not be matched by any other pastry in texture and flavor. Early that day, Daddy had closed the grocery store's front door to block the heat from the street, turning on the overhead fan and an oscillating fan on the floor. Despite the closed door and humming fans, we heard shouting in the street, totally unexpected in a neighborhood where sounds of car motors and train engines predominated.

Mama came out of the back. "Allie, what's happening?"

Daddy sent me to find out.

A boy was walking down Wright Avenue shouting, "EXTRA! EXTRA! Read all about Will Rogers's death. Will Rogers dies in an airplane accident!"

Daddy opened the cash register and gave me three pennies to buy a paper. When I came back, Mama read the front-page story out loud, her eyes filling with tears. "I just can't believe he's gone. We always lose the good people too soon."

The front-page story in the *Democrat* described how Will Rogers and his friend Wiley Post, the daring one-eyed pilot, crashed in Post's bright red Explorer airplane attempting to take off from a lagoon near Point Barrow, Alaska. Just a few weeks before the accident, I had seen Mr. Rogers in his last movie, *Life Begins at Forty*, and could still see him grinning and scratching his mussed gray hair.

With a lump in my throat and tears in my eyes, I turned to hide my face from Buster. I loved and admired Will Rogers as a person and an actor; he was my kind of hero, a man who could truthfully say, "I never met a man I didn't like." And he had proved it by traveling all over the world raising money for the Red Cross and Salvation Army.

In the fall, Buster found his kind of happiness despite the store's poor business. The big black-and-white female cat from our first store had a litter of kittens, providing him once again with cats to pet and to control our rats and mice. Buster gave all the litter but the solid black kitten with white mittens to customers. For some peculiar reason, he cut the kitten's tail off! I protested his unnecessary cruelty, but he insisted the kitten was too young to feel pain in its tail. Maybe that was Buster's way of having the Manx cat he always wanted but couldn't afford. Shorty, the cat, proved a very smart attraction for customers, who found his playfulness amusing.

Several months after Shorty joined our family, Mama asked why I had used but not emptied the little baby's pot from my babyhood that sat beside the commode in the bathroom.

"Mama!! Why would I do such a thing?"

"I thought you might have carried it to your bedroom to use in the night."

"Mama, I can walk to the bathroom, even in the dark. I'm not guilty."

The next day, she called me into the bathroom to show the pot had been used again. When the puzzling liquid deposits continued for several days, I figured it one of Buster's silly jokes. Then one day, I was washing my hands when Shorty strolled into the bathroom, placed his paws on the sides of the pot for balance, and urinated. Nobody believed me until he deposited again while Mama was cleaning the tub. I was sure Buster had trained the cat; it would be like him to do that.

Shorty was always feisty and eager to go outside the store, so we had to watch him carefully to be sure he didn't depart with customers. I was not home the day the cat slipped out the door while Buster and Daddy were busy. Buster saw him on the sidewalk in front of the store and hurried out in time to see Shorty chase a wind-blown paper under the wheels of a speeding car. Heartbroken, Buster didn't protest a funeral for the cat similar to that for my goldfish in Warren.

One afternoon, when Mama substituted for Daddy and Buster, a peculiar-looking black woman entered the store, her hair rising above her head like a halo. It had been bleached in peroxide so often that it had the color of a new copper penny. Mama talked with her several minutes before motioning me to care for the store. The women entered our apartment and left the door slightly ajar, and I peered in. They were sitting at opposite ends of our dining table, staring silently at the wall, the dark woman mumbling something. I had to leave the door to wait on a customer.

The women eventually came back out front, and Mama filled a sack with a loaf of bread, luncheon meat, and can of coffee.

As the woman closed the door, I said, "Mama, she didn't pay for those groceries."

"She'll pay later. We just bartered for a reading."

"A reading? What's she going to read?"

"The future. She's Madam Lillian, a clairvoyant who sees the future."

"Mama, you don't believe that silly stuff, do you?"

"Madam Lillian offered a reading for a few groceries. I'm taking her up on it."

"Mama, Daddy always says you're gullible enough to believe fortune-tellers. Now I believe him. Why didn't she read for you while she was here?"

"Madam Lillian couldn't read the writing on *our* wall. I have to go to her house."

After supper, as Mama prepared to leave for Madam Lillian's house on Howard Street, I begged to go along, but she insisted Lillian could read the wall only when alone with a client. Even though Daddy laughed at the reading, he was eager to know what the wall said about our business.

When Mama came back, she described how Lillian, in a kind of trance, stared at a blank wall and told about Daddy's several jobs, wrecking our car, Mama's near death from pneumonia, and Buster's dropping out of school. At least, Mama assumed as much from Lillian's general comments. Even though nothing was said about our failing business the first night, Mama hoped Lillian would refer to it at her next reading. Daddy told Mama any connection between her predictions and events was purely coincidental and conjectural.

Mama's attitude toward Lillian didn't change until she walked home with her one evening for another reading. Lillian continued talking to Mama as she stopped beside a wall, lifted her skirt, and peed. That act and her lack of underwear shocked Mama so that she told only Daddy, who told Buster in my presence. Imagining Mama seeing such a display, we laughed until we hurt.

Daddy told Buster, "Madame Lillian's going to miss living off Floy's fees."

She may have been the most unusual black person living in the ramshackle houses on unpaved Howard Street, but she wasn't the only black customer living south of us. Many came to our store to buy smaller items. One evening near closing, a little brown boy came in and stood in front of the main counter without speaking. Buster, eager to close and see his girlfriend, asked what the kid wanted.

The boy's eyes widened as he pointed at the big glass cookie jars on top of the front counter. "I wants a cookie."

My brother asked if he had money, and the boy opened his hand to reveal a penny.

"Well, we've got lots of cookies. What kind do you want?"

The boy smiled. "I wants one of dem round cookies with a cockroach in tha middle."

Buster reached into the jar and pulled out a big sugar cookie with a large, flat, oblong raisin pressed in the center. The little boy picked off the raisin, bit the cookie, and raced out the door.

The girl my brother was so eager to visit lived in an apartment on Park Street. She had come in to buy bread and coffee soon after we moved to this store, and they got to talking. She was from Beebe, where her family still lived, and had gotten a job downtown after finishing Draughon's Business College. Slender and dark-complexioned, with brown hair and eyes, she resembled all of Buster's previous girlfriends. He really liked her but had so little money he seldom dated, so Mama was convinced their relationship wasn't serious.

Christmas prospects sure didn't look good for our family; I assumed there might be no presents at all on the day. As the holiday approached, business fell off so badly that my parents had tense talks in my presence about how much they needed customers who owed to pay their bills. Then Daddy, who was usually so calm, began lashing out over the least thing, shouting as if Mama and Buster caused our troubles.

The climax came after school the day I asked, "Daddy, can I have some liverwurst?"

Ordinarily, he smiled and cut a thin slice of meat, but that afternoon, he grabbed a knife from the rack on the side of the butcher block, shouting, "I'll give you some damned liverwurst. I'll give you enough liverwurst to choke you."

I tried escaping into the apartment, but he demanded, "Stay where you are!"

Flinging open the refrigerator, he slammed a whole loaf of meat on a butcher block, and split it into two huge chunks with one blow. Handing a chunk to me, he shouted, "There! That'll keep you from starving. Now, stand there and eat the whole goddamned thing!"

In tears, I held the liverwurst out, begging, "Take it back, Daddy. What's wrong?"

He didn't answer; he stood with the knife in his hand, glaring at me.

Mama hurried through the apartment door. "What's the matter, Allie? What's he done?"

"I'm so goddamned tired of him asking every damned day for a slice of that stinking liver. He hits that front door asking for it."

"Well, Allie, let him get it himself. You don't need to shout curses or bawl him out."

Daddy turned his back and plunged the knife into the rack, picked up a wire brush, and began scraping the surface of the butcher block.

Mama took the chunk of liverwurst from my hands. "We'll put it in the icebox in the kitchen. Then you can have a piece anytime you want, without bothering your daddy." She put her arm around my shoulders and led me into the apartment.

The quiet ending couldn't conceal something more serious was wrong. At supper, I sat like a condemned man at his last meal, keeping silent, although lots needed to be said in the man's defense before his execution.

Mama tried talking about Madame Lillian's last reading.

Silence.

She repeated a customer's remark, "There's bigger things than money—bills, for instance."

Daddy didn't laugh. Buster said nothing. All of us concentrated on our plates as if eating our last meal in this world. Even though afraid to speak, I wanted to remind my father that I wasn't responsible for his outburst. After supper, I helped Mama clear dishes before joining Daddy and Buster beside the radio.

During a commercial, I couldn't restrain myself any longer. "Daddy, I'm sorry I bothered you asking for liverwurst, but you didn't need to yell at me."

"Don't tell me how to behave, young man!"

"I will if you're not being fair."

Daddy leaped up and jerked the piece of rope I was playing with from my hands and hit me across my back, legs, and butt.

Buster said, "Ho, Dad, take it easy."

He dropped the rope and went to my folks' bedroom before Mama could run out of the kitchen.

"Mama, I don't know what's wrong with Daddy. He scares me. Why's he so angry?"

"We're in real trouble, Cleveland. Your daddy's as afraid of what's happening to our business as you are of him."

Later, Mama joined Buster and me listening to the radio, but Daddy never came back. I could not forget, after being lashed with a piece of rope, the threat of my father's displeasure. Lying beside my brother, feeling and hearing the rhythm of his breathing, I couldn't sleep, only ponder my mother's defending my father and me at the same time. Even though she reproached my father for his behavior, she had the knack of disagreeing without being disagreeable.

As Christmas approached, Mama found work as a temporary clerk at Bracy Brothers Hardware Store on Main Street. Proving to be a dynamo in both good and bad times, she gave us a warm home, good meals, and affection while working from eight in the morning until six in the evening on weekdays and until nine at night on Saturdays. She earned just enough to pay bills and buy small presents for me: a tiny demitasse cup I had admired one night when we picked her up at Bracy Brothers and a copy of the Christian fantasy *At the Back of the North Wind* by George MacDonald.

But the best gift for me on Christmas morning was having each other.

Sales of groceries and meats at our store had almost stopped, except for customers buying items they forgot while shopping at Piggly Wiggly, only four blocks east of us on Wright Avenue. My father and brother began talking about bills, debts, losses, making ends meet, and bankruptcy, none of which I truly understood. What I did comprehend was the deep silence in our store and back apartment, the loss of happy workaday sounds—the bell tinkling as customers entered, the telephone ringing with an order, the cash-register drawer banging after a sale, and the cleaver's rap and butcher paper rolling in the meat market.

Trying to collect money enough to pay household bills, Mama picked the names of debtors in the neighborhood who owed the most. Then, dressed in her Sunday clothes, she visited them, occasionally taking me along to stand beside her, believing, I suppose, that the appearance of a potentially "starving child" might persuade a debtor to pay. Some customers were embarrassed enough to make a payment, but most sent her away empty handed.

Yet she still excused them. "They're struggling just like our family."

When she found that Mr. Britt, co-owner of Britt and Bowe Dry Cleaners, a thriving business, had the biggest outstanding bill, she decided to collect from him. He had never come to the store to discuss or pay his bill, so one morning Mama went to his shop on Battery Street, between Ninth and Tenth.

She asked, "May I speak to Mr. Britt?"

The clerk disappeared, and returned to say, "Mr. Britt hasn't come in this morning."

Suspecting he was in back of the shop, Mama said, "All right, I'll wait until he gets here."

She remained on a bench in the front of the shop until late afternoon, when Mr. Britt emerged and made a payment, promising to settle completely later.

Mama taught me a lot about persistence, but going face-to-face with debtors embarrassed her, and business losses wore my father's waning spirits so much that he couldn't deal with anything without his temper flaring.

With most of their cash exhausted for supplies from wholesalers, Mama declared at supper one night, "Allie, we have to do something right now to keep a roof over our heads and food in our mouths. Heaven takes care of those who help themselves."

Daddy nodded, without a word, his assent.

After Buster and I went to bed, Daddy and Mama must have had a long talk, because the next day my father sold our car, the grocery stock (except for the canned goods), and the store's equipment. The only piece he couldn't sell was the long wooden counter from the store at the foot of Rice Street, which had been as essential to our past as it seemed irrelevant to our future.

Even though I hated moving again, I knew by then that living in different neighborhoods taught me more about various types of people and ways of living than my classes at school could ever teach me.

PHOTO OPPOSITE PAGE:
Cleveland in last year at Rightsell while living at 322 Spring Street downtown.

CHAPTER 6

Rooms for Us
and Roomers Too

THE NEXT MORNING at breakfast, Mama, in her sternest voice, said, "I firmly believe Heaven helps those who help themselves!"

After making that statement, she washed and dried the dishes, put on her best dress, shoes, coat, hat, and gloves, and rode a streetcar to W. B. Worthen Bank at Fourth and Main. The man in charge of rental properties walked her two blocks west on Fourth Street to a house he called "the Mary Worthen home," purportedly built in the late nineteenth century by a member of the banking family. The lot was part of the city's original plat, and the house faced Spring Street. Mama believed the house was big enough for our family and lodgers, and leased the property in her name only, without consulting Daddy.

A few days later, Arkansas Transfer Company moved our belongings from the store, and I rode a streetcar from Rightsell School to the front of the Pulaski Theater on Capitol Avenue at Spring. Searching for 322 Spring, I passed Boosey's Sandwich Shop, Jenning's Motors used car lot, a private home, Coates and Raines Insurance Company, Pla-Mor Bowling Alley, and Crow-Burlingame Automotive Parts.

Then I saw a house matching Mama's description on the northwest corner of Fourth Street: a soiled gray Colonial Revival bungalow, with a dark red tin roof, fenced front and side yards, and a two-car garage at the back beside an alley. From the broken front gate, I gazed north at a two-story, red-brick Italianate house next door, the front of a vacant drug supply store, the Karcher Candy Company, the Pearson Sign Company, and the towering Rector Building. We were, once again, in a neighborhood of residences mixed with businesses.

I climbed the house's wide front steps, passing our old swing already hanging on the porch. Inside the long front corridor, half the length of the house, were three tall doors; the ones on my left had small hinged windows, or transoms, above, and in the rooms were fireplaces, walk-in closets, and medicine cabinets, with mirrors above the sinks. The larger room at the front had a bay window. The big room on my right, without a lavatory or closet and stacked with furniture, had a large fireplace framed by a handsome mantelpiece with colored decorative tiles. The windows in all rooms reached almost from floor to ceiling.

Located at the end of the corridor, the largest room in the house was obviously originally intended to be the dining room, for it had rails on the walls for plates or ornaments and a large fireplace at one end that had a wide mirror above a mantel embossed with flowers and fruits.

At the door to a smaller hall, between the dining room and bathroom, I saw Buster on his knees waxing the floor. Looking up, he said, "Found your new home, did ya?"

Returning his smile without speaking, I walked toward our parents' voices. At the rear of the house, Mama was also on her knees, with a can of Old Dutch Cleanser, vigorously scrubbing the kitchen woodwork and fading linoleum with elbow grease. Daddy, standing beside the shelves he built in the kitchen for canned goods brought from the store, was collecting his tools to erect a counter in the rear bedroom.

Mama, relieved I had found our new home, stood up to guide me through the house. She stopped at the pantry door in the kitchen to say, "Here's your and Buster's bedroom."

Our old double bed was again butted up against two walls, accessible on only one side. And the room had no closet. Mama, seeing my disappointment, said, "Cleveland, we just have to rent as much of this house as possible. You and Buster will find it cozy here in winter, and cool on the screened back porch in summer."

I could protest, *Sure, this pantry's "cozy" if you mean tight!* Instead, I asked an important question. "Mama, how can a family of four and at least three renters manage with only one bathroom?"

In a tone of impatience, she said, "By being flexible, that's how!" Adding in an airy voice, "We'll share without too much trouble, you'll see."

Leading me through the house, she revealed her plan to make the front room a parlor-bedroom for her and Daddy, and the big "dining room" a lounge for the family. She'd serve formal meals to guests there and daily meals in the kitchen.

After living in three small apartments and the back of a store, I found the old house spacious and handsome but worn. Crown molding was in every room except the kitchen and back bedroom; six-foot-long chandeliers ("log chains" to Daddy) hung from the center of the twelve-foot ceilings; gas jets and asbestos panels provided heat in the fireplaces; and mirrors and the original oxidized-bronze gaslight sconces, wired for electricity, added light over the wide, high mantles. The sconces were still connected to gas lines, but when Daddy lit one, Mama had a fit. Fearing an explosion, she forbade anyone to ignite the gas again. When gas jets didn't heat the dining room adequately, Daddy installed a wood stove on the hearth of the fireplace.

Our early weeks in the house involved a succession of fix-ups. The first Saturday, Daddy taught me how to apply high-gloss enamel without leaving brush strokes, so I could paint the kitchen, bathroom, and bedroom shelves and cabinets after school. Mama, on her 1911 Model 66 Singer sewing machine, a wedding gift from her parents, sewed curtains and drapes. Since we didn't have furniture enough to furnish all the rooms, Daddy went to Seventh Street and bargained with his former customers for bed frames, springs, mattresses, chests of drawers, dressers, and chairs. That left so little money for linens and towels for the roomers that Mama had to wash daily. To save money, Daddy and Buster began rolling their own cigarettes.

After the furniture, curtains, and drapes were installed, Mama had me paint and hang a sign on the front porch, FURNISHED ROOMS FOR RENT, and our first lodger, a middle-aged woman who wore black crepe dresses and too much makeup, rented the back efficiency bedroom. No problem with that, except she bathed, shampooed, and set her hair in one long session, which disproved Mama's case for the ease of sharing one bathroom. Then the lanky truck driver who rented the middle room took long baths on Saturday afternoons and left a dirty ring around the tub and water on the floor. Rather than speak to him to prevent the scourge happening again, Mama had me paint and post a sign in the bathroom: PLEASE WRENCH THE TUB!

Taken to task for my misspelling, I pleaded, "Mama, that's *how* you said it!"

"Never mind how you *think* I said it. Paint the sign again and spell the word correctly."

From then on, I checked the dictionary for the pronunciation and spelling of even the simplest word before painting a sign. Of course, Mama knew the correct spelling, but her pronunciation of *rinse* represented her inability to make certain sounds correctly, like she said "crish-uhl" for *crystal* and "chirren" for *children*.

Once all the bedrooms were rented, Mama was right about our making do with a single bathroom. We coped easily, for there were lavatories in each lodger's room for washing, shaving, brushing teeth, rinsing underwear, and applying makeup. And our family bathed in the evening and before dawn each day.

Mama was so busy with a house full of roomers that she sent me to pay bills at Arkansas Power and Light at Fourth and Louisiana, across from Union National Bank. Standing in line to weigh myself on the giant scale at AP&L, I noticed the sign at Kansas City Steak House covered the whole wall on Fourth Street, the largest sign I'd seen in Little Rock. Sent to buy cigarettes and hardware for Daddy, I got acquainted with Boosey's Sandwich Shop at Fifth and Spring and Ellis Fagan Electric Company, across from Tate's Loan Shop on Center. Daddy had grown up with Mr. Fagan in Beebe.

I paid the gas bill at the Arkansas-Louisiana Gas Company at Fifth and Center, and wandered across the street to the toy counters, soda fountain, and Christmas displays at Sterling Department Store. I already knew about the bicycle racks at Western Auto at Third and Louisiana but not about Mildred Reamey's dance studio above the Packard Automobile show rooms (*Ask the Man Who Owns One*) at Third and Center. I ran into Eddie Aldrich, one of my rubber-gun opponents on Rice Street, and although we had fought with play guns for months, he didn't remember me. Maybe taking dance lessons with girls embarrassed him.

There wasn't much time to play while helping Mama and Daddy in our first months on Spring Street. As far as I knew, there were no other guys, like Jim and Arthur, close enough for games. So I explored my old toy box, which was full of odds and ends from my childhood, searching for something to do in the cold weather. Finally, I found my solid-wood, homemade airplane, which had no landing gear, only wings and a propeller. Holding it in my hand above my head, I ran around the house and in the yard, spinning the propeller until I was breathless. To spare getting winded,

I attached a string to the tip of one wing and whirled the little plane around my head, spinning the propeller while dipping and diving.

In the kitchen, I saw how many burnt matchsticks stacked up after Mama lit the burners and oven of the gas range, and an idea sprang to mind. I could use the matchsticks to construct a small village of pioneer cabins and barns. I put little rail fences between the buildings and pretended the pioneers were farming the land quite successfully until Indians went on the warpath after their land was taken by the white men. After exhausting the fun of building the farm, I asked Mama for a few live matches so the Indians could attack the village with flaming arrows. The Indians set one barn aflame, and the fire spread along the rail fence between the barns and cabins. The Indians destroyed the whole village.

When Buster saw me playing with matches, he said, "Mama, you know what they say about kids playing with fire. They pee in their sleep." He looked at me. "Better not happen in our bed, buddy boy!"

"I'm not a baby in diapers, Buster!"

Searching for playmates, I stumbled upon a little friend and a new food. Mr. Thomas Musticchi, co-owner of Tom and Andrew's Restaurant on Capitol Avenue, lived with his family in a yellow house on Spring Street, across from the Pulaski Theater. I stopped by the front fence to look at the house's unusual roof, shaped like an upside-down cone, and a chubby, dark-skinned little boy came to the fence and invited me into his yard. We played until noon, when Mrs. Musticchi came out and invited me to have lunch with little Angelo.

Their big midday meal was the first Italian food I had eaten and first time I had observed Italian family life of parents, grandparents, and children. I sat at the large round dining table and watched Mrs. Musticchi pile a mountain of spaghetti on an enormous platter in the center of the table for everyone to fill his plate with pasta and meat sauce. Holding, passing, and scooping spaghetti bathed in olive oil from a plate at the Musticchis' was awkward. Also, the Italian way of scooping spaghetti into my mouth without cutting it seemed impossible, for I hadn't mastered rolling pasta on my fork. The pasta, meat sauce, and green salad, with black olives and peppers, which I had never eaten before, were delicious. With everyone at the table focused on his food, no one cared how I ate my food.

When Mr. Musticchi put wine bottles on the table at the beginning of the meal, I paid special attention, because Mama didn't allow alcoholic spirits of any kind. Angelo and I had glasses of watered-down wine, which gave me a chance to see if wine warmed me behind my knees as it did with Mama. Sweet little Angelo, half my age and too young to be a regular playmate, began stopping at our house on his way home from Peabody Elementary School, but our family wouldn't eat at Tom and Andrew's Restaurant until Daddy found a job.

Other places along our block commanded my attention, too. Karcher Candy Company, three doors north of us, made and sold candy in wholesale and retail lots. Without pennies from Mama anymore, I just looked through Karcher's window, wondering which of their two best candy bars on display I would someday buy: the Almond Nugget, a vanilla nougat shaped like a quarter-pound stick of butter, filled with almonds and covered by strips of parchment paper; or the Bunte Tango, a thin maple-sugar wafer topped by fluffy marshmallow coated with thin, dark chocolate. Months would pass before I would have money enough to sample either one.

But inspecting the lobby of the ten-story Rector Building on Third Street didn't cost anything. It had elevators in the lobby and a cigar stand presided over by a blind proprietor selling cigarettes, cigars, gums, candies, newspapers, and magazines. He made change as if his eyesight were as good as mine. A rather fancy-looking liquor store at the building's entrance displayed ornamental bottles of whiskey. Despite wanting to, I was reluctant to board an elevator without a specific objective in the building.

Even though it was one of the tallest buildings in town, the Rector Building didn't intrigue me as much as the yellow-brick Temple B'nai Israel, two blocks from our house, at Fifth and Broadway. One afternoon, I had nerve enough to enter its dark vestibule, and I ran into Rabbi Ira Sanders, a short, baldheaded man in dark-rimmed glasses. Surprised to encounter me, he asked in a deep, mellow voice what I was doing in the building, and I revealed my curiosity about the interior of the Jewish synagogue. He immediately invited me into the sanctuary, where I saw a dark spectrum of colored lights streaming through the tall, wide, cut-glass windows, filling the sanctuary and enveloping our short figures in a brilliant play of colors.

Even though I whispered my questions to him, the Rabbi answered in a full, resonant voice, explaining the Ark and the Torah scroll as the central focus of Jewish worship. At the front of the sanctuary was "the eternal light" hanging above the Ark, the symbol of God's eternal presence in the temple. Instead of a lectern and pulpit, as in a Christian church, the Jews had an elevated platform for a reader to lead prayers and separate pulpits for the rabbi and the cantor.

I asked if a *rabbi* was the same as a *preacher*, and Rabbi Sanders said there was some similarity in what they did. "A rabbi is mostly a leader of a congregation, like B'nai Israel, but the title may also be a sign of respect for a Judaic scholar or teacher."

"Are *cantors* comedians and singers like Eddie Cantor?"

"They may be comic, but they are the singing leaders of Judaic choirs."

Then Rabbi Sanders said he had to go, and for me to remember that "Temple B'nai Israel is the largest Reform Jewish Congregation in Arkansas."

Even nearer to us, another yellow building fascinated me as well, the two-story frame house across Spring Street from us, a rambling Victorian house with an ornately lettered sign above the front steps—MRS. HIGHTOWER'S BOARDINGHOUSE—and high-backed rocking chairs on the wraparound porch. In the front yard beside the porch was a dirty white caravan mounted on bricks with a hand-painted sign on the roof, WIMPY'S HAMBURGERS. I entered the caravan, and there was barely space enough for the cook, counter, cash register, grill, icebox, and me.

Mildred, the owner, who was built like half a barrel with keg legs, wanted to sell me a hamburger, but the powerful odors of onions and grease spoiled the mere thought.

"Then how 'bout a chance on the punch board?"

"What's a punch board?"

She whipped out a thick cardboard square filled with thin slips of rolled paper you bought and pushed out to read the prize. Obviously, very few slips would give a prize. But I risked a penny and punched out a slip. The phrase on the slip read *Better Luck Next Time.*

Mildred's ruddy fat face beamed. "Even if you ain't won no prize, you git a chocklit candy wafer with a pink or white center. If the wafer's pink, you git another punch free." Even though I sold empty bottles for pennies to try again, my only reward was the prospect of cavities.

Across from Mrs. Hightower's and Wimpy's, the white, three-story frame building on the corner resembled a New York City tenement, like those I'd seen in *National Geographic.* The walls rose straight out of the sidewalk, and the Spring Street entrance smelled of urine and disinfectants.

As I climbed to the second floor, someone yelled, "Hey, squirt, whatcha doin' here?"

Turning to see a hulking teenager whose brow was covered by greasy hair, I said, "Just looking around."

"What tha crap ya lookin' for?"

"Nothing, I guess. I just wanted to see what this building looks like inside."

"Haul your butt out of here! If I catch you here again, I'll whip your ass!"

A large girl on the steps yelled, "Lee-roy, pick on someone your own size!"

Taller than me, with a large nose on a pasty face, she asked, "What's your name?"

"Cleveland. We just moved into the house across the street at 322 Spring."

"I'm Mary Goforth. Lee-roy goes to East Side. Thinks he's better 'cause he's bigger."

Leroy warned, "Watch out, boy! She'll be all over you. She ain't named Goforth fer nothin'."

Mary whirled to face him. "Shut your nasty mouth, you dirty-minded fink!"

During their standoff, I slunk downstairs, vowing to stay away from the tenement.

At home, Mama was putting on her hat to go to the school board to determine whether I had to transfer to Peabody, only four blocks away, at Fifth and Gaines.

"Why do I have to leave Rightsell, Mama? I dodged Centennial riding the streetcar!"

Mama answered by taking me to the school-board office, at Eighth and Louisiana, and asking Superintendent R. C. Hall (his middle name was the same as mine) to grant permission for me to remain at Rightsell. But Mr. Hall insisted school-district rules required me to transfer to Peabody. We left and walked very briskly until we were nearly home.

Mama stopped abruptly, took an audible breath, and declared, "You'll stay at Rightsell, with your friends and teachers, by continuing to ride the streetcar!"

During our first winter on Spring Street, weather turned severely cold. Nobody had noticed gaps in our house's foundation or thought of insulating the bare water pipes underneath until the first freeze. After living in apartments and houses with basements, neither of my parents expected pipes to freeze, but one morning, as Mama prepared to cook breakfast, she was unable to draw water at the kitchen sink. Luckily, water still flowed in the bathroom where Daddy was shaving. So he decided to defrost the frozen pipes by drawing pans of water in the bathroom, heating them on the kitchen stove, carrying them under the house, and applying rags soaked in the boiling water to the pipes. But Mama, fearing he might strain his hernias and despite his objection, rolled up the legs and sleeves of his fishing clothes to crawl beneath the house and do it herself. She left the spigots at the kitchen sink open so we'd know when frozen clots in the pipes broke.

I carried pans of hot water outside and slithered beneath the floor joists to Mama's side; she was short enough to sit upright and apply the hot rags to the pipes. She found, by guess and by gosh, the icy clots and wrapped steaming rags around the frozen pipes to unclog them. In the cold blasts funneling under the house, she soon had soaked her gloves, shirt, and pants. I warned her about catching pneumonia again, but she persisted until water flowed in all the pipes. Even though Mama and I resembled exhausted dirt daubers crawling out from under the house, Daddy sent me to Black and White and Safeway stores on Fifth for cardboard boxes to cover the openings in the foundation. Luckily, the temporary patches couldn't be seen from the street.

As our family struggled for cash, I collected glass bottles and jars— milk, beer, NuGrape, Nehi, and Coca-Cola bottles, as well as Mason jars with lids—and other items, like wire coat hangers, to get refunds from merchants. Mama emptied boxes of her belongings, searching for items she no longer used or needed—old clothes, hats, dishes, vases, and costume jewelry—and sent them with me, a block and a half, to Tate's Loan Shop to get whatever Mrs. Tate would pay for them. I begged her not to sell a painted chalk figure of my favorite pug dog, the bust of Hiawatha (the Indian warrior in Longfellow's poem), and her sewing basket that was decorated with perforated nineteenth-century Chinese coins. But she insisted we needed money more. She would have sold her best sewing basket, covered in colored Indian beads, if she weren't using it making our clothes.

For months, when we couldn't afford ready-made clothes, Mama bought cheap fabrics at Sterling Department Store to sew wash dresses for herself and shirts for us, chores she added to her housekeeping.

She had very little cash to buy groceries, so our meals changed, too. At first, Mama opened cans of vegetables and soups from the stock brought from our grocery, but Daddy and Buster didn't feel they'd eaten if they didn't have meat of some kind. So Mama bought hams to stretch them in many different ways for as long as she could, from sliced ham steaks to ham hocks, frying the meat for redeye gravy on biscuits, and boiling it to make cornmeal dumplings with the liquor. She also bought cheap cuts of good beef and pork until dwindling cash forced her to fry flour-battered slices of salt pork and combine milk and cracklings for gravy over hot biscuits. She could hardly wait for summer to come when the African-American farmers who picked up garbage would sell fresh vegetables. Mama managed the food and budget so well, we were seldom bored with her choices or hungry.

The aromas of Mama's cooking sometimes lured tramps from the alley to knock on our back porch door. Though Mama was working in the bed-rooms or the bathroom some distance from the back door, she heard their knocks and greeted them with a cheerful, fearless "hello," in her special way with black and white tramps and yardmen. No matter how threadbare and threatening they might appear, she never showed any fear. She had the same manner as with a neighbor she knew who came to borrow sugar. Even though the men usually offered to work for the meals, Mama just asked them to rest on the steps until she brought them a plate heaped with our family's next meal, along with a cup or glass filled to the brim with coffee, milk, or water. It was as if feeding strange black and white men meals in our yard or on the porch was normal.

Mama's rapport with the men who asked to do yard work was similar. In the early weeks of our first spring, an elderly black man assumed the role of our yardman, even though our grass and money were short. Old Luke took the job for twenty-five cents and a midday meal, and he could share more of any dish or drink he fancied, but he rarely asked. When other black men later asked for more money to cut our yard, Mama candidly told what Luke charged and they left. But one younger man said, "Mizziz, he gonna open his eyes one day!" If Luke "opened his eyes," he still cut our grass for the same fee until Mama raised it.

Watching Mama organize our house, I realized how decisively she ran everything while tending our family, how rapidly she summed up what needed to be done in all situations, and how quickly she accomplished things, never ambling, especially doing household chores, leaning forward as if facing a high wind and almost running as if time were running out. She had amazing physical strength in her chubby, short body, too. So why she never lost weight to match Daddy's slender muscularity, I couldn't imagine. He had weighed the same since reaching his full growth, even though he was what Buster called a trencherman, eating three full meals a day.

Strangers occupied all the rental rooms for short periods before Mama began taking in relatives who were struck a blow by the hard times, helping them get back on their feet. The less money, space, or anything else our family possessed, the more she gave to others, especially providing a roof over a poor relation's head. When Cousin Billy Terry sold Aunt Betsy's home after her death, the first to stay rent free with us were Aunt Jane and Uncle Lafayette Jones, both in their seventies. Great-Aunt Jane, in my mind, was the "Little Old Lady" in a popular song of the day:

> *Little old lady passing by*
> *Catching everyone's eye,*
> *You're a perfect picture in your*
> *Lavender and lace.*

The couple had married in Cabot when she was nineteen and he twenty-one, and they spent most of their married life in Little Rock. Uncle Fayette, a house painter and carpenter, worked at Terry Dairy Company for twenty-five years until he retired. A slender man, slightly taller than Aunt Jane, he invariably wore white overalls and smelled of paint and turpentine. When I first saw the elevated epidermis of his fingernails, I assumed paint had built up under them. Later, in science class, I learned he had a skin fungus.

When a Wonder Bread truck slowed in front of our house, I knew Grandpa Honea had arrived. Mama's cordial greeting would have made a stranger passing our house think the family had been praying for his visit. Grandpa, who moved from McRae to Cabot where he had a smaller grocery store, came to join two of his brothers in the celebration of Aunt Jane and Uncle Fayette's fiftieth wedding anniversary. The occasion was my first and only chance to meet my great uncles.

Of course, Grandpa came to stay awhile after the celebration, which added to Mama's workload and changed our family schedule. Since all but the family bedrooms were rented, Grandpa slept on the daybed in the dining room and sat in the wicker rocking chair near the stove, observing whatever took place in the kitchen, dining room, or living room. He rose from bed so early that he disturbed even the lodgers.

To accommodate Grandpa's snuff dipping and corncob pipe smoking indoors, Mama kept a brass cuspidor by the family-room stove. Outside, his elevation over the front banister was questionable. If his snuff ran out, I went to the store for more, fearing the clerk considered me "country."

After drinking from a common dipper all his life in McRae and Cabot, Grandpa filled a glass from a tray on the kitchen cabinet with water, drank from it, and put the glass back on the tray.

When I saw him do it, I said, "Grandpa, please don't put a dirty glass on the tray."

Picking up and holding the glass toward me, he asked, "Do you see germs on this glass?"

"No, sir, they're invisible. The rim is covered with germs from your mouth."

He put the glass on the carousel, protesting, "There's no such thing as germs."

"Grandpa, how can you deny the theory of germs? It's an established fact."

"Can you see 'em? "

"No, sir."

"Can you feel 'em?"

"No, sir."

"Can you taste 'em?"

"No, sir."

"Then, aye, gonnies, Grandson! There's no such thing as germs."

While the Joneses lived with us, Mama read in the *Gazette* that Rabbi and Mrs. Samuel Katzenellenbogen, their neighbors on Sherman Street during the Great War, had returned to Little Rock. Daddy suggested having them to dinner, but Mama said she couldn't cook a kosher meal.

"What's *kosher*, Mama?"

"Food suitable for Jews to eat. They're orthodox, you know." No, but I didn't pursue it.

"They're permitted to eat only the meat of animals that chew their cuds and have split hooves. And they never eat food containing meat prepared with milk."

"That sounds silly to me!"

Mama reminded me that we should respect the religious beliefs of others.

"Then, why don't you have 'em for dessert and coffee?"

Since I had never talked to a Jewish person other than Rabbi Sanders, I was eager to greet the couple. At the front door, the small, dark-complexioned couple introduced themselves in a formal but friendly way. The rabbi removed his homburg, revealing a small skullcap on his head, a yarmulke, worn at home and in the synagogue. The conversation with my parents suggested how close they had been on Sherman Street when the rabbi headed the Orthodox Jewish Synagogue, at Eighth and Louisiana. He told us of resigning in 1932, after sixteen years at the synagogue, and buying a small farm in Palestine to retire in peace and comfort in Jerusalem. But three years tilling the soil in the Holy Land proved so taxing that the couple and their son, Sam, decided to return to Little Rock. Unfortunately, Sam, who was Buster's classmate at Kramer Elementary School, died of pneumonia one week after arriving in New York City. So the Katzenellenbogens' reunion with my parents was a sweet but sad occasion.

Soon after their visit, Uncle Fayette and Aunt Jane moved to Memphis to live with their married daughter. Then Daddy's second-oldest sister, Naomi, and two small sons replaced them in the large front room. Aunt Naomi's husband, Gordon Crane, had left the state to search for a job. I was first acquainted with her when she and Aunt Marguerite would arrive unexpectedly and spend the night in Buster's and my room on Gaines Street, putting me under the dining table and Buster on the living room sofa. I remembered Aunt Naomi's wonderful smile before she became so solemn after Uncle Gordon lost his job.

My cousins—slender seven-year-old Jimmy and chubby five-year-old Charles—were the liveliest souls in our house. They demanded lots of attention and Mama encouraged giving it to them, so I invented games for them, dragging out my old toy cars and showing them how to build roads and play in the sandy loam under the eaves of the house. For his safety, we had to corral Charles inside the incomplete front-and-side-yard fence to play cowboys-and-Indians, and we warned Jimmy about hiding his little brother's toys, scaring him, or blaming him for something objectionable Jimmy did but wouldn't admit.

If the brothers hadn't been so close in age, they would have resembled Buster and me. I sympathized with Charles when Jimmy teased him until he cried, and I wanted to tell Aunt Naomi to punish Jimmy. Mama wouldn't hear of it. She warned, "No matter how much you love little Charles and want to protect him, it's their family's business. You keep your nose out of it."

When they left to join Uncle Gordon in Jackson, Michigan, and all the Harrison sisters and their husbands who worked in the automobile industry, I regretted seeing them go.

For several months, another parade of anonymous lodgers stayed for short periods of time. Distracted by my last term at Rightsell, I remember only a few of them, such as Donald and Margaret Cartwright, from Chattanooga, who spent a few months in the middle bedroom until they found jobs and moved into their own home on the west side of town.

After the Cartwrights left, William and Elsie Cockrum, from Corning, Arkansas, rented the middle bedroom. Nicknamed Doc, William attended the Arkansas Medical School and trained in the Civilian Military Training Corps at Camp Robinson on weekends and for full weeks in the summer. His wife, Elsie, a small, shapely brunette, worked at a downtown office. She and Mama, despite the difference in their ages, became close friends, shopping and seeing afternoon movies together after Doc went into the army.

Doc invited our whole family to the inaugural reception at the new building of the University of Arkansas School of Medicine on McGowan Street east of the city park, but Daddy pleaded too weary to go. We rode there on a trolley, and Doc led Elsie, Mama, and me through the building, showing us classrooms, laboratories, and surgical arenas where surgeons demonstrated procedures to students. He warned us about unpleasant sights in the morgue before he led us to the deep vat of corpses immersed in formaldehyde, mostly bodies of indigents and criminals. Doc said very few people willed their bodies to the school for medical research. I had to pull Mama to the wall above the deep tank, but she refused to look down at the cadavers.

Doc explained that each "med" student was assigned his own cadaver to dissect and examine in detail to learn firsthand the anatomy of the human body. To show his specimen, a criminal killed by a shotgun blast that left small birdshot under the skin, Doc led us into a laboratory holding dozens of operating tables covered by white enamel tops. I hadn't yet seen any resemblance between Doc and Buster until he led us to his table and, without warning us, lifted the cover off the partially dissected body of a large naked black man with exposed genitalia. Mama recoiled, inhaling so deeply that I grabbed under her arms, fearing she'd faint. Doc only laughed.

To worsen the situation, on our way home, he continued describing and laughing at Mama's reaction, forcing Elsie to apologize repeatedly for his persistent ill manners. Though not physically strong like Buster, Doc had a manner of teasing to equal my brother's. Elsie later told Mama, who told Daddy, how sexually adventurous Doc was—he wanted a nurse at medical school to share their bed.

In 1936, the Arkansas Centennial celebrated the hundredth anniversary of the state's admission to the Union. For Rightsell's part in the city pageant on the stage at Little Rock High School, our sixth-grade teachers, Misses Whaley and Brown, conceived and directed a song-and-dance number based on the Floradora Sextet, the famous Victorian vaudevillians in New York City at the turn of the twentieth century.

Our mothers, using homemade patterns, cut and built the costumes for the sextet—girls in matching floor-length dresses, with wide-brimmed picture hats and parasol accessories, and boys in morning trousers and frock coats, with top hats and canes. All the boys' mothers found sewing the trousers of blue and white striped bed ticking and heavy black broadcloth frock coats very difficult. Mama struggled with the thick fabric for the trousers and intricate coat construction until she had to have Aunt Ethel fit the shoulders and sleeves of the frock coat and double-stitch seams to keep the pants from ripping.

The pupils in sketches from so many different schools didn't get to practice on the high-school stage, so performing in the enormous space with legions of kids standing in the wings was distracting. The sight of the huge stage and the audience of 2,000 took my breath away. To help us feel secure, Misses Whaley and Brown had us grip each other's hands tightly while lining up on stage and waiting for the narrator's cue.

Tripping on stage in time to the melody of "While Strolling through the Park One Day," the girls whirled parasols and the boys canes as we sang.

At the end of the Floradora sextet episode, we waltzed with our partners, singing "After the Ball," which, even to this elementary-school boy, captured the gaiety and melancholy of couples parting at the end of a ball.

After the ball is over,
After the break of morn,
After the dancers' leaving,

After the stars are gone,
Many a heart is aching,
If you could read them all;
Many the hopes that have vanished,
After the ball.

For the cavalcade's grand finale, we wore flower costumes to repre-sent the state blossoming at the dawn of the next one hundred years, our upraised faces greeting Arkansas's new century. How appropriate it was to end my happy days at Rightsell in a theatrical pageant on the largest stage in Little Rock, perhaps the whole state! I owed so much to Misses Whaley and Brown, whose musical and dramatic exercises helped me develop an ability to plot, stage, and act in plays, and to all the other teachers who developed my strengths in reading and writing.

The artists, historians, and writers employed by the Works Progress Administration also celebrated the Centennial with a tabloid booklet dis-tributed by the *Arkansas Gazette*. And they presented a pageant at Fair Park on June 10, 1936, of the Federal Theater Project—a cast of thousands tracing the history of the southwest United States. Aunt Ora, a devoted Democrat, drove Mama, Daddy, and me out to see and hear President Franklin D. Roosevelt speak at the climax of the pageant. The crowd was so large that Aunt Ora had to park at the edge of the former Fair Park racetrack, so far from the wide, tall stage that Daddy had to lift me up on top of her car to see the president speaking to the crowd, estimated by the *Gazette* to be 30,000 men, women, and children. Even though we were too far away to distinguish Mr. Roosevelt's features, I heard his voice in person for the first time, his distinctive delivery in a confident high baritone, with phrases ending in a rising inflection with a ringing timbre, just like the fireside chats over the radio.

Going home, Aunt Ora and Daddy spoke confidently of the country's economic recovery after seeing and hearing the president speak in person. Their expectations, at least for our family, proved warranted when my father and brother found jobs soon after, their patient searches paying off. Walter N. Brandon, the owner of Brandon Stove Company on Markham Street, hired Daddy to sell natural-gas space heaters, appliances, and hardware. Daddy had met Mr. Brandon while working for Ray-Glo. Buster was hired as a soda-fountain counterman by the manager of Walgreens Drug Store, at Fifth and Main, after he demonstrated skills developed at

Glasgow's Confectionary in Warren. His tuna salad sandwich convinced the fountain manager he was the man for the job.

Buster had always prepared supper for himself after work or dates, putting together delicious snacks or a meal from leftovers in the refrigerator. So the skill he developed in his homely efforts became the art he practiced at the drugstore fountain. Mama, when out shopping, had fun stopping to visit him at Walgreens because his coworkers first mistook her for his sister, an honest mistake. Mama had teased her older son, who was twenty-four by then, for the common error. Buster, who was an imaginative, industrious, and dependable worker, soon replaced the fountain manager who hired him.

When my father and brother were checking the classified employment ads, they never failed to read the *Gazette* sports pages, searching for news about Joe Louis, a black boxer who won many professional heavyweight bouts very quickly. Even though he was born in Alabama, the sports writers called him the Brown Bomber of Detroit. He was set to fight the German Max Schmeling, the former world's heavyweight champion from 1930 to 1932. If Louis defeated him, he would fight James Braddock for the heavyweight title.

Until the night of June 19, 1936, I had no idea how many people besides my father and brother listened to the fights on the radio. The night of the Louis–Schmeling fight in New York, Daddy stretched out on the sofa, Buster lolled in an easy chair, and I sat on a footstool by a living room window seeking a breeze. When the radio announcer named the sponsor, he seemed both inside and outside the house. I went out on the porch to see why he was so loud. Porch lights and loud radios were on at Hightower's, Arrington's, and the houses along Fourth to Center. It was cooler outside, so I sat in the swing with Mama to listen to the fight.

Gravel-voiced Clem McCarthy intoned, "In about five seconds, the fight will be on." The first-round bell rang, and both the New York and Little Rock crowds roared. McCarthy growled, "The men step into the ring cautiously. Louis lashes out with a left very lightly. Schmeling sends over a hard but short right. Sparring, Louis lashes again with his left and Schmeling throws short rights."

The cloud of cigarette smoke curling through the window screens behind us in the porch swing suggested Daddy and Buster had lit up and were tense. On other porches, pinpoints of lighted cigarettes and cigars blinked as two rounds passed without much change.

In round four, McCarthy snorted, "Schmeling stepped out slowly to the center of the ring. Louis came out cautiously. They're feinting with left hands, doing no damage. They've been in there eight seconds without landing a solid blow." Two minutes into the round, Schmeling shot a right hand high on Louis's jaw, making the Brown Bomber rock his head. Then McCarthy shouted, "Joe Louis is down! Not waiting, he's up on the count of two. Schmeling pounces on Louis, blow after blow. There's the bell, the men are still fighting. The referee stepped between them. Louis's manager looks worried."

In the eighth round, Louis closed Schmeling's left eye slightly, and crowds in New York and on the porches in Little Rock yelled louder. At Arrington's, someone shouted, "Close both his damned eyes, Joe!" But Schmeling crashed his right hand over Louis's head, carrying the fight to Louis, which didn't please the neighbors. Then Louis was caught off-balance and hit Schmeling low, with the referee cautioning him as the round ended.

A shout from Mrs. Hightower's urged, "Git him any way you can, Joe!"

From Arrington's porch, "Come on, Joe, get the lead out."

In the eleventh round, McCarthy commented on how Schmeling danced and Joe shuffled. When Louis shot another left hook below the belt, the referee cautioned him a second time. The crowd shouted, "Keep 'em up, Joe. You don't have to hit no Kraut low to beat him."

In the twelfth round, Louis went down.

From Hightower's porch, "Get up, Joe, you can do it!"

McCarthy: "He's hanging on to the ropes, blinking his eyes, shaking his head. The count's done! The fight's over! The twelfth round ended in two minutes and twenty-nine seconds."

Someone shouted, "I can't believe a dirty Nazi knocked him out!"

Neighborhood radios fell silent, probably flicked off in disbelief, judging by my father's and brother's disappointment. All the porch lights flipped off, too. The most exciting public event on Spring Street since our arrival had just ended.

By the time Louis and Schmeling fought a rematch on June 22, 1938, the fight had become *Joe Louis versus Adolf Hitler*. But by then, Mrs. Hightower's and the other houses along Fourth to Spring had been torn down. Only ours and the house next door remained; no crowds would ever listen to fights on Spring Street porches again. By the second fight, Daddy was convinced Louis had learned not to lean way over while jabbing, "putting his kisser out, begging to be socked!" And Daddy was right! After correcting that fault, Louis defeated Schmeling so decisively that even suspicious Germans examining the fight films didn't contest the Brown Bomber's win.

Still isolated from my former companions, I had to invent games to play by myself that summer. In the evenings, when lightning bugs appeared, I gathered enough in a fruit jar to have a faintly glowing lantern. Out catching them, I overheard roomers on Mrs. Arrington's porch talking and laughing. What they talked about I didn't understand, but the women's voices were rough and their laughter shrill and the men's growling and threatening. Traffic in and out of the Arrington house seemed far greater at night, particularly as my bedtime neared. Something fishy was going on over there that resembled activity at the tourist court where my buddy Maynard and his mother lived on Wright Avenue.

During early summer, June bugs were also abundant. Robust adult June bugs were nearly two inches long and had powerful wings protected by a wing case. I caught a good number of them during the day and tied a string of thread on the hind leg of the strongest-looking bugs, preparing them to fly. Usually, when I threw a beetle into the air, it flew in an arc and buzzed. But if one was stubborn and didn't fly quickly enough, I gave him a few hard swings in the air around my head. I tied the best-performing bugs to a thread and attached them to a bush. Tethered, they sometimes started buzzing and entangled the threads.

"Whoa!" I screamed, diving to stop them, usually too late. The strings were a hopeless mess as the bugs buzzed in and out, plaiting each others' threads together before I could separate them. When I desperately cut them loose, they flew away with strings dangling behind like kite tails. The next day, I would find the poor things caught on a limb or a bush, buzzing madly. If they were not out of reach, I tried to free them before they became a bird's delectable dinner.

After June bugs disappeared, I turned my attention to the winged maple seeds that were meant to scatter and produce more trees. Placing maple wings upon my lips and tongue, I could make a piercing whistle.

One afternoon, I was playing under the house's eaves after a rain shower when a kid in the yard next door yelled, "Hey, you're new around here, ain't ya?"

"Yeah! We just moved in a few months ago."

"I didn't see you at Peabody, though. Why didn't you go to Peabody?"

"Cause my momma says I didn't have to. Want to come over and play?"

We drove toy cars around puddles of water that had collected beside our house's foundation and built dams and roads in the mud. Crawling on our knees, pushing cars over and under the roots of the black locust trees and across the causeway of our largest dam, I learned that Claude Holland and his mother had lived at Mrs. Arrington's next door for some time and that he didn't know where his daddy was, or where his mother worked. I told Mama about them, and she asked if he was nice. I said he talks nicer than Leroy Horn. She didn't encourage playing with him, without saying why.

My father continued following his favorite athletic events on the radio; there wasn't money or time enough to attend events. Besides boxing on Friday nights, he wanted me to join him listening to Little Rock Travelers baseball, and encouraged me to join the Knothole Gang for boys my age that the Travelers baseball management organized. The club's name referred to the times when boys watched games through knotholes in fences without paying admission.

Claude, a fan who carried a glove and ball around in the summer, went with me to the Knothole Gang organizational meeting at the Boys' Club, at Eighth and Scott. In the big gym, we were surrounded by boys wrestling and shouting at the tops of their lungs. Finally, Mr. Billy Mitchell, director of the Boys' Club, and his assistant, Mr. Coy Adams, came out of their office and managed to quiet the crowd by introducing Doc Prothro, the manager of the Little Rock Travelers baseball team, dressed in his player's uniform. I was reluctant to join, but Claude was an immediate card-carrying Knothole Gang member.

We rode the streetcar to Travelers Field in Fair Park to witness our first free game from the bleachers. Neither of us ate or drank anything because we had only money enough to pay for trolley rides home. Claude didn't notice the conditions, but I didn't like all the waiting in the broiling sun. I decided that baseball of all the team sports—with its long breaks in the action, its immense, tranquil field sparsely populated by relaxed men in grayish-white uniforms—was the least dramatic and compelling athletic event ever for a loner like me. Even with professional players in a Southern Association park, everything that led up to a hit and run was too slow. But

Claude, like most other guys, was so excited about every play, he didn't need a place to sit.

Buster practiced his kind of sport only two blocks away at "The South's Most Beautiful Ballroom." The Rainbow Garden, on the top floor of the 555 Building, occupied a square block between Second and Third on Broadway and Spring. Buster and the brown-haired girl he met at our grocery store on Wright Avenue danced there regularly on Tuesdays (Bargain Night) and Saturdays (Whoopee Night), the dance-hall specials when dates were admitted free.

Buster saw this same girl every night after work, which was an unexpected change of pace for him. We seldom knew if, when, or whom he was dating until he brought this slender, attractive girl home one night to wait in our living room while he changed clothes for their date. Mama, Daddy, and I talked to her, particularly Mama, but none of us perceived the big event coming so soon after. A few days later, Buster and Ada Bess Fryer showed up at our house after marrying in a civil ceremony at the county clerk's office, without either family knowing. Both were excused from work the next day and moved into a rented room downtown for a honeymoon.

Twenty-year-old Ada Bess, like Buster, was born and grew up in Beebe. Slender and taller (without heels) than Buster, she had aquiline features, an olive complexion, a large mouth, even teeth, and dark brown, shoulder-length hair. Like movie actress Ann Dvorak, she was vivacious and good looking without being pretty. She instantly treated me as her equal, for our senses of humor matched and her infectious laughter at my remarks suggested she thought me witty. Buster smiled, even laughed, more than I had seen since we left Warren. Any reluctance my folks may have had about their marriage in such hard times was never revealed.

We liked Ada Bess even more after she and Buster moved into one of our rooms while searching for an affordable apartment. Living in the one-room efficiency at the back of our house, with little money for outside entertainment, Buster and Ada Bess played cards and dice games in the evenings with Daddy and sometimes me. To spike their interest, they bet pennies on their hands in cards or tosses of dice. When they allowed me to play the game, Mama, who was never a player, had to referee. Buster regularly cheated just to hear me complain and beg for my money back, and when Mama asked him to return my coins, he refused.

Daddy said, "If you can't stand to lose, Cleveland, fair or not, don't play."

I followed his advice. The only game I regularly played with our family was Monopoly, a new game, introduced in 1935, centering around ownership of property in Atlantic City, New Jersey. Daddy thought a game involving mortgages and interest would teach me something practical, so the seldom-used formal dining room table always had a Monopoly board on top with a game in progress.

After Buster and Ada Bess moved to an apartment on the east side, we saw them only on weekends. They appeared happy to me, but I overheard Mama's remarks to Daddy that suggested some kind of personal difficulties between them. Several months would pass before Buster came home one night after we were in bed and asked to spend the night. He and my folks had a long talk about his marriage problems. Even though Daddy advised him to go home to his wife immediately, Mama let him stay. So for a few nights, he (smelling of alcohol) again became my roommate before returning to Ada Bess. When their blowups continued, my father reminded Buster that he and Ada Bess should work matters out between themselves, that he and Mama shouldn't be involved. But our mother continued to sympathize and allow him to come home after their disputes.

I hadn't seen my favorite girlfriend, Jeanette Adair, since Rightsell School dismissed for the summer. When I visited her house on Gaines Street, my partner in the sextet was gone, and Jim, who lived two houses from her, didn't know when she left or where she went. Weeks later, my curiosity about a famous gangster's car accidentally led to her. While we lived on Wright Avenue, I was sure Bonnie and Clyde Barrow raced past our store one night. When I read an article and saw a photo in the *Gazette* and *Democrat* that the same car the outlaws drove the day they were killed—a gray, four-door Ford Deluxe sedan—was on display at a car dealership at Third and Broadway, I had to go around the block to see it.

I stood outside the front window looking at the car until a salesmen came out and invited me inside to see the car close up. The car in the window, riddled with bullet holes and displaying an Arkansas license plate, convinced me that Bonnie and Clyde had indeed sped past our store pursued by police firing their guns while I was in bed.

I started back home on the sidewalk along Broadway when I saw a familiar feminine face on a girlish figure sitting in a swing on the front porch of a boarding house. Jeanette, my secret girlfriend, was living less than a block from my house without either of us knowing. When I stopped at the foot of the sidewalk to the house and shouted her name, she signaled for me to join her in the swing. Chatting, I learned that she and her mother were rooming at the boarding house while her father looked for a job in Florida. Just think, there was a chance that they might have lived at our house if we had had an empty room.

Mr. Adair, to entertain and distract her during their wait for him, gave Jeanette a pet spider monkey, which was hanging on the chain of the swing above her head as we talked, nervously blinking and furrowing his tiny brow. The monkey reminded me of Henry Armetta, a character actor who played hunch-shouldered Italian roles in movies, sometimes a hurdy-gurdy man with his monkey. After promising to come back again soon, I called less than a week later, and the landlady said Mr. Adair came back and moved his family to Florida. I didn't know that after our accidental meeting, I would never see her again.

Even though studying and listening to radio shows at the same time was difficult, Mama never objected when I tuned to my favorite comedy and music shows in the evening. Bobby Breen and Dinah Shore, on Eddie Cantor's show, inspired my wish to sing solo, and Cantor's stooge, the character actor Parkyercarcus, provided me yet another impersonation.

Boy actors in movies stirred my acting ambitions. Even though I saw Shirley Temple in *Bright Eyes* and heard her sing "On the Good Ship Lollipop" in her first major movie role, I thought she had too many cute tricks to be a good actor. Jackie Cooper, with his pug nose, pouty lower lip, deeper voice, and ability to cry on cue, strongly influenced me. And I set out to master Freddie Bartholomew's articulate British accent to make my own speech equally precise. But Mickey Rooney's compelling energy, concentration, and upbeat humor in both dramas and comedies were the strongest influence on me.

One rainy afternoon after coming home from school, I twisted the radio dial and stumbled upon a radio show for kids with kids. The announcer's voice said, "This is radio station KGHI, atop the Pyramid Life Building, in Little Rock, Arkansas. Stay tuned for Uncle Mac's Kiddie Hour coming up. Time is 4:00 p.m."

Following his voice, another, more resonant, mellow voice drawled, "Hello there, kids. This is Uncle Mac, joining you for another hour of fun and music." What seemed like dozens of kids in the radio studio squealed hysterically and applauded, nearly drowning out Uncle Mac's comments. For an hour, I listened to him interviewing kids, mostly girls, who sang solos. Between the numbers, he offered bits of fatherly advice—be courteous to elders, do your lessons willingly, and help others worse off than you.

Mama, passing the living room, asked, "Why don't you sing on that program?"

After school the next day, I followed her suggestion and went to the Pyramid Building, only two blocks from our house, climbing the steep, narrow stairs to KGHI's small studio on the second floor. Through the studio window, I saw kids milling around a thin, long-faced man sitting on a high stool beside a microphone on a stand. Another man was sitting on a bench at an upright piano, absent-mindedly running his fingers across the keyboard while talking to a little girl. Once a young assistant admitted me to the studio through a thick door, he asked my name, age, and talent.

Ready to sing without rehearsal, I asked, "Will I sing today?"

He smiled. "If there's time."

The sign over the control booth window flashed red, ON THE AIR, and Uncle Mac repeated his opening spiel and the kids hollered and clapped. He interviewed a procession of kids who sang popular songs of the day: "Blue Moon," "June in January," "Red Sails in the Sunset," "Deep Purple," and "The Object of My Affection." The pianist knew the music for all the songs, or faked it, without rehearsal, but several kids sang unusual songs without accompaniment because he did not know the music.

In the middle of the hour, as another kid sang, Uncle Mac gestured for me to come to his side. The applause for the previous singer faded, and he said, "We've got a new boy with talent today. What's your name, young man, how old are you, and where do you go to school?" I answered his questions and chose to sing Mama's favorite song of mine:

When I grow too old to dream,
I'll have you to remember.
When I grow too old to dream,
Your love will live in my heart.

Uncle Mac said my voice was bell-like, and the kids applauded as though they agreed.

I appeared on the show regularly thereafter, Uncle Mac calling me on the air "his little Bing Crosby." Even though my soprano hardly resembled his resonant baritone, I favored sentimental ballads as he did.

As a part-time evangelist, Uncle Mac asked Mama if she would let me accompany him to nearby towns of England, Sweet Home, Benton, and Bauxite to sing before he preached his sermons. Mama agreed after Daddy reassured her that Uncle Mac was a good man and I would be safe with him. Uncle Mac always talked with me in front of the crowd about school and other matters before introducing my religious and popular songs that were right for a boy's voice and his favorites. Uncle Mac also sent me to sing at civic clubs, like Lions International, in the Hotel Marion ballroom, and with Bill Goodrich, the *Arkansas Gazette* reporter-photographer who was his kid-show piano accompanist.

More surprises popped up our first summer on Spring Street. During breakfast one morning, a short-haired, middle-aged lady in a mannish suit knocked at our back door and introduced herself to Mama. Miss Eunice Compton, a certified public accountant at the Rector Building, wanted to rent parking space in our backyard, and suggested others in the Rector Building would also pay to park there, too. At lunch, Mama and Daddy discussed the idea and decided parking fees would furnish my allowance. Daddy and I measured the space in the backyard, and he estimated it had space enough for ten cars, with easy entry and exit. Happy to run a parking lot, I whipped out my paint and trusty brush to post a sign saying PARKING 5 CENTS facing Fourth Street by the driveway.

The next week, I sat on the back steps reading comics, waiting for someone besides Miss Compton to park. They never came. But over ensuing weeks, enough drivers dribbled in to fill the yard. Some came back from lunch and didn't want to pay another nickel. I told Daddy, who thought it would be fair to allow parkers to come and go all day for a nickel. Eventually I tired of waiting in the parking lot for parkers to come and pay, so I painted a sign asking them to drop their fees through a slot beside the screen door, trusting they wouldn't cheat me.

After parking in the yard for a month, Miss Compton rented one side of our two-car garage during the day for five dollars a month. Word of mouth brought more parkers from the Rector Building and the U.S. Engineers' Office on Broadway, filling our backyard every day. As my income accumulated, Mama took me to open an account at People's Savings and Loan, in the old Commercial National Bank Building, at Second and Main. Every week, my account grew, even though I bought candy, soda pop, and movie tickets.

The parking lot income, access to nearby movie houses, low admission price (ten cents for children under twelve), and an abiding interest in theater led me to the study of acting and direction of moving pictures unconsciously. The seven movie houses within seven blocks became theater classrooms for me over the next seven years. All the "acting" I did before moving to Spring Street was spontaneous and uninformed, but the movies would introduce the basic principles of acting and directing without my being conscious of it.

The Pulaski Theater, a block from our house, was the flagship for Arkansas Amusement (later Robb and Rowley), with administrative offices and a screening room above its lobby. The first movie theater in Little Rock with air conditioning displayed a banner on its marquee: REFRIGERATED AIR. During that first summer on Spring, the weather was so hot I sometimes stood under the fine spray from the fans in the wooden cooling tower behind the theater.

At first, Mama was afraid to let me go to movies by myself, so Daddy, while out of work, took me to see Tom Mix and his horse, Tony, on stage at the Pulaski between showings of the cowboy star's latest movie, *Rustler's Roundup*. The horse nickered constantly, lifting his foot on cue to count. Appearing aware of his special accomplishment, he outshone Tom Mix's pistol tricks in my estimation.

Months later on Saturday afternoon, Daddy took me to the Pulaski again to see Cab Calloway and his orchestra. The band members weren't allowed to lodge at Little Rock's white hotels until someone gave permission to stay in the Lafayette Hotel, at Sixth and Louisiana, which was closed during part of the Depression. When Cab Calloway—a long, lean, cocoa-colored singer in formal white tails—swirled on stage to lead his orchestra, he smiled broadly, displaying a remarkable set of brilliant white teeth. He led the orchestra, danced, and sang "I'll Be Glad When You're Dead You Rascal You," and ended with "Minnie the Moocher":

> *Hey folks here's the story 'bout Minnie the Moocher.*
> *She was a low-down Hoochie Koocher.*
> *She was the roughest toughest frail,*
> *But Minnie had a heart as big as a whale,*
> *Hidey Hidey Hidey Hi / Hodey odey odey oh*
> *Heedey Heedey Heedey Hee / Hidey Hidey Hidey Ho*

The totally white audience wildly applauded Mr. Calloway's spirited singing, for even their prejudice didn't diminish recognition of his talents as a singer and dancer. For weeks, I tried to imitate "Minnie the Moocher," preparing for Uncle Mac's show, but Bill Goodrich, his accompanist, insisted it was inappropriate for me and for the kiddie show.

At first, Mama hesitated to let me go to the Royal (the smallest first-run movie house in town), which showed modest family films and comedies from smaller studios. So my father took me to *The Biscuit Eater*, a film about a birddog like those he raised and trained in McRae. Later, he took me to *Fireman Save My Child*, starring Joe E. Brown, who shaped his enormous mouth so daintily, triggering Daddy's big laugh that made the audience laugh. Mama, finally convinced I was safe to go alone, sent me to *Ten Nights on the Barroom Floor*, because a picture stressing the ill effects alcohol had on men, like my Uncle Cleve, would teach me a lesson. Her point was serious, but the old-fashioned "stage-acting" in the movie detracted from it. Whether my ridiculing *Ten Nights* affected her decision, I don't know, but she didn't let me go to *Reefer Madness*, about young couples smoking marijuana, the only movie she banned me from seeing.

I enjoyed movies most at the Capitol, at Sixth on Main across from Pfeifer's Department Store. Only first-class movies were shown in its compact auditorium, which had a balcony near the screen. I first noticed the Capitol in 1932, when, passing on the streetcar, I saw a man in native African regalia beside the box office, which was decorated like an African hut. *Trader Horn* was showing, and I persuaded Mama to take me.

The scenes of African tribes pursuing a white safari and wild animals stampeding on the veldt frightened Mama but thrilled me. Harry Carey, the leading actor, was so believable, and Duncan Renaldo, later jailed for manslaughter, quite handsome. I was aware that the Capitol, more than other theaters in town, illustrated the marquee and lobby to match a movie's theme or locale. Sometimes the ushers, who guided patrons to their seats holding flashlights behind them, like illuminated tails, wore uniforms keyed to pictures. And the Capitol's distinction was midnight previews and the first popcorn machines in town. The other midtown theaters had previews at irregular intervals, but the Capitol had one every Saturday night. It was also the site of Senior Previews, a graduation ritual of Little Rock Senior High.

The Capitol opened at 12:30 p.m. on Sundays, a half hour before its first movie showing. When *Mutiny on the Bounty* was shown, I rushed home from church for a sandwich and then to the theater to be among the first to see a movie based on the *Bounty Trilogy* and filmed in Tahiti with Tahitian natives. Clark Gable and Franchot Tone were ideally cast as Fletcher Christian and Roger Byam, but Charles Laughton had the demanding role of Captain Bligh, the tyrannical, sadistic officer who flogged even the body of a dead sailor before the ship sailed from England.

The movie and Laughton's performance were so compelling, I stayed to see the picture twice. As I left the theater, the dark streets were empty; I had forgotten about time. I ran to Capitol Avenue, turned the corner, and saw trouble coming! The small figure marching toward me had the rhythm and silhouette of Mama. I had been away from home for five hours, and she was coming to get me. Before we reached home, she accepted that I was at the theater the whole time and listened to my impersonation of Captain Bligh, beginning, "Mr. Christian ... come here!" She never again showed concern about my physical, mental, or moral safety at movies, as long as I returned home at the time promised.

The oldest, largest theater in town was the Arkansas, which had a balcony on three levels. Originally a theater for stage plays, named Kempner for the family who built it, the theater was closed during the Depression, opening only for special live performances. Soon after we moved to Spring Street, a troupe of Princeton University students opened a musical revue, *Hades' Ladies, or Hell's Belles.* I wanted to go, but the title convinced Mama it was too mature for my eyes and ears. After I promised to leave if anything was "nasty," she allowed me to go to a matinee.

But Mama didn't object to another act, *The Weaver Brothers and Elviry, with Their Great Big Bashful Brother Oswald*, which later appeared on the same stage. Furthermore, she even let me walk on Fifth Street alone after dark to see the act, her subtle acknowledgment I was growing up. I first heard the Missouri hillbillies, three men and one woman, perform on the *Grand Ole Opry* broadcast. All the men played stringed instruments, and Leon Weaver also played a musical saw with a violin bow, which distinguished them among country music groups.

I went to one non-theatrical event at the Arkansas. The Terry Food Stores chose the theater to announce the winner of their grand prize for collecting the most sales receipts for groceries purchased from the chain stores. Employees of the company and their relatives were not eligible for the prize, a gasoline-powered motor scooter, and since Buster was chief checker at the store on Prospect Terrace, I was ineligible, but I discounted that, believing he and Ada Bess were a family separate from ours. I accepted the sales receipts Buster saved when customers left them behind, and entered the contest feeling only slightly guilty.

The winner was to be announced on Saturday morning at the Arkansas, where I joined hundreds of kids and parents in a line extending along Louisiana around the corner to Fifth. Once inside the theater, I found a seat on the balcony, where I could see most of the orchestra and the balconies above mine overflowing with kids, most under twelve and accompanied by parents. The ritual of sorting out which kid held the most receipts was bedlam, but after the dust from the receipt estimates settled, the winner's total sales proved mine piddling in number. The slight total of my ill-gotten receipts kept me honest by default.

The only truly unique seating arrangement in Little Rock movie houses was at the New Theater on Main, between Markham and Second streets. The movie screen was on the back of the wall separating the lobby from the auditorium. The seats were located in the center of the house and the aisles along the outer walls. Movie-goers entered facing the faces of the audience rather than the screen. The New showed the "B," or low-budget, pictures Hollywood produced by the hundreds in the '30s and '40s, chiefly murder mysteries, soap-opera romances, and low comedies, starring second-level actors, like Sally Eilers and Kent Taylor. As an eleven-year-old, I wasn't interested in strictly romantic movies, and went to the New only on a few occasions as Mama's escort in the afternoon.

Around the corner from the New, across Second Street from the Canton Tea Garden restaurant, was the Crescent, the seediest, most rundown movie house in Little Rock. The Crescent was cold in the winter, hot in the summer, and dirty in all seasons. My buddies insisted that rats shined your shoes and bats combed your hair while you watched their double features, all of them cowboy and horror movies with sleazy plots and second- or third-rate performers. It was the perfect atmosphere for Bela Lugosi–Boris Karloff horror pictures and the knockdown, drag-out, farcical silliness of the Three Stooges. I often saw John Wayne in movies at the Crescent, working his way up the scale in unheralded Westerns to major pictures.

But the premier cowboy-movie house was the Roxy, next door to the Western Union Telegraph office, on the southeast corner of Second and Main. The Roxy showed double features, serials, and short comedies (no newsreels, travelogues, or sing-alongs) aimed at kids twelve and under.

I frequently spent entire Saturday afternoons there watching the greatest screen cowboys of the times: Tom Mix, Ken Maynard, Johnny Mack Brown, Hoot Gibson, Bob Steele, Buck Jones, and others. About two hundred boys could be crammed into the narrow theater on Saturdays. Their actions in the movie house often surpassed that on the screen—boys moving up and down the aisles during the screen gun battles, horseback chases, and cattle drives. The front row, within a few feet of the screen, had an undivided, unpadded bench, like a church pew, which may have encouraged the fights simulating the main action on the screen. The theater manager controlled the rowdies only when fights spread to the shallow stage below the screen.

The only romantic gestures boys tolerated at the Roxy were between a cowboy and his horse. No kid willingly suffered the hero kissing a girl at the show's end; only a cowboy nuzzling his horse satisfied him. Girls, who preferred romantic kisses, rarely went to the Roxy.

By the end of that first summer on Spring, we had learned more about the house next door to us. We saw a scrawny black woman living in a shanty in Mrs. Arrington's back yard and assumed she was a full-time maid. But one Saturday morning, she knocked on our back door and asked Mama for work.

Mama asked her name and then invited "Cora" to come in and offered her a Coke. Cora's mouth split wide open with a wild laugh, revealing her missing front teeth and snuff stains on the rest.

She said, "Missus, how 'bout a shot uh whiskey."

Mama, pretending she didn't hear, asked Cora what kind of work she did next door. Whatever Cora mumbled, I saw Mama's disapproval on her face.

After Cora left, Mama suggested that I not play with Claude Holland anymore, and I figured it had something to do with his mother and adult sex.

In our backyard, sitting on the platform I built in the crotch of the big mulberry tree, I could watch Cora crossing in and out of the Arrington house next door every day. Once, as she crossed toward the house, I sang a song to her:

Co-reene, Co-reena, where yuh bin so long?
Ain't been no lovin' since you bin gone.
Oh, Co-reena, where'd yuh stay last night?
Listen here, Corinna, tell me where'd you stay last night?

Stopping with her hands on her hips, she shouted, "Lissen heah, yo little ole white boy, I'm tellin yo momma on yuh, if you don't quit dat makin funna me!"

"I'm not making fun of you, Cora. Nothing's wrong with singing a song with your name. It's a popular one on the radio. Isn't that something?"

However, not long after, my gentle teasing of Cora took a different form. One evening, Mary Goforth and I were standing under the corner streetlamp, watching bats cut, wheel, and dive after insects and swish into chimneys, when big Leroy Horn sauntered up, dragging a long tail of something behind him. He had broken into the vacant medical supply store and stolen bundles of the wide elastic bandages stored there. He wanted to wrap Mary in bandages, just for fun.

"It's too hot! Besides, I don't want your nasty hands near me, Lee-Roy."

When I saw the reels of bandages he had in his hands, I remembered cringing in my theater seat watching Boris Karloff in *The Mummy*. Why not let them wrap me in bandages to scare Cora in her cabin? Mary and Leroy eagerly agreed and wrapped my arms, legs, torso, neck, and head. By the time they encased me in bandages, it was completely dark. Leroy had to lead me to the front of Cora's shanty before he crossed into the alley behind it and scratched on her window screen, moaning.

Cora shouted, "Who dat? Git on way frum he-uh!"

At the front, Mary knocked on Cora's door—tap … tap … tap—as I intoned in my chest, "Cooo-raaa … Cooo-raaa. The mum-mum-mummy has come to see you."

Cora cracked her door to peer out, and I stalked toward her door, seeing only the dim light from her coal oil lamp through my bindings. Her door swung completely open, and a smear of liquid slashed the air, barely missing me—the foul-smelling contents of her slop jar.

She screamed, "You ain't no hants. I knows who you is. I'se gonna call duh po-leese!" She slammed her door.

Leroy, laughing, disappeared, never to accost me again. Mary helped me unwrap my body before she left, though.

I sat on the back porch steps, hoping Cora wouldn't tell Mama. But mostly, I was ashamed for repeating my brother's fault, teasing someone weaker than me.

I didn't tell Mama what I had done; I felt bad enough without her trying to make me cry for harming someone with words or actions. For you see, as I would later decipher, Mama had an attitude about emotional display she wasn't conscious of. She believed human beings are under all sorts of external pressures and have to display their emotions to relieve the pressures. Since her ideal emotions were sympathetic, she believed that weeping proved one's virtuous nature.

In the summer, Mama bought fruits and vegetables from the same black farmer who picked up our garbage in the back alley. She was convinced that she saved money by canning fresh fruits and vegetables, even though the heat in the kitchen nearly made her sick. In fact, her total savings must have been pennies after she first purchased cartons of new Mason jars. But she believed a penny saved is a penny earned.

She was caught in the midst of one of her canning projects when Cousin LaDell, Uncle Albert Honea's daughter, and her husband, Herbert Moody, dropped in unexpectedly from Bald Knob. LaDell, Mama's favorite niece, bore a striking facial resemblance to her—a round face, smiling mouth, bright blue eyes, and black hair—except LaDell was tall and big boned. Herbert, average in height and square shouldered, had sandy hair and a pleasant manner. She was assistant principal at the elementary school where she taught, and he practiced law in Bald Knob, a trading center near Searcy on U.S. Highway 67, twenty-seven miles north of McRae.

As the women prepared lunch, Herbert talked with me in his quiet, restrained manner, which contrasted so much with LaDell's shrill, high-pitched voice and bounce. When I kidded about their hometown matching his father-in-law's head, he laughed, explaining the town's name derived from the low ridge, or bald knob, the town sat on, a landmark that guided early travelers. In the kitchen with LaDell, Mama learned that her brother, Uncle Albert, was moving his grocery business from Beebe to McGehee, Arkansas, which was a surprise.

Daddy arrived home expecting to have lunch in the kitchen, but Mama had set the table in the dining room for our guests. In the conversation at the table, Herbert expressed political opinions: why the Supreme Court declared the NRA unconstitutional, how the Works Progress Administration was succeeding, and the Depression's effects in White

County. He sounded a lot like a politician to me.

LaDell invited Mama and Daddy to take a break by visiting Bald Knob. She wanted them to see the antique furniture and accessories she had collected from white and black farm families, paying them cash in the hard times. When my folks couldn't leave the house untended, LaDell invited me, probably assuming my absence would be a break for them. I expected Mama to say, as usual, "He'll be too much trouble." But she didn't. After lunch, she helped me pack my clothes in the old Gladstone bag for a two-week visit in Bald Knob.

I had traveled in the old Chrysler to White County so often that the countryside was familiar, but I rode in a fancy new car this time. We'd been without one for nearly two years, so I felt like a prince in their shiny black 1935 LaSalle sedan, plush as a king's carriage, with white sidewall tires, silver hubcaps, the trunk enclosed in the car's body, and parking lights on the front fenders. The torpedo ornament on the hood, shaped like a rifle's telescopic sight, seemed to be either a silver bird or a bullet in flight. I relaxed in back as Herbert demonstrated the car's speed and smooth drive.

In Bald Knob, they put me in a room with a full-size bed, with only the headboard touching a wall. It was beside two big open windows that admitted cool breezes and moonbeams that marked out windows of light on the floor. The first night, I lay for a long time in the absolute silence of the small town: no all-night street traffic like home; no loud laughter from next door, or across the street; only the soothing sounds of tiny night peepers in the front and back yards.

The next day, LaDell, who seemed to know every kid in Bald Knob, introduced me to new friends who filled the days with outdoor and indoor games. I attended Sunday School with them and the main church services at the Central Baptist Church, where LaDell was a teacher and a deacon.

The really special event for me came on the weekend before they took me home. At Friday night supper, Herbert said we'd go to something special on Saturday. The next morning, he drove us to Searcy to show me the unusual White County courthouse, which has a ground floor faced with white limestone and second floor faced with red brick.

Before lunch, he drove around the small campus of Harding College of the Christian Church. That afternoon, he drove to Judsonia and parked in lines of cars at the edge of the city park, very near a big brown canvas tent. Herbert left LaDell and me in a crowd that had gathered around a Model T truck to listen to a man calling himself "Doctor Rudasill." He stood in the truck's bed pointing at colored drawings of a human body, explaining how his concoction cured various ailments. He ended his spiel about the remedy with the Indian name, and his big wife climbed on the truck bed to sing as he sold the stuff.

Herbert returned holding tickets to a Toby show in the big brown tent. He said, "Cleveland, you'll laugh at these comics, hate the villains, and love the heroines. I know they're silly looking in make-up and wigs, but I want you to see the musical Gray family and the Gray Sisters, Skeeter Kell, and his comedians. I've seen all the stock companies coming through Judsonia and Searcy since I was a kid your age."

LaDell said Toby shows in tents always came during berry season. We walked on sawdust covering the ground inside the tent and sat on a backless wooden bench, facing a rickety curtained platform stage. The tent was nearly full of adults and children when the scruffy-looking musicians in costumes began playing "Lookie, Lookie, Here Comes Cookie" and "Goodie, Goodie" on piano, bass, violin, guitar, and drum. A drum rolled, and the curtains opened on the first short play. The hero in three short sketches that followed was a red-haired, freckle-faced country boy named Toby. In each scene, the rural characters were suspicious of city characters, made fun of their manners, and won out over them using common sense in simple ways. With my stage-struck antennae out, I imagined myself playing all the parts and singing all the songs, deciding what I'd do the same or differently.

On our Sunday drive back to Little Rock, I repeated the skits' funniest lines, hoping LaDell and Herbert would invite me to Bald Knob again next summer. When we arrived home, Mama hugged and kissed me so much she embarrassed me. It was as if I'd been gone a month instead of two weeks. But I decided 322 Spring was more of a home than any place we'd ever lived.

Before the summer ended, Daddy introduced me to principles of effective selling at furniture stores by taking me with him. He chatted awhile before checking to see what stock was low and allowing managers time to make up their minds before placing orders. Of course, if no one placed orders, he could survey all the furniture stores on Seventh Street in less than a week. Then what would Dad and I do? Except for his infrequent trips to Pine Bluff, Benton, and Hot Springs, his principal territory was Seventh Street.

Most stores had little light at the entrances and in the showrooms. We often walked halfway through a store before seeing anyone, before a bodiless voice said, "Why, here's Al Harrison. Probably thinks we're outta somethin'. Who've you got with you, Al?"

By then, we had reached the back of the store, where the manager, salesmen, and lady bookkeeper spent their time between customers. The bookkeeper was usually a woman with a matronly figure and graying hair who seldom left her desk, which was piled with ledgers, orders, and invoices. All the salesmen spoke as if equal to the owner or manager. After conversations began, the men sat on floor-samples: couches, chairs, or glider-swings at the back of the store.

After setting down Dad's satchel, I stood there until Dad responded to the inquisitive stares. "This is my boy, Cleveland. I brought him along to see what his daddy does for a living."

As the manager and salesman shook my hand, the lady bookkeeper walked from behind her desk and stood beside me. She said, as if I weren't present, "I declare, Mr. Harrison. You can sure tell he's your son, he's your spittin' image."

The owner-manager pointed to a chair. "Take a seat, young man, while your dad and I do business."

"Business" turned out to be hunting or fishing stories, or both, each man outdoing the others relating stories everyone had shared in times past. But no storyteller minded the anticipated and familiar endings, laughing as if hearing them for the first time. After three-quarters of an hour, Dad said, "I think I'll check your stock in the back." And like a hunter on a well-worn trail, he disappeared into the dark reaches of the store to check the inventory.

While Daddy was absent, the owner-manager and bookkeeper asked what grade I was in at school, what I'd been studying, what I wanted to be when I grew up. The bookkeeper said, "If you become a salesman like your daddy, you'll be a good one." The owner-manager nodded agreement, no doubt wondering what else there was to say to a callow school kid.

Daddy returned from the stock room, mentioning short supplies— valves, flue pipes, connections, space heaters—and recommending new items—hassock fans, tabletop radios, refrigerators. The owner-manager would sign orders to replace supplies and accept delivery of a few new items, promising to order more depending upon his sales. I was ready to leave but, like courteous dinner guests, we didn't eat and run; we sat a bit longer, making observations about weather, discussing hunting or fishing trips, before rising and slowly wending alongside the manager to the front door.

We repeated the ritual at several stores before going home for lunch. As we ate, Mama insisted on hearing about our morning. Dad, concentrating on his meal, laughed at a few of my observations and corrected others. After the meal, he smoked a cigarette at the table and then lay down on the couch in the living room for his daily nap. Astonishingly, he fell asleep as his head touched the pillow, lying flat on his back without changing position, and waking precisely twenty minutes later, without any prompt from an alarm clock or Mama.

Observing the way my father earned a living didn't help me understand him any better. There were rarely playful moments like those I enjoyed before he went broke; I suppose that revealed how deeply hurt he was by failing in business. But he never spoke of events that had pained him emotionally, and I didn't know how to draw him out of his reserve. Whether his silences when alone with me were introspective, I never knew. Upright, hardworking, and honorable, he was reserved most of the time in public, even while telling favorite stories to family and friends. My brother, also a taciturn working man, understood something of our father's quiet personality and related to him better than I ever would.

With a tight family budget, we still had to buy items for me to start school in the fall at East Side. To replace clothes I'd outgrown provided a good reason to buy my first long pants, which I had wanted since Jim wore his to East Side at mid-term. Mama said we couldn't afford trousers, that we had money enough for shirts, socks, and shoes. I was still wearing knickers but old enough and big enough for long pants.

The other purchase she mentioned surprised me. We had to *buy* textbooks for subjects, which we never had to do at Rightsell. Mama said, "We'll take your list to Berry's Bookstore, where the old Majestic Theater used to be, between Eighth and Ninth on Main. They specialize in second-hand books for all the schools."

"Oh, Mama, I don't want soiled books other kids wrote all over. Let's go to Allsopp & Chapple, between Third and Fourth on Main, for new ones. That's where Jim bought his books. Old books from Berry's are awful looking."

Mama said, "I don't see what difference pencil marks will make on books."

"Please, Mama. It makes lots of difference to me."

"Well, we'll see what your daddy says when he comes home."

Daddy said exactly what I expected. "If used books have all their pages and the type's readable, they're as good as the new ones from Allsopp & Chapple."

I really shouldn't have faulted anything or anybody. So much good came to me in such a short time on Spring Street, especially our rooming house, which had been our shelter and income until my father and brother found jobs. Mama, working before dawn to late evening every day, seemed happy with the house and our lodgers. Daddy had returned once again to the gentle, soft-spoken father I had always known, working for a man he respected. And my brother and his sweet wife both had good jobs.

Ever since I first appeared in Rightsell's skit in the Centennial pageant on stage at high school and sang on Uncle Mac's radio show, I had looked forward to performing at junior and senior high schools. Living so close to downtown movie houses provided the best of all possible worlds for a boy with my theatrical urges.

Cleveland on a fishing trip while at East Side Junior High School.

CHAPTER 7

Matters Old and New

AS I LAY IN MY pantry bedroom contemplating the coming school day, a sliver of light fell across my face. Mama was starting breakfast in the kitchen and soon wafted into my room, along with aromas of frying bacon and percolating coffee, to suggest wearing my best corduroy knickers for the first day at East Side. Yes, I was going to my brother's old school, which was closer to 322 Spring than either West Side near the Arkansas Baptist Hospital or Pulaski Heights in the far western hills, which a few kids called "pew-nasty heights" while pinching their noses shut.

Eating breakfast with Mama and Daddy, I didn't conceal my trepidation about going to a bigger school, expressing the hope that my first day at East Side would be ordinary. But not even the streetcar ride turned out to be "ordinary." The motorman, stopping at Fifth and Spring, released brake sand on the tracks in rhythm with "shave and a haircut, two bits!" Instead of sitting with a motorman's usual distracted expression, he stood by his stool, smiling and speaking as I climbed aboard.

"Tell old Sparky where you're heading this early morning, young man."

When I rode to and from Rightsell for a year, a streetcar motorman never once spoke or uttered his name. So I dropped my token into the fare box and held on, talking about living downtown and going to junior high school for the first time.

Turning to take a seat, I saw a sign on the vestibule wall of the ancient streetcar: "Do Not Expectorate on the Platform!"—a relic of times when male riders chewed and spit tobacco. Kidding, I said to the motorman, "Mr. Sparky, even before I saw your sign, I didn't expect to rate on a streetcar!"

With a forbearing grin, he said nothing. But when we stopped at East Side, he treated me as an equal again. "See ya same time tomorrow, kid."

Hopping off at Fourteenth and Scott, I looked a block south and saw our old apartment in Professor Rosenberg's yellow duplex.

At East Side's entrance, I walked between tall classic Greek columns through wide double doors into a cavernous foyer smelling of sweet cedar floor sweep and reverberating with echoes of shouting kids scrambling to homerooms. Most boys wore long pants and dress shirts, and the bigger guys, in heavy blue-knit sweaters embossed with giant white and blue school letters, must have been athletes. Little guys like me were dressed in ordinary corduroy knickers and camp shirts.

When I reached 7B Homeroom 208, I saw the wall shelves bulged from floor to ceiling with books. A broad-hipped, square-shouldered woman with short, steel-gray hair was standing behind a big desk on a low platform. I smiled at her and eagerly joined old pals from Rightsell to joke about our new school.

Miss Griffin interrupted us. "Boys, I'm Miss Lois Griffin, your homeroom teacher. Please respect this room as you do your home. Remember, it's a *reading* room, not a *play* room."

Ducking my head, I said quietly, "What she really wants is a *tomb* room."

When every boy snickered in his own way, Miss Griffin, in a solemn, deep voice, asked, "What's so funny, boys?"

United in a treble voice of innocence, we chirped, "Nothing, Miss Griffin!"

It seemed strange that only boys showed up, but Miss Griffin explained that girls had their own homerooms for attendance checks and announcements. We would join them later in our academic classes.

Our very first morning, she marched us in alphabetical order to the balcony of a large auditorium in a separate but attached building that I had first seen as a three-year-old. The shouts and babble of the classes filing in abated when a thin, dour-faced man stepped out of the wings and crossed to the center of a stage wide and deep enough for concerts and plays. At the microphone, he introduced himself.

"I'm S. C. Swearingen, the principal, and I want to introduce your teachers, if they will stand when their names are called."

When he named "Ernest J. Gold," a lanky, older teacher awkwardly leaped up and loped toward the stage, triggering laughs and scattered applause among the students. His scrawny face beaming beneath his shiny bald head, he encouraged us to develop *spizzerrinkdom* in support of East Side's academic, artistic, and athletic activities. Whatever that unusual word meant, his own big gestures and florid terms proved the *spizz* in his *rinkdom.*

Joe Hart, the boy next to me, said, "I hear old Mr. Gold teaches science and keeps detention hall after school."

Venturing a joke, I said, "Surely, 'Old Gold' must allow smoking there."

"As sure as I see hair on top of his bald pate," Joe snapped back. We became instant buddies.

Arriving early in homeroom each morning, I joshed around with old and new friends from Rightsell, Parham, and Kramer before Miss Griffin's arrival. I got to school early because our family had been up since dawn so Mama could begin household chores and Daddy could open Brandon Stove Company. Joe arrived at school early, too, because his father, a plumber, made early morning calls. And Boykin Pyles's father opened Bush-Caldwell Sporting Goods every day. Both Joe and Boykin, a recent transfer from North Little Rock, were unpretentious and fun; our camaraderie and the regular change of classes made going to junior high school far more interesting than elementary school.

But neither Joe nor Boykin joined me in music class, my first class each day. I didn't miss them, though, for my eyes and mind were glued on Miss Helen Romine, who had replaced Miss Whaley as my most beautiful teacher. Gazing at her alabaster skin and shiny black pageboy as she directed the glee club, I hardly glanced at the sheet music. In my mind, her image replaced that of Lily Pons, the diminutive Metropolitan opera singer pictured on the album covers of the opera recordings she played in class.

Through her recordings, Miss Romine introduced the emotions of romance, pain, exhilaration, and triumph in serious music by American orchestras and singers, like Arturo Toscanini and the New York Philharmonic, Leopold Stokowski and the Philadelphia Orchestra; and Lauritz Melchior, Helen Traubel, Lawrence Tibbett, Grace Moore, Marian Anderson, and Todd Duncan. Alas, my romance with Miss Romine would end after Christmas when she retired and married.

In library class, my second class each day, we were free to read any book we chose. Miss Griffin, despite her severe appearance, kindly searched for books to fit my expanding interests. I fell into a delirium of reading anything and everything in print: morning and evening newspapers, front page to classifieds; magazines at drugstores and newsstands, including advertisements; placards above trolley windows; and instructions and ingredients on washing powders, cereals, and condiments.

Engrossed first by Joseph Altsheler's adventure books for boys, I imagined myself the young hero tutored by a native Indian boy in the lore and aboriginal ways of American Indians. In "the virgin wilderness" of locust, mulberry, and sycamore trees in our backyard and on the "plains" of the nearby empty lots of razed houses, I explored the frontier. Wearing Daddy's fringed hunting jacket and Buster's brown canvas slacks (buckskins), I wandered our downtown neighborhood on Saturdays, BB gun in hand and homemade bow across my shoulder, silently treading "woodland trails," never snapping a twig or rustling a leaf to warn enemies or wild animals.

Ending my treks walking beside surprised pedestrians on Saturdays, I ventured onto the Seven Seas when Miss Griffin recommended *The Collected Poems of John Masefield*, and I memorized the three stanzas of "Sea-Fever."

Sea images also led me to read Charles Nordhoff's and James Norman Hall's trilogy: *Mutiny on the Bounty, Men against the Sea,* and *Pitcairn's Island.* When I perfected an impression of Charles Laughton, as Captain Bligh in *Mutiny on the Bounty,* I performed it for any willing listener. In the guise of an eighteenth-century English gob, I imagined a carefree life in the thatch huts of Tahiti and on Pitcairn Island in the South Pacific.

Completing a thousand pages at sea the first semester, I landed on a short peninsula of dry land in the second, Harold Kellock's *Houdini: His Life Story,* which taught me how the escape artist and magician exposed fake claims made by spiritual mediums. I mastered the trick two sisters invented to convince their family and visitors that "beings from the spirit world" inhabited their home. When Harry Houdini exposed them, he found the sisters, sleeping together in a solid oak bed, had snapped their toes against the thick footboard under the covers, making resonant thuds that seemed to have no apparent source.

Attempting their trick on the library floor, I snapped my toe joints against the inner soles of my shoes, thumping as the girls had done, without revealing the sound's origin. I knew I achieved the proper effect when Miss Griffin lifted her head with a quizzical expression, and walked down the aisles, listening. Before she reached my row, I stopped, and she did, too. Thereafter, when bored in any class, I simply snapped my toes inside my shoes and watched the teacher's head bob.

In addition to Library, I had English, history, and math. Miss Mellie Martin, a maiden-lady English teacher, her light brown hair in a bun and wearing no facial make-up, wore ankle-length dresses with lace collars held by cameo pins. She taught both composition and literature in her gentle fashion, introducing us to Sir Walter Scott's poetry, which inspired my first patriotic recitations:

Breathes there the man with soul so dead
Who never to himself hath said,
This is my own, my native land!

The day we finished reading *The Lay of the Last Minstrel*, Boykin asked me, "What does a minstrel look forward to after his *Last Lay*?"

I didn't understand the racy allusion, so he delightedly revealed the sexual meaning of *lay*, another word I added to my unspoken, secret vocabulary. Boykin, as unusual as his name, was a whirling dervish of funny expressions, word distortions, and jokes. For example, "gourd head on," for "go ahead," and his watchword "allah-paw-longee," a call of salutation and recognition that spread among all the guys in our small gang.

But he was as subdued in history/civics class as I. Our teacher, Miss Corinne McMahan, of Scots and Presbyterian ancestry like him, demanded our full attention. Slight of height and weight, with auburn hair bobbed and banged, she had pale, freckled skin, and wore orange lipstick to harmonize with the earth colors of her dresses, skirts, and blouses. To match her wardrobe, she wrote with a peacock-green Parker fountain pen in her large, rounded handwriting in brown or green ink. If someone's hand, male or female, clean or grimy, touched the surface of her desk after we had all been warned never to touch it, she whipped an immaculate white cloth from her center desk drawer and wiped the entire top. Mr. Clean's female equal zealously guarded her antiseptic citadel!

Until I went to East Side, arithmetic was simple as a song for me, but mathematics proved a far more complex tune I didn't sing in equal harmony with three different teachers: Mr. Clayton Elliott in seventh grade and Misses Irvine and Cobb in eighth and ninth. Mr. Elliott, erect and muscular, possessed the square jaw of Dick Tracy and had brilliantined hair, parted in the middle, like Chester Morris in the movies. Always in handsome suits, starched dress shirts, colorful ties, and polished shoes, he was the fashion plate for faculty men. But his sartorial splendor captured my attention in his class, making his math lessons less comprehensible. Miss

Irvine, lean and elegant, and Miss Cobb, chunky and formless, though less memorable than Mr. Elliott, posed the same mathematical word-problems, the real puzzles I struggled with.

Physical games and sports I liked, but I disliked gym class. After mastering the combination of my first lock (turning the dial the proper number of times and stopping at three different numbers), I approached gym class, spic and span, only to cringe facing the tangy odors of sweat, urine, and disinfectants and hearing the clanging of metal doors on lockers and shouts reverberating under the room's low ceiling. Changing clothes under the pale, naked bulbs in recessed overhead pockets still exposed you to boys who spied on others and would see my birthmark.

I asked, "Why are some boys wearing a stretchy belt and tight cup under their shorts?"

Laughing, Joe said, "Protecting their family jewels!" Only recently turned twelve, I hadn't yet felt a need to protect my "jewels" with a jockstrap.

Once we were on the basketball court, Mr. Whitten, the slender, middle-aged coach, lined us up to shoot baskets, which stirred huzzahs for shots sunk, groans for misses, and ridicule if you missed the backboard. Then Coach formed two teams for each basket. The nearest I'd ever been to a basketball was playing dodge ball at Rightsell, so I chose to guard the goal. I ran, leaped, and bounced with my skinny arms outstretched until Coach's whistle sent us to shower in soapless, cold water. Walking in puddles on the slick concrete floors, we sat on a wet bench, dampening our shorts, buttocks, and enthusiasm for gym before going to the next class.

The crowning blow of gym was contracting itch. Taking a hot tub bath one night, I itched all over as a red rash sprouted between my fingers, toes, crotch, and arm pits. After consulting Daddy, Mama adopted her role as home-grown Hippocrates, mixing a concoction of bacon grease and sulfur powder to rub on my torso, finger and toe creases, wrists, and waistline folds. To reach the scabies mites under my nails, she applied the mix with toothpicks. But before she reached my buttocks, genitals, and belly button, I insisted on applying the salve with neither toothpicks nor her presence.

When I complained of smelling like a wet match head, Mama said, "Cleveland, you have to be covered from neck to toes to kill the little mites."

What a pain! I took two baths a day for three days, until Daddy declared me cured. Fed up with gym class, I blamed my itch on a stinky guy who changed clothes beside me, even though Daddy said the boy's lack of personal hygiene wasn't the cause. Nor was wearing damp gym suits, storing sour clothes in lockers, rubbing against boys with body odor, or drying on soggy towels, all of which I suggested.

Besides gym, first-year boys had manual training, just as first-year girls had home economics. I chose woodwork and metalwork, because we had no car so I didn't need to know about auto mechanics. Nevertheless, the greasy motor block and bare car chassis mounted on a rack above an oily swatch of cement floor in the room next to our basement metalwork shop aroused my curiosity, faintly reminding me of viewing cadavers in the formaldehyde pit at medical school.

Our woodwork teacher, Mr. H. T. Ziegler—wider and thicker but no taller than seventh-grade boys—demonstrated shop safety with both manual and automatic tools before assigning our projects. Along with everyone else, I had to construct a *taboret*, the French word for a small, cylindrical stool without arms or back. Until I came along, Mr. Ziegler probably assumed boys with two hands and average intelligence could cut wood squares and strips and attach them with nails to make a stool. I certainly thought so.

After meticulously measuring and drawing pencil lines on the wood, I sawed along the lines precisely and assembled the pieces with the prescribed nails. My completed *taboret* looked perfect—that is, if you wanted a miniature replica of the Leaning Tower of Pisa. How'd that happen? I sawed the legs the same length, so why wouldn't it balance? Measuring again, I found one leg infinitesimally longer and shortened it. But the stool still wobbled. After more sawing, rasping, and sanding, the stool legs and Mr. Ziegler's patience were both shorter.

Mama placed the teetering *taboret*, topped by a potted fern, under the dining room window beside our lone wicker rocking chair, where it was hardly noticeable.

After shop each day, I was relieved and happy to recuperate in study hall. Everyone had at least one study hall each day with Miss Jewell Stone, who was called "miss" like most woman teachers, whether married or single. Short and gray-haired, she was probably the smallest and oldest teacher (male or female) at East Side, based on the evidence of her trembling lips and hands. Her duty was maintaining order in a large classroom packed with teenagers whispering, passing notes, tapping feet, drumming desk tops, and napping face down or with heads on forearms.

Miss Stone's only power, besides her piercing gaze and grumpy presence, was a slender baton, a long, unsharpened lead pencil with a metal extension and rubber eraser at the end. Carrying the wand in her tiny hand, she approached offenders from the rear and snapped their crowns sharply before bestowing her verbal reprimand. The punishment might be a change of seats, a visit to the principal in the main office, or Miss Stone's *coup de grace*, condemnation to detention hall after school with Mr. Gold. She punished me for my tendency to talk a lot during study hall, which she perceived as a lack of self-control, only by giving me demerits for citizenship on my report card every six weeks—gentle mercy for my otherwise smiling, courteous behavior.

I loved reading, and one of Mama's good friends from Beebe lent me books other than textbooks, a luxury our family couldn't afford. When Aunt Nanka and Uncle Dick Watson first invited us to visit them on East Fourth Street, near where my parents lived on Sherman Street in 1917, Daddy wasn't eager to go; he didn't like Uncle Dick. We walked to their house, where a large, gruff-voiced, bulldog-faced man, accompanied by a feisty white Spitz named Trixie, greeted us. He took us to their family room to meet Aunt Nanka, a tiny woman with black eyes and hair and exceptionally white skin, who introduced a replica of herself, their daughter, Nan.

Their two-story home of many rooms had a wide front porch with a swing, rocking chairs, and the first Hunter ceiling fan I'd seen outside a bus or train station. Their back porch, wide as the house, was enclosed by floor-to-ceiling latticework. The surprise on the back porch was a five-gallon glass bottle of Roc-Arc spring water in a stand. I was so taken by the setup, I drank paper cups of water repeatedly, dividing my time between the cooler and the bathroom.

For me, the best things in their house were the books that lay about—in bookcases and in piles—and stacks of magazines: *Liberty, Colliers, Look, Modern Romances*, and *True Romances*. On a lark one afternoon, I made up inclusive titles for their popular detective and movie magazines, combining the adjectives used: *The Inside-True-Real-Daring-Startling Detective Stories* and *The Photo-Picture-Play, Modern-Silver-Screen, Movie Life-Mirror* Stories. Recognizing detective magazines as trash preceded recognizing movie magazines as such because of my interest in acting. Aunt Nanka's collected works of Mark Twain filled many empty spaces in my mind. My favorite books—*The Adventures of Tom Sawyer, The Adventures* of *Huckleberry Finn*, *The Prince and the Pauper*, and *A Connecticut Yankee in King Arthur's Court*—were adapted for movies at the time, which I also loved.

Leaving for school one morning, I saw moving vans in front of Mrs. Hightower's, and they were still there in the afternoon. When I asked Mildred at Wimpy's Hamburgers, who always knew what was happening in the neighborhood, she was cleaning out her caravan, preparing to have it towed away the next day.

"Raymond Rebsamen Motors at Third bought Hightower's property to enlarge his lot."

"Where are you moving your cafe to, Mildred?"

"Across the street by the big tenement. Say, Cleveland, do you think your dad will sell that counter you say he has in your backyard?"

"I don't know, Mildred. But I'll ask him at supper and let you know."

Several days later, the movers at Hightower's finished loading the furniture, and a wrecking crew began the dismantling, revealing the Victorian house's inner structure and materials. They removed many parts intact, stacking them at the back of the lot to sell for use in other buildings: doors, window frames, stair steps, exterior clapboard, studs, railings, mantelpieces, gas and water pipes, tubs, sinks, and plumbing fixtures. Watching our neighbors and their house disappear was sad, even though I had never entered the house or met any of the roomers.

The crew dismantling churned the soft, dry dirt underneath the house into deep, clinging mud mixed with wood lathe and plaster. A worker explained that the lathe, nailed horizontally between the studs, had held the plaster covering the walls. So workers destroying the inner walls left piles of loose plaster and broken strips that were difficult to walk across without stepping on pieces of lathe.

The white plaster that was churned-up in the mud gave me an idea. I saw Clark Gable, Loretta Young, and Jack Oakie in *Call of the Wild*, which featured Buck, a heroic St. Bernard dog pulling a heavy sled. Nailing lathe runners on an orange crate I copied Clark Gable, shouting, "Mush!" as I pushed the sled through "Alaskan snow." But running through the mud and plaster riddled with lathe strips full of nails, I wasn't cautious. Something sharp stuck my foot! I lifted my foot to step forward, and a piece of lathe rose with my foot! A nail had pierced my shoe sole and ball of my foot. Balancing with my "ski poles," I held my injured foot above the street and crossed to our house.

Luckily, Daddy was home, for Mama was beside herself. He pulled the nail out, washed my foot in soapy water, doused it in alcohol, and poured turpentine into the puncture to prevent lock jaw. Miss McMahan would have praised him for a pioneer remedy that prevented infection. I was pleased that Mama had no reason to give me a laxative, and she was pleased no more gobs of mud would be tracked in the front hall to the back porch.

I then made my orange-crate sled the body of a race car like the one I saw in the movie *The Crowd Roars*, with Jimmy Cagney and Joan Blondell. I removed the lathe runners and nailed two-by-fours at opposite ends of the box for axles and attached old roller skates for wheels. The two-by-four at the front pivoted on a center bolt with a rope attached at the right and left ends for steering. But my race car turned out to be a drag. Only by pushing, pulling, and scooting did I circle the block once, attracting the puzzled stares of workers and pedestrians. As the only boy playing on the sidewalks in the neighborhood, I was a curiosity.

We were closer than ever to the Second Baptist Church and rarely missed services. Ever since I was five, Sunday school, church, Royal Ambassadors, and revivals had been regular parts of my life. When Marshall Measels and Bob Halley, my best church friends from Pulaski Heights, turned twelve as I did, Mrs. Langston, our Sunday school teacher, persuaded us to join the church together. We had done everything together at church for years, including sitting in the balcony looking down upon Dr. Waller, the choir, and the congregation. So, when Dr. Waller issued his weekly invitation to join the church, we descended side by side from our perch, walked down the aisle, faced the congregation, and professed our faith in Jesus Christ as our personal savior, a commitment our parents expected from our births.

The next week after professing, we were prepared for baptism by Dr. Waller. He asked us about our individual beliefs. Did I believe the Bible is God's word? Did I understand I was a sinner? Did I understand the significance of being baptized? I answered him sincerely and positively, for, growing up in the Baptist Church, I accepted church beliefs without questioning.

Dr. Waller said, "Sunday, your total immersion in water will signify to others your personal faith in Christ's death, burial, and resurrection."

That Sunday, we brought our baptism outfits. Just before Dr. Waller ended his sermon, we quietly retired behind the baptismal font and changed into our white shirts and slacks, preparing to be dunked into the baptismal pool one at a time. I crossed through the curtain first, stepping into the icy water of the pool up to my waist with a pale idyllic scene of land, sky, and a single tree painted on the font wall behind me. Oh, how I wished I had relieved myself before entering the water!

Dr. Waller, in a stiff white suit, guided me to the middle of the pool, clasped his right hand over my mouth and nose, and with his left hand behind my neck dipped my head and shoulders completely beneath the water. He pronounced, loud enough for the congregation and me in the gurgle of water to hear, "I baptize you in the name of the Father, the Son, and the Holy Ghost."

As he lifted me upright again, I realized he was much stronger for his age than I expected. I pulled the curtain aside to exit and allowed Bob Halley to enter.

Other than being cold and dripping wet, I had the same warmth that I always harbored in my head and heart for Jesus Christ and the Lord, loving them with all my heart, mind, soul, and strength ever since Mama first instructed me and I observed her behavior. But I wondered, after what I had just undergone, if I should have deeper or different feelings.

Retiring to change into our Sunday-best clothes, we looked like bedraggled white rats, even dear old Dr. Waller, whose hair I saw mussed for the first time. Marshall's hair stood like quills on a porcupine's rear, and Bob's long, black, wavy locks hung in his face like a Hassidic Jew's.

Once dry, we returned to the sanctuary to stand proudly beside our parents facing the congregation. The older church members came forward and grasped our hands and patted our backs, acting as though we had been transformed into minor saints in a few wet moments.

Daddy's business life entered a different phase, too. Mr. Brandon of Brandon Stove Company bestowed a company car upon him, a new blue Chevrolet coupe, with a space for stove samples and catalogs behind the front seat. Daddy would no longer have to walk Seventh Street but would add Pine Bluff and Hot Springs to his sales territory. Soon after getting the car, Daddy built a dog run in the back yard on the Arrington-house side and shopped for a dog in hunting magazine ads. The night he bought a hunting dog from a breeder in Shelby County, Tennessee, he made a long-distance phone call, speaking so loudly that roomers in the farthest room heard his arrangements.

Then, with Mr. Brandon's permission, he drove the Chevy to Tennessee late Friday afternoon and returned Sunday with Joe, a rich chestnut-red setter, whose aristocratic air didn't look promising at all. Even though Daddy took care of Joe's health—shots, bathing, and exercise—Mama was his daily caretaker. Every day, she parceled his dry feed into his dish and filled his water bowl, but as she did it Joe growled and curled his upper lip. Lying on his stomach, his head raised and his front paws crossed, he gazed at her in regal splendor, rumbling deep in his chest.

Mama, in a quiet voice, said, "Now, old Joe, you don't need to growl at me."

As Daddy's sales increased, he began going hunting for game again and assumed duties of "chef for Saturday evening." He prepared quail breasts and squirrels, whose little naked bodies aroused more sympathy than appetite in Mama and me; finding crunchy buckshot in them did not enhance meals either. Daddy's other specialty was battering and frying huge fresh oysters from Food Palace.

If Daddy didn't cook on Saturday night, he took Mama and me to Tom and Andrew's Restaurant for ham sandwiches—thick slices of sweet baked ham, garnished with slaw, mayonnaise, and mustard—or spaghetti and meatballs dripping with a delicious tomato sauce. It gave Daddy a chance to drink a bottle of Budweiser beer without Mama frowning. We sat at the end of the dining room with a view of *Custer's Last Stand*, courtesy of Anheuser-Busch, on the wall.

The most memorable Saturday night at the restaurant involved more than taste buds. As usual, I was sent to place our order at the refrigerated counter in one corner of the restaurant. Waiting for the order in front of the counter to pick up our sandwiches, I looked down and saw a folded monetary bill on the floor. Without unrolling the bill to determine its denomination, I stuck it in my pocket and carried our plates to the table. I examined what turned out to be a twenty-dollar bill! My parents, in their adult wisdom, advised asking the counterman if anyone had reported a loss without identifying what I found, and leaving my name and phone number. After nibbling my sandwich and sipping my Coke, I tiptoed home on tenterhooks, expecting a phone call for its retrieval at any moment, but the hall phone never rang.

Daddy said, "If you showed that bill to the counterman, he would claim it." The next time we celebrated on Saturday night at Tom and Andrew's, dinner was on me.

Another special eating place on Saturday nights was the Shack Barbecue at West Seventh and Marshall, practically part of the State Capitol grounds. Once Daddy had parked in the lot, I went inside to order two sandwiches each for Daddy and me, one for Mama, and bottled Cokes for all. Ordering, waiting, and picking up the sandwiches was an aural and olfactory treat. The knives chopping hunks of barbecue pork and heads of cabbage for the sandwiches sounded like a house a-building, and the aromas of the juicy lean meat and hot, brown, vinegary sauce emanating from the kitchen set my gastric juices flowing. Because there was so little room to eat inside the Shack, my mouth watering, I carried out the tray of sandwiches and Cokes and attached it to Daddy's side window, like a carhop. In the winter, the car windows fogged over, and in the summer, the rolled-down windows admitted mosquitoes, but we didn't mind. I sat in the sample space behind the front seat so everyone had elbow room to eat.

At school in the spring semester of 1937, Mr. Nolan Minton replaced Mr. Ziegler as my manual training teacher, concentrating on metalwork, teaching us to read patterns, cut tin with tin shears, and use a soldering iron heated over a Bunsen burner to join pieces. I chose to make a kitchen match holder for Mama's gas cook stove, which had no pilot light. Fashioning pieces of metal required strength and wore blisters and abrasions on my hands. Mama hung the finished match container, shaped like a fireplace with an open hearth at the bottom for burnt match sticks, by the gas burners and oven.

My second project was a twine box shaped like a cat's head. I drew the outline of the head and the box for a ball of string on a tin sheet to cut out. Bending the tin along trace lines to form the box required strength I didn't know I had. Then heating the solder to weld the cat's head to one side of the tin box burned blisters on my fingers, which made drilling a hole for the cat's mouth difficult. I painted the cat's head white, eyes blue, and mouth red, and pulled the loose end of a ball of string out the cat's mouth. Mama had a string holder she didn't need and put it in an obscure spot on a back-porch shelf. Her judgment didn't pain me; I had completed manual training satisfactorily.

As my understanding and appreciation of music deepened in class, listening to recordings and singing in the glee club, I wanted to whistle, hum, or sing in manual training, but it wasn't permitted. Even though East Side had a marching band and orchestra, I chose the glee club because others seemed to appreciate my singing voice. Miss Romine's replacement, Mrs. Cleta Scott, a short, blonde, athletic woman who directed the glee club and coached girls' sports, held tryouts at the beginning of spring semester for a musical version of Robert Louis Stevenson's *Treasure Island.*

Even though I was the smallest boy auditioning, I wanted the part of Jim Hawkins, a young boy who befriends an old pirate. Even though I was the only boy who spoke the dialogue conversationally, Mrs. Scott cast Melbourne Miller, who was slightly taller, for Jim and gave me the role of the pirate's mascot, Wee Willie Winkie, a little Scotsman who laughed a lot when he wasn't whining to go home to his mother. I was the only boy who could laugh believably on cue. Wee Willie is not in Stevenson's novel, but his laughter to cover his insecurity provided comic relief for the play. I solved intuitively at the first reading the technical acting problem of laughing believably on cue. At rehearsals, I discovered that *laughing* is only an expulsion of air while forming an *h* before vowel sounds—*a, e, i, o, u*—holding the mouth in different shapes.

When I practiced laughing at home, Daddy asked, "What the devil does that boy find so darned funny, Floy?"

At rehearsals, Mrs. Scott approved the movements and gestures I devised without her direction: "Yes, that's exactly what Wee Willie would do."

Her approval of the ideas spontaneously springing into my mind built my confidence. In fact, I seemed to sense what the other actors should do, too. Without her instructing me, I studied the script for characterization clues, a concept that had never occurred to me acting a part in grammar school.

As usual, the mothers of the cast members, except for mine this time, made costumes from material they purchased, using patterns Mrs. Scott furnished. The mothers cut costumes from colored sateen, a smooth, glossy cotton material, and constructed wide-brimmed tri-corner hats, patent leather belts, and silver foil shoe and belt buckles from a variety of other fabrics. But in my case, Mama took my parking fees and bought a cheap plaid skirt, black tie, and knee-high black stockings at Sterling Department Store for my costume, and borrowed a black beret (or tam) from Nell Watson. For the *sporran*, the fur pouch at the front of a Scotsman's kilt, Mama hung a new cotton floor mop below my waist.

The week before we performed the operetta, I was sent to Mrs. Scott, who had me put on my operetta costume to accompany Coach Jess Matthews to Little Rock High School to announce the dates of our show at their Friday assembly. I had never been close to Mr. Matthews before, and the size of his large body and big, square head surprised me. He told me I was supposed to laugh and dance the highland fling as I did in the show.

Walking on stage to face hundreds of expectant faces, I felt short of breath, not from fear but excitement. I followed Mr. Matthews onto the huge stage and stood beside him at the microphone as he talked. I laughed at the ends of his sentences, falling into a paroxysm of laughter when he finished his speech.

Standing back, he pointed at me and said into the microphone, "Well, that's what'll happen to you if you see the show!"

After that statement, I flung myself into the highland fling, light and agile as I could be. Stopping, I looked at the audience, laughing as if they were the joke. The audience was silent. But I continued laughing and cavorting until they broke into laughter and stamped their feet. Mr. Matthews and I turned and crossed the wide stage accompanied by applause. I wished my family had been there, but Mama and Daddy never attended my performances. Going back to East Side, Mr. Matthews lifted my spirits by suggesting I go out for track.

Though small for twelve, I didn't need any more encouragement. I was determined to be on the East Side track team like my brother, to wear the blue and white uniform of the East Side Hornets. I was convinced I'd be chosen even though East Side teams on the field, track, or court were bigger and better developed physically than boys of the same age at West Side and Pulaski Heights. I mentioned this difference to Mrs. Whitten in the office, and she said many boys dropped out of school during the first of the Depression, returning older and more physically mature when their family finances improved.

Light, quick, and fast enough for sprints or relays, I was so sure of my running ability that I used parking fees to buy expensive spiked track shoes from Boykin's father, Mr. Noah Pyles, at Bush-Caldwell Sporting Goods on Main. Joe Hart and I practiced in City Park before the season started, learning to run in the spike-toed, heel-less track shoes. After a few weeks, Joe also ran hurdles on the track, as eager as I to be on the team. One afternoon, though, exhausted from his efforts, he straddled a hurdle, landing on the most tender spot a boy has. As he lay on the ground in pain, the older guys teased him about becoming a "gelding" and "eunuch," words I didn't yet know. Happily, Joe wasn't permanently injured.

His accident escaped my mind until I got home. Mama was talking to Mrs. Hart, who had called her after Joe's accident. Mama, fearing I'd have a similar accident and be injured, ordered me to turn in my track suit and sell my track shoes, reacting as strongly as I'd ever seen her. Even though I asked Daddy to intervene, he didn't. He said Mama was undergoing a physical change, called "menopause," and was too disturbed to change her mind. I didn't understand but didn't protest.

Overnight, my athletic ambition changed to the business of sports—selling drinks, candy, and popcorn at football, basketball, and softball games in their seasons. I had already assisted lithe Lucille Beaumont and buxom Vivian Beauchamp selling drinks and popcorn at basketball games, where I entertained coworkers and customers with imitations and wisecracks that came to me so naturally, I never resisted them. Lucille had a long, smiling face, framed by brown hair, and tended to bend her figure into angles laughing, which delighted me. Blonde and curvaceous Vivian, who lived near me between Fourth and Fifth on shady Arch Street, laughed at anything I said or did, persnickety only about the correct pronunciation of her last name—"Beachum, *not* Bow-Champ." Teasing and kidding them before halftime at basketball games was my warm-up for customers to come, razzing and getting acquainted with East Siders, popping Coke and Nehi bottle caps, and scooping buttered popcorn into bags.

When summer came, so did my cousins, Uncle Cleve's teenage sons, Ralph and David Honea. They drove from Beebe for the day to buy magic tricks at a specialty shop in the 200 block on Main Street. As usual, they stopped at our house to play tricks on their much-loved, naive Aunt Floy, the perfect victim for any trick. They purchased Bakelite puddles of spilled ink and dog excrement, cloth-and-spring snakes in cans, rubber chickens and turkeys, chattering sets of teeth, and packets of itching and sneezing powders. Mama grabbed a rag to sponge fake ink off the table, and gasped, hand over mouth, when a coiled snake in a basket uncoiled in her direction. I was never sure whether Mama was fooled by their childish tricks or if she played along to please them.

My Honea cousins lived with their mother and her second husband on a farm high on a hill at the junction of Highway 65 and State Road 64 to Conway, west of Beebe. We visited their white, two-story house, with its pretentious southern columns, only one time. I didn't see inside the house because, when we reached the top of the hill, Mama sent me to play with my cousins while she and Daddy talked with Aunt Naomi, Uncle Cleve's widow, the daughter of Dr. W. E. Abington, a state senator in the Arkansas legislature for years. Mama's sister-in-law had been her dearest friend throughout their early years in Beebe and McRae.

My Honea cousins thought chasing me down the hillside, like hounds after a fox, without letting me know the destination, was entertaining. I realized when we reached the farm's large pond that I should have stayed on the porch. The boys, after stripping off their clothes and diving into the pond, invited me to do the same. With no swimsuit and a genuine fear of water, I watched them cavort in the murky water and wander around naked until Daddy hollered we were leaving.

Their older brother Charles was Buster's age and Grandpa's favorite. He had joined the army for want of anything else to do, but restless and without my brother's work ethic, he soon disliked the service and asked Grandpa to buy him out. In the pre–World War II army, there was a unique option that permitted an enlisted man to buy his discharge for $120 after twelve months' good time, no questions asked. Grandpa couldn't wait to satisfy Charles's wish.

Ralph and David were good enough not to put itching powder on Mama or me during their visit. Fortunately, my cousins' visits were brief and infrequent. I always wished Jimmy Elliott lived nearby; he'd outdo them.

Later that summer, I passed their house on the hill again on my way to Beebe to spend two weeks with Big Daddy and Grandma Harrison. Daddy drove me to the bus station on Markham, across from the Marion Hotel. The bus stopped in front of a drugstore in Beebe, and Big Daddy and a friend were there in a car to pick me up. I expected a long drive to Big Daddy's farm, but we drove only a few blocks from downtown to a cottage.

I hadn't known that Big Daddy was in poor health. Tall, smiling Grandma was on the porch to welcome me. She carried my suitcase inside, set the bag down in a bedroom, and asked what snack I wanted.

Big Daddy, following us, suggested she give me "peanut butter and soda pop." Grandma laughed at his joshing and served fresh cherry juice, my favorite.

My grandfather, a garrulous and entertaining conversationalist, enjoyed jokes and had opinions on any subject. At well over six feet tall and more than two hundred pounds, his appearance and manner were commanding. If, beneath his forelock of coarse, iron-gray hair, he fixed his piercing eyes and unwavering gaze upon you, he seemed threatening. And his powerful baritone voice could drive mules, command farm workers, and control children, near or far. Even though he never held elected office, White County Democrats sought his opinions on issues and candidates.

My grandma, Florence Virginia Nations Harrison, equaled my grandfather in every respect. A sturdy, good-humored woman, tall as his chin, with broad shoulders and erect back, her assured presence and energy calmed Big Daddy's high temper. Like a frontier woman, she lost children in childbirth, raised ten, and cared for her family—cleaning house, washing and ironing clothes, tending garden, milking cows, churning butter, feeding chickens and pigs, canning fruits and vegetables, baking bread, and fixing meals for the family and farm workers.

When I asked Big Daddy about my father as a boy, he described all their children. Their first three babies died at birth; their fourth child, Earl, came a year later, and my father was born in Antioch, Arkansas, on January 12, 1892. He began formal schooling at four at the private Maple Springs School and transferred to Antioch public schools in 1897, just before the Harrison family moved to Beebe, where his four younger brothers and three younger sisters were born.

Grandma's story of my father's big appetite sounded like Dickens's *Oliver Twist*, who asked for "more." She told of Daddy visiting an uncle and aunt on a small farm in the backwoods, near Reno in White County, where he learned to ask for only what he was capable of eating. After eating a big supper, he begged for a biscuit with butter and sorghum molasses, but his "eyes were bigger than his stomach," and he ate only half the biscuit. At breakfast the next morning, his aunt served him the same plate with the half biscuit encapsulated in butter and sorghum.

The next morning when I got up, my grandparents had eaten breakfast and left mine in the dining-room safe, a cabinet with metal doors punched with a country tulip design. While I ate, Grandma carried a bowl of hot water into her and Big Daddy's bedroom.

Big Daddy jovially growled, "Finish breakfast, boy, and come see how a man shaves."

From the door, I saw he was sharpening a straight razor with a leather strop like the barber's. Daddy and Buster shaved with safety razors, tissue-paper-thin steel blades in a holder. Big Daddy sat at a table with a bowl of water on his right and a standup mirror in front of him, dipping and circling his shaving brush in an ornate soap cup. Peering at his image over his glasses, he lathered his coarse, grizzled beard. While his beard soaked in shaving cream, he stropped the razor again, then applied more lather. Laying the blade flat on his cheek, he stroked his whiskers, which were stiff as the wire in a scrub brush and rasped like sandpaper sliding off.

After wiping soap off his face, he took a hypodermic needle and vial of clear liquid from the dresser drawer.

"What're you gonna do with that big needle, Big Daddy?"

"Take an insulin shot for my sugar diabetes, grandson."

He pulled his shirttail out of his trousers, pinching a fleshy fold of his large stomach between his thumb and index finger before stabbing it with the hypodermic needle.

"Ooh, Big Daddy, I'll bet that hurts."

"Not if you do it as often as I do—every day."

Even as a kid, I sensed the pathos of his once strong body now dependent on help.

Big Daddy warned, "Boy, if you're going to eat Grandma's good meals and listen to my best stories, you'll have to earn your keep driving our Bossy and May to pasture."

He sent me out to guide the cows to pasture. I stopped at the lot gate facing the two cows. Both were taller than me and gazed so directly into my eyes that I hesitated to make another move. Grandma, praising the obedient bovines for following their set routine, urged me to open the fence gate. The cows, their huge, round eyes still set on me, ambled past and turned down a lane between high hedges. Feeling more secure watching them amble away, I fell in behind them. At that very moment, the cows began gathering speed, loping down one side of the lane while leaning against the hedge. Assuming they'd broken loose, I ran ahead of them to prevent their running into the street.

Big Daddy, on the front porch, laughed loudly enough at my bewilderment to be heard a country mile. "Ha, ha, whoop-de-do! Boy howdy! You should see your face, boy! But I'll give you this, you can really run fast."

At the end of the hedge, the cows slowed down, straightened up, ambled across the street, and stopped at the pasture gate. That afternoon I went back to get the cows, and Bossy and May reversed their act going to the barn, running against the hedge. But this time I wasn't intimidated.

Grandma, despite her age, milked the cows sitting on the right side of the cows on a low stool with a milk pail between her knees and her head pressed against their sides. Grasping two teats (she called them "tits") at a time, she squeezed and pulled downward squirting milk in a long stream at me and laughing. Showing me how to milk, she repeated the motions, pulling, pressing, squirting, and releasing the stream of milk in the pail.

Once she finished milking the cows, she placed the bucket of warm milk in the root cellar behind the house to cool in a tank of cold well water. Later, after skimming cream off the milk's surface with a ladle, she poured the cream into a crock in the root cellar, the coolest place available without a refrigerator or icebox.

A week's worth of cream made clabber enough to churn butter. I poured the clabber into a dash churn, a tall, narrow, nearly cylindrical five-gallon wooden tub, and pushed the wooden plunger handle through the hole in the churn's cover. Plunging the dash up and down in short cycles, I pumped until my arm muscles ached and fat globules of butter had clumped together. Grandma drained the buttermilk and washed the butter off in cool water before forming it in a compact mass in a wooden mold that had a false bottom that allowed her to push an intact cake of butter out to wrap in wax paper.

My daily routine was set: herding cows to pasture, watching Grandma milk, talking with Big Daddy in the swing on the porch, and walking in the fields near the house. I found a plant Grandma called a "may-pop," which had an egg-shaped yellow berry that she told me I could suck the sweet jelly-covered seeds from. I sat in the porch swing behind the morning glory vines on the trellis, watching hummingbirds hover, flit, and dip their long beaks into the blossoms sipping sweet nectar.

Big Daddy sat beside me on the porch in a large rocking chair filled with pillows.

"How do you make a living, Big Daddy?"

"I contemplate the problems of the world, Grandson."

"You mean you don't do any kind of work?"

"Not anymore."

"Why not?"

"Well, Cleveland, I'm saving myself to be a really good *old* man."

By the end of the week, I had explored every inch and item in their little five-room house. The kitchen had a cast-iron, wood-burning cook stove with a reservoir for heating water, a work table, and a sink with running water. They had machines I'd never seen before—a mill for grinding coffee beans, a meat chopper and food cutter, and a fruit-wine-and-jelly press. The dining room had a large sideboard, a food safe, and a large oak table with matching chairs. We ate there under the severe gaze of a bearded man in a framed photograph on the wall. Despite James Garland Harrison's remarkable resemblance to our twenty-third U.S. president, Big Daddy insisted that my great-grandfather wasn't Benjamin Harrison, the Republican, who lost the popular vote but defeated Grover Cleveland in the Electoral College. Big Daddy would never allow even a token of Republicanism in his home. He said my name of *Cleveland*, a Democrat, and *Harrison*, a Republican, made me a "mug-wump"—my face and my butt on opposite sides of the political fence.

My grandparents wanted to know about my schoolwork, our family's different moves, Daddy's new job, and what I did for fun, obviously wondering how to entertain me for another week. The next morning, Big Daddy felt good enough to walk several blocks to downtown, pausing now and then because after losing several toes to diabetes, his feet were extremely tender. We ended up at the Racket Store.

He introduced me to the owner. "This is Allie's son, Cleveland—a city boy who survives on peanut butter and soda pop."

Even though he kidded me, Big Daddy arranged with the manager to borrow an air rifle, a Daisy BB gun, and bought pellets for me to shoot. Like my father, he thought firing an air rifle was preparation for firing a real weapon and hunting game. With the BB gun in hand, I followed Big Daddy to a drugstore where we sat at a marble-topped table drinking fountain drinks—cold water for him and Coke for me. I sipped as Big Daddy introduced me and talked politics with other customers.

At home again, he suggested, "Why don't you sit in the porch swing and shoot at the hummingbirds?"

That may have been another joke of his, because I couldn't hit a hummingbird caught in a net. By the time Big Daddy saw me off for home on the bus, my intense devotion to him and my grandmother matched my immeasurable appreciation of city life.

Back in Little Rock, anticipating the start of school, I asked for long pants to look grown up, but there wasn't money enough for them and school supplies, too. But something I could do without money was conquer my defiant cowlicks, which went every which-a-way at the front and rear of my head. Without saying why, I smeared enough rose hair oil on my head to look slick as a black rat and smell like the bathroom after lodgers bathed. But my errant hair refused to lie down. Mama, observing my efforts, gave me her jar of setting gel to try.

Buster, beside me in bed, reacted to the gel. "You're making our bed smell like a whore's!"

I told him how much I wanted my hair to lie down like his, and he understood and eventually tried to help me. But first, he teased me about primping for a girlfriend, which I protested wasn't true. Then he suggested I part my hair and hold it in place with a stocking cap. He made one by cutting off the wide upper end of one of Mama's old silk hose and tying it in a knot at the cut end, forming a cap snug enough to hold the cowlick down—a valiant effort that didn't work.

After Buster divorced Ada Bess and came back to live with us on Spring, he stayed out after work every night past midnight or later, drinking heavily and frequently fighting at night spots. Daddy called him a "mean drunk," a little guy eager to fight men physically larger than he, as if to prove his manhood. If true, Buster asserted himself too often, coming home with bruises, black eyes, and raw knuckles, which I saw at breakfast the next morning before he went to work.

Then, without giving us a clue, Buster had a new girlfriend. Shortly after we found out, he married her and moved into his new wife's small, rented apartment in an old Victorian mansion at the corner of Fifth and Cumberland streets. The woman was a divorcee who had a six-year-old daughter living with her grandmother in Marmaduke—a small town in the northeast corner of Arkansas—but the child was not part of the marriage.

Weeks passed before we met Buster's new wife, Ozena Houston. A brunette, about our mother's height and plumpness, she had a pretty face, good taste in clothes, and an arrested case of tuberculosis.

The longest time I spent in Ozena's company was painting the bathroom in their apartment when Buster was too busy to do it. Mama volunteered my service because I gained skill painting the walls and woodwork at our house. Over two Saturdays, I applied coats of "apple blossom" enamel to the walls, observed by Ozena for a few minutes without comment before she prepared my lunch without eating anything herself.

Months later, Buster unexpectedly went home at noon and found Ozena in bed with another man. Their marriage had lasted less than a year. After their split, Buster moved back home to share my tiny pantry-bedroom again and found a new job as the head checker at Food Palace, the fanciest grocery store in town, on the east side of Main Street. He would work at Food Palace until he was drafted.

My own life began changing in the fall of 1937 after Mr. Bill Bramlett rented the small efficiency bedroom at the back of our house. He was of medium height and so thin I secretly called him "the wafer man." With his shirt sleeves rolled up, winter and summer, Mr. Bramlett revealed the stringy sinews of his skinny arms, so unlike the smooth muscles of my father's forearms. His pale, bony face with the sharp edge of his nose and dark circles around his eyes made him resemble a raccoon. Talking easily with Mama, who worried about his health, he habitually twisted the cap off a tube of mentholatum and swiped his little finger over the neck to dab a bit of salve in each nostril. Then, pressing his lips together, he sniffed deeply while recapping the tube. The routine he practiced so unconsciously forced Mama to look away.

Mama revealed our recent family history to Mr. Bramlett—that our store went broke and we rented rooms to make ends meet. He suggested he'd get me a job selling newspapers to help pay for my clothes and school expenses. To encourage my interest in a job with the newspaper, Mama and Daddy sent me to watch Mr. Bramlett set type in the *Democrat* building at Fifth and Scott.

I found him setting type on a Linotype machine in a hot second-floor room foggy with cigarette, cigar, and pipe smoke. Operating a keyboard similar to a typewriter's, he depressed a key releasing a matrix from a magazine, and a small rod with a letter die on its vertical edge fell into the line-composing box where little wedges automatically adjusted the spaces between words. When a line of matrices was set, it was carried off and cast in metal slugs the width of a newspaper column. Another worker assembled the slugs inside a form, and compositors handset headlines and illustrations readying the form for the press.

Watching Mr. Bramlett at work, two thoughts struck me: the hot air and the Linotype's pool of melted lead dried his nostrils and led to his mentholatum habit, and working for an afternoon newspaper was what made his skin so pale.

The next afternoon, I dropped my books at home, ate a peanut butter sandwich, grabbed my raincoat, and walked in a misty rain to the *Democrat* building. Entering the open basement door, I saw narrow loading platforms along three walls with swinging doors behind them. Old men and boys had spread out like an amoeba and were scuffling, jumping off and on the dock, yelling like lunatics, the scene underscored by the deafening rumbles of presses bouncing off the concrete walls.

I saw no one I knew and squatted in a corner to wait for Mr. Scroggins, the circulation manager. Suddenly the double doors by one platform swung open, and men in dirty white painter's caps and aprons dumped the newspaper stacks on dollies at the dock's edge. The paper boys, like sprinters responding to a starter's pistol, scrambled for their daily allotments.

One man, surrounded by yapping boys, had to be the circulation manager.

"Mr. Scroggins?"

"Yeah?" He looked down at me. "How can I help?"

"Mr. Bramlett told me ..."

"Oh, yeah, you're the kid Bill mentioned, his landlady's son."

"Yes, sir. Where am I going to sell papers?"

"Fifth and Center ... in front of Sterling Store. It's a good spot, kid."

What a relief, I thought! I'd be only two blocks from home.

"Papers are three cents a piece. You get a penny for each one you sell."

He stuffed a stack of papers into a dirty white canvas bag with ARKANSAS DEMOCRAT printed on the side. Carrying the heavy bag across my shoulder, I went outside into the mist that had turned to rain. The walk to Sterling left my knickers and socks wet below the raincoat. If Mama knew, she'd make me change clothes. Now, I was my own boss. Standing in the rain didn't suit me, so I got under cover between the glass display windows at the front of the store, where I was dry but not seen, and unable to thrust newspapers into customers' hands. My position beneath the overhang had the same result—the people hurrying to get out of the rain either looked down or away.

Late getting home for supper, I told my folks everything that happened, and Daddy advised stepping in front of pedestrians or walking beside them, speaking loudly but politely, stressing the headlines. The next day, following his advice, I stood beside people waiting on the corner for traffic signals or walked beside them; eventually, I was brave enough to pursue and cajole the more likely looking customers.

If a passerby protested, "I can't read, kid!" I was quick on the uptake and cracked, "Well, you can look at the pictures!"

After such a retort, a few chuckled and bought a paper, but most walked on by. When a potential customer had only a large bill and no coins, I went inside Sterling to the soda fountain beside the front doors to change the bill. The counter boys and girls soon became my buddies, kidding me when I asked for change or sat at the counter warming up or asked for water to soothe my parched throat from yelling "paper!" On Saturday afternoons, I ate the Sterling lunch "special," the cheapest combination on the menu: a hot dog with all the fixings, washed down with a mug of root beer. One young waitress liked me so much, she slathered the wiener with extra mustard and slaw and refilled my mug free. After eating the lunch, I spent a nickel at the candy counter buying two "opera drops," pieces of fruit-flavored fondant coated in dark chocolate.

Before picking up papers at the *Democrat* on Saturday, I surveyed the toy counters at the back of the store's first floor, examining the miniature cars, lead soldiers, party games, fancy yo-yos, toy pistols, and whatever else was new. The young women clerks soon recognized me and never showed any concern about my stealing a toy. But one afternoon, I silently watched a boy put a toy car in his pocket.

In a second, he hurried around the counter and faced me. "Hi!" he said. "Wanna help me fix my bike?"

"What's the matter with it?"

"I don't know. The front wheel jist don't turn right. Come outside 'n I'll show you."

We walked out the side door to Center Street, where his bike was leaning against a light pole.

After looking at its front and back, I said, "Your bike looks okay to me."

But he insisted, "Go on, look down close at the front axle."

When I bent over to look more closely at the front wheel, something smashed my nose! Raising my head to see what hit me, I saw the boy on his bike riding away. He had lured me outside away from the clerk, afraid I'd report his stealing. Hitting was a diversion and a warning that permitted his clean getaway. Back inside at the toy counter, I told the clerk to keep her eye on him if he returned. But at supper, I didn't tell Daddy. He'd want to know why I hadn't hit the boy, taken the toy from him, and returned it to the clerk.

Growing more comfortable in my newsboy role, I developed an "eager salesman" characterization. But even then, I didn't enjoy plying my trade in cold rain, sleet, and snow as the winter deepened. My kidding prospective buyers increased my sales, and a few workers passing daily became regular customers. But whipped by frigid winds, my nose stopped up or ran from bad colds for four months. As Christmas approached, Mama, worrying about my health, suggested I quit. But selling newspapers, I learned good lessons: a job requires honesty, regularity, promptness, and dependability, regardless of feelings or the weather.

After Daddy wrecked our Chrysler in 1934 while he and Buster worked on Big Daddy's farm, he never drank anything stronger than beer with a sandwich at Tom and Andrew's. As far as we knew, furniture dealers on Seventh Street never offered him alcohol of any kind during the holiday season, or if they did, he refused it. Daddy never smelled of whiskey, because Mama, with the nose of a bloodhound, would have detected even a beer from the back door. Well, at least until Christmas 1938.

But on December 23, Daddy worked only half a day on Saturday as usual, and he came home from Seventh Street after imbibing generous holiday libations with various customers. Daddy was such a quiet man (except on long-distance phone calls) that when he slammed the back screen, stomped onto the porch, and greeted Mama in a loud voice, I knew something was different.

Mama said, "Why, Allie Harrison, you've been drinking."

"Yes, I have, Floy. Every dealer offered me wassail of some kind, and it didn't seem companionable to refuse."

"Well, we'll sit down and get some food into you and sober you up."

"Aw, Floy, don't make out that I'm drunk. I'm not, and you better believe it."

Daddy put his arms around her and tried to kiss her, but she pulled away. "You go wash up and sit down to eat. Then you'll get sober and be fine."

"I'm fine already," he protested on his way to the bathroom.

When he returned and sat at the table, he stumbled through the blessing before eating slowly but heartily. His eyelids were drooping before the meal ended.

Mama said, "Now, Allie, you just go into the living room and lie down on the sofa until you sober up."

"Dammit, Floy, I'm not drunk, sleepy maybe, but not drunk."

"Well, whatever you are, a good long nap will make you feel better."

After Daddy lay down, Mama presented her usual ruminations on the dangers of whiskey.

In the middle of the second year at East Side, my homeroom moved from Miss Griffin to Mr. Harris Hogue, a general-science teacher. He had a long, half-inch-thick leather strap on his desk similar to Mr. Webb's at Rightsell, which he slapped on the desk top to start or silence classes. Even though he left the subtle impression of applying it elsewhere, he knew that we knew he never would strike us.

Mr. Hogue wasn't as serious as Miss Griffin; he got his way by joshing and playing practical jokes. He initiated new class members into physical science by using our whole class. We stood in a circle holding hands, the uninitiated student last in line and grasping the contact wire of a small electric generator. Mr. Hogue cranked his small generator vigorously, sending a harmless electric current through the line to shock the new boy in his first lesson in basic physics. Yet Mr. Hogue had a personality, like Miss McMahan's, that engaged everybody.

Miss McMahan insisted Latin would help us understand English grammar and prepare us for college, which I had never given any thought to. But when I saw Miss Hettie McCaul, the Latin teacher, with her lovely facial features and strawberry-blonde hair, and heard her sweet voice, I was attracted to Latin. Since language study required memory work and drill in vocabulary, word genders, declensions, and conjugations, my quick retention drew me to the subject. Her best vocabulary-building drill was "Latin baseball," two teams with pitchers hurling either English synonyms or Latin terms at team members at bat. From C+ in my first six weeks, I advanced to an A- before leaving East Side and the fair grace of Miss McCaul.

Miss McMahan, besides teaching local, state, and federal government, provided job counseling, seeking to make us think about what we intended to do for a living as adults. Most students stated that they wanted to be a doctor, lawyer, merchant, or chief of some kind. I was the only one with aspirations in the arts; I aimed to be an actor.

Miss McMahan, pursing her orange lips, chuckled, "Be serious, Cleveland, pick an occupation!"

In other words, choose a job to match her printed information. My unwavering insistence on acting tested her patience, with information on the profession proving difficult to find in 1938. I supported the points in my report with stories about the careers of successful movie actors and radio performers: Slim Summerville, an Arkansan, who starred in *All Quiet on the Western Front* and other movies, and Dick Powell of Little Rock, star of movie musicals and *Hollywood Hotel*, a dramatic radio series. My Aunt Ora, a friend of Dick Powell's mother, visited his home in Hollywood, where his many clothes were organized in chests and closets, like the garments of royalty. To add variety to my argument, I did vocal impressions of Ronald Colman in movies and Fred Allen and Jack Benny on the radio. I stressed the chancy nature of the acting profession but emphasized the potential rewards of popularity and wealth. I entertained with more froth than facts.

I felt born to be an actor. I had invented substitute worlds for fun and imagined different personalities from the beginning, firmly convinced that making up stories and imitating others was my calling. My parents probably shared Miss McMahan's attitude about acting as a vocation but never discouraged me. They tolerated my theatrical ambition by assuming it was a phase that would end soon. But if, as some sociologists argue, we invent ourselves by seeing ourselves through the eyes of others, I was fortunate my parents were nonjudgmental.

From the eighth grade until my graduation from junior high, they never had to worry about my applying myself to my lessons. I also kept busy by working for the principal's secretary, Mrs. Dorothy Whitten, Coach LeRoy Whitten's wife. In the main office one class period a day, I collected and checked attendance slips; issued excuses for students to leave the school grounds, lunch permits, and readmission-to-class slips; delivered packages sent to the main office; and used the schedule cards for several purposes. I also reported for the *East Side Journal*, acted in the dramatics club, and served as vice president of the National Junior Honor Society. When I ran for student body president against Delores Fuller, Herbert Reamey, and

Bert Gaster, I didn't try to win, because I had no political interests and wanted time to act, sing, and see movies.

I either walked or rode a streetcar home after school, depending upon the weather and my plans. Walking north on Main, I sometimes bought an enormous double-dip cone at Summerfield's Ice Cream shop at 1123 Main for a nickel. (Mr. Summerfield and my Uncle Billy Terry were partners in the dairy business at one time.) Stopping at the Capitol Theater, I checked the black-and-white photographs of current and upcoming movies out front, and walked west on Sixth past the empty Lafayette Hotel on Louisiana before checking the Arkansas Theater marquee on the way to Capitol. Along that avenue, I passed Kroger, Sterling, Arkansas-Louisiana Gas Company, Safeway, and the Pulaski Theater.

A few kids who lived or shopped downtown sometimes joined me. Charles Shapiro walked with me now and then; his father, the rabbi at the orthodox synagogue at Seventh and Louisiana, owned a small delicatessen between Center and Spring on Sixth Street, where Charles occasionally invited me to share a kosher snack. Later, when Marx's Deli opened across from Sterling, our whole family shared kosher delicacies and special coffees.

Most days, though, I waited for a streetcar beside the Villa Marre, the home of my classmate Mary Ann Kinsworthy. (From 1986 to 1993, the house appeared in the opening credits of *Designing Women*, the popular CBS television series by native Arkansan Harry Thomason and his wife, Linda Bloodworth-Thomason.) Since the house's mansard roof didn't match roofs in their own neighborhoods, kids thought the house "looked weird."

Girls waiting for the streetcar held neatly stacked books in their arms across their chests, leaning against the ornate cast-iron fence, while boys carried a few books in one hand against their hips. Some jockeyed to board the stubby streetcar first, filling the seats and leaving boisterous riders standing firmly wedged between the seats and each other in the aisle, arguing, flirting, and cracking wise.

At the end of such a streetcar ride on Friday, April 1, 1938, a bunch of classmates in olive-drab uniforms and campaign hats surprised me in front of the empty Crow-Burlingame Auto Parts Store across from our house. Though it was April Fool's Day, the boys weren't there to trick me;

they were in Troop 40 and had joined other troops in a Camporee, demonstrating the projects that earned merit badges and advanced them in rank. Boykin and John Pyles, Zach Bair, Joe Hart, and Billy Prichards literally dragged me inside to try to lure me into the Boy Scouts of America.

Troop 40 from the First Methodist Church, at Eighth and Louisiana streets, was led by the manager of the Dictaphone Corporation in the Riegler Building, Scoutmaster W. Clarence French, and Assistant Scoutmaster John H. Rule, the co-owner of Manufacturer's Furniture Company on Seventh Street. My pals were preparing to go to a summer Camporal at Camp Robinson and asked me to join them. The troop met weekly in the assembly room north of the church on Saturday evenings. I was reluctant to commit myself to Boy Scouts, fearing interferences with my singing, acting, and movie going.

After my acting success in *Treasure Island*, I expected a leading role in *Up in the Air*, a two-act operetta about love and travel. So Mrs. Scott surprised me with the tiny role of a sightseeing bus spieler with the boys' and girls' glee clubs. My friend Earl Nichols, whose singing voice was beautiful, was given the leading role. I settled for the focus on the bus ride, and a fun costume of khaki shirt, riding britches, Daddy's brown leather leggings, and a billed cap. The bus was a long platform three feet above the floor with a bus cab and wheels painted on cardboard profiles, with chairs on top. The tour guide welcomed passengers on board, and walked the aisle, singing:

> *Gentlemen, please take your seats!*
> *Ladies, hold your chapeaux!*
> *As we travel the city streets*
> *Please watch the way we go.*

I sang verses about the church with the tower, the courthouse on the square, and the statues of city heroes, pointing at the sights we passed.

Even though the role of the sightseeing tour guide was small, every second I was on stage counted.

When spring came, Mama encouraged me to attend my first tea dance, accompanying Mary Louise Schweig, whose blue-black hair and faultless white skin made her one of the prettiest girls at East Side. Her father, who owned a furniture store, was one of Daddy's customers. Mary Louise and I joined her cute friend, Rosemary McCoubry, and Boykin Pyles, a real pal-o'-mine.

On Saturday afternoon in dress-up clothes, our junior-high crowd gathered in the echoing ballroom on the second floor of the Woman's City Club, at the corner of Fourth and Scott. I agreed to go because Mama insisted it would help me learn how to behave with girls on a date, as well as meet boys and girls from other schools. The live band on a low, shallow bandstand against the ballroom's fourth wall was directed by Tommy Scott and played well enough for us rank amateurs. Many boys came alone dressed to the teeth but didn't dance, and some only sat beside the girls who invited them in chairs against the three walls of the ballroom.

A middle-aged lady, whose voice was big as a man's, formed us in a circle in the middle of the ballroom to learn a new dance for ten or twelve dancers. It combined steps from the Charleston, the Black Bottom, Truckin', the Suzie Q, the Shag, and the Virginia Reel and took its name from a nightclub in South Carolina where it originated, the Big Apple. After imitating Stepin Fetchit for years, I was adept at Truckin'.

There were other steps, but Mary Louise and I concentrated on the simple ones, dancing beside each other.

The longer the dancing lasted, the more boys and girls broke away from our circle until the few left stopped. A few girls headed to the second-floor lobby to be near the refreshments. Other couples, including Mary Louise and me, gravitated to the bandstand to listen after leaving the dance floor. Then we heard loud laughter behind us, and saw boys squirming past the girls in the lobby and out the French doors onto the balcony overlooking Scott Street.

Curious, Mary Louise and I drifted toward the balcony that was packed with noisy boys on their knees shooting craps, overlooked by more boys smoking and passing a common cigarette among them. I recognized the boys on the balcony as socially ambitious guys in my class—Roland Frazier, Clifton Smith, Bert Gaster—flirting with membership in high-school fraternities. When refreshments were served, the guys on the balcony stomped out their cigarette butt, pocketed their dice, and joined the long line inching toward the cake and punch.

Besides learning some steps of the Big Apple and enjoying the companionship of Mary Louise, Rosemary, and Boykin, I am not sure what social graces I absorbed.

In May, I was a Tenderfoot Scout, and, by July, a Second-Class Scout, wearing an olive-drab uniform I bought at Blass—shirt and shorts, knee-length hose, brown shoes, web belt with brass buckle, and a silver slide with the Scout logo to hold the end folds of our troop's patterned green-and-yellow neckerchief. The felt campaign hat, similar to ones army and marine corps drill sergeants wore, had a broad brim and four dents in the crown. It was hard *not* to wear that hat every day.

At our troop's fall and spring meetings, we often went to the city park (which later became MacArthur Park) to play serious games of capture the flag on the great green lawns around the old Armory. Patrol members divided into two teams of equal numbers, and the scoutmaster flipped a coin to determine which team would first hold and defend the flag, for the aim of the game was to steal the flag from the opposing team by various maneuvers. In a rough-and-tumble game that involved a lot of running, tackling, and tussling, I realized for the first time that all Scouts in our troop did not have equal physical health and strength. Albert Boehler had a heart condition from rheumatic fever when he was a child and couldn't participate.

I looked forward to the two-day, statewide Boy Scout Camporal starting late Friday afternoon in the middle of June at Camp Joseph T. Robinson. Under a cloudless sky, the temperature had reached a hundred degrees in a dusty open field of tall prairie grass by the time we erected the pup tents furnished by the National Guard. We already felt sweaty and miserable with mosquitoes humming about our heads and chiggers from the high grass digging into our legs. Mr. Rule, the assistant scoutmaster, had us rub kerosene on our legs and arms to ward off the insects. Our camp smelled like a kerosene refinery, and Scouts allergic to coal oil suffered caustic burns.

Fortunately, we didn't need fires to cook but picnicked on lunch meat sandwiches, fresh fruit, and lemonade for supper. Twosomes in tents talked a lot that night or spent their sleep time playing tricks on boys in other tents. At Saturday breakfast, still reeking but not flammable, we fried bacon and eggs in heavy iron skillets propped on rocks over coals.

Scouts from all over Arkansas gathered for the opening ceremonies at the center of the Camporal grounds, beginning two days of activity. A long line of Scouts stood at attention, their hometown flags flying, as Governor Carl E. Bailey and his official party passed us to review our ranks. The photograph of our troop as the party passed appeared in the *Arkansas Gazette* on Sunday.

I competed in the dressing-undressing relay and was hailed as Troop 40's "Gypsy Rose Cleve." The race involved two posts set about fifteen yards apart, and contestants alternated between posts, removing one garment at one post, then crossing to the other post to remove another garment, until we wearing only our skivvies. Then we reversed the procedure, putting our uniforms back on. The Scout completing the routine in the shortest time won; I placed second in my contest.

I also competed in fire building, which required the use of a single match and a handful of dry tinder to build a fire. Other fire-building contests depended upon striking flint with carbon steel for sparks to set a punk on fire, or a bow with a thong rotating a wooden drill in the hollow of a fire board for friction enough to ignite a spark and set tinder ablaze.

That night, I took my turn as cook. Frying chicken, I tilted the heavy iron skillet sideways, splashing hot oil on my right hand and wrist. Boykin quickly righted the skillet without losing any chicken parts in the fire, and Mr. French applied gauze soaked in Unguentine ointment to my burns. Even though the burns were painful, I forgot my discomfort after supper, gathering in an enormous crowd around a huge bonfire for a community sing, including "My Darling Clementine."

By Sunday morning, the brilliant red burns on my hand and arm were blisters, as gray as casket lining. When I got home and Mama saw them, she urged me to drop out of the troop to avoid such dangers, but Daddy insisted that was no reason to drop out of the Scouts. With his encouragement, I set out to be an excellent Scout, and I fulfilled requirements for ranks and merit badges as rapidly as I could for First Class, Star, and Life Scout before finishing junior high school. I fell short of attaining Eagle Scout by failing to pass life saving. But I had earned the fourteen merit badges on the khaki sash across my right shoulder and left hip: woodwork, basketry, cement work, metalwork, public health, personal health, first aid, handicraft, textiles, pioneering, plumbing, civics, scholarship, and athletics.

Later that summer, my parents drove me and my pack of clean play clothes and swim trunks to spend a week at Camp Quapaw on a wooded promontory above the Saline River in Benton County. Mr. E. A. Bowen, the camp director, greeted us—a slender, middle-aged man of average height, he wore a short-sleeved T-shirt, long pants cut off at the knees, and ankle-high socks. Except for Dr. Wassell, he was the first grown man I had seen in short pants.

The cabins were scattered around the camp grounds with the large dining room and kitchen in the center. I joined Boykin, Joe, Billy Prichards, and Arthur Stranz, who were at camp for the first time like me, sleeping on cots with metal springs and thin mattresses in the Silver Fox Cabin. The screened cabin, with a hipped roof and half walls of natural rock, was open to fresh air, the light of the day, the dark sky and stars at night, and the sounds of insects and woodland creatures around the clock.

By mid-week, we felt confident enough after lights out to compete to see who could leap farthest from one cot to another. The game was safe enough if you landed in the center of a mattress, but my right foot hit the cot's edge, catching the big toe of my right foot between the springs and metal frame, almost ripping off the toenail. My mates helped me hop to the camp doctor, a University of Arkansas medical student, with an ironic name for someone in the healing arts—Savage. He removed the whole nail and bathed my toe in alcohol. Wrapping his arm around my shoulders, he reassured me that the nail would grow back, which it did.

Learning to swim was my aim, so the waterfront filled an essential part of each day. A small "swimming pool" was built in the waterfront dock opposite a raft moored twenty-five yards out in the river. The pool was for non-swimmers, whom good swimmers derisively referred to in unmention-able epithets, rather than the kinder allusions of "pollywogs," "tadpoles," or "sinkers." The pool's wooden floor was under four feet of water, and the two-by-fours of the sides with spaces in between allowed water to flow and furnished hand holds while kicking from the hips to develop muscular power. In the pool, we learned to relax and float on our backs, as well as to hold our breath rolled up in a ball, our heads beneath the water. The "buddy system" allowed us to keep constant touch with our companion, holding our clasped hands aloft when a counselor whistled and counted partners.

The narrow, steep dirt path down to the dock was not precipitous but surrounded by vines that crept to its edge. One day as I started down the path, a beady-eyed snake was coiled in the path, appearing ready to strike. But I observed the sixth Scout Law, standing quite still until the snake slith-ered away to safety in the weeds: *A Scout is kind. He is a friend to animals.*

He will not kill nor hurt any living creature needlessly, but will strive to save and protect all harmless life.

From the top of the path, we could see an open field on the other side of the river where Quapaw Indians had purportedly camped or settled. Later, Boykin and I rowed across the Saline River in a canoe to comb through the soft dirt between the rows of corn stalks searching for arrowheads and fragments of flint.

During the breaks between camp activities, we could buy half pints of sweet or chocolate milk and a variety of soda pops for a nickel: Coca-Cola, Pepsi, and Royal Crown colas, NuGrape, and many flavors and colors of Nehi. The most popular soft drink was R-Pep, a local prune-flavored beverage similar in taste to Dr. Pepper. It had more carbonic gas than other soda pops, and we used it for something more than drinking. Free of dining-room etiquette, we used R-Pep's explosive properties for a whoop-de-do. Placing our thumbs in the bottle necks to control the fizz and trajectory, we shook the bottles and fought sticky battles with R-Peps until we exhausted ourselves and our counselors' patience.

One night, the counselors took us neophytes on a snipe hunt. Gathering in the dark without flashlights to hunt "snipes," we followed a traditional ritual for beginning campers. The counselors claimed moonless nights, such as this one, were excellent for capturing snipes, the mysterious game bird that harbored in heavily wooded, somewhat marshy land around the camp. Warned to be extremely quiet, we each carried burlap bags walking single file into the deep underbrush, dropping off one at a time to sit separated from each other holding our bags open to catch snipes.

The silence, except for the wood's peepers, was slightly threatening, and the stinging mosquitoes had a field day with our exposed arms and legs. Yet no snipes came or were seen by anyone. We sat in the clammy dark until it dawned on us that we were the pawns in a staff trick. Back at camp, the counselors greeted our varied reactions to their hoax with great rounds of laughter and wisecracks.

During the months Mr. Bramlett roomed at our house, he shared news before it appeared in the latest editions of the *Democrat*. When Mama generously invited him to Sunday dinner, he began to feel like a part of our family. I liked him well enough, but my parents, probably as a result of their ages, really enjoyed his company. He was divorced and had a twenty-year-old son in Jonesboro, Arkansas.

One evening, Mr. B introduced our family to "Bert," or Bertha, the shapely daughter of "Willie," short for Wilhelmina, his lady friend. When I later accompanied Mr. B to Willie's apartment on Seventh Street, across from the State Capitol grounds, he bestowed a smothering Hollywood-style kiss on Willie, who was dark haired in contrast to her daughter's dishwater blonde. I didn't want to see it. His kiss for Bert was only a peck. Listening to them talk, I sensed some kind of shared secret.

Another day, Mr. B took Bert and me fishing. Even though I didn't want to go, Mama thought I'd enjoy the outing. Later I learned that Willie had called Mama and insisted I be sent along with them as chaperone. I outfitted myself for the fishing excursion in the same kind of fishing clothes Daddy wore: a pair of my old slacks, a knit shirt, Daddy's old felt hat, and his old shoes, with a bandana around my neck. Mr. Bramlett drove out State Highway 10 to a narrow creek back in deep woods. When we arrived, I was surprised to find he had no fishing equipment. I had Daddy's fishing kit and knife to cut a pole for hooks and lines to fish. After we sat on the shady bank a while, Mr. Bramlett took Bert for a walk, leaving me alone for a long time. When they returned, Mr. Bramlett was red faced, and Bert made too much of a fuss over me.

In the summer, Mr. Bramlett's son visited him for several weeks. John was taller than his dad, well built, and brown as a farmer. One afternoon, while his Mr. B was at work, John took Bert and me driving in his father's car, all of us sitting snugly in the front seat, with Bert snuggled up close to John. There was a Powerhouse candy bar on the dashboard which John offered me, even though he wasn't sure how fresh it was. The bar was large enough to share, but they didn't want any.

After an hour just tootling around letting John see the town, my stomach didn't feel right. And the longer we drove, the more my stomach roiled and my head swam. So they dropped me at home before John drove to Bert's apartment. I barely made it through the front door and to the toilet before vomiting and fainting. I don't know how long I lay unconscious before I woke up, cold and clammy, lying on the daybed in the lounge–dining room. Mama, Daddy, and John were all standing beside the bed staring at me, as if in dread about my condition.

Mama was helplessly wringing her hands, and Daddy, who usually showed no emotion, appeared tightly wound up.

From their silence, Mama suddenly exclaimed, "Oh, Allie, he's never been like this before. He's so white and his eyes look set."

Daddy quietly said, "Maybe we better call Dr. Gray to come see him."

Mama said, "There's no telling what he'll charge for a house call at night."

For the first time in my life, I thought I might be dying. What convinced my family I wasn't dying, I don't know. But John mentioned the candy bar, and Daddy identified my symptoms as an extreme case of ptomaine poisoning. He persuaded Mama to give me a massive dose of castor oil and permitted me to stay on the daybed for Mama's and my convenience. She looked after me while doing housework, and I had a beeline to the bathroom. Who knows how long that candy bar under the windshield lay in the sun fermenting with bacteria before I ate it?

During the weeks after John returned to Jonesboro, I heard odd sounds in the early morning hours in Mr. B's room next to mine. The whispering voices, thuds, and scraping sounds occurred several nights before I realized I was an absent witness, without any intention on my part, to Mr. B's sex life. I heard sounds I'd been told were part of the ritual of sex: anticipatory whispering, lip smacking, bedsprings creaking, sighing, moaning, and groaning. The aural repertory of lovemaking was very potent as I lay in the dark of my tiny bedroom next to Mr. B's. The sounds excited in my mind obscure pictures of sexual coupling.

Soon after hearing those episodes, I noticed the window screen at the back of Mr. Bramlett's room had fallen out. Trying to set the screen back in place, I found scuff marks on the outside wall and footprints on the ground below the window. At supper, I told Mama and Daddy what I saw, and Mama said she had suspected Mr. Bramlett was bringing a woman into his room secretly after finding lipstick on his pillowcases and the odor of perfume on his sheets. She and Daddy decided, then and there, to ask him to find another place. I don't know when she spoke to him, but he failed to make his usual visit in the lounge one evening. I knew without asking that he was gone.

Hemmed in by office buildings and sidewalks, I bicycled or skated to play in the vacant lot beside Joe's home, at Fifteenth and Broadway. Lots of guys gathered there for football, baseball, pole vaulting, or hanging out, a loud bunch that argued constantly, even pushing each other around but settling arguments with words not fists. I never had an urge to fight anyone, firmly convinced that disagreements could be settled by talking things over.

At one of our regular weekend tackle football games, a new boy appeared on the field. No one knew him or had invited him; he just showed up. John Tuberville, a tall, thin, sinewy boy said he had just entered East Side and wanted to play ball with us. He didn't say where he lived.

Joe said, "Sure, come on, join one of the sides and play."

Everyone mumbled agreement. Who cared if another guy who was a stranger joined the game? Most of us didn't block, only ran downfield to catch passes from whoever had a turn as quarterback. John Tuberville, though, played as if he wanted to hurt the fellow opposite him, blocking viciously, aiming at testicles, stomachs, and chins rather than tackling opponents at the knees and ankles.

After his many unnecessary collisions, boys shouted, "Take it easy, guy. It's only a game!"

But Tuberville persisted, managing to tackle and hit everyone so hard that some guy, certainly not me, told him he couldn't play anymore and everyone seconded the motion.

"Jesus Christ, what a bunch of sissies, " he sneered.

As Tuberville walked away, Joe said, under his breath, "Good riddance to bad rubbish."

Tuberville heard him, raced back, and swung a haymaker, hitting Joe squarely in the jaw. As Joe rubbed his face, I stepped between them, in the role of peacemaker, and protested, "You shouldn't hit Joe. The rest of us decided you're not welcome."

Tuberville smashed his fist into my nose, as well. Surprised by the blow that didn't hurt, probably because my nose is soft and flat, I stood face to face with Tuberville, naively claiming I hadn't done anything to deserve being hit. I expected to be hit when he cocked his fists to strike again.

That's when Joe's mother, to my relief, pushed through the circle of players. Tall and broad shouldered, Mrs. Hart accepted nonsense from no one. "You hooligan! Get off this lot and don't come back again. These boys don't need your kind around."

Tuberville shouted, "Old woman, I've got as much right to be here as anybody." Turning to us, he snarled, "Just wait, I'll get even with you sissies!" After he left, the game broke up, and I rode home on my bike, my nose still stinging slightly from the blow. At lunch, Mama asked why my nose was so red, and I described the fight. Daddy asked what I did to the boy who hit me, and I told him I tried to reason with him. Daddy insisted I should have knocked his block off.

"You'd find he's a yellow-bellied sapsucker, if you called his bluff."

He was obviously disappointed in me for not fighting back. He didn't say so, but I assumed he thought me a coward, because he never mentioned the episode again. For weeks, I assumed I *was* a coward, wondering whether not wanting to hurt someone or to be hurt by someone makes one a coward. I may have been scared, too, for I adjusted my daily habits to stay out of Tuberville's way. I wasn't really afraid, just ashamed of being defeated.

John Tuberville's bullying at East Side ended one afternoon after school. I was standing at my locker kidding with fellows when someone yelled, "There's a fight on the corner of Fourteenth!"

A larger, nosier crowd than usual had gathered at the streetcar stop on Scott. Standing at the edge of the mob, I saw Tuberville lying on the ground with another boy sitting astride him, pounding his face. Tuberville was struggling to get up when my streetcar arrived and I left. The next day, Harry Page told me that a bully from North Little Rock had come over to beat Tuberville up. I thought it's fair enough for him to meet his equal and lose. I never saw John Tuberville again.

Men in barbershops always teased me about girls, alluding to relationships with them that had never entered my mind. I decided I didn't possess the peculiar abilities girls liked in boyfriends—the ability to dance, play football or baseball, smoke cigarettes, or drive a car. So I never thought of taking a girl to a drugstore for a soda or to a theater for a movie. When girls hinted about us doing something together, as if I might be a proper companion, I noted but didn't acknowledge their hints. Girls probably thought me too thickheaded to understand.

One afternoon, I came home and found Mama talking animatedly on the telephone in the hall. As I entered the door, she smiled at me in a peculiar way. I sensed something disastrous taking place when she hung up and grabbed my arm.

"I've just talked to Martha Jane Cole's mother. She invited you to take Martha Jane on a hay ride next Saturday evening. I told Mrs. Cole you'd love to."

"Mama, why did you say that? I hardly know her. We only have math together."

"You need to go with girls as well as boys. Do something besides movies."

"But, Mama, you shoulda asked me before you agreed."

"If I had, you'd have said you didn't want to. You'll have fun."

"I don't even know what a hay ride is."

"You get to ride in a wagon with young people and have a nice picnic."

During the week, thinking of what to wear, I settled on my best shoes, sports coat, sport shirt, and slacks. I knew what Martha Jane looked like but little else, and that worried me. What would we talk about? Why go sit or stand in a wagon filled with hay? Why hay?

Late Saturday afternoon, I was dressed and sitting in the swing when a car driven by a woman pulled up to the curb, facing the wrong direction, and honked. I walked down the front steps as Mama came out waving at Martha Jane's mother.

Leaning out the window, Mrs. Cole said, "Cleveland, honey, I think you don't want to wear good clothes. Change into old knockabouts."

Martha Jane in the back seat had on slacks, a denim shirt, and a short jacket. Mama stood by the car and started a conversation with Mrs. Cole as I ran inside and put on corduroy pants, plaid flannel shirt, jacket, and old shoes. Back in the car, I tried to appear comfortable on the outside but nothing altered my discomfort inside. On my second date with a girl, what would I do next that's wrong? Driving us down to the banks of the Arkansas River, west of the Broadway Bridge, Mrs. Cole kept up a steady conversation, mostly questioning me. We reached a long sandbar where boys and girls were milling around two wagons filled with hay and hitched to mules.

Martha Jane said, "Isn't it exciting? We'll ride out on the sandbar by the river under the stars." That did, indeed, sound like romantic movie stuff. What would we do riding on a sandbar when we can't see anything?

While it was light enough as the sun was sinking slowly behind the high cliffs around the bend across the river, we stood in line for hot dogs and Cokes. Following Mama's advice, I told Martha Jane to find a comfortable place to sit on a driftwood log while I got our refreshments. Almost all the other boys in line were ninth graders, talking eagerly about the dark and their girls.

Martha Jane asked for seconds, and I complied. As we ate another hot dog, many couples had already boarded the hay wagons, and others, like Martha Jane and me, stood gazing into the bonfires.

A male chaperone (a new concept, since I had never attended an adolescent boy-girl party) yelled, "Load up, kids! We're heading up the sandbar."

I helped Martha Jane onto the wagon bed, and we crossed to lean against the siding behind the driver's seat, stepping carefully to avoid the kids already snuggling up close lying in the hay. Away from the bonfires, we could see how really dark the night was without a moon and only stars, with a brisk, cold wind blowing off the river. Even though talking to Martha Jane was easy, especially about movies, the other couples weren't talking. They were embracing, whispering, and kissing—not noting the stars in the sky at all. Martha Jane pushed against me as if she wanted to sit in the same place I was sitting.

She said, "It's so cold. If I'd known, I would have worn a heavier jacket."

I said, "Martha Jane, let me put my jacket over your shoulders."

"No need, Cleveland. Your arms in the sleeves around my shoulders will do."

"I can't put my jacket's arms around your ... oh, oh, I know what you mean."

And I scooted over and pulled her into my arms, like any good movie hero. She turned her face and brushed her cheek against mine, but I couldn't kiss her. There were enough examples around to inspire me, but I couldn't kiss her. I just smiled and said, "This is warmer, isn't it?"

She didn't answer, so I assumed the problem was solved. Of course, it wasn't. She wanted to exchange the same kisses and groping we saw or heard on all sides. I was relieved when the wagons turned to return to where we had started. Mrs. Cole, waiting in her car, wanted to hear about the fun we had had together.

At our house, I thanked Mrs. Cole for the car ride and Martha Jane for the hay ride, concealing an urge to leap out, race up the steps, and escape into the house.

I was more comfortable at the world premiere of a movie at the Pulaski with a couple of boys. The star in the movie was Bob Burns, a native of Van Buren, Arkansas, and a regular cast member on Bing Crosby's *Kraft Music*

Hall. When Arkansas Amusement Company announced the opening of *The Arkansas Traveler* in October of 1938, I was eager to see the droll comic actor who talked so naturally on the radio and puffed on a "bazooka," a primitive musical instrument he invented that sounded like a slide trombone hoarse with a bad cold. How he looked and acted were mysteries to me; I had only heard him talk about his kinfolks in an Arkansas drawl on the radio.

By the time Joe, Clifton, and I met at the Pulaski and bought tickets, the end of the ticket line extended a block from the box office. We didn't want to wait so long getting in, so Joe suggested dropping to our knees to act as though we were looking for lost tickets and crawling to the theater entrance. We knelt, crawled, and asked to be excused. Surprisingly, the crowd, accepting our pretense for real, parted as we advanced on our dirty knees "searching for our tickets." Believe it or not, no one objected to our slow advance to the lobby. Did that reflect people's low opinion of the movie or of Bob Burns's personal presence? We found Mr. Burns on stage was a close-up of what one heard for free on the radio, but he wasn't bad looking and was beautifully dressed.

Mr. Bramlett kept his promise and arranged a job for me at the *Arkansas Democrat*, perhaps making me the first in our gang to work at a regular job. My parking lot certainly hadn't required my presence or effort. Billy Prichards, who lived nearby, didn't have a job, and I didn't know Boykin delivered the *Arkansas Democrat* until he asked me to carry his route for a week when his family went on summer vacation. For me it was an opportunity for excitement more than money, for his route was on Scott and Cumberland between Thirteenth and Fifteenth, the neighborhood of my early childhood.

Boykin and I rode our bikes and walked his route on foot two afternoons before he left. I wasn't to collect fees; Boykin would do that when he returned. Most papers would be thrown but a few dropped at the subscribers' front doors. After making his deliveries on Saturday afternoon, he left eager on his trip. I was tense as I could be, wanting to do my duty properly.

Early Sunday morning, I rode down Fifth in the dark to the *Democrat* building at Scott Street, my new handlebar lights gleaming on the pavement ahead. The bicycle lights were my first ones, because I rarely cycled after dark. Pumping to Boykin's route, I was slowed by the bags of Sunday papers, which were heavier than afternoon editions, and spooked by the dark silence and soft halos of street lamps.

Tossing papers into yards and onto porches was a snap, but laying papers at rooming-house and duplex doors was slower and filled with unexpected sounds and smells. I anticipated snoring (one of my father's superior attainments) and cooking odors, but sneaky, silent cats rubbing my legs and leaping off railings in the dark gave me a few starts. After experiencing Sunday morning deliveries, weekday afternoons were a breeze, and it was fun for subscribers to greet me and question me about Boykin's absence. If he asked me, I'd do the job again.

Boykin's fellowship chiefly meant we spent a great deal of time together, instinctively and unconsciously enjoying each other's presence, and always reinforcing each other in public arguments.

During the coldest winter month of 1939, Troop 40 took an adventurous camping trip one weekend, sleeping overnight in an enclosed cabin at Camp Quapaw. At bedtime, a guy pulled two small cartoon booklets out of his knapsack, one colored and the other black and white, to pass among us in our bunks. The reactions were instantaneous.

"Wow, I never saw a thing as big as that."

"Let me see! Let me see!"

"Goll-lee, will you look at what they're doing."

Their intensity and exclamations captured the attention of the rest of us, and we gathered around the bunks at one end of the cabin, waiting for our turn to see sex pictures. When a few guys wouldn't pass them along, we bent over them, sneaking peeks at the first pornography, other than hand-drawn pictures on the sidewalk or toilet walls, I had seen.

Suddenly, we were aware of a new presence; Mr. Rule had entered while we stared in fascination at the dirty booklets, aroused by what we saw.

"Boys, what's so everlasting interesting that you didn't hear me come in?"

"Only some comic books, sir."

The books were thrust into sleeping bags.

"They must be really strange comics for such attention and no laughs. Mind if I have a look?"

The guys with the booklets pulled them out and handed them to him.

"You won't approve of what you see, Mr. Rule."

"Maybe I don't approve of what *you* see, young man."

Of course, Mr. Rule knew instantly the books' contents, flipping hurriedly through the pages. Then he silently stared at his feet for the longest time, making us uncomfortable, before he looked into the eyes of each of us in turn.

"Fellows, I know how exciting sex is and that you've reached the age to be seriously concerned with it, but I don't believe you'll learn what you need to know about girls looking at cheap, silly distortions like these cartoons. Let me take them, and I'll return them later. But right now, all of you need a good night's rest before a busy day tomorrow. Good night, and turn out the lights."

Mr. Rule's reprimanding us as if we were adults preserved our dignity. After lights out, we expressed concern about his telling Mr. French and our fathers and embarrassing us further. When Daddy let me know he knew, he said there are other books that are worthy of your thoughts and time.

Even though neither Mr. French nor Mr. Rule ever spoke to us as a group about the episode, I think they substituted the father-son banquet organized a month later for that. As many fathers as could helped troop members prepare a spaghetti dinner in the kitchen and banquet room at the church. Organized in teams, we prepared the salad, bread, meat sauce, and spaghetti courses, and set the tables and cleaned up after the meal. For the first time, Daddy joined me doing something together outside our home. He knew a lot about cooking and showed his great sense of humor working with the other fathers and Scouts.

At the banquet, the Reverend M. H. Sikes, pastor of the Highland Methodist Church, suggested that a closer relationship between fathers and sons would help solve problems of juvenile delinquency. In a provoking reversal of what we did reading dirty books, he said:

Every boy is born with the idea that his father is all good.
When a father's conduct causes his son to lose faith in him,
he has done much to damage the boy's faith in humanity.
Every boy should make his father his closest pal
and take him into his confidence.
No man is better than his son, and not many boys
are better than their fathers.

Another memorable occasion at Camp Quapaw was a one-mile race along the dirt road leading from the highway to the camp, pitting teams of the same age and size against one other. There was little likelihood anyone would beat Zach Bair, a distance runner on the track team, and no one did. But I finished right behind him and felt his equal.

Zach's father provided shelter for our next camping trip that winter. Mr. Bair and a group of Little Rock businessmen who owned a hunting-fishing lodge gave Mr. French permission for our troop to spend Saturday night in the old farmhouse after we completed our pioneering exercises.

Boykin, Billy, Joe, and I bedded down to sleep outside on the farm-house's deep porch, but when the temperature dropped achingly low we moved into the common room beside the large fireplace. After someone lighted the fire, smoke billowed from the fireplace and filled the room with smoke that seared our eyes. No one had checked to be sure the flue was open. Even though the doors and windows were opened, the smoke continued stinging our eyes and making our throats sore.

So Boykin, Billy, Joe, and I picked up our blankets and trudged back out on the porch, placing our sleeping bags close to each other for added warmth, yet that didn't prevent us from waking at intervals throughout the frosty night with our chattering teeth. We ate breakfast the next morning still stiff from the cold night on the hard porch floor, and then took off on a cross-country trek. We reached a wide stream and had to cross by leaping from one wet boulder to another. My foot slipped as I leaped between stones, and I plunged into the icy water. Even though I protested, Mr. French sent me back to the farmhouse to dry out by the fire, where I remained until we loaded into the cars for the trip home.

A few weeks later, senior members of the troop spent a day and night of real pioneering in the low-lying bottomland of the Arkansas River backwaters, not far from Scott. The sunless day that Saturday and below-freezing temperature froze the moisture in the ground into icy flakes.

Upon our arrival, we dug a deep hole at the center of the campsite and built a big fire in it. After warming our bodies and hands, we dug a slit trench some distance away in the deep brush for a toilet, erecting a small tree trunk as a horizontal rail for a toilet seat. Most of us set up pup tents, but a few boys seeking pioneering merit badges made ground covers of branches, leaves, and needles under lean-tos of logs and branches to sleep under. When the fire had burned down to a bed of glowing coals, we filled a Dutch oven with beans and ham hock, put the cover on, and lowered the pot into the hole at the center of the campsite, heaping coals over it. We left the beans to cook slowly while we completed our projects, explored the woods, and played games. At day's end, we uncovered the pot, lifted the lid, and ladled the ambrosia of ham and beans into our mess gears for supper. After all the delicious beans we could eat, we sat around the fire singing and telling stories before bedding down.

We didn't know, of course, but we would be the right age for military service if a war ever came. Hardly anyone could imagine that scouting was preparing us for service in an unforeseen conflict. When Boykin and I, as Life and Star Scouts, raised the American flag at the front of East Side before school every morning, lowering and folding the flag after school, hardly anyone paid a bit of patriotic attention to us or the flag.

One person who paid attention to our patriotic duties was our long-time roomer Doc Cockrum. Even though Doc started at the medical school with great enthusiasm after he and his wife rented one of our rooms, he found the requirements tough and the nights long as he prepared for exams with the help of Elsie, who worked to help pay for his schooling. She told Mama that Doc seemed less and less inclined to remain in med school, and he'd been talking about quitting and joining the army with the lieu-tenancy he earned in the Citizens Military Training Corps on weekends and in summers. So he appeared one evening in our family room clad in his U.S. Army military uniform to announce he had been commissioned a second lieutenant and was on his way to join the 31st Infantry Regiment in the Philippine Islands. Sweet Elsie would remain at our house just as she had for four years.

In the last few weeks before our class graduated, the dramatics and music students rehearsed what the *East Side Journal* called "a three-act entertainment": the girls' and boys' glee clubs with the East Side Orchestra; *Two Crooks and a Lady*, a one-act play by the Dramatics Club; and a three-act operetta, *The Galloping Ghost*. For me, the Spring Festival on May 12 was an actor's heyday; I had leading roles in two different plays, since I had to replace one of the actors.

Two Crooks and a Lady was set in the library of the New York mansion of wealthy Mrs. Simms-Vane (Betty Jo Kinsolving), whose maid (Martha Rose Cox) and her young man, Miller, plotted to steal the old woman's jewels. George Lieper, who was first cast as Miller, disapproved of Miss Irma

Davidson's direction and quit the cast the week before the performance. His temperamental withdrawal was typical of him, so Miss Davidson, the director and my art teacher, who had heard I was a "quick study," asked me to replace him. I accepted without even reading the play, eager to play two different roles in one show. Miller required realistic acting, which meant playing his emotions much as I felt them at fourteen.

In *The Galloping Ghost*, I played Lemuel, an eccentric old ranch care-taker. A rancher's high-school son brings a group of friends to the ranch house for the weekend, and Lem gathers the young people in the gloomy living room to tell them a ghost story. A mischievous boy, who is an inge-nious radio hobbyist, brings the ghost in the story to life through a radio broadcast. Before the girls and boys become hysterical about the ghost, another young guest, Messy, discovers the source of the mysterious threat. Playing Lemuel, I had a chance to play an older man and sing three songs.

Preparing my characterization, I drew the following suggestions from a book on character acting: wear clothes similar to those the person would wear; use physical actions to create emotions in yourself; copy a picture of an older person, and use mental images to inspire behavior. I recalled the old men in McRae and Beebe, and chose elements from their appearance and behavior: their bent postures, unkempt hair and beards, and country dialects. Since I didn't know where to buy Stein's sticks of greasepaint make-up, crepe hair, and spirit gum, I fashioned a mustache from the fur of a toy monkey and formed a loop of tape with the adhesive on the outside sticking both to the fur and my skin.

The stage manager's "Places, please!" at *The Galloping Ghost* provided the most exciting warning I ever heard, for Lemuel was the fattest role I'd ever had and a character of my own creation. The *East Junior Journal* printed "Harrison Stars," and the faculty sponsor of the student newspaper wrote a personal note:

> *I'm not saying it with flowers—but I want you*
> *to know how much I enjoyed your performance.*
>
> *—Miss D. Davidson*

Wow! I was already on my way as a serious theater craftsman. But I was prouder still when my classmates voted me "the most talented boy" in our class.

A day or two before our graduation, I was teasing Lucille and Vivian, my female pals, at the foot of the stairs beside a classroom, grabbing their arms and pulling them to my sides. An instant later, a steel hand gripped my neck, suspending me in my tracks. I released the girls and turned to face the grim face of Mr. Ziegler, the manual arts teacher, at the door of his classroom beside the stairs. The girls tip-toeing up the steps looked back as Mr. Ziegler whirled me into a corner.

"What do you think you're doing, grabbing and hugging those girls in the hall, mister?"

I wondered if he preferred I do it somewhere else. "I wasn't doing anything wrong, Mr. Ziegler, just teasing."

"Pushing girls around isn't teasing. You're not so funny, mister. I don't wanna see you do that again. You need to treat girls properly."

I wondered what he knew about treating girls properly. To Mr. Ziegler I wasn't funny, but the girls thought I was entertaining and that I treated them properly.

In late spring, graduating ninth graders were herded without preliminary warning into the cafeteria to take a battery of standardized tests to determine our academic placement in English, math, and science at high school. The room still smelled of lunch—like an empty tin soup can—and the space was still humid from the steam of dishwashing in the kitchen. The overhead lights had been adequate for eating but were not sufficient for reading and interpreting test questions. I faced a blank wall in my seat at a cafeteria table, and the kids on either side squeezed me so tightly, I could hardly bend my elbows to write. Those conditions certainly didn't help raise the test scores, which would never be revealed to us.

Our graduation ceremony was in East Side's auditorium on the bare stage where I had appeared so often in some disguise over the past three years. Mr. Swearingen, of course, presided, presenting our diplomas and shaking our hands on May 30, 1939.

My three years at East Side had been busy ones; I was a general news reporter on the *East Side Journal* staff, clerk in the main office, chapter secretary of the National Junior Honor Society, and actor-singer in three spring festivals. I also won letters for scholarship five out of six semesters. At graduation, the Sons of the American Revolution awarded me a certificate for excellence in leadership and patriotism, and my classmates voted me "the most talented boy" in our class. The unexpected social coup was Shirley Vestal, the daughter of Little Rock's most prominent florist, inviting me to a party at her home in Sylvan Hills. Luckily, Mama had bought me new slacks and a sport coat to wear at graduation.

That summer, I played with Billy Prichards, who lived between Broadway and State on Sixth Street, behind the Hotel Frederica. Billy had brilliant red hair, pale skin, and freckles, and had attended Peabody Elementary before East Side. The first time I played at his house, I found its compact arrangement unusual; the bedrooms, dining room, and kitchen were around a large central living room. He and his mother shared a bedroom, his sister and grandmother had the other two, and a fourth was reserved for his absent father. In his father's room, he showed me his dad's hair brush and comb, cuff links, and ties. His father's photograph on the bureau resembled actor Lewis Stone, who played Judge Hardy in the Andy Hardy movies.

His mother, Mrs. Bess Prichards, a milliner, owned Madeline's Millinery Shoppe, which was named after Billy's sister. Her shop, at the back of the first floor of the Hollenberg Building on Capitol Avenue, was two rooms filled with sewing machines, work tables, dressmaker model and hat forms, and mannequins. I enjoyed going there when Billy asked for money to go to a picture show with me.

Madeline's friend Sherry spent a lot of time at the Prichardses' in the summer when Billy and I were hanging around listening to music on the radio and his grandmother's Victrola. If "Stairway to the Stars" or "Deep Purple" played on the radio, Sherry and Madeline sometimes danced with each other, but one day Madeline wasn't interested. Sherry liked me, maybe even in a slightly romantic way since I was nearly a foot taller, and reached out to me. Whatever her reason or feelings, she volunteered to teach me how to dance. Madeline and Billy were busy elsewhere when "Stairway" began playing softly on the radio, and Sherry grasped my left hand and put my right hand at her waist and embraced me, the first time so much of my body had been so close to a girl's.

Sherry said, "Let me show you how to foxtrot. It's a combination of simple steps, slow moves to two beats of music, and quick to one beat of music."

Caught in her firm but tender grasp, not certain which foot to place where, I traveled counterclockwise around the living room in her embrace, as the singer on the record dulcetly suggested:

Let's build a stairway to the stars
And climb that stairway to the stars
With love beside us to fill the night with a song.

Once I had the knack of the movements, I relaxed and realized how soft and warm her body felt against mine, and how delicate the scent of perfume in her hair. Pulling her head away from my chest, she looked into my eyes and kissed me on the lips. What a rush but how embarrassing that was!

"You're a good kisser, Cleveland, " she said, laying her head on my chest again and guiding my steps to the beat of the music:

We'll hear the sound of violins
Out yonder where the blue begins
The moon will guide us as we go drifting along.

PHOTO OPPOSITE PAGE:
Cleveland at the beginning of his high school career.

CHAPTER 8

Around the Corner but Uphill

IN THE AUTUMN of 1939, the beginning of Charles Dickens's *A Tale of Two Cities* epitomized my life and the state of the world:

It was the best of times, it was the worst of times...

After seeing the movie of Dickens's novel about the French Revolution, I added Ronald Colman, as Sydney Carton, to my repertoire. I changed his character's name to "Cigarette Carton" and changed the word *rest* to *place* in the last statement he made while riding to the guillotine in a tumbrel beside a frightened little seamstress:

It is a far, far better thing that I do, than I have ever done;
it is a far, far better [place] that I go to, than I have ever known.

With no tumbrel but many a streetcar, Little Rock Senior High School seemed a far, far better place to go from East Side.

Eager for funny material and to learn more about acting, I went to *Ninotchka*; *Wuthering Heights*; *Goodbye, Mr. Chips*; *Stagecoach*; *Gone with the Wind*; and *The Wizard of Oz*—the best movies of the most celebrated year in American film history. I borrowed Bert Lahr's Cowardly Lion accent, tremolo, and outrageous caterwauling "gnaang, gnaagng," which matched "allah-paw-longee!"

When *Gone with the Wind* opened at the Pulaski Theater, the long, noisy ticket line snaked far back from the box-office on Fifth, turned the corner onto Spring, went one block north, and turned again at Fourth reaching all the way to Center. Before the movie started, there was unexpected overture music, with the audience sitting as quietly as churchgoers only to explode in chattering and applause when the Old Mill at Lakewood in North Little Rock appeared on screen. I liked the first two-thirds of the movie, but after Scarlett and Rhett married, frankly, I didn't give a damn!

Gone with the Wind, like every movie Hollywood released in 1939, competed with the reality of the newsreels showing the German army overrunning Europe and threatening the British Isles. The whole world seemed split, convulsive, and damned even though the United States hadn't yet come under fire. Then Britain and France declared war but didn't attack Germany, perpetuating the deceptive calm of a "Phony War."

A real calm prevailed at our house. The routines of long-term lodgers and our family members rarely collided at the bathroom door. Daddy's professional life had been eased by his new Chevrolet, and his stove and appliance business grew in an enlarged territory. Buster had risen to head checker at Food Palace. Though crammed into the pantry beside me again, he seemed settled, his only indulgence being late supper and beer after work at the Triangle Cafe.

The in-and-outers and regulars in our backyard parking lot continued adding "moola" to my bank account. Miss Compton and a male lawyer in the Rector Building rented both sides of our garage from seven a.m. to six p.m., five days a week. And Mr. Martin of the U.S. Engineers and his wife, in the Rector Building, still rented space for their car in our backyard as three-year regulars.

I was worried about the demands of high school when Boogie (our classmate Clifton Smith), who joined a fraternity while at East Side, offered me a ride to a get-acquainted party at Spring Lake Country Club, a private club in deep woods off the Pine Bluff highway beside a shallow lake filled with tree stumps. The boys I met there were mostly strangers, so when Clifton disappeared, I felt like an awkward impostor. But Boogie sprang out of the bathhouse door without a stitch of clothes on and dived into the water. He swam a lap among the stumps, emerged, and walked among the guests talking in what seemed an immodest predicament to me. Of course, the occasion had been planned for frat members (in clothes) to judge potential pledges.

Shortly after the Spring Lake affair, the fraternity pledged its new members. Arthur Stranz, who pledged Delta Sigma, revealed that Jimmy Wassell, the son of Commander Corydon Wassell (the Little Rock physician and naval officer who later performed a heroic rescue of servicemen and civilian women from the Island of Java in World War II), blackballed me. So my chance to be in a social fraternity appeared and vanished in a weekend. Despite Arthur's sympathy for me and impatience with Jimmy, the blackball was a stroke of good fortune that removed financial obligations I couldn't afford and social obligations I would never wish to meet. His blackball was my highball.

After the frat's rejection, I expected other guys might have misgivings about me. Yet as I shopped for books at Berry's Book Store and Allsopp & Chapple, my old friends and new acquaintances treated me cordially as always.

On the first day of school, I rode a trolley to Sixteenth and Park to behold the buff-brick high-school building glowing in the early morning sunlight like an Italian Renaissance castle. The neatly trimmed carpet of green lawn along the two blocks of Park Street out front lay dappled with dew rather than sprinkled with gravel like East Side's grounds. I walked through a tiny copse of cedar and pine trees, past an oblong fishpond flashing with pink carp under the water's surface, and stopped by the colonnade to stare at the central tower of "America's Most Beautiful High School," which was clamoring with the ruffle of snare and boom of bass drums, squeals of clarinets, clarions of trumpets, and oompahs of tubas.

Climbing to several sets of double doors at the main entry, I was breathless, not from physical effort but from the social scene: scores of boys and girls standing, sitting, and lying down—alone or in groups—on the wide steps and balustrades at every level, the low vocal rumble interspersed with shouts and screams of recognition. I passed the 2,000 students enrolled in the most extensive curricular program of any high school in Arkansas to wait for Joe at one of the front doors.

Then a high-pitched, prolonged cry of "allah-paw-longee!" rose above murmuring-laughing-shouting students lolling on the landings. In an instant, Boykin slapped my back and feinted a goose that made me miss the four Greek figures of *Personality, Ambition, Preparation,* and *Opportunity* above the front doors. Weeks passed before I would see them.

Boykin, Joe, and I stopped by the athletic trophy cases outside the auditorium doors to decide how to reach our homerooms. I found Room 307 with Mr. Everett C. Barnes, the chemistry teacher, standing beside a black-topped lab table, his smile as brittle as cold toast. Judging by his long face and bald head, he was in his early forties. The sign he posted on the frosted glass of his lab door reflected his attitude:

LABORATORY: *Observe the first five letters! Avoid the last seven!*

Since chemistry wasn't one of my courses, Mr. Barnes rarely spoke to me.

My homeroom included last names beginning with *A* through *K*. Sitting with boys from well-known Pulaski Heights families, I didn't kid about "pew-nasty heights!" They were mostly strangers: Bobby Gosdin, Thomas Hackler, Jimmy Gammill, Arch Heim, Waymond Elrod, Jimmie Huie, Tommy Hurt, Earl Fuqua, Ellis Fagan, Max Heiman, and others. Our business the first day was choosing homeroom officers, as well as a student council representative, Bible reader, attendance checker, and seller of tickets and *Tiger* newspapers.

Peppy Bobby Gosdin was elected president, and a handful of East Side boys helped elect me vice president—maybe because I kept my mouth shut and had a presidential aura to my name. Weeks later, when Bert Gaster, our new student council representative, moved, the class elected me to fill the dull position with responsibilities no one wanted.

Bobby ran a tight schedule, keeping order and making announcements. Arch Heim, our secretary with the look of a little boy, demanded all items be repeated to record in the minutes. The similarity between his and Max Heiman's names was confusing, although their personalities were as opposite as salt and pepper. Earl Fuqua, our salesman, regularly accosted us with hot tickets. His pal, Frank Schay, from another homeroom, visited him every morning to check the accuracy of his chemistry and math homework. I directed idle attention at Ellis Fagan's ears, whose lobes daily sported dabs of cream from a shave he didn't need. Ellis wore dress shirts every day; but the fancy broadcloth with French cuffs confirmed it was Monday.

Joining a mix of popular boys and girls with bright minds and spirited personalities in the student council appealed to me. Without political ambition, I offered no suggestions to improve student life, only kibitzed *sotto voce* to relieve the boring routine by waylaying Robert's Rules of Order, just happy to be there.

My attitude in academic classes had more serious objectives. Sharing high-school math with Boykin guaranteed my earning a better-than-passing grade. The first day of class, our teacher, the assistant principal—short, stubby, and round faced—reminded me of Hugh Herbert, a dithering movie actor. After a week, I saw no resemblance between them. Gentle, modest, and soft-spoken Mr. J. H. Bigbee treated our stumbling efforts with the algebraic equations and inequalities as patiently as a mother hen with chicks. Word problems was the most frightening phrase until quadratic equations were introduced.

Boykin, a whiz bang at college algebra, explained ideas Mr. Bigbee didn't cover in class or explore individually. His ever-ready advice helped me earn Bs, which would have been Cs, or worse, without his assistance. I became better acquainted with Mr. Bigbee, a happy precursor to his unsympathetic math successor, on a drive to Memphis the following year.

Even though I loved to sing, in or out of school, I feared my tenor was too weak to get into the glee club, for the squeaky notes I hit sounded like a squealing clarinet. My speaking voice was a high baritone like my father's. But we learned a tryout song, and Earl Nichols, my singing pal from East Side, could hardly wait for the solo auditions. We newcomers gathered under the low ceiling of Room 127 in the basement, with the choir members who were in tenor, baritone, and bass sections. We were ready to sing for Mrs. Settle and establish our voice placement.

A tall, angular lady entered the room and sat at the piano. As we stood beside Mrs. Settle, the music supervisor for the public schools, at the piano, she smiled a toothy smile like Mrs. Roosevelt's, looking into our eyes as we sang a verse and chorus of "Here's to the schooner and the cup, and a log on the fire." I thought she was sharp as a razor's edge.

She asked me to repeat the high notes I had mastered listening to Stuart Churchill, a singer and arranger, on Fred Waring's Chesterfield cigarette radio show weekday afternoons. I sang along with him until I knew how to sing falsetto. Even though mine, in the range of a boy soprano, wasn't very loud, Mrs. Settle placed me with the first tenors, while Earl's rich, well-supported voice joined the second tenors.

Much as I liked music, academics had first priority. Short, stout Miss Laura Pedersen, my teacher for ancient history, had a plain face and the short haircut of a Russian peasant, perhaps appropriate to her political interests. On Fridays, after our weekly history exams, she explored recent novels and current events. She and Miss Elizabeth Pape, a biology instructor at Little Rock Junior College, had visited Soviet Russia in the mid-1930s to witness the results of the Five-Year Plan of 1928.

They saw on the spot how the collectivization policies affected lives in the Soviet Union. The abolition of free markets brought shortages of food, clothing, and consumer goods. Peasants fleeing collectivized villages created acute shortages of housing in the major cities, leading to jamming whole families into single rooms in communal apartments, filling the overcrowded country with endless queues, broken families, and hollow promises of future abundance. When she read from *Native Son* by Richard Wright, the editor of the *Daily Worker* since 1937, I wondered if that was a clue to her political leanings.

What it was like to live surrounded by other people, intimate strangers, night and day, I understood better than most of my classmates did.

Miss Pedersen also introduced contemporary American literature by reading aloud from novels and short stories such as those in *My Name Is Aram* by William Saroyan, which detailed the escapades of a rambunctious, irrepressible nine-year-old boy in an immigrant Armenian community in rural Fresno, California. Then she read from *You Can't Go Home Again* by Thomas Wolfe, a serious southern writer who left New York and lived in England, Germany, and his Carolina hometown, and was dismayed by social decay in American society. Wolfe's last novel would be the first one I read.

When Miss Pedersen's readings didn't fascinate me, I sat transfixed by a beautiful senior sitting ahead of me who was late fulfilling her sophomore history requirement. Sydney Stifft, the daughter of the owner of Stifft's Jewelry Store downtown, often turned to ask me questions about the lesson. Gazing into the eyes of a classmate as faultless and attractive as Hedy Lamarr, I asked her in wonder, "Lesson? Which lesson?" before sputtering any kind of reply.

Ironically, Miss Pedersen had more effect upon my understanding of the English language than Miss Janette Harrington, my English teacher. My work in English was good but not outstanding in a class of scruffy boys who committed grammatical and usage errors with pride, not apology. If Miss McMahan had been there, she would straighten them out and fill their minds with grammatical principles. Miss Clean playing Miss Mean could convert them all!

Near the fall semester's end, Miss Harrington casually mentioned that my skill in reading aloud and writing essays had convinced her I should be in a more advanced class. When I recalled the extremely poor physical conditions for placement tests in the East Side cafeteria, I wasn't surprised. Yet changing English instructors had to wait until next year.

Even though I had an ear and tongue for imitating foreign accents and American dialects, I wasn't equally adept at languages. After two years of classic Latin at East Side, I could fulfill the high-school foreign language requirement with one more semester of Latin. Unfortunately, I was assigned to Miss Essie Hill, who was considerably older than Miss Anne Chandler, the other Latin instructor. Miss Hill's appearance and manner proved far more memorable for me than her Latin lessons. Surely near retirement, she appeared to be a gray bird on fragile legs in her "dressy" dresses and stiff shoes, their heels spiked and toes turned-up. Her cautious walk led a class wag to claim her toes were wooden.

After reading Julius Caesar's *The Gallic Wars* in Latin and English, I recall that "Gaul is divided into three parts," and "Veni, vidi, vici" (I came, I saw, I conquered). We also read about Roman art and architecture and brief essays in Latin by Virgil, Horace, and Ovid. Even though she never faulted my efforts, she gave me a B for the first six weeks, which sank to a C+ by the end of the semester. Whatever our mutual inadequacies, the study of Latin shaped my use of English.

On Halloween night, Boykin, Joe, and I met at the carnival sponsored by the East Side faculty to keep their students off the streets and out of mischief. Even though we only recently and happily left the junior high behind, perhaps we already longed to return. And maybe we wished to see again the teachers who helped us cross various thresholds. Probably we matured sufficiently in four months to recognize soaping windows, ringing doorbells, and moving lawn furniture were wastes of our time.

We arrived at the carnival without masks or costumes, revealing that we needed to be acknowledged as older guys from high school. Strolling the halls as a trio, feeling our seniority, we greeted the younger girls and boys we knew, stopped at booths to throw balls at pyramids of wooden bottles, tossed embroidery rings around prizes atop pedestals, fished for negligible prizes behind a curtain, or heard our fortunes read from cards by an outrageously disguised teacher. To record our return, we had our photographs taken by the Science Club. Even though our former teachers recalled our names and asked for opinions of high school, our return was bittersweet for us.

Departing without prizes or loose change but with the faint taste of hot dogs and root beer on our tongues, we hoped the Science Club mailed our pictures as promised. Going back to East Side helped me understand Thomas Wolfe's point in *You Can't Go Home Again*: you cannot recover the past; what appears everlasting is changing. Even my own image in the photo received in the mail the following week differed from the plainer, younger person I still thought I saw in the mirror.

Joe had waited impatiently for the football season to begin, sports being as compelling to him as the arts were to me. He imposed his obsession upon me by discussing players and their abilities and speculating on LRHS's chances against our school's arch rivals, Pine Bluff and North Little Rock. When football practice began, we bicycled to the practice field beside the new stadium to see and judge the players. It was the first time I saw the gray, concrete bleachers—a roofless, rectangular concrete-and-steel stand of tiered rows of seats—that replaced the weather-beaten wooden bleachers of old Kavanaugh Field.

While we didn't yet know the names of sophomore team members, we had heard of a superb senior running back named Howard Hughes. We read in the sports pages how he scored touchdowns with the same ease the well-known flyer of the same name did with Hollywood starlets, both men famous for their passes. We knew by sight several guys in our class—Earl Bowman, Jim Crafton, Bill Simms, Carl Dillaha, and Bill Graham—on the team. Even if we had wanted to play, we lacked the physiques and strength even to sit on the bench with those guys.

The Little Rock Tigers, coached by Clyde Van Sickle, had winning records for many years, supported by our cheers at pep rallies in the auditorium and in the stands beside the field at home games. But Joe didn't think our presence and cheering were sufficient; we had to promote the team in more concrete ways. So we first cut tiny paper squares neatly with scissors to match the confetti we saw tossed at New Year's Eve parties.

But Joe blurted, "Why are we doing this? It's not a darned girl's tea party!"

So we gathered old newspapers, ripping them any which way and filling large grocery sacks with the litter for each game. Tearing the newspapers filled the pores of our hands with black printer's ink which, if laid on a clean sheet of paper, imposed black palm prints. At every game in the stadium, we left debris, wet and dry, in our wake.

Even though the 1939 Tigers were underdogs against the Pine Bluff

Zebras, the team slogged on soggy turf in Pine Bluff to a 0–0 tie. Joe said if we'd been there tossing a shower of newsprint, the Tigers would have squeezed out at least one point to win. In 1940, we helped the Tigers come from behind and beat the Zebras 14–12. Then Coach Van Sickle joined the staff at the University of Arkansas in 1941, to be replaced by Clarence Geis of Jonesboro.

Coach Geis's first game at Pine Bluff was my first and only opportunity to see the Tigers away from Little Rock stadium. Jim MacFarlane and Betty Romick double-dating with Patsy Rimmey and Jack Whisnant were going to drive to Pine Bluff for the game in Jim's pale green 1938 Pontiac decorated with black and gold show card signs on the side windows and trunk: "Hail to the Tigers, Hell to the Zebras" and "Wipe out the Stripes."

When Jack's medical school professor sprang a last-minute exam, Jim asked me to escort Patsy, a bright, dainty, pert blonde, to the game. Jim already had corsages of yellow mums with black and yellow ribbons from Vestal Florist's on Broadway, and Jack's approval for me to escort Patsy. She and I enjoyed each other's company, but since Jim and Betty talked very little, Patsy didn't know what to make of my constant chatter and impressions. All of us quietly submitted to the Zebras' overwhelming victory of 33–0 over the Tigers. Later, the North Little Rock Wildcats would also beat the Tigers 26–0 on Thanksgiving, the usual day for the capital city rivalry. Joe had a paroxysm of grief.

When school resumed in 1940, after our Christmas break, I expected to see the same old faces in biology; to my surprise, a new, prettier one showed up in Homer Berry's 10B class. She quietly sat at the lab table in front of Jane Hamilton and me, observing the boisterous reunions of classmates from the fall semester. The slender newcomer, in a moss-green dress with a pale green and orange scarf, had a round, pretty face, gold-rimmed glasses, and brown hair sparkling with red highlights. Before the new girl joined us, Jane, my eleventh-grade partner, was the only glamour in our ordinary class.

Mr. Berry usually wore a sweat suit and tennis shoes with a whistle at his neck, but he taught biology with a white smock over his suit trousers, dress shirt, and tie. The large, sweet-spirited man, who excelled as assistant football and track coach rather than academic biologist, called the class to order. After a few remarks, he released our class, and I had an opportunity to meet Marian Gammill, a mid-term transfer from Pulaski Heights, called "Tumpy" by Jane. How did such a cute girl get such an odd nick-name? There was a question to ask her! It turned out she had been a chubby child her family called "Humpty Dumpty," which was shortened to Tumpy. We shared hellos, goodbyes, and comments but no other courses for the rest of the semester. Separated, we saw a year pass before encountering one another on campus again.

The second semester, I joined the A Cappella Choir with some girls and boys I knew at church and East Side: Jean Moreland, Eleanor Schweig, Eloise Weir, Jackie Franke, Louise Atkinson, Earl Nichols, Pat Riley, Edmund Taylor, and Bill Hollopeter. Mrs. Settle first organized the choir in 1938 and won state championships every year thereafter. At our first meeting of the spring, she said the choir's appearance at the National Music Educators' Conference in San Antonio, Texas, in spring 1939, resulted in an invitation to the Southwestern Music Educators conference, in April 1940, in Wichita, Kansas. She warned us that we'd miss classes from April 15 to 19 and needed to ask our teachers for permission to go.

I wanted like the dickens to sing in Wichita! I hadn't been out of Arkansas since Denver when I was five. Mama and Daddy favored the trip, which would be more educational than five class days. I had done well in all my courses in the fall, and had a B+ in algebra through the second six weeks before beginning to struggle. Mrs. Ethel Rivers said that my recent work was too poor for me to miss classes. I asked for an incomplete that I would make up quickly, and she reluctantly agreed. I was off to the races! Singers in the choir rehearsed long, odd hours preparing for the ambitious program Mrs. Settle chose from our repertoire of religious, international, folk, operetta, and contemporary songs.

On April 15, before sunrise, Daddy drove me and my Gladstone bag packed with clothes and toilet articles to the small parking lot at the north end of the high-school building, where the bus stood with motor running waiting for choir members to board. Mrs. Settle, traveling separately in her own car, was conferring with a middle-aged man I assumed was the bus driver. By seven, the bus was fully loaded and had departed on the long trek through the Ozark Mountains and Oklahoma to Wichita, Kansas.

At the beginning of the trip, choir members played an informal game of musical seats, changing partners several times between Little Rock and the Ozark Mountains. At first, girls sat beside girls and boys with boys, but boys were soon more likely to sit by girls. For us younger, more recent choir members, we sat together rather than with older girls and boys until farther down the road. Some kids who had heard me do impersonations at East Side asked me to repeat my routine of voices. Since it was difficult to hear over the road noise, I performed for three or four people at a time, meeting every choir member before we reached Wichita.

We arrived in the still of the night at the Broadview Hotel beside the Arkansas River in Wichita, and were assigned four to a room. Earl Nichols, R.V. Bethay, Dick Adamson, and I, all of us tenors, were together. Traveling on the bus, sleeping in the same room, and dining together had welded the choir more firmly together, socially and musically. Early the next morning, we ate breakfast in the hotel dining room, then gathered in the lobby for our vocal warm-ups. The other hotel guests formed an enthusiastic audience in the lobby, applauding even the scales we sang. Separately, the men warmed up with "Stout-Hearted Men" and the women with "I Heard a Forest Praying," followed by applause that was deafening. Already a success, we happily boarded the bus to go sing at several conference sessions, each time receiving standing ovations.

The second night at the hotel, everyone felt so high after such enthusiastic receptions, we had trouble sleeping, except for low-key R. V. Bethay, who turned in early and remained asleep even with his roommates and their friends talking. Earl Nichols, with the smile of an elf, quietly suggested dipping R. V.'s bare hand in a glass of water to make him pee. Of course, the liquid tickle didn't force a trickle, but we all ended wet in a water fight after R. V.'s vituperative response.

The next day, the choir toured Wichita, which was the geographic center of the forty-eight contiguous United States and was called "the air capital of the world." Shopping for souvenirs downtown, I bought a small engraved vase for Mama. The next morning, after our short informal concert in the lobby, the choir boarded the bus and departed for home. I sat beside someone who would become my lifetime pal, Earl Nichols.

Choir members at the front of the bus noticed the bus driver's erratic steering and passed the word to the rest of us. When we had our rest stop at Fayetteville, the older boys decided the driver was too drunk to drive and waited for Mrs. Settle's arrival to decide what to do. It seems the driver, after his final celebration in Wichita, continued to nip more drinks on the way through Oklahoma back to Arkansas. Mrs. Settle and J. P. Van Pelt spoke to the argumentative driver, who didn't want to be relieved. But they established that he was a war veteran and persuaded him to remain at the Veterans Administration hospital in Fayetteville until he recovered.

J. P. Van Pelt, the choir's president and bass soloist, replaced the driver and drove the bus home safely.

Daddy met me late that night at high school and asked, "What the devil took you all so long getting back?" I didn't tell him about replacing the drunk driver; Mama didn't need to know about that.

When I reported to algebra on Monday, I recognized how unsympathetic Mrs. Rivers was about my going to Kansas and how far behind I was, even missing only two class days. I had As and Bs in biology, English, and history but received a D (the only one I made at school) for the third six weeks in algebra. Fortunately, with Boykin's help, I pulled my grade up to C+ by the end of the semester, but I never established a positive rapport with Mrs. Rivers. Even though I recovered my equilibrium with her and algebra, it wasn't the happy relationship I shared with other teachers. I wondered if I reminded her of a former student.

At school, if no assemblies were scheduled on Fridays, we attended clubs. Some were honor societies—LR Club (athletics), National Honor Society (scholarship), Quill and Scroll (journalism), Graphic Arts Society (printing), Junior Classical League, French, Spanish, and Latin. Each intramural sport and athletic boosters group had a special club. The array included aviation, hobbies, reading, first aid, knitting, gardening, engineering, scrapbook, stamps, foreign correspondence, art appreciation, photography, and Forum. Teachers sponsored the clubs, but a few had private citizen advisers.

Joe was a member of the downtown YMCA, so I joined him in the Hi-Y Club for 1939–40. The sponsor, Mr. Billy Kramer of the YMCA staff, was a short man with rapidly receding kinky black hair. His massive shoulders, chest, and short legs looked like a medicine ball on gnarled stumps. Speaking to us in a throaty, raspy voice, he distorted the pronunciations of words as every molecule of his muscular body burst with energy. Propounding convictions with a revivalist's ferocity about health and physical exercise, he commenced club meetings as the first boy showed up, then, growling endlessly about the values of "fidge-ee-kull edge-uh-kashun" when the group formed, he permitted few opportunities for club members to interrupt with their observations or questions.

Even though we laughed at Mr. Kramer's manner when we were away from the club meetings, he was so sincere and vigorously entertaining as he related stories of his boxing career that we liked him. We accomplished nothing at our meetings beyond listening, horsing around, and adding Kramer anecdotes to his legend. Even though Mr. Kramer disappeared from our lives after Hi-Y Club, I recalled him the next summer when Boykin fell for a girl named Frieda, who worked with Mrs. Kramer at the Millwood swimming pool.

Boykin kept his private rapture a secret, but he was reported seen cozying up with Frieda at the pool. Jim and I wanted to see the girl who had swept our friend into a "hot and heavy" pursuit, so we bicycled many miles out the Hot Springs highway to get a view of her. Perspiring and weary at the ride's end, we hurried to the snack bar beside the large bathhouse for cold Cokes, though the pool hadn't opened for the day for swimmers. We asked a beautifully tanned, curvaceous girl at the counter for Cokes and she waited on us, even though the bar was closed.

The boss came out to remind "Frieda" to serve only during the posted hours. Nevertheless, we had found the flame scorching Boykin's libido and understood the attraction.

With our curiosity and thirst satisfied, we checked out the laughter and screams of pleasure coming from the pool. At one end of the pool, a large, robust woman was conducting a swimming class for kids, floating like a hilly island surrounded by an archipelago of children. The lifeguard said she was Mrs. Carolyn Kramer, our good old Hi-Y Billy's wife. Even floating on her back, she radiated the same energetic presence teaching swimming as her dynamo husband had teaching boxing at Kramer's summer day camp.

Millwood had more attractions than White City in the Heights—a unique toboggan slide from atop a water tank to a small pool beside the larger one, and water games on a big, spinning top, a cable across one end of the pool with ring handholds to swing across, and, of course, a diving board. Jim and I didn't stay long our first day at Millwood, but we returned many times in his car to swim and picnic in the shady bowers around the pool.

Our other destination on the Hot Springs highway, between Little Rock and Millwood, was Brodie, the cottage of Mr. Heinie Loesch and his wife, who were friends of Jim's mother, Eleanor, and her second husband, Mr. Clemens. Even though he was the night editor of the *Arkansas Gazette*, he asked us teenage boys to call him Heinie and visit their country place often: "Where the sun rises at 10 and sets late ... you may do the same." The Loeschs invited us to play tennis on their court with their two young nieces. So during Boykin's fling with Frieda, Jim and I played tennis at Brodie in the morning and spent afternoons at Millwood.

One afternoon on our way home on our bikes, Jim and I turned off Asher Avenue at Thirty-six Street to go through Boyle Park to Twelfth Street. The park had parallel asphalt roads, one higher than the other, running from Thirty-sixth to Archwood where they intersected. The higher road to the east ran through woodland, and the lower one to the west led past the large pavilions in the heart of the park. The high road joined the lower road at the foot of a steeply banked curve bordered by widely separated gray boulders along the shoulders.

Taking the high road, Jim challenged me to race to the intersection of the two roads. I eagerly accepted, assuming that my newer Western Flyer, with balloon tires, could run faster than his old thin-tired bike from another era. We started the race at the highest point on the road before it descended to the intersection. Racing, we were even at least two blocks. Approaching what is now Archwood, I pulled ahead going downhill without braking on the curve, assuming I could take the curve going as near the boulders as possible. My estimate of the proper speed and space to turn safely was mistaken. I struck the second roadside boulder squarely and flew off the bike over the boulder, landing on my back.

Jim was at my side so quick, I assumed he had the same accident. He had anticipated my poor judgment trying to win.

I hurt all over, but my injuries were only abrasions and bruises on my arms and legs. My bike's front wheel looked like a doughnut with a bite removed. Relieved I wasn't injured, I wondered how I would get home with the broken wheel. Jim suggested I remove the front wheel and push the frame on the rear wheel, carrying the broken wheel on top. Instead of abandoning his awkward friend, he walked beside me, pushing his own bike, to my house. That's a real friend! Unfortunately, Jim spent the rest of that summer with an uncle in St. Louis

After he left, I biked to Joe Hart's house, sometimes staying all day. His folks, who owned the two-story apartment house, lived in the downstairs apartment and rented out the one upstairs. Ellie, the older sister of a popular girl at East Side, lived upstairs. In the middle of the summer, Joe's mother visited relatives in another town and left Joe and his father to fend for themselves. Joe's dad, a plumber, was usually away working on house calls and came home after I left, so Joe had the apartment to himself all day. We'd been playing ball in the vacant lot beside his house or checkers and card games in the house until our classmate Clifton Smith joined us.

Even though I admired Clifton's athletic ability at Rightsell, we were never close after I abandoned my athletic ambitions and pretensions at East Side. I played at his house on a high terrace on south Chester Street once, but my personality didn't meld with a boy as adventurous as he, a risk taker. When, where, or how he earned his nickname Boogie (pronounced *Boo-jee*) were mysteries.

Until Boogie joined us, Joe and I paid no attention to Ellie Buchanan, who occupied the Harts' upstairs apartment. But Boogie was like a birddog scenting a covey of quail and noted her presence the first day he stopped at Joe's. Then, if he knew she was home, he talked loudly enough to Joe and me for her to hear him on the upstairs porch. One morning, although there had been no plan to play tennis, he arrived with his racquet and can of tennis balls, juggling them in the yard below until one "accidentally" fell on her porch. Of course, he rang Ellie's doorbell and ran upstairs to reclaim the ball and meet Ellie face to face.

Apparently, Boogie was as attractive to her as she was to him, for they spent a lot of time smooching in the swing together at night after I went home. The next morning, Boogie would brag about his time with Ellie the night before, telling just enough about his maneuvers as a lady's man to leave a lot unsaid that excited our imaginations. Joe and I were spellbound by his exploits, real or imagined, until Ellie found a job and moved away.

Boogie's presence lent something sexual to anything he was involved with. For example, the "Poe show" that succeeded the Buchanan episode. The well-to-do Poe family—father, mother, daughter, and son—lived in a large two-story Victorian house on a big lot on Broadway, between Fifteenth and Sixteenth. I never once saw the parents who left their fourteen-year-old daughter, Irene, and ten-year-old son, Charley, in the care of servants, who also seemed absent most of the time. Though I never passed beyond the Poes' front porch, Boogie spent an afternoon inside the house with Irene, opening her father's liquor cabinet and sampling his whiskey. Since her little brother was present, she and Boogie didn't go beyond liquid spirits.

But when Irene heard we were hanging out at Joe's house, she came without her little brother, and Boogie, letting one experimental idea lead to another, persuaded Joe and Irene, before I arrived one morning, to play strip poker. Without joining them, I saw Joe, poor kid, without his shirt, barefooted and in shorts. Irene had likely seen more of him than he would see of her. Yet it was Boogie's intention for all to see all of Irene when he suggested the game. I observed their game until the cards fell Boogie's way, forcing Irene to shed her shoes, socks, and dress before preparing to remove her brassiere. I felt guilty for everyone and had no intention of being a voyeur; I was embarrassed for her and disappointed the guys took advantage of her. Joe later told me their game of strip poker ended after I left, and we never referred to it again.

Boogie had started smoking while hanging around with Ellie, offering Joe and me cigarettes when he lit up. Joe refused after smoking several cigarettes, but I grew up in a house filled with my father's and brother's smoke. Imitating them, I had played cowboy games smoking grape vines and Cubeb "medicinal" cigarettes from the drugstore. Even though Mama discouraged my play-like smoking, she didn't stop me. Anyway, I began accepting and smoking Boogie's real cigarettes—that is until Mama and Daddy unexpectedly drove up and stopped in front of Joe's house one Saturday afternoon. Boogie and I were sitting on Joe's front steps smoking, puffing away big as you please, when I saw Daddy's car. I handed my cigarette to Boogie and ran out to the car, hoping to distract them. But I also feared Mama would smell the tobacco on my breath, so I didn't lean into the car window as usual. She didn't detect anything, probably because her nose was desensitized to smoke, living with smokers. Nor had she seen me as they drove up.

Mama said, "We just visited your Aunt Grace at the other end of the block and wanted to see what you do spending so much time at Joe's."

Guilt made me hot all over, and I was afraid my face blushed conspicuously.

"Mama, we live so far away from my friends that I have to play over here to be with them." Trying to change the subject, I said, "I didn't know Aunt Grace lived around here."

"Yes, on the next corner. She married Max Breen after your Uncle Harold died. Mr. Breen's a very nice man but nothing like Harold."

Dad said, "Too bad you've got your bike here with you, son, or we'd take you home with us. We're eating at the Shack tonight, so don't come back too late."

Guilty and eager to distract them, I said, "I'll follow you home, Dad. You take Broadway and I'll take Spring, and we'll see who gets there first."

My only advantage in the race was a lack of traffic signals on Spring. If they saw me smoking, they didn't mention it, and I vowed not to smoke anymore.

Once I knew Aunt Grace lived on the corner at Fifteenth and Arch, I watched for her. I saw her one morning in front of her house sweeping the sidewalk and stopped. Ten years had passed since I last saw her; now she looked shorter, puffed like a pigeon from gaining too much weight, but still had those slender bird legs.

I walked up to her. "Hi, Aunt Grace." Narrowing her eyes, she looked into my face questioningly.

I said, "It's Cleveland."

She dropped her broom, grabbed me around the waist, and practically pushed her face into mine. Squinting, she said, "Why, of course you are! Floy told me how much you've grown. My, you're such a big boy, Cleveland!"

She took me inside her house, which was just as colorful as the one I remembered on Cumberland, and introduced me to her short, stocky husband, Mr. Max Breen. Recognizing his and her age revealed to me how much time had passed since she, my favorite "aunt," led me to my elocution lessons.

Feeling guilty about my experiences at Joe's, I began playing with a bunch of boys in an empty lot on the corner of Wright Avenue and Chester Street, near Boykin's home. When his family took a summer vacation, he asked me to deliver *Democrat*s for him again. Working out of Station B at Twenty-third and Arch, he had a large route southeast of Sammy's Drive-In, at 103 Roosevelt at the foot of south Main. The black subdivision there, off Roosevelt Road, was called "Tuxedo Junction." Boykin showed me how to roll and put rubber bands on papers before riding over there and guiding me through his delivery route.

He stopped us at the edge of Tuxedo Junction beside a honky-tonk, a dark, tumbledown shack that backed up to Roosevelt Road. We ducked our heads entering, and Boykin greeted a squat, round-faced black man standing behind a bar, sliding into a cozy exchange of jests in the patois of black folks, which Boykin used adeptly without giving offense. That special ability explained why his circulation manager had assigned the route to him. Boykin frequented the honky-tonk to play the electric pinball machine, hopeful of winning a cash prize. I watched Boykin manhandle the pinball machine, applying elbow grease in his effort to fool the electric tilt mechanism, while sending the metal balls rolling, pins pinging, and lights flashing on the colored backboard.

But Boykin kept track of time, checking his wristwatch, and eventually quit pinball to deliver papers. Tuxedo Junction, like a tiny country village that just grew like Topsy in *Uncle Tom's Cabin*, had no block grid pattern but was a haphazard layout of irregular dirt streets and distorted lots on the down-slope side of a big hill. On our bikes, we whizzed along the subdivision's formless dusty roads tossing papers on porches, into yards, and, if a subscriber was outside, delivering hand-to-hand. Each dilapidated shack had a barrier around it, a collapsing fence of some kind—wood, brick, or wire—for corralling animals, fowls, or children. The street lamps on leaning light poles in the subdivision were few and far between and shed little light on the streets after dark.

I felt fairly secure after Boykin had identified his customers' houses, particularly those with dogs, and he left his debit book of subscribers and their house numbers for making collections. He believed that if I collected the weekly fee, customers would make regular payments without the excuse of his absence. I threw papers every afternoon, delivered Sunday morning, and collected once.

The first day, large birds I hadn't seen touring his route attacked me. They were the size of large hens, and covered in dark gray feathers with small white dots, their bare heads white and their necks with red wattles under the throat. When I threw the newspaper, they uttered shattering screams of alarm and flew at me. As I rode away, they squawked continuously, "put-wheat, put-wheat." I asked the owner later what kind of birds they were, and he said guinea fowls.

Other houses were guarded by big white geese that proved territorial, acting aggressively like watchdogs. The birds spread their huge wings, extended long necks, and thrust the serrated edges of their yellow bills forward, hissing and honking at me hysterically. In the deafening blast, I stopped and got off my bike and walked slowly backward, staring into the goose's eyes as I inched out the gate. The owner coming out to check on the fuss said I was right to maintain eye contact backing out since geese rarely flew over the fence. After being confronted by geese hissing, guinea fowls squawking, dogs barking, children squealing, Victrolas playing, and grown-ups arguing and laughing, I truly understood the meaning of "cacophony."

These feathered guards were in their way more intimidating than dogs. Most dogs could be sweet-talked into submission, but guinea fowl crying "Come back, come back" chased me, and geese squawking waddled hastily after me. The same confusion reigned when I went back to collect. Boykin had introduced me to only a few subscribers, for most weren't home when we first called, so I was a stranger trying to collect money, and their suspicion was understandable. I didn't press too firmly too soon and let them see me making deliveries before asking again.

To deliver in the dark on Sunday morning in Tuxedo Junction frightened me, so I waited until nearly sunrise. With my bicycle loaded with bags of Sunday papers, front and back, that weighed a ton, I approached Tuxedo Junction in the dark. The first thing I heard was jazzy blues and nasty laughter from the honky-tonk, so I avoided any drunks outside the shack by going roundabout to deliver the route backward. By the time I finished throwing papers and passed the honky-tonk heading home, it was closed.

At supper one night, Mama mentioned shopping at Baker's Shoe Store for a new pair of shoes and having to wait an extra long time while a heavy, jovial salesman searched for her size in the style she preferred. Apologizing for taking so long, Sonny Cohen, the salesman, said Baker's really needed a stock boy.

Now Mama said, "Cleveland, you'd be a dependable stock boy. Why don't you apply for that job tomorrow after school? It's a good way to make a little money."

Daddy said, "No, Floy, he should apply for a sales job. That'll earn him a commission on sales."

But I preferred to be a stock boy; I didn't think I could handle sales. I had never applied for a job before and didn't want to embarrass myself. And I had my usual mix of wanting to be liked and hired, yet hoping to be liked and *not* hired. Why? Weekend employment would wipe out bicycling, skating, tennis, movies, and the total freedom I enjoyed. Getting older wasn't nearly as much fun as I anticipated. For, at fifteen, I needed more than small change from the parking lot to cover the cost of my clothes, books, and odds-and-ends. I needed a job that would last longer than a newsboy's and would be indoors.

On my way to the shoe store the next day, I wondered what I'd be asked and what I'd say. It was easier to impersonate someone in front of an audience than to be myself asking for a job. With Mama, I'd been in Baker's Shoe Store, which was between Lerner's at the corner of Fifth and Main and the Palais Royale, but I paid no attention at all to its interior. Now I saw the marble floor of the foyer and pink and beige background in the display

windows filled with women's dress and casual shoes in different arrangements. Beside the front door, a curved front counter had a cash register and
pretty girl behind it, and shoe shelves filled with pinkish-beige shoeboxes
covered the walls of the shop. Scattered about were stools for salesmen to sit
on fitting customers. The stools had side mirrors and Brannock foot devices
beside them for taking heel-to-toe, arch, and width measurements.

A short-waisted, chesty little middle-aged man in a two-piece suit
stood by the counter talking to a young woman at the cash register. The
quizzical smile on his shiny face seemed to ask if I had come into the
women's shoe store by mistake. I asked for the manager, and he was it.
Mr. Rosenberg asked me several innocuous questions before asking me to
fill out an application, on which I named my scoutmaster, Mr. French, as
a reference. But the interview and application were unnecessary; when I
handed the form to Mr. Rosenberg, he asked me to go to the federal building on Capitol Avenue for a Social Security Number before coming to work
next Saturday.

Months later, Scoutmaster Clarence French, the branch manager of
the Little Rock Dictaphone office, sent me a copy of the glowing recom-
mendation he had written and sent to Edison Brothers Stores Inc., in St.
Louis, Missouri, on my behalf.

When the copy of his letter reached me, I had already been working for
weeks as the stock boy. My Saturday hours were from seven in the morning
until nine thirty or ten in the evening, depending on how many shoes had
to be shelved after the store closed. When I worked after school on Fridays
before and during holidays, I stocked shelves from five until nine in the
evening on sale days.

All the employees, except the young woman cashier, were young men
and older teenagers, a mix of permanent and part-time salesmen. Once
the store opened each day, the salesmen stood in a line against the wall
near the front counter waiting for customers. Mr. Rosenberg, poised like a
maître d' near the front door, greeted each customer and introduced her to
a salesman. The salesman led the prospective customer to a seat, removed
one of her shoes, measured her feet with a Brannock foot plate and asked
what style she wished to try on.

Of course, each salesman's approach and spiel differed, depending
upon their respective personalities. With older white women, all the salesmen observed a certain degree of proper decorum. However, if a customer
was young or black, the salesmen would guess what her reception to humor

would be and proceeded accordingly, kidding about various colors, fabrics, and styles, especially on Saturday nights just before closing. The salesmen within my hearing might claim the color of green shoes was "the new gangrene," or, after measuring a young woman's foot, exclaim that no shoe would fit her, but the tiebacks and boxes would. This kind of sales behavior deserved to be called "footle," a pun using a rare word for someone talking or acting foolishly.

I performed my stock-boy chores on two different levels, working mostly out of the basement, carrying stacks of boxed shoes up and down the narrow, steep stairs with poise and balance. Pulling stock off the basement shelves, I attempted to keep those on the showroom floor fully supplied with every style of shoe, keeping a constant check of inventory on both the main floor and the basement. Often, with my hands holding a dozen boxes of shoes carefully stacked and balanced, I had to dodge frantic salesmen, eager to make a sale, incautiously descending or climbing the narrow stairs to search for shoe styles that I hadn't yet replaced. Considering the awkwardness and excessive size of some salesmen and my slight build, acrobatic juggling was a necessity.

On Saturday mornings, if I awoke and found it either sprinkling or pouring down rain, I knew I'd spend my first hour at Baker's carrying galoshes and umbrellas up from the basement before the doors opened. When Christmas sales started, I brought up the entire stock of house slippers every Saturday.

Since I provided the product they sold, the salesmen cultivated or teased me in various ways. Not content with "Cleveland," they had several different names for me based upon their most compelling interest—the subject of sex. They had concluded I was sexually innocent, consequently calling me "Virgy," "Little Dicky," and "Nooky." The more decent-minded older salesmen, though, chose a nickname emphasizing my underground job, "The Mole."

The most frequent refrain among salesmen on sale days at Baker's was, "Ask the Mole to fetch that shoe style in such and such a size!"

One of their favorite tricks was to wait until I had shoe boxes piled high in both hands and goose me, particularly as I climbed steps from the basement. Or they made me part of their tricky ruse of stretching shoes enough for customer comfort to sell them.

Not long after I began at Baker's Shoe Store, the Brandon Stove Company expanded its stock of hardware and home appliances, including

Stewart-Warner refrigerators, radios, and fans. In October, the Brandon truck pulled into our backyard and delivered a handsome Stewart-Warner electric refrigerator to our kitchen, with a special cookbook that included recipes for "Florida sherbet"—a frozen mix of orange and lemon juice with milk—and "Sea Foam"—a poetic name for fluffy divinity candy. I developed real skill preparing both recipes for our family.

Soon after, Stewart-Warner honored Daddy for his sales by putting his picture with a citation in the *Gazette*. Daddy, in turn, gave Buster and me small Bakelite Stewart-Warner "Campus" radios, red and black for him, and tan and brown for me. My gift was especially appropriate since I listened to Horace Heidt and his Alemite Brigadiers on a program sponsored by Stewart-Warner every evening.

In the fall, my new English teacher, Miss Emma Scott, taught English literature and composition with discipline and imagination. Miss Scott, an appealing middle-aged blonde, had a sunny disposition and encouraged each of us to explore his or her individual interests in literature. Her method of interpreting works set my habits for a lifetime, for she joined our compositions to the literary pieces we read and memorized, such as portions of Milton's companion pieces *L'Allegro* and *Il Penseroso*, Shakespeare's *Julius Caesar* and *Macbeth*, and Coleridge's "The Rime of the Ancient Mariner."

To the consternation of many, Miss Scott required us to learn poetry and play excerpts by heart for class recitation. Her favorite number to memorize of each piece was 120 lines. Some students, particularly boys, really howled in protest outside class! What was the point of memorizing Shakespeare's "Is this a dagger which I see before me?" speech from *Macbeth*, or "Friends, Romans, countrymen," from *Julius Caesar*? Miss Scott never answered that question for students who memorized those big painful chunks by rote repetition.

The process of memorizing any poem is fairly mechanical at first. You cling to the meter and rhyme scheme (if there is one), declaiming lines in a sort of sing-songy way without worrying too much about their meaning. But then something organic happens. Mere memorization gives way to performance. You begin to feel the tension between the abstract meter of the poem—the "duh DA duh DA duh DA duh DA duh DA" of iambic pentameter—and the rhythms arising from the actual sense of the words.

It's a deeply pleasurable physical feeling. You can get something similar to that pleasure reading the poem out loud off the page, but the sensation is far more powerful when the words come from within. (The act of reading the printed page tends to spoil the physical pleasure.) It's the difference between sight-reading a manuscript and speaking it from memory, when you somehow feel you come closer to channeling the writer's emotions.

Miss Emily Penton's history courses also made deep impressions upon me; they were like an introduction to college courses. Miss Penton, her slender back straight as an arrow, had fine brown hair in a bun and pince-nez on her nose, an appearance that made her seem like a rather prim and formal person. But that was what you saw before she went into action, for she charmed us—displaying an open, energetic, and vivacious manner—treating us as intelligent adults. My old report card shows my first grade in her course was a B, but for the remainder of the two semesters, I received As.

She equaled college professors I subsequently studied with: thorough familiarity with the subject, an up-to-date bibliography to guide research, and thought-provoking delivery in lectures. She complimented me in Latin American history by asking me to "teach" her class while she was at a conference. The school district paid me two dollars on October 31, 1941, for my day's work.

In the spring of 1941, Miss Penton again taught me Latin American history; Miss Scott concentrated on Shakespeare's plays, particularly *As You Like It*. And rotund, pleasant Mr. Ivy, who had tried his best to instill the principles of plane geometry in our minds, found me seemingly immune to any form of mathematics. My mind and energies were focused on Miss Harris's speech-course activities.

I always enjoyed assemblies featuring my classmates. Student responses to my own performances in the choir, variety shows, sketches, and stand-up routines in assemblies in the tenth and eleventh grades convinced me that other students felt that way, too. In fact, I think my own appearances in assemblies were responsible for the student body electing me the student council president.

My biggest acts included Charles Laughton as Captain Bligh in *Mutiny on the Bounty*, Ronald Coleman as Sidney Carton in *A Tale of Two Cities*, Sweetie Face and Mr. Wimple on *The Fibber McGee and Molly Show*, Prissy in *Gone with the Wind*, and the tenor of the Inkspots singing "If I Didn't Care."

In one assembly program, I again replaced George Lieper, who dropped out as he had at East Side, and played Patty Andrews, alongside Bobby Jackson (Maxine) and Preston Carradine (LaVerne) singing a medley of Andrews Sisters' hits. In drag, using recorded music and our own voices, doing dance steps and gestures, we sang "Boogie Woogie Bugle Boy," "Beer Barrel Polka," "Don't Sit Under the Apple Tree," "Bei Mir Bist Du Schoen," and "Beat Me Daddy, Eight to the Bar." The applause shook the roof and almost brought the chandeliers down!

Miss Harris's dramatics class wrote and produced an assembly about a Hollywood producer making a movie. Cecil B. DeWheelerdealer had his staff of weird flunkies audition actors for roles in a screenplay starring Swedish actress Carmina Lavensdatter. The casting auditions, including singing, dancing, skits, and impersonations, were our show. Inspired by Charlie Chaplin's singing waiter in *Modern Times*, I impersonated Hitler making a speech composed of double talk and German gibberish—*wiener schnitzel, gesundheit, knockwurst, liverwurst, und sauerkraut*—punctuating a flurry of words with Nazi salutes and a preening camel walk.

Until the spring of 1941, Tumpy Gammill and I had never seen each other in the halls or on campus, even by chance. Then, in Miss Alberta Harris's speech class, a miracle occurred—she sat down at the desk next to mine, close-up and friendly, as if we'd never been apart. She was so natural, with none of the fake mannerisms girls so often adopted around boys. And she was good to look at, too. With brilliant white teeth and lovely lips, a shapely little nose, and green eyes, her face simply lit up in a smile. Yet she seemed shy, seldom speaking in her well-placed voice.

Drawn to Tumpy, I still didn't have nerve enough to ask for a date. I always enjoyed girls, trying to entertain them. Yet, alone with a girl who interested me, I was shy. Besides, dating was too expensive. I had money for snacks and movies for myself but hesitated about asking my parents for more money. More importantly, I had only a bicycle for transportation and only the everyday clothes for school.

This speech course in the second half of eleventh grade was my first chance for formal acting training. Miss Harris, the teacher, a plain lookalike of Claudette Colbert, had a face of similar shape and features, short bangs, and a slender figure. She tried to set an example of what was required when she conducted vocal drills, displaying the proper method of breathing and good breath control, softly resonant vocal quality, and carefully placed lips and teeth articulating consonants and enunciating vowels. In fact, hers was the most studied manner of speaking I ever heard, which made her sound and seem rather distant and cold.

Early in the course, she introduced us to the use of a wire recorder, called a Mirrophone, Western Electric's wire/ribbon recorder and player, which had one minute of continuous loop wire for recording. The Mirrophone recordings of our voices gave us our first opportunity to hear how we sounded to others. My voice shocked me, too high pitched, less resonant than the voice I heard, and with a pronounced Arkansas dialect. No wonder my rural dialect impersonations seemed perfect to others.

The other courses I had in the spring were civics, American history, and English. Miss Daniels in civics firmly believed all students should memorize portions of major American historical government documents and reproduce them word for word, especially the Declaration of Independence, the preamble to the U.S. Constitution, and the Bill of Rights. But Miss Emily Penton wanted us to explore in history the philosophical sources of our federal principles. Miss Celia Murphy in her English literature and composition course focused on Victorian authors and their works. And I finally had an opportunity in Miss Harris's dramatics class to explore theater ideas from Stark Young's *New Republic* column.

One Friday morning in early May, Mr. Larson called a mysterious meeting of the student council, which ordinarily met at midweek. He asked the council to nominate candidates for the offices of student president and vice president for the next year. I didn't expect anyone to nominate me, because I had only represented the eleventh grade at the Arkansas Association of Student Government at Hendrix College in Conway, in October 1940, along with Betty Tracy, Jean Jones, and Bob Trieschmann.

At the convention, I found discussions about student government there so boring I concentrated on listening to the dialects of students from Arkansas's smaller towns. For the first time, I paired with Betty Tracy, whom I first met while at Rightsell when my folks visited Jess and Bess Weidemyer, next door to the Tracys on North Palm Street, and had become her friend for life. And I enjoyed kidding Jean Jones, the senior delegate who was thinner than me, calling him "Clean Bones" on the trip. So you'll see why I was hardly prepared for what was coming.

Mr. Larson asked the council to nominate two members of the council for the offices of president and vice president of the student body for 1941–42, with the provision that whoever received the most votes would be president. The council chose Orville Henry and me as the candidates. Even though flattered, I didn't have an iota of interest in winning either position. There was no time to withdraw, so we left the meeting and walked directly to the auditorium where the student body had already assembled. Henri Julian, the current president, introduced Orville and me, and we each spoke briefly to the students, before they returned to homerooms to cast their votes.

In election returns that shocked me, I received the majority of votes and was named president of the student council for 1941–42. The only explanation for the outcome was my being better known than Orville after so many appearances on assembly programs acting, singing, and impersonating, while Orville, an excellent student, had worked unobtrusively behind the scenes throughout the year as the council secretary and on the *Tiger* newspaper staff.

In the summer of 1941, my teenage pals and I sitting astride our bicycles on shady South Broadway watched long convoys of trucks filled with soldiers, Arkansas National Guardsmen called into federal service. We yelled and waved at them enthusiastically, and a few soldiers tossed little silver tins stuffed with resin-like wads of dehydrated coffee at us. Where the soldiers were headed, we didn't know. Nor did we foresee that the war was drawing nearer our country each day and that we, like the passing soldiers, would soon be in military service, too, heading to unknown destinations.

My first duty as president of the student council in the fall of 1941 was to host the seventh annual convention of the Arkansas Association of Student Governments, which Mr. Larson founded. I realized on my way to the opening session in the auditorium on the morning of October 9, 1941, that I had failed to prepare a welcoming speech. I had to speak to the delegates from across the state impromptu:

"Faculty and members of the Association of Student Governments, here's my official greeting: Welcome to Little Rock Senior High School. Let's get this show on the road!"

Those simple words brought all the delegates to their feet in a tumult of happy yells and applause. An impromptu speech had rescued us from the usual formalities. But, leaving the lectern, I turned to face the wrathful stare of Miss Middlebrook, the assembly sponsor, and the baleful head-shaking of Mr. Larson.

Mr. Larson reminded me, after I sat beside him, that the school host had to welcome delegates again at the mixer in the cafeteria that evening. Since the delegates had no dates but had to have dance partners, I didn't know who to dance with. Never secure dancing with a partner, I had practiced several steps of the Big Apple, and could do a kind of solo dance. So when the band played "The Big Apple," I launched into my Stepin Fetchit impression. Totally caught up in the music and steps, I forgot the others until they had stopped dancing with their partners to watch me. Embarrassed, I stopped, too, but the crowd encouraged me to continue until the music ended and the crowd applauded my dance.

Friday of the following week, I had more student government business facing me. As the head of our delegation to the Southern Association of Student Government meeting at Central High School in Memphis, Tennessee, I rode with Mr. Bigbee, the assistant principal, who drove Betty Tracy, Orville Henry, and me along the narrow, beat-up concrete two-lane road to Memphis. We missed the morning session, but met in Central's auditorium from 12:30 to 4:30 p.m., where I spoke to the delegates from ten Southern states on "The History and Purpose of SASG." The set speech didn't receive the same response as my welcome at home. The text I memorized was written by convention sponsor Mr. Charles F. Allen of Little Rock.

At that evening's banquet in the Peabody Hotel's Continental Room, for the first time, I ate chicken a la king (a dish I subsequently consumed at school banquets for the next fifty years). Even after suffering through four hours of flag ceremonies, R.O.T.C. bands, invocation, introductions, speeches, and stunts in the afternoon, we submitted after dinner to more speakers, choruses, and sponsors' questions and answers. The dance that followed did not appeal to Orville and me, so our high-school host, Max Pearl, called his father, who came to get us.

We were overnight guests in Max's recently built family home, which was beautiful. Our guest room had its own bath, quite a coup for a boy who shared a toilet with his family and three or four roomers. The next morning at breakfast, Mr. Pearl recalled an Arkansas cotton broker he knew by the name of Cleveland who turned out to be Mama's brother, my Uncle Cleve

Honea. Mr. Pearl remembered him as the cleverest storyteller and jokester he could recall.

Before becoming council president, I enjoyed assemblies without paying much attention to their details. But presiding, I realized they fell on Friday mornings after meeting in homerooms. Assemblies for seniors alternated with those for tenth and eleventh graders. Only the most unusual occasions or special guests brought the entire student body together. Homerooms were seated by academic level, classes moving from upstairs to downstairs, from back rows to front rows as their grade advanced. The auditorium had a gigantic stage that served as several basketball or volleyball courts, side by side, for gym classes. When the electrically controlled steel fire curtain was lowered, the stage apron was wide and deep enough for any show, and a public address system made participants audible in all kinds of programs.

Miss Edna Middlebrook, the rather tall, raw-boned woman, with a long, solemn face heavily powdered to conceal whiskers, chairing the assembly committee, wielded power over program selection. As a student, I knew what students found entertaining in a way she did not, and I sometimes opposed her suggestions, which led to a sparky but relatively friendly relationship.

Miss Middlebrook chose a theme for assemblies each year and decided, after World War II began, on "Patriotism and Tolerance." Assemblies followed a set procedure. For example, when Dr. Gaston Foote, pastor of the Winfield Methodist Church, spoke on "Citizenship and Character," I presided and Orville Henry, as vice president, was in charge of the curtain. Ted Richardson and Charles Dietz carried and set the American and Arkansas flags on stage, Mary Carolyn Cherry read from the Bible, and Mrs. Settle directed the audience in school and pep songs. Special assemblies might introduce recent scientific discoveries. The first I heard of the coaxial cable and its effects on telephone communication was at a special assembly by technicians of the Bell Telephone Labs in the spring of 1941.

When a condensed version of Shakespeare's *Macbeth* by the Ben Greet Players, a famous English acting company, was announced, I expected a really exciting assembly. Miss Harris, who hadn't seen the group, primed her dramatics class by telling us about famous actor-managers such as David Garrick and Sir Henry Irving in the eighteenth and nineteenth centuries. Our class assumed Sir Philip Ben Greet and his company, who toured in England and the United States, would bring the highest quality performance of Shakespeare.

Presiding over the assembly, I felt fortunate to witness the performance close-up, backstage beside the lighting board. Imagine my surprise when only four persons were backstage to perform a play with a cast of more than twenty-five. The assembly committee had booked the company without knowing there were only Macbeth, his Lady, a utility player for other roles, and the stage manager. It now seemed unlikely that Sir Ben Greet was playing Macbeth, which had been implied. The three actors performed selected scenes with the stage manager relating plot narration and operating the lighting switchboard and offstage rumbles on a bass drum and thunder sheet. Most of the characters, just as Birnam Wood was in the plot, were invisible upon the stage.

The elderly actor playing Macbeth had applied thick make-up in an attempt to appear a robust soldier, but he looked and sounded old enough to be Ben himself, especially in the quivering, hollow tone of his voice. The actress playing Lady Macbeth, his ancient equal, also wore heavy make-up and was clothed in dreary plaid robes. The witches three were reduced to one, who was male.

The cast performed the entire action on the extreme right corner of the gargantuan stage. When I asked why, the manager explained that they needed to be near the lighting board so he could shine the red-purple-green lights falling on the folds of black drapes arranged for players to appear and disappear quickly. In the limited "action," the actors assumed such grand manners, extreme vocal vibratos, thick dialects, and exaggerated gestures and stances that the impatient athletes seated in front of the stage apron snickered loudly. As the scenes proceeded, the jocks began tossing pennies at the feet of the old players.

I sought Mr. Larson's advice about what to do, and he suggested collecting the pennies during the narrative intervals to prevent the old players from slipping on the floor. I followed Mr. Larson's advice during the narration, waddling like a mute duck picking up the change, cheered by the boys. I apologized to the cast at the end of the show for the disgraceful behavior of a small segment of the audience. The cast graciously accepted my apology, voraciously accepted the fee, and departed.

On Sunday afternoon, December 7, I stood alone in the backyard enjoying the crisp air and cold light, and heard the lonely drone of a small, single-engine airplane flying over. Sunday afternoon always seemed lonely if I didn't go to a movie. I went back inside and lay on my bed, flicking the radio dial to CBS, which usually broadcast music by the New York Philharmonic at 2:00 p.m. on Sundays, but John Daly's tense but mellifluous voice reading the news releases that preceded the Philharmonic broadcast had an urgent tone.

"The Japanese have attacked Pearl Harbor, Hawaii, by air, President Roosevelt has just announced. The attack also was made on all military and naval activities on the principal island of Oahu."

I couldn't believe it. Especially when the Philharmonic broadcast continued without any more news about the attack. It might be another Orson Welles's *War of the Worlds* hoax. Not long after I heard the announcement, the hall phone rang, and I answered, because my folks and the roomers were away that Sunday afternoon. Mr. Larson, on the other end of the line, said he planned a special assembly the next day for the student body to hear the president's address to Congress.

The next day, students filled every seat in the school auditorium and some students and faculty had to stand at the back and in side aisles before the program began. At 11:30 a.m., December 8, the president started speaking to the joint session of Congress, his voice engraving these crucial sentences upon my mind:

> Yesterday, December 7, 1941—a date which will live
> in infamy—the United States of America was suddenly
> and deliberately attacked by naval and air forces of
> the Empire of Japan ...

> With confidence in our armed forces—with the
> unbounding determination of our people—we will
> gain the inevitable triumph—so help us God. I ask that
> the Congress declare that since the unprovoked and
> dastardly attack by Japan on Sunday, December 7th, 1941,
> a state of war has existed between the United States and
> the Japanese empire.

The Senate's declaration of war was unanimous; in the House, only Jeannette Rankin of Montana dissented. As far as I could tell, every student approved of Congress's action. When Germany, a day later, also declared war against the United States, our high-school days would match no others since 1917.

The international catastrophe so near Christmas changed the usual pattern of local events. Ordinarily, we presented our Christmas festival in the school auditorium during school hours, but after the declaration of war, the faculty changed the time and place from afternoon on the campus to evening at the Joseph T. Robinson Memorial Auditorium so families and townspeople could join our students and faculty. That night, anything performers did brought tumultuous applause, surely an emotional outpouring of patriotism and honoring of the lives lost in Malaya, Hong Kong, Guam, the Philippines, Wake Island, and Midway Island in the world conflict.

The crowd's biggest applause greeted the A Cappella Choir and "The Donkey Serenade." A Mexican boy is walking in rhythm leading a burro, clippity cloppity, toward a marketplace south of the border. But the burro suddenly balks, refusing to follow the boy, even when he patiently pulls at its bridle. Straining against the reins, the boy leans back on his heels, tugging with all his strength and weight. Yet the obstinate animal won't move. So the boy walks behind the burro and puts his shoulder under its hindquarters, attempting to shove him along. But the burro is firmly planted.

Then the playful boy, not to be outdone, takes an apple from his back pocket, holds it under the animal's muzzle out of reach before turning away, pretending to be biting the apple. The donkey, curious about the boy's move, nudges him under first one elbow and then the other, seeking to share the apple. With the burro's attention, the Mexican boy holds the apple under his nose and leads him to the marketplace as the musical serenade fades.

Applause swelled throughout the massive auditorium and didn't diminish, even though I bowed and disappeared in the wings. Signaled by Mrs. Settle, I returned and bowed five more times to the choir and to the audience as the applause continued. Then Mrs. Settle motioned us to repeat the song and pantomime. At the sixth and final curtain call, I was breathless from the tumultuous ovation that left my skin tingling and body hair bristling. Only the orchestra, glee club, and choir performing Handel's "Hallelujah Chorus" of the *Messiah* enjoyed an equal response that evening. Certain in my mind and heart of my life's calling, I was determined to act on the stage.

———~m~———

During the first five months of 1942, before our graduation, one Allied military disaster followed each month. In January, a German U-boat offensive took place off the East Coast of the United States in sight of spectators on land. In February, the Allied forces in the Java Sea were destroyed; in March, the American forces at Corregidor surrendered; in April, the Japanese led the Bataan Death March; and in May, German U-boats sank Allied ships off our coast in the Gulf of Mexico.

Even though Congress declared war against Japan and Germany after Pearl Harbor, it did not change the upper and lower limits of the draft age, which led me to assume I'd go to college for several years after high school. I helped collect scrap, bought war bond stamps, and participated in all the patriotic war efforts without any anxiety about going into the army.

In late April of 1942, Elsie Cockrum received a telegram from the War Department that her husband, First Lieutenant William L. Cockrum, of the 31st Infantry Regiment, had died at a POW camp at Cabanatuan, on the island of Luzon in the Philippine Islands, 118 miles north of Manila. The first major land battle of the United States in World War II was for the peninsula the Japanese took in January 1942, cutting American and Filipino troops off from help and supplies after ninety days. The sick, starving, and bedraggled prisoners of war walked sixty-six miles to the prison camp, where we assumed Doc succumbed to starvation or disease or both. Elsie received a letter of condolence from the army chief of staff, General George C. Marshall. Our whole family shared Elsie's grief, for Doc had been like one of our family despite his sometimes crass behavior.

The only relief from the bad news about the war and Doc's death was my part in a show over National Broadcasting Company radio. On April 12, 1942, on "Music and American Youth," a weekly radio program sponsored by the National Broadcasting Company, Mrs. Settle, Miss Harris, and Mr. L. Bruce Jones, head of instrumental music, created a program entitled "The Epic of Arkansas" based on John Gould Fletcher's long poem *South Star*. Seven scenes with music and narration described the state's evolution from a wilderness to statehood: "Indians," "Spain in Arkansas," "France Founds Arkansas," "Under Three Flags," "Pioneers," "The South," and "Today."

The performance of the Little Rock High School band, orchestra, A Cappella Choir, and speech students took place on the high-school stage before a full house, under the direction of NBC producers and technicians. For the "Pioneers" section, I portrayed in Arkansas dialect the old man in the legend of the Arkansas Traveler.

I don't know exactly what month Merlene Lybarger rented a room at 322 Spring, nor when she and my brother married. Judging by the date of their daughter's birth, February 17, 1943, as well as their dress and appearance in snapshots, it's safe to assume they were married sometime in May 1942. Buster was inducted in July and given the usual three weeks leave to straighten out his civilian affairs before reporting to Camp Robinson. He was sent to Keesler Field in Biloxi, Mississippi, for training in the Army Air Corps.

In February, in the midst of great excitement at 322 Spring, we received a "little bundle" from her mother, who was at a loss about naming her. At Merlene's request, I invented "Diana Gail" for the little pixie in the bassinette with almost no hair on her head. The tiny nymph, Diana Gail, was the answer to Mama's prayer; although her baby (me) was now nearly an adult, she had a new baby and new title of Mamaw.

When the Office of Price Administration opened in Little Rock in 1942, Professor Olsen, an economics professor from the University of Wisconsin, rented a room at our house to be near his office in the federal post office building on Capitol Avenue. The federal agency established in April 1942 to prevent inflation set a maximum-price regulation based on prices charged in March 1942 as the ceiling for most commodities, and it imposed ceilings on residential rents. The regulations, later modified and extended, froze almost 90 percent of retail food prices. Besides controlling prices, the OPA rationed scarce consumer goods: tires, automobiles, sugar, gasoline, fuel oil, coffee, meats, and processed foods.

A stout, rather solemn bachelor who always needed a shave, the professor had only two dark wool suits, which were much too heavy for Little Rock's climate and left his nearly bald head shiny with perspiration. He had two shirts that he rinsed in the lavatory in his room which were always wrinkled, and his gravy-stained ties never quite covered his collar button. He had brought more books than clothing from Wisconsin and, to judge by light coming through the transom over his door, he read late every night.

Mama, cleaning his room, asked what he wanted to do with the pile of *New Republic* magazines on the study table in his room, and he suggested, "Your son might want to read them. It has a column about theater."

His casual suggestion introduced me to Stark Young's dramatic criticism. I knew the critic's name from reading *Theatre Arts Magazine* and seeing *So Red the Rose*, the film based on his novel. Young's thorough knowledge of dramatic literature, technical production, and nuances of the spoken word, and his sensitivity to color, line, form, and tone opened my eyes to the *art* of theater. Reading Young's dramatic criticism in the *New Republic* completely altered my understanding of theater.

My courses that spring included economics with Miss Hatch, Latin American history with Miss Penton, and dramatics and radio, both with Miss Harris. My senior English teacher was Miss Celia Murphy. Until I had her course, no teacher had ever sent me to the school principal for any reason. Of course, I had frequent contact with Mr. Larson, who advised the student council each week, and I knew through frequent contact that he was a gentle, scholarly man. His position and conspicuously bald head made him a target for students' jests.

His administrative secretary, Miss Ernestine Opie, was the school's majordomo, reputedly storing as much information in her head as the Encyclopedia Britannica. Referred to as "Opie" out of her earshot, she was a threat if you were summoned to the main office. For facing Opie, at her paper-strewn desk behind the long, chest-high office counter, was like standing before a judge in court, innocent or not, fearing the judgment. Her round face was framed by a mannish haircut, her eyebrows often lifted above piercingly sharp eyes, and her wry, flat voice snapped you to attention. At her nearby desk, Mrs. Artie Mae Cartwright, her smiling assistant, leavened Opie's effect.

One spring afternoon, Miss Celia Murphy, my teacher in senior English, stood by her first-floor classroom window gesturing at the cedars and reflecting pool on the front lawn, when suddenly struck by an artistic revelation. Lifting her arm and pointing out the window, she exclaimed, "There's poetry in those trees ... that breeze ... that pool!" Turning back to the class, she looked straight at me. "Say a line of poetry, Cleveland!"

"I don't know any poetry to recite, Miss Murphy."

"Indeed, of all the boys in this class, you're most likely to know poetry."

I protested I didn't know any "appropriate poetry" to recite.

Raising her thin arm, she pointed at the door. "Go directly to the principal's office for your lack of cooperation."

I dragged out of her room, down the hall, and entered the main office. Opie, pretending puzzlement, asked, "Why is the president of the student body here in the middle of a class period?" After I explained the circumstances, she laughingly ordered me to sit on the bench reserved for delinquents and wait for the principal. When Mr. Larson returned, she enjoyed pointing at me waiting on the bench outside his office for the first step to detention or suspension. We retired to his office, where he laughed and suggested complying with Miss Murphy's request, even if it meant stooping to poetic doggerel.

Fortunately, twelfth-grade students with good grades had the privilege of a "book packet," which allowed reading books beyond the standard requirements. Instead of going to the library or a reading room several times each week during a semester, I could check out a half dozen books of my choice, read them, and write reviews of them. The most fascinating nonfiction adventure story in my 12A packet was *The Unveiling of Timbuctoo*, based upon the records of Rene Caillie, a member of the French Geographic Society. As the first white man, disguised as a religious pilgrim, to enter the holy city, he returned to write about his tribulations. Another book, *Enchanted Vagabonds*, described Dana and Ginger Lamb floating down a river in a sixteen-foot canoe through the unexplored jungles of the lower Baja Peninsula of Mexico. In their hazardous adventures, they survived malaria, snakebites, insects, and tiger and wild boar attacks. They were lost in caves, tossed by storms at sea, and attacked by primitive tribes, which removed any wish for travel adventures I had beyond camping along the Saline River with the Boy Scouts.

My 12B reading packet had a more enduring effect upon my vocation—Scribner's twelve-volume collection *The Plays of Eugene O'Neill*, bound in green buckram, on the bottom shelf of the library's drama section. My ambition to act on Broadway and O'Neill's reputation as America's greatest playwright made us perfect companions; I vowed to read the whole shelf of his plays before graduating. Even though I finished *Anna Christie, The*

Hairy Ape, The Fountain, Beyond the Horizon, and *The Emperor Jones,* I found there were too many long plays to fulfill my vow. However, the plays convinced me that theater was a serious endeavor worth a lifetime pursuit.

One feature of Arkansas weather escaped my notice until one sultry afternoon in late April. If the twisting funnels of air called tornadoes had ever loomed over Little Rock before, I wasn't aware of them. On my way home from school at about four, I saw black clouds hanging low over town. Expecting rain, I scooted fast as I could to the streetcar stop at Fourteenth and Park, but not a drop fell. By the time the streetcar had reached the Pulaski Theater, the greenish-black clouds had swelled to mammalian protuberances that scared me into running home.

In the kitchen feeling safe, I ate a cookie to hold me until mealtime while Mama was preparing supper, remarking how hot and breathless the day had been. When a startling flash of lightning was followed by a mighty clap of thunder that shook the house, Mama and I went out on the back porch and opened the screen door to look at the sky; the clouds were dark scallops hanging seemingly close enough for us to touch. It was unusually quiet as a gentle breeze blew into our faces.

Mama declared, "It's gonna storm. Oh, Allie, please get home before the storm."

As if on cue, Daddy's old blue coupe turned into the driveway and drove into the garage. A few moments later, Daddy, carrying his order satchel, ambled in his usual way toward the back porch.

Mama, holding the screen open, shouted, "Hurry and get in here, Allie, a bad storm's coming."

"Well, it does look like rain, Floy. A good rain'll cool things off. This has been a mighty hot day."

The canvas curtains over the back porch screens flapped and popped, and a long, low roll of thunder followed as Daddy came through the screen door and kitchen and dropped his satchel in the sitting room. I slipped another cookie out of the jar, flipped the light switch in the pantry, and plopped down on my bed, glad the day was over. Mama followed Daddy into the front room, talking about how smothery she felt. I heard the mumble of their talking when the canvas curtains on the back porch outside my window popped again, like the slap of a wet bag on pavement. Then—silence and utter stillness.

Mama shouted, "Cleveland, Cleveland! Hurry in here and lie down on our bed!"

The back porch curtains snapped again, as a roar coming our way grew louder. Jumping to my feet, I headed to my parents in the living room. I raised one foot and then the other to walk out of the room, but I remained in place, as if suspended in the air, lifted and held by the nape of the neck.

WHAM! My body slammed into the dining room doorjamb.

Freed, I ran to the living room, as Mama rose from the bed, where she lay when the mighty wind struck, and raced to the front door. Daddy and I hurried to the back porch, where we had heard the roaring wind and the breaking and crashing sounds. The screen door was blocked by huge limbs and the thick foliage of the two mulberry trees in the yard. Pushing the limbs aside, we saw our garage on top of the mulberry trees, and a downed power line draped across Daddy's coupe and Miss Compton's La Salle sedan parked beside it in the garage.

The whirlwind had stalked along the path of the Arkansas River until it crossed Broadway and trailed down Fourth Street, lifting and dropping its whirling leg erratically on the way to Main Street.

The wind had lifted our garage, the porch of a cottage on Fourth, and one wall of Raymond Rebsamen's car repair shop off their foundations. The electric power in our part of town was off, but when I suggested lighting the gas sconces, Mama wouldn't hear of it. She lit candles for the table and served supper in their faint, romantic glow. We spent the rest of the evening without light, but AP&L restored the power during the night. The next day, Tumpy told me she had been at the YWCA, on the corner of Fourth and Scott, when the storm struck.

In our last five months before graduation, students at high school sponsored metal, paper, and rubber salvage weeks, food-canning programs, sweater and glove knitting, war bond and defense stamp sales, and Red Cross classes. But the largest activity supporting the war effort also involved students from the junior high schools. A Victory Carnival was organized to raise money for the Little Rock chapter of the American Red Cross by nominating pretty girls for queen—Fern Pevis, Betty Jean Schmuck, Robin Miller, Emma Lou Atherton, and Joanne Patton—and popular boys for king—John Windsor, Jack Ginnochio, Jack Rule, Jim Crafton, Don Hudson, and me. Each penny paid for the tickets to sideshows and the main show counted as a vote to cast for the Valentine King and Queen, with all the money going to the local Red Cross chapter.

High school and the junior highs dismissed at two o'clock on Friday, April 17, and students from all over town soon jammed the high-school halls, lining up for the side shows and refreshments. The Hawaiian Night Club, in the large chorus room in the basement, featured an orchestra, magic stunts, and the *pièce de résistance*, pretty Betty Jeanne Grayson in a cellophane skirt dancing the hula. (She later became "Gail Davis" and starred as Annie Oakley in a 1950s TV series, as well as in movies.) The biggest hit, though, was a Womanless Wedding, with Jim Crafton, the football captain, as the bride, and Breck "Midget" Campbell, the head cheerleader, as the groom.

At 11:00 p.m., Harry Crow, the emcee, crowned the queen and king of the carnival. That ticket-buyers chose Betty Jean Schmuck as the Queen of Victory was no surprise, but for me to be chosen King of Victory defied explanation. I certainly hadn't campaigned for the honor. We closed the Victory Carnival singing "The Star-Spangled Banner" without knowing that simultaneously with our school's carnival, sixteen B-25 bombers under Major Jimmy Doolittle took off to bomb Tokyo and Yokohama, Japan.

In May, before our senior play, we celebrated Senior Class Day, combining an assembly in the auditorium with a luncheon in the cafeteria. At the all-school assembly, 12A students presented a hypothetical radio broadcast of skits based on popular radio characters: Mr. Wimple and Sweetie Face, Dr. I.Q., Junior and His Mommy, and the Quiz Kids.

Afterward, we strolled to lunch in the school cafeteria, where I had rarely eaten in three years at high school. Since the Depression for our family hadn't ended, Mama usually prepared a sack lunch to save lunch money. A group of mothers and the school dietitians prepared and served a spaghetti dish, fresh salad, and cake. Big, burly Jimmy Crafton, president of the graduating class, presided over an awards ceremony that featured Herbert Reamey, vice president of the class, reading the class prophecy, an exaggerated set of expectations about class members' future attainments in art, business, medicine, and politics. Marcele Roberts, the class secretary, read the class history. When Jimmy awarded the class distinctions, six of them were awarded to me: the wittiest, cleverest, most talented, accomplished, and entertaining, and bachelor boy. Now really, for one person to receive so many distinctions in a class of 650 graduates was unfair; who made the choices?

I hadn't seen much live theater on stage as I grew up, and theater didn't enter my mind unless I was performing. But I became aware of professional productions in our city when Alfred Lunt, Lynne Fontaine, and their company of actors (which included Richard Whorf and Sydney Greenstreet) presented *Amphitryon 38* on the Little Rock High School stage. I wanted to go but didn't know where to buy tickets—yet Mrs. Vaughan at the Women's City Club, who booked professionals and sold tickets for their events, was only four blocks from our house.

After entering high school, I had seen two senior class plays directed by Miss Alberta Harris. In 1939, Elsie Cockrum, the long-time roomer at our house, bought tickets to a senior play at high school to help some kid. Since her husband Doc was missing overseas, she asked me to go. We saw Kaufman and Hart's *You Can't Take It with You*, with Boyce Drummond playing Grandpa Vanderhof, the central character. Elsie and I had fun together and, for the first time, I realized how huge the auditorium and stage were from the audience's viewpoint. The play setting in the middle of the stage looked like a stamp on an envelope.

The next year, I went to *Beggar on Horseback*, by George S. Kaufman and Marc Connelly. Obviously, Miss Harris liked Broadway shows and comedies by Kaufman. In this play, an impoverished composer loves a poor girl but, fearing poverty, proposes to a rich girl. When she accepts, he has a nightmare about life with the wealthy girl and her eccentric family. James Clifton Williams acted the role of the composer playing the piano, and his poor girlfriend, Betty Lou Kramer, was vice president of the student council in 1939–40. (Williams became a professor of theory and composition at the Universities of Texas and Miami.)

In my first chance to be on a play production staff, I assisted Miss Harris directing a short play with six seniors in the mid-term graduating class of 1941: Lee Toney, Carl Quaintance, J. P. Van Pelt, Louise Walker, Patsy Rimmey, and Sarah Louise Steed. *King Sargon's Jars*, my first opportunity to direct even a portion of a play, led me to a creative sense of stage space, character relationships, and dialogue clues to movement and gesture.

I don't know whether Miss Harris chose our class's senior play before or after Pearl Harbor, but *Margin for Error* was already out of date on

December 7, 1941. To fill the nine roles, she held a week of auditions and cast students from her dramatics class. The play revolves around several suspects who had reasons and opportunity to murder the German consul (me) in New York City: the consul's wife (Betty Jean Schmuck), the consul's secretary (Tess Reda), and his physician (Sumner Rodgers), a newspaper columnist (Bob Loomis), the head of the German American Bund (John Pounders), and the consul's German maid (Marian Gammill). After the consul is murdered, the suspects gang up on the Jewish policeman (Charles Shapiro), who had been assigned to protect him, making it difficult for the cop to expose the murderer.

The only two characters requiring German accents were the consul and the consul's maid. I played the role of the arrogant Nazi consul, which furnished my first direct contact with the philosophical conflicts of the war with Germany. Gertrude Selz, a classmate and German Jew from Berlin who was helping me develop an accent and speak the German dialogue, revealed in our daily sessions her harrowing escape from the Nazis. She immigrated to the United States under the sponsorship of the large, influential Jewish community in Little Rock.

While we rehearsed the play, a production crew of faculty sponsors and senior students prepared the set, furniture and drapes, properties, make-up, costumes, and lighting. Bob Halley was stage manager and Charles Meltabarger ran the lighting switchboard, both my Second Baptist Church Sunday school classmates. One of them had the great idea of mounting the scenic flats with their back side to the audience, allowing the wooden frame and crossbars of the flats to suggest a wood-paneled office. Placing the consul's desk up center forced Miss Harris to keep actors facing the audience to be heard by the audience in the big auditorium, which made scenes static and awkward. She didn't use microphones and amplification to reinforce our volume, and many players, especially the girls, had trouble projecting sufficient volume. But I think the main difficulty was static stage pictures. We performed the evenings of May 14 and 15, instead of the usual matinee and evening of a single day.

The consul died at the end of the first act, but I remained on stage throughout the second act at a desk with my back to the audience while the policeman interrogated the six suspects. The American Bund leader spouting Nazi slogans drew audience groans and laughs. The love affair between the consul's wife and the newspaperman captured the audience's sympathy. The flirtation between a Jewish cop and a German maid got laughs, and Charles's loose-ankled big feet and Marian's cute swing dancing to "The Back Bay Shuffle," by Artie Shaw's Gramercy Five, drew applause. So the first night's performance proceeded without a mishap of any kind.

But the second act on the second night saw Charles's performance wander in a different direction before he recovered. Shapiro, as Moe Finklestein, swung in the part until he came to Clare Boothe's built-in actor snag, identical lines in two different spots in the second act. When the line appeared the second time, Charles went back and repeated the dialogue he had already passed. Sitting with a fictional dagger in my back, rope around my neck, and glass of poisoned whiskey in my gut, I was a breathless corpse listening to the cast struggling to lead Charles back on track. His repetitions provided a longer performance for the audience and the heebie-jeebies for the cast.

On our graduation night, May 29, 1942, it was difficult to reconcile the horrors of war sweeping across the world with the peace and beauty of the ceremony. On an exceptionally hot, humid evening, the concert band played before the ceremony at eight, while a fire-red sun slowly melted west of the stadium and a cool white moon rose in the east.

Sweating in our summer graduation outfits—dark trousers and white shirts with ties for boys and white street-length dresses for girls—we entered the stadium to the strains of "Marche Pontificale" by Gounod and sat on risers on the playing field facing the crowd in the stands. As buglers played "To the Colors," flag bearers placed the American and Arkansas flags in stands on either side of the speakers' platform. Then we all sang "The Star-Spangled Banner" and pledged allegiance to the flag before Lowell Dabbs, a graduating senior, pronounced the Invocation, and the A Cappella Choir responded with "The Lord's Prayer."

Mrs. Ruth Klepper Settle led songs from the combined boys' and girls' glee clubs and choir before William Sibley reminded us of "Youth's Responsibilities." With the war under way, we boys knew military service beckoned. After the concert band played Tchaikovsky's Sixth Symphony, John Larson Jr. spoke on the "Priorities of Youth," and Mr. E. F. Jennings, the president of the school board, presented the scholarship awards and diplomas to our class.

Despite my excellent academic and service records (20th scholastically in a class of 650), I would have to find a job to save enough for tuition at

Little Rock Junior College in the fall. Our class sang "Hail to the Old Gold" one last time as students, and I was sad but relieved to graduate. Then the loud hurrahs and Rebel yells erased any momentary sentiment. Graduates rushing from the stands to their parents and friends and bestowing hugs, kisses, handshakes, and congratulations clogged the stadium's exits. Mama and Daddy weren't there, because I had dismissed the event's importance and told them not to bother coming in the heat.

Sweating, I headed home while others were going to celebrations. Then I bumped into Tumpy Gammill, who had stopped directly in front of me. One of the bugs flying in the powerful stadium lights had lodged in her eye. She had stepped to the side of the crowd and was standing with tears pouring down her cheeks, looking so fragile and helpless. I instantly whipped my clean handkerchief from my hip pocket to remove the bug. While I held her eyelid down and inserted the tip of the hanky, I impetuously asked her to the senior preview at the Capitol Theater, and she accepted.

What was I going to do? The only transportation I had was my bike, and I couldn't take Tumpy to the senior preview on the streetcar. Fortunately, when I revealed my dilemma to Jim, he asked us to join him and Betty Romick at the preview, and he picked us all up in his 1938 Pontiac sedan.

Spring activities had been fun, but now I had to concentrate on finding a summer job. Mama mentioned my job search to Mrs. Martin when she paid her parking fee, and Mrs. Martin suggested that her husband at the U.S. Engineers district office might know of an available clerical job. The next morning, Mr. Martin knocked at the back screen door and recommended I apply to Mr. Pilcher, the director of the finance division. I was surprised to hear the finance director's name, because his daughter, a mature, dark-complexioned girl, had graduated with me.

That afternoon, I went to the office two blocks from our house on Broadway, where I first encountered Mr. C. O. Wilson, the chief accountant, who took me to Mr. Pilcher, whose shirt was rumpled and tie askew. After a brief interview, I was hired so quickly as an under clerk for the summer that the job appeared arranged. When Mr. Pilcher and others filled my first workday with only simple tasks a junior-high kid could do, I realized my job and duties were undefined. So in the first week, anyone in finance used my services as a stacker, puller, and go-fer.

In the second week, Mr. Richards, the assistant director, in an office next to Mr. Pilcher's, discussed a specific job with me and arranged my permanent assignment. I was to compile a document the Little Rock office didn't have but needed—an index of War Department circulars, bulletins, and U.S. Army regulations presently scattered in all the division offices. I collected the bound and unbound documents and assembled them in a separate office assigned to me alone. There, I sat recording topics and integrating all the information for easy access. Since I couldn't type, I was given permission to hand print the index, a tedious job that convinced me typing was the first course I would take at college.

My other job was depositing everyone's paychecks at downtown banks on payday, twice a month. Mr. Wilson instructed me on how to avoid being waylaid carrying the checks to the banks. He gave me a zippered five-by-ten leather money bag for dozens of checks banded together for the different banks—People's, Union National, Worthen—and suggested taking different routes to the banks each payday. The prospect of danger excited me, but no one ever accosted me or made a threatening move.

Shortly after I began working at the U.S. Engineers district office, Miss Harris telephoned suggesting I try out for *The Royal Family*, by Edna Ferber and George S. Kaufman, being produced by the Little Rock United Services Organization (USO). I didn't know the play or roles that might be right for me, but the unusual chance to act, like a big carrot in a rabbit's face, set my heart racing. The opportunity was close to home—only three blocks away at the Robinson Auditorium.

I found tryouts in one of the convention halls in the basement. The men auditioning were mostly soldiers from Camp Robinson, all older than me, Jewish, and from cities like Los Angeles, New York, and Chicago. One lanky cast member, Orville Sherman, who assisted the director, had been a bit player in Hollywood movies and a supporting player on Broadway before the war. (He later appeared occasionally on *Gunsmoke*, the TV series, as a bartender.) Among the women, only Martha Merryman, an especially talented actress who graduated a few years before me from Little Rock Senior High School, had semi-professional experience, in Dallas. The other younger and older women were stage-struck civilians from in town.

After rehearsals started, we moved to the small stage at St. Andrews Hall, at Ninth and Louisiana. A few nights later, to my utter surprise and pleasure, Tumpy Gammill showed up, slender and tall in a starched pink and white striped summer frock, making me think of sweet peppermint candy. She shared her disappointment at not being informed of the auditions, but she still flashed her pretty smile that exceeded any Ipana toothpaste ad. I couldn't imagine why Miss Harris told Laura Belle Baker and Helen Wilkey but not Tumpy, who would have been far more effective as the ingénue opposite me in the juvenile lead, rather than double casting.

Rehearsals for *The Royal Family*, though a bit disorganized, lasted through July without becoming tedious. The soldiers were a lively bunch who invited me to join them before and after rehearsals for a snack, drink, or supper at Breyer's, a fine old restaurant on Markham Street, where for the first time I ate borscht and a boiled potato.

We performed the play in early August in a large convention room in the basement of Robinson Memorial Auditorium. Both the *Gazette* and *Democrat* reviewed the play and praised my performance as Perry Stewart, the juvenile lead, even though I only performed an underwritten character in handsome clothes.

The really important event that had long-term consequences occurred the night Arkansas historian and chairman of the Little Rock Junior College Scholarship Committee, Professor J. H. Atkinson, came to our house. We didn't know the reason for his visit, but he didn't hesitate to reveal his purpose. The college scholarship committee had awarded me the largest scholarship the Junior College offered, the Lamar Porter Scholarship, which guaranteed my tuition, books, and fees for two years. Receiving a full scholarship before the draft age of twenty-one simplified my financial future, guaranteeing half of my college education.

PHOTO OPPOSITE PAGE:
Cleveland at Little Rock Junior College.

CHAPTER 9

Fulfillment before Farewell

WHEN I GOT HOME from work at the U.S. Engineers office at five, Mama said, "Miss Harris telephoned about play tryouts this evening at seven at Junior College."

I certainly didn't want to miss that, but why Miss Harris called instead of Jaycee's director of dramatics, I couldn't imagine. Maybe because she failed earlier in the summer to tell Tumpy about auditions for *The Royal Family*.

I let Mama know I was going and had just enough time to eat, bathe, and bicycle to Junior College on Thirteenth Street. I hadn't seen that campus since Jim and I were kids pretending the college front porch was a sailing ship and later watching boys play football on the college grounds. I was excited about tryouts but worried about competing with older actors.

Astride my old Western Flyer bike, I pumped south on Broadway Boulevard toward Thirteenth, racing against the slowly fading sunlight. The car traffic was lighter than I expected, probably because most folks were eating supper, like the young people in cars parked at Old King Cole's at Capitol and Broadway.

At the corner of Thirteenth and Broadway, I pulled my bike onto the sidewalk, next to Mount Holly's high wall, to avoid the street's broken surface, and passed our old apartment at 1301 ½ Gaines and the White family's old shack behind Springfield's empty grocery store before arriving on State Street. Where would the auditions be on campus, anyway?

Then I saw a noisy group by the gym behind the main building, answering my question. I leaned my bike against the high tennis court fence and walked toward the group, expecting only strangers. But there was Tumpy Gammill! Whoopee! Her presence made the evening great before it started. I hadn't seen her since *The Royal Family* rehearsal at St. Andrew's Hall in the summer.

Sidling up as close as I dared, I said, "Hi! I'm glad someone told you about the play auditions."

She said, "Miss Harris did! I've kept in touch after missing *Royal Family* auditions."

I didn't really know the others standing in a lopsided circle at the stage door; they had been grades ahead of me and only casual acquaintances at high school—Ed Rowland, Mary Katheron (K. K.) Harris, Douglas Wells, Dick Upton, Helen Ann Worthington, Margaret Davies, Rita Joy Mouton, and Jane Abbott. Oh, there's Helen Wilkey!

"Hey, Helen, short time no see!" We played the young love interests Perry Stewart and Gwen Cavendish in *The Royal Family*.

Waiting for auditions to begin, I kidded around and lost my anxiety. After we filed into a small, dimly lit room beside the stage, I thought Mrs. McDermott, the director, was sitting at a table behind a tall pile of play scripts. But taking my seat, I realized that the stubby little lady, her head the size of a soccer ball and covered in tight brown curls, was standing. With her chubby cheeks and pursed, un-rouged lips, she was a female facsimile of movie director Alfred Hitchcock.

She greeted us with a smile and summarized, in an offish voice, the play plots before selecting pairs of us to do "cold readings" from both scripts. No one appeared familiar with *Lady of Letters*, a light drawing-room comedy, by Turner Bullock, or *Night Must Fall*, a dark melodrama, by Emlyn Williams. After we stumbled through reading various scenes until nine, "Mrs. McD" (as older students called her) released us without saying who was considered for particular roles.

Even though Tumpy and I were convinced we read well, we said good-night assuming that freshmen had little chance of being cast in leads. She offered a ride in her shiny black Studebaker, and I regretfully declined, suggesting she ride on my bicycle, helping me pump up the hills to her home in the Heights.

The first complete day we spent in classes at Jaycee convinced me that the tree-shaded campus was a world of its own, a quiet haven unlike any school I had attended before. The square block of the campus, nestled in the midst of private homes on West Thirteenth Street, was bound north and south by Twelfth and Thirteenth, and east and west by State and Izard.

The main building was the old U. M. Rose School, built for elementary-school kids, which had been Junior College's home since 1931. The graceful two-story, red-brick building had offices for the dean and registrar and eight classrooms (two for biology and physics labs) on the first floor; the library and two classrooms on the second floor; and the grill, game room, and toilets in the basement. Behind the main building a combination gymnasium-auditorium, designed by engineering faculty member Guy Irby, had at its north end a music room, stage and backstage area, speech room, and typing lab. On opposite sides of the gym were a physics-chemistry laboratory and a regulation tennis court.

Searching for a drinking fountain in the basement, I stumbled upon the college grill, which had a few tables and chairs, a long counter, and a steam table. The menu, posted on a small blackboard, featured vegetable soup, chili, hamburgers, hot dogs, soft drinks, and coffee. The woman behind the cash register introduced herself as "Mom Wooten," the manager of the grill, who also served as cook, waiter, cashier, and unofficial student counselor.

The grill, harboring odors of sour coffee grounds, cigarette butts, and old cooking grease, was the scene of a bridge game in progress. Alice Cooke and Helen Ann Worthington, a lanky blonde and a tall brunette, both smoking cigarettes, were engaged in what I later learned was an unending bridge game, with male and female partners coming and going throughout the day, depending upon their class schedules.

Helen Ann said, "Sit down, Cleveland, and take Susan's place."

"Helen Ann, I don't know how to play most card games, much less bridge."

"Never mind. Have a seat! Alice and I'll give you a quick course."

"Thanks for assuming I'm smart enough. But it's too much sitting down."

Since I didn't play bridge, smoke, or eat much, even at mealtimes, the grill wasn't a hangout for me. I merely drank Cokes and yakked with friends there.

I found doors to the men's and women's toilets on opposite sides of the basement's rear entrance. In the men's room, I confronted the tallest, widest urinal I'd ever seen, a spectacular white ceramic bowl the length of a wall and tall as an average man. I saw, in my mind's eye, the tiny elementary boys standing dwarfed and intimidated by the basin tending Mother Nature's call and felt sympathy for them.

Across from the toilet, I looked into a small recreation room that had a lone ping-pong table that my friends, avid doubles-champion Jean Jones and singles- and doubles-champion Bob Taylor, presided over. Glancing into a nearby utility closet, stacked with toilet paper, brooms, mops, soaps, and cleansers, I surprised Mr. Smith, or "Smitty," in his "office." The short, grim-faced, gray-headed custodian responsible for buildings and grounds crossly asked what I meant by looking into his closet.

When I told my pal Ed Rowland about Smitty's reaction, he said, "So you met the invisible man! He seems hidden on campus, but wait 'til you do something he disapproves. He'll be on your case like a hawk."

Transferring from Senior High to Junior College was like moving from a metropolis to a village.

Once the class routine was under way, I realized that college hardly resembled high school, where we remained on campus all day meeting in classes continuously. At college, we met in scheduled classes and afterward were free to do as we pleased. My courses in English, Spanish, speech, zoology, and typing (fulfilling my summer vow!) accounted for seventeen clock hours in class each week; the rest of my time I managed as I chose—total freedom that demanded self control and adult responsibility.

Tumpy and I, if she was free of class, could eat lunch, drink Cokes, or buy a "walking sundae" at King's Drugstore. We were being pursued by a sorority and fraternity. Battlecriers, the only sorority on campus, wanted Tumpy, but she seemed content to remain independent and busy in her own way, like me. I favored independence, too, ever since seeing part of a Jaycee fraternity initiation as a kid, even though my friends and acquaintances pledged or were members of Delta Kappa and Phi Alpha Beta. Maybe being blackballed at high school affected my outlook. Fraternities were okay if you're more comfortable on campus in a social organization.

But I had changed my mind about other activities at college. After three years in the student council at high school, one as president of the student body, I was no longer interested in campus government, certainly not in its politics. And despite my happy experience in the A Cappella Choir at high school, I didn't wish to sing in a campus choral organization anymore. Instead, I planned to devote all my energies outside class to play production in the Trojan Theater Guild—acting, directing, and stagecraft.

My first priority after suffering writer's cramps while working for the U.S. Engineers was Commerce 135, Beginning Typing, to avoid a similar pain preparing papers for courses. I was lucky to have congenial Mrs. Edith Scopp as my typing teacher. A slender brunette with an olive complexion, aquiline features, and a ready smile, she had graduated from Hunter College in New York and was married to an army officer stationed at Camp Robinson.

When she excused herself from class in the first few weeks to go outside to smoke, I attempted to impersonate her captivating Manhattan dialect for the class. A chain smoker, she took rather frequent breaks during our typing sessions to indulge her habit in a gray cloud on the porch beside the typing room. As the only boy in the class, I teased twenty girls as best I knew how during her absences, wisecracking about faculty and students, such as Mr. Atkinson, the history teacher, whom students called "Put-Put" for his mispronunciation of "put," or Marjorie Sharp's bare-back allure when she wore a sun dress on hot days. Whether my behavior accounted for my mediocre typing, I can't say. But thirty-eight words per minute, error free, provided adequate competency for term papers.

English 160a was a different matter; vitally interested in words, with an above-average background, I had some understanding and skill in the subject. Miss Dorothy Yarnell—my teacher, whose last name conjured in my mind images of Yarnell's double dips, the popular ice cream from Searcy County near where Cousin LaDell lived—was purportedly a member of the ice cream family. She had pale, translucent skin, fine features, and short, black, wavy hair. She was, without doubt, the prettiest teacher I'd seen since the Misses Romine and McCall at East Side.

In a soft-spoken, gentle manner, she led our class through expository prose, poetry, and the writing of essays, sympathetically guiding every step in the preparation of a research paper, my first extended writing assignment in college. Our brief essays at high school were written without observing the research techniques Miss Yarnell outlined: choosing topics in areas particularly personal and suitable, following a strategic search to support a thesis, and organizing notes from books in the library.

My topic search ended under my nose with the box of Kleenex I had while tending a bad cold, a frequent feature of my adolescent life. So I decided to explore the origins and treatment of the common cold and wrote "The Myths of the Common Cold."

I grew up subscribing to the same myths my mother believed about susceptibility to colds, and the results of my research surprised and reassured me: colds don't develop from dry mucus membranes when a room is overheated, being outside in extremely cold weather, having wet feet, sitting in drafts, having a weakened immune system, or being chilled or overheated. People spread more than 200 existing cold viruses by touching contaminated skin and surfaces and the eyes and nose, as well as inhaling viruses from the air. Some viruses live in the air for as long as two hours, so being inside enclosed spaces with infected people helps spread cold viruses. After ridding myself of my belief in the myths, I had to persuade Mama to dismiss them also, which would be a much more difficult task.

The term paper provided my first chance to practice my new typing skill preparing the long essay. But I had to use a typewriter in Mrs. Scopp's classroom, since I didn't have one of my own. After filling the first pages of my essay with messy erasures, I wrote my research paper, including footnotes, in my best Palmer longhand, without attention to Miss Wherry's concern about the circular movement of the elbow. I am forever grateful to Miss Yarnell for introducing me to *The Elements of Style* by William Strunk Jr.

Unfortunately, Miss Yarnell was not to be a joy of mine forever. Before the fall semester ended, a harbinger of things to come reached me through the student grapevine. The rumor was that Dr. Granville Davis, the former Jaycee history instructor who was now a sergeant in the army at Camp Robinson, was enamored of my favorite teacher, but Miss Yarnell had chosen another man for a husband. She married a mysterious stranger at semester's end and was never encountered by me again.

In my new science course, zoology, I tried to make up for having only biology in high school; Zoology 140 at Jaycee offered an opportunity to reach into another scientific corner. The instructor, middle-aged Miss Mary Elizabeth Pape, appeared in class from the first day wearing a white (well, almost white) laboratory smock, a dour look, and a crooked smile. (Or was that the shade of my own shirts, and my expression in her class?)

Her deeply shadowed eyes and dark hair, flat at the temples with a tight bun at the back of her head, suggested humorlessness. Yet, if I inhabited a dreary classroom filled with black-topped tables and had a dark storage closet behind me suffused in the fumes of a preservative sustaining dead specimens, my face and mood might match hers. When the atmosphere in our class sank to an unforgivable low, I tried to divert her by asking about her tour of Soviet Russia in the 1930s with Miss Laura Pedersen, my high-school history teacher.

We sat two at a table in her class, sharing a single four-and-a-half-inch grass frog, reeking of formaldehyde, and one dissection kit—with a scalpel handle and blades, scissors, forceps, and pans in which to store the disassembled frog parts. The lab tables, assigned alphabetically, placed me at a table behind brunette Jane Abbott (daughter of the assistant superintendent of Little Rock schools) and blonde Alice Cooke (the scholar–bridge player who regularly headed the honor roll). Perhaps our exchanges, scientific and social, wiped out memories of my own lab partner, who may have been just another boy.

When I chose Spanish 140, I not only subscribed to knowledge of a foreign language but to a portion of daily entertainment. The instructor, Señora Hemans (widely known as "Madame" because she was French), was a thin, angular woman of indeterminate age, with tinted gray hair in a Dutch bob and thin stringy bangs over her high forehead. She taught class energetically, alternating between sitting on a high stool with her elbows on the desktop and standing behind the desk, leaning forward braced upon her wiry arms. On the first day of class, I took a seat occupied in the previous year by a student of another name and sex, and she proceeded to address me as "Senorita Thompson" every day for my next two circus-like semesters in Spanish.

Even though Señora held no academic degrees, she had studied French at several European universities, and with private French, Belgian, and German tutors. But she made no similar claims for her preparation in Spanish. From time to time, she impressed upon us her relation to the famous poet Felicia Dorothea Hemans, reciting "Casablanca," a poem beginning with "The boy stood on the burning deck." And when some class wag dared finished the poem's opening line with doggerel, "eating peanuts by the peck," she exploded in French and Spanish.

She was intent on teaching us "proper" Spanish and chose the Castilian dialect, certain features of Spanish culture, and Spanish songs rather than Mexican. During each class period, she left her desk and sat on a high stool at the upright piano at the front of the room. With her back to us, her splayed legs in pink cotton stockings rolled below her knobby knees, she pounded her gnarled, arthritic fingers on the yellowing piano keys, singing in a croaking voice to lead us in the Mexican songs "Cielito Lindo," "La Cucaracha," and "El Rancho Grande."

When she excitedly rose from the stool, Señora sometimes caught her skirt hem and exposed her pink bloomers. A slightly embarrassed girl student in the front row tried to warn her with hand signals, but her efforts only disturbed Señora, who didn't understand until the girl rose and covered her teacher's posterior.

When any holiday approached, Señora hauled a colorful papier-mâché Mexican burro from the closet, a piñata that a student suspended from a hook in the ceiling at the back of the classroom. Then we played the piñata game. After she blindfolded and turned us, one at a time, in circles two or three times and faced us toward the piñata, she placed a broom handle in our hand, and we tried to break the candy-filled piñata. Swinging the stick repeatedly, we attempted battering through the surface of the paper piñata to scatter the goodies across the floor.

For students in our hemisphere, Señora should have taught practical Mexican Spanish instead of Castilian Spanish, because *gracias* (thank you) in Spain is pronounced "grathias," like someone with a lisp would say it, rather than "grass-see-ahss," as in Latin America. Another difference: *vosotros* (meaning "you others") in formal Spanish and *ustedes* in Mexico. Sorry to say, I learned vocabulary and grammar for reading and writing rather than worked to gain fluency speaking Spanish, whichever dialect she insisted upon.

Over the weeks, I slowly identified the college's individual staff and faculty members at assemblies, in halls, and in classrooms. I missed Mr. Larson, the principal at high school and president of the college, who came to campus for major events only. But Dean E. Q. Brothers, fulfilling various academic duties, was more ubiquitous on campus than Smitty, whose maintenance duties the dean often assumed. He was the only administrator I saw as often as Mrs. Allie Green, the librarian, to whom I noted when first checking out a book that we shared the same first name.

All administrators and teachers addressed us as "Mr." and "Miss," but despite that formality, they were accessible in and out of classes. I wondered as more male draftees and volunteers departed for different branches of service if the faculty worried about losing their jobs. Mr. Larson offset some student losses by arranging for academically able twelfth graders to complete the final year of high school and the first year of college simultaneously. Even though he arranged the accelerated program to help young men complete as much college as possible before being drafted, he extended the option to young women as well. Two friends, Clint Albright and Jeanne St. Aubin, enrolled at Jaycee in their senior year of high school.

A few other students were added when families brought their daughters home from other schools to enroll at Jaycee. For example, Mary Trieshmann from Texas State College for Women, Elizabeth Reap from Hendrix College, and Mildred Strauss from Goucher College in Maryland enrolled at Jaycee. Before the war, Jaycee's day and night students exceeded 300, but in September 1942, there were only 217 students—twenty-eight men and forty-three women sophomores, and 146 freshmen, equally divided between the sexes.

The first day of speech class, Mrs. McD revealed that she had cast Tumpy as the pixilated wife of a college English professor in *Lady of Letters*, and me as the psychopathic killer in *Night Must Fall*. The roles were the longest, most challenging ones either of us had ever had, and we took a long stroll around the neighborhood, talking about our good fortune. I loved talking to Tumpy, but she didn't say much.

Rehearsals for *Lady of Letters*—the story of a small-town college professor's wife who buys a manuscript from a young writer and publishes it in her own name—began immediately. Since rehearsals for *Night Must Fall* were a month away, I went to rehearsals almost every night to watch Tumpy, eager to be around her and the theater, and to see how Mrs. McD directed plays and how other actors performed. Watching Tumpy, I realized she had a great comic sense, a kind of screwball reality reading the lines and reacting to others. She had been cute as the German maid in our senior play, *Margin for Error*, and danced wonderfully, but her lines in German provided no chance to reveal her comic skill.

I was also particularly interested, after acting on the huge high-school stage, to determine how the much smaller Jaycee stage affected performances. Mrs. McD, on the other hand, was interested in keeping men in parts before they were taken by unexpected draft calls. She dared the system by casting Bobby Bryan in the part of Mr. Ainsley, a New York publisher, despite his uncertain draft status. Then, ironically, she couldn't find the right girl to play the role of the black maid, Henrietta. I helped out at rehearsals by acting the maid similar to one in Thurber and Nugent's *The Male Animal*, who struggled with French, calling hors d'oeuvres "whore doves."

As a stunt one night, I dressed the part of the maid, and my disguise and vocal impression convinced Mrs. McD I could play the maid's part in drag and solve her casting problem. But potential for that surprise ended when Bobby Bryan was drafted, setting off a game of musical chairs. I took his role of Mr. Ainsley, Mary Katheron Harris became the maid, and Helen Ann Worthington replaced Anne Wright as Stella McDonald, who filled Mary Katheron's original role as Winifred Shaw. Does all of that seem confusing? Well, you can imagine what rehearsals were like.

Eager to learn how to direct plays, I searched the library and found Alexander Dean's book *Fundamentals of Play Directing*, probably one of the first books on play directing in the United States, written by a professor at the Yale School of Drama. I knew nothing about the procedures directors followed staging full-length plays, especially how they blocked the action on stage based on characters' motivations—when, how, and where actors moved in relation to other characters and the setting—because movement and gesture convey so much more of a play's meaning beneath the dialogue.

Mrs. McD offered few specific blocking suggestions to actors; she let them move, instead, according to their uninformed urges rather than a character's motives. She didn't seem to know what movement or gesture to add to a line to reinforce the thought and emotion or make an action strong or weak. And it was difficult to relate the position and moves the actors made to their importance in a scene, to determine where an audience member should focus his or her attention.

I watched rehearsals from the deep shadows at the back of the auditorium, as Mrs. McD stood midway in the auditorium rigid as a post or pacing in her short measured tread without looking at the stage, listening. When she detected something amiss—an actor fumbling lines, picking up cues slowly, or speaking too softly—she whistled. If her whistling grew persistent and piercing, actors with puzzled faces stopped and stared across the stage apron into the dark auditorium. With the cast's attention, Mrs. McD offered her criticism or advice. If she was quiet, they were either doing everything just right or it was not important enough for her to make any criticisms, but we wanted to hear that from her.

With only a small part in *Lady of Letters*, I performed first at Jaycee in an assembly in October. We rehearsed two short plays in the afternoons to be free in the evenings, since almost everyone in the casts was involved either in the cast or crew of *Lady of Letters*. In *The Deceivers*, a one-act about a couple whose distrust of each other threatens their marriage, I played Amos Little, the husband, opposite my cousin, Mary Vincent Terry, the wife, Flora. On the same program, I both directed and acted in *The Still Alarm*, by George S. Kaufman, a comedy about two men in a hotel room continuing a conversation even though firemen arrive after the building catches on fire. Dick Upton, a chubby guy who played Hubert in *Night Must Fall*, was in the other role in *The Still Alarm*. It was my first chance to direct since assisting Miss Harris with the mid-term senior play at high school in 1941. During the rehearsals and performance of one-acts, I realized that directing and acting simultaneously in a play diminishes your critical faculty.

When we finally performed *Lady of Letters*, for one night only, on November 20, it was a waste for the actors, who learned nothing about playing to an audience. There is very little to be learned in one performance of a play for a single audience. Actors need to know how different groups respond and how they react if they are to grow in performing a role.

The review in the *College Chatter*, Jaycee's weekly newspaper, praised Tumpy, just as any perceptive reviewer would have:

> Marian ("Tumpy") Gammill plays excellently the
> difficult part of the wife Adelaide Willifer, who wants
> to do something to make people respect her. Miss
> Gammill made the audience not only laugh at poor
> Adelaide but feel a little sorry for her, too. She looked
> like a child-wife, but she was a lovely one.

The same reviewer suggested that my performance "added dash and color to the whole production ... dapper and poised as the hand-holding publisher from New York ... an excellent and amusing characterization."

To everyone's surprise, two references to the play appeared in Sunday's *Arkansas Democrat*:

> Miss Marian Gammill was the scatterbrain wife of
> a college professor ... Even the scene-stealing antics
> of Ann Wright and the versatile Cleveland couldn't
> top the mimics of Gammill as she used every trick
> within her far-reaching power to overshadow other
> members of the cast.

Positive comments in a separate story, titled "Over the Week End," also appeared in the same issue of the *Democrat*. I assumed Lee McLean, a Delta Kappa and friend of mine who worked as a stringer for the paper, wrote these remarks.

The cast's late-night stop at Hilltop surprised me. I had never been inside any night club, on a plain or a hill. Glenn Roberts drove us out to the nightspot on Highway 365, south toward Pine Bluff, and I felt guilty even approaching one of Buster's favorite hangouts, especially when Glenn stopped at the liquor store at the foot of the hill owned by the father of our classmate Harvey Walthall. Some Jaycee guy with our party who was old enough, or had credentials suggesting he was, purchased a bottle of blended whiskey, probably Four Roses, to add flavor and punch to everyone's drink. Once in the club, we all chipped in for Cokes and 7 Ups and a bucket of ice for the necessary "set-ups." The liquor and the terms used were all new to me.

After the car climbed the dusty, unpaved road to Hilltop, we all piled out and entered the oddest arrangement of space that I had seen for a dance party. There was a raised duckboard platform around a small dance floor, and on the platform were deep booths with tables and high-backed benches separating the booths for privacy. The unpadded benches made of duckboard similar to that covering the floor probably prevented trash from accumulating. The small band playing that night sat with their backs against the wall at the opposite end of the building from the entrance.

Tumpy and I, under pressure to pledge Battlecriers and Delta Kappa, had been given a ride by Glenn Roberts, DK pledge master, and his date, K. K. Harris, a Battlecrier officer. When Tumpy and I were served Cokes with whiskey, we drank them, but the taste didn't appeal to either of us enough to accept "a second round"—another new term to me. Tumpy and I danced a couple of times, but since I wasn't much of a dancer, I insisted she dance with Doug Wells, a lanky brunet tall enough for most girls, who commanded a wide variety of dance steps and was probably the best male ballroom dancer at Jaycee.

Glenn Roberts, ordinarily a very responsible guy, for some reason didn't drive us back to town until long after midnight. Mama was waiting up for me when I got back; she never did that with Buster. Tumpy, on the phone Sunday morning, told me that her mother had been worried sick and let her know in no uncertain terms that she had stepped out of line. Neither of us had ever stayed out so late, and I hoped this instance didn't ruin my reputation with Mrs. Gammill.

I didn't date while at high school, but I enjoyed friendships with many girls. Now, I shared part of every day and every weekend with only one girl, Tumpy. As long as we were together, we didn't care whether we were on foot, my bicycle, or the streetcar.

Going to dances was a new experience for me. Since I didn't belong to a fraternity or drive a car, or have male friends who dated much, I had attended only two dances at high school, each time in my official capacity as student body president. But going to dances with Tumpy in the Jaycee gym became a significant part of my social life. I learned a few simple dance steps, and we regularly attended sock hops, informal dances held in the late afternoon or early evening on weekends. It wasn't dancing I enjoyed so much as it was having Tumpy, with whom I had fallen overwhelmingly in love, in my arms.

Is there any love purer than a first love, when you don't even know what makes you feel the way you do? I wanted to be constantly beside Tumpy, to hold her warm, soft hand in mine, to gaze directly into her bright, smiling hazel eyes, and to see the shining halo of reddish brown hair crowning her lovely head. Tumpy's smile, like Mona Lisa's, suggested a knowledge of something I didn't know, and since she was by nature quiet, she never revealed what it was. When she spoke, I found her vocal pitch perfectly placed, and her speech bore none of the ugly provincial Arkansas dialect I heard on all sides, only certain pronunciations she inherited from her mother's Nashville, Tennessee, heritage.

Our frames of five feet eleven and five feet seven inches made us a perfect match physically. Tumpy, something of a loner, was distinguished, fetching, thoughtful, and in a state of longing analogous to my own—for what, neither of us could have said. I appreciated that she showed none of the brash qualities the more socially self-assured girls from the Heights did. Some assertive girls pounced on certain boys, like Catherine Rightsell did with Flip Daugherty in his parked car on the street at the front of the campus. My first declared affection for a young woman was so serious, my parents and my brother did not tease me.

Even though shy about dancing, I felt more comfortable dancing with Tumpy at the sock hops. We observed none of the program dance's formalities, and we had the added pleasure of moving our feet in socks across the hardwood floor without shoes. (Sock hops began after the basketball coach and janitor complained that shoe soles marred the gym's hardwood surface for games.) You could also exchange partners with greater ease and less formality than at program dances, although many couples danced only with each other, which was certainly the case with Tumpy and me. We danced to big swing band phonograph recordings, especially Glenn Miller, Artie Shaw, Harry James, Freddie Martin, and the Dorsey brothers, playing "Beat Me Daddy, Eight to the Bar," "Take the A Train," "Jersey Bounce," "Cow Cow Boogie," "A String of Pearls," and "Serenade in Blue."

The formal or program dances at college, on the other hand, featured music by either Tommy Scott's or Harris Owens's orchestra. And we had a lot of arranging to do before the formal affairs. Since the women came in long evening gowns, the men wore their best business suits and dress shirts and ties. We chose and sent fresh corsages to our dates, arranged to double- or triple-date with a guy who had a car, and at the dance filled the blank spaces of our date's dance card with the names of other girls' escorts and our own names for the specials, aiming to fill our date's card but still dance with her as often as possible. The program dances pretty well kept every "flower" blooming on the dance floor rather than beside the garden wall.

At intermissions, guys and their dates usually piled into their cars and drove to eating places fairly near the campus for food and soft drinks. Some favorite food stops were King's Drugstore on Gaines, The Blue Goose on Eighth, HobNob on Main, and Sammy's on Roosevelt.

As blithe as we seemed every day on campus in the fall of 1942, there was no escaping the news that the war was going badly for the Allies in all parts of the world, and the armed forces of the United States needed men in all its branches. So Congress fulfilled the inevitable by lowering the draft age for males to eighteen in November, two short months after I entered college. Eighteen in August and eligible for service, I registered on December 16 at Pulaski County Draft Board B in the Boyle Building. My college career at its very beginning appeared at its end.

Doc Cockrum's death was on my mind when I registered. When President Roosevelt nationalized the Guard in 1941, Doc had dropped out of medical school and entered federal service as a second lieutenant to be sent to the Philippine Islands. Elsie had read parts of his letters to us about his adventures with Filipino scouts before Pearl Harbor, which didn't stir the slightest military ambition in me. When the War Department notified Elsie of Doc's death, our whole family shared her loss when the war came closer to our household, even before Buster was drafted and assigned to the Army Air Corps.

The casting problems that delayed the performance of *Lady of Letters* shortened preparations for *Night Must Fall*; rehearsals didn't begin until Monday, November 23, 1942.

From the moment Mrs. McD cast me in the role of Danny, I set out to speak an authentic Welsh dialect as the hotel bellhop, and I memorized the dialogue of the whole play before rehearsals. To learn an authentic Welsh dialect, I borrowed *The Survey of English Dialects*, published by the English company of Linguaphone. For some reason, it was shelved in Mr. John Adams's music classroom, and the exceptionally accommodating teacher allowed me to use his room to listen to recordings of British county dialects. I chose the vernacular speech of Cardiff, Wales, for Danny, and practiced with the recordings, slowly mastering the Welsh melody of speech—the lilt and upward inflections at the ends of phrases and sentences, and the lengthening of all vowels, which in many respects is more important in rendering a dialect.

Night Must Fall, a psychological thriller, had been performed first in London in 1935, with the playwright Emlyn Williams in the role of Danny. From the play's beginning, it is obvious that Danny is a murderer and easy to tell who his most likely victim will be. Wealthy, autocratic old Mrs. Bramson, living her final days in a cottage in Essex County, is surrounded by her beautiful but penniless niece, Olivia Grayne, her personal assistant and companion; affable Hubert Laurie, Olivia's would-be suitor; and the bumbling, pregnant maid, Dora Parkoe. Mrs. Bramson, in her determination to find the child's father, draws Danny, the bellhop at the Tallboys Hotel, into her household. Then, the cheerful lad skillfully insinuates himself into the old woman's affections, and Olivia's physical attraction to Danny prevents her giving him away to Scotland Yard.

When Danny arrives at Mrs. Bramson's cottage, he reveals in his opening lines the simplicity and innocence of manner that ensnares women. Looking at Mrs. Bramson, Olivia, Dora, and the housekeeper, he says:

"Mornin' all. I must apologize to all and sundry for this fancy dress, but it's me workin' togs."

Then, looking at his hands, as if they belonged to someone else, he innocently smiles at the women, saying:

"And me hands isn't very clean. You see, I didn't know as it was going to be a party."

Soon after Mrs. Bramson invites Danny to stay at the cottage, his personal belongings, including a mysterious leather hatbox, arrive. Only then does anyone suspect a connection between him and the headless body of a woman found in the nearby woods. When Olivia confronts Danny with her suspicions, he reveals the capacity for violence subtly established in small ways in the first and second acts.

As Mrs. McD blocked the scenes on stage, setting movements and positions of actors in relation to each other and the setting, I realized the strong contrast between working on the smaller stage and the one at high school but continued projecting vocally to 2,000 rather than 200.

Mrs. McD stopped me immediately and asked, "Why are you shouting, Cleveland?"

"I didn't know I was shouting, Mrs. McDermott."

"Well, you are. There's no need to shout. You're easily heard."

At high school, I was so accustomed to powerful projection, I had lost control of vocal modulation. Finally, in rehearsals, I projected but with more subtle nuances of meaning rather than concentrating on making myself heard.

At Wednesday evening rehearsals came a surprisingly unexpected musical underscoring of scenes. A small African-American church on the property line behind the gymnasium-auditorium held choir practice on Wednesday nights. Their sound was not so much vocal as instrumental, an easily recognizable piano, bass, violin, drums, and tambourine behind our dialogue created a steady, if somewhat muffled, beat through the back wall.

That unexpected score gave me an idea. A deep-dyed movie fan, I was aware of how many motion picture effects depended upon background music for emotional appeal, and decided to rehearse Danny's revelations of abuse by his parents and by upper-class patrons at the Hotel Tallboys like a film's score. I thought using a portion of Igor Stravinsky's *The Rite of Spring* on phonograph backstage provided punch to the psychopath's threats, and Mrs. McD agreed. Since tape and wire recorders were not easily available at the college, I marked the surface of a 78 rpm record with white crayon pencil indicating where to begin and end, and Tumpy, responsible for cueing all sound for the play, gradually faded the music in and out under my lines.

Rehearsals for *Night Must Fall* were as exciting as any I was ever involved in, because my role was the center of the play. Unfortunately, Margaret Davies, the small sophomore girl playing Mrs. Bramson, had a huge ego and assumed her character was the play's central figure. She "upstaged" me in our scenes, moving her wheelchair to force me to face the back of the stage. I made minor adjustments in my position, assuming her moves were accidental, but she continued to do it even after Mrs. McD corrected her.

In our only public performance, Margaret, seeking to bedazzle the audience in scenes with me, forgot her lines. Suddenly she had that blank stare that appears as the lines of dialogue disappear from an actor's conscious mind. Since I knew all the lines of all the characters in my scenes, I rephrased Margaret's to try to help her back on track. When I came offstage, she was so "grateful" that she accused me of forgetting my own lines.

We performed *Night Must Fall* on Wednesday, December 16, before the Christmas break, so the *Chatter* didn't publish a review.

Despite the changes the war brought to almost every aspect of our lives, Jaycee celebrated traditions as usual. Students held the annual Stunt Night, originally conceived in 1930 by Mrs. Helen Hall, the journalism instructor, and this year's *Chatter* staff members Orville Henry, Douglas Wells, and Anne Wright arranged the concessions, stunts, and door prizes. Clubs, honorary and otherwise, prepared stunts and sponsored booths along the shallow platform around the auditorium. Concessionaires sold hot tamales, hot dogs, Cokes, popcorn, cotton candy, candied apples, and layer cakes and sponsored games like nail driving and fishing.

Weeks before Stunt Night, individuals and organizations began competing to collect the most items from merchants to give away between stunts as door prizes to audience members holding ticket stubs with lucky numbers. Friday night, December 4, the concessions of the thirteenth annual Stunt Night opened at 7:00 p.m., with stunts to begin at 8:00 p.m. Alan Jackson of Phi Alpha Beta won the gift from Stifft's Jewelry Store for gathering the most prizes as an individual, but Delta Kappa collected the organizational award. Pretty girls, including Tumpy, helped deliver the prizes to winners in the audience.

Rather than perform a stunt, Battlecriers contributed a war bond to the Student Loan Fund, and three members—Louise Floyd, Sarah Louise Steed, and Betty Jean Schmuck—sang "Dancing in the Dark" and "Whispering," and led a community sing; and Alva Love Chauvin performed a cancan dance.

For La Sociedad Espanola, I wrote and directed "A Night at El Beano Cafe," and played a drunken bandit, "the souse of the border," holding guests and employees prisoner while serenading them. Dick Adamson, formerly in the tenor section of the A Cappella Choir, impersonated the Latin American singer Carmen Miranda, wearing a headdress piled high with real fruit he distributed to audience members at the cafe tables. Helen Ann Worthington pretended to be Señora Hemans as a tourist, and Alice Cooke, in Spanish shawl and mantilla, and Douglas Wells, in tight black slacks, multi-colored vest, and oversized sombrero, danced a slapstick Spanish dance. As the bold, bad, mustachioed bandit, I held the cafe customers at bay while they performed, then sang to the tune of "South of the Border":

> *Souse of the border*
> *At El Beano Cafe,*
> *Is where I drank the drink*
> *That makes me walk this way.*
> *And now as I wander*
> *And continue to sway*
> *I'm the souse of the border*
> *From El Beano Cafe.*

The Battlecriers, trying to pledge her, invited Tumpy to their fall prom. Of course, I was her escort to what was my first formal dinner-dance, and had to buy my first business suit. I planned to shop at Baumans Men's Store on Main, where Jack White, Buster's old schoolmate at East Side, was a salesman. I trusted him to help me choose the right suit. When told where I was headed, Mama insisted on going with me, which would embarrass me, even though she knew Jack. She reminded me that she and Daddy were paying for a garment considerably more expensive than my usual outfits, but agreed to let Jack and me choose before going to the store to approve it.

At the store, I recognized Jack even though I hadn't seen him in years. In height and physique, he was a blond version of Buster, about five eight and muscular, dressed in a beautifully fitted three-piece suit, dress shirt with French cuffs, and brilliantly shined shoes. I wanted him to help me find an outfit that looked as good on me. Mama approved the medium blue, hard-finish wool, three-piece suit Jack recommended and I chose. She bought a white shirt and beautiful tie for me to wear with it. I also bought black socks and oxfords at Kenny's Shoe Store from the father of my classmate Bill Hollopeter.

A second first for this big occasion required me to choose a corsage for Tumpy to wear with her black lace evening dress. The day before the dance, I went to Vestal Florists, between the YMCA and Old King Cole's drive-in on Broadway, and chose the flowers. The lady asked and I described what Tumpy was wearing. She went to the refrigerated display case and brought out a bouquet of roses with small, deep yellow (almost golden) petals with pink edges, just right for Tumpy's black dress and her own coloration. Satisfied with my choice, I had it delivered.

Boykin and his busty, blonde-headed date, Shir Lee Henderson (hubba-hubba!), picked me up in his dad's pale green four-door Willys Overland sedan and drove us to 220 Crystal in the Heights for Tumpy. Even though I had passed the Lafayette Hotel, at Sixth and Louisiana, a hundred times, I had never been inside. The banquet was on the mezzanine level above the lobby, where they served the usual hotel dinner of green salad, Chicken a la King, and Parker House rolls.

Alan Jackson, president of the freshman class, welcomed everyone, and Warren Scott, president of the sophomore class, who possessed the kinkiest blond hair I ever saw, responded. Miss Elizabeth Hardin, a Jaycee speech teacher, who was scheduled to present a gossip column about students and faculty under the title "Conversations," asked Helen Ann Worthington and me to replace her. We tried to be clever and funny relating the latest tales we had heard about various couples or single guys wanting to be part of a couple. Louise Floyd and Betty Jean Schmuck sang, and Mr. Russell T. Scobee, superintendent of schools, spoke on "Here and Now."

Boykin drove us to the dance in the gym on campus, and the boys exchanged dance cards, filling the empty spaces for ten of the dance numbers before the intermission and ten after, and the four specials for Battlecriers, Phi Alpha Beta, and Delta Kappa. Tommy Scott and his band were on stage playing after the male partners had filled their date's cards with the names of other guys for specific dance numbers. Usually a guy danced the first number, the specials, and final dance with his date. On my program, I danced the first, the thirteenth, two specials (Battlecriers and Delta Kappa), and the twentieth with Tumpy.

During the Christmas break, Boykin and my other frat friends finally persuaded me to pledge Delta Kappa, a logical decision since Tumpy and

I attended all their social events and all my closest friends were members. But my natural tendency to be a loner in social and other matters had been an obstacle, because I didn't want any group or individual to tell me what to do with my time or to have to spend my allowance on assessments for activities that didn't appeal to me.

Tumpy had felt very much the same way before joining the Battlecriers.

Though I palled around with girls, I really hadn't ever pursued one until I fell in love with Tumpy. Now that we were seeing each other constantly, she told of persuading her parents to let her go to Jaycee rather than the University of Arkansas, where her sister Kathleen was studying in the School of Business. She didn't add that she had wanted to spend her freshman year with me. I shared the same devotion to her, and now the expectation of any separation from her was painful.

The moment you find you love someone is like the moment of knowing you will never see that person again; it alters everything—not just everything that comes after, but everything that's gone before. I approved Tumpy's affectionate nature that did not smother me with gush, and her restraint, reserve, and instinct for privacy that matched my own. A good deal of her quiet personal charm was revealed in the graceful way her shoulders and neck carried her beautiful head.

Christmas vacation introduced me to all members of the Gammill family. Even though Tumpy and I dated more and more frequently after *Lady of Letters* at sock hops, Stunt Night, movies, tennis, biking, and walks, I rarely went beyond her front door when I picked her up. But as Christmas vacation approached, I began tossing my porkpie hat at the hall tree inside the front door and visiting her in the living room. When I brought her home, we stood close to each other outside the front door reluctant to stop kissing and say goodbye until Mrs. Gammill, on the other side of the door, cleared her throat warning me to clear off.

During Christmas break, Tumpy's sister Kathleen, who had graduated from Stephens College in Columbia, Missouri, as a Four-Fold girl, representing the ideal of Honesty among the senior women, came home. She was home from the University of Arkansas in Fayetteville, where she was majoring in business administration on the Hill.

One evening, Tumpy and I double-dated with her sister and red-headed Sloan Finley, a would-be crooner and local radio announcer. Kathleen first met Sloan when her home-room sponsor, Mrs. Sewell, took seniors to Paragould, Arkansas. Smitten with Kathleen, he came to Little Rock at

Christmastime bearing an engagement ring to ask the tall, slim, vivacious Kathleen to marry him. I understood why she enchanted him, but only his curly red hair and persistence distinguished him, and her interest in him was casual.

Sloan drove us downtown in his car, talking uninterruptedly, to see a movie and afterward to the Blue Goose Drive-in for barbecue sandwiches and drinks. Tumpy and I felt very grown up doubling with the older couple, and we ended our date smoking cigarettes, a habit I hadn't developed, even though my father and brother had smoked for as long as I could remember.

After driving back to the Gammills' home, Sloan and Kathleen went to another room to talk privately, and he accidentally left his cigarettes on a table in the sun parlor. When Tumpy found his pack, we dared each other to smoke a cigarette. Doing my best impression of Paul Henreid in *Now, Voyager*, I tamped the pack against my hand, withdrew and placed two cigarettes between my lips, lit them simultaneously, and extended one to Tumpy. Shortly after, my grown-up feelings began fading like smoke rings in a drafty room; I felt dizzy and slightly sick at my stomach from inhaling. But Tumpy, trooper that she was, was not affected by the nicotine and showed compassion by driving me, disgraced and limp as a rag, to my home in her Studebaker with all the windows down, hoping fresh air would prevent my throwing up. Luckily, it did.

Mama was distraught about my smoking, but Daddy was amused when I went to bed to recover. The irony of my reaction to the cigarette is that Kathleen told Tumpy that my dark hair and appearance with hat, overcoat, and white scarf at my neck reminded her of a mobster.

During the Christmas break, I also met Tumpy's father, Major Lee C. Gammill, chief of hospitalization for the Army Air Force. When I headed home to Spring Street, Tumpy walked with me from Jaycee to Gus Blass Department Store to buy presents for her family. On the way, she talked about her father, who was a chief pharmacist's mate in the regular navy before and during World War I, and had become the superintendent of the Arkansas Baptist Hospital after the war, remaining there until the army reserve called him back into service in World War II. Major Gammill, back in Little Rock on leave, joined Tumpy at Blass's Fourth Street exit. Meeting Major Gammill, I was, to say the least, intimidated, although it wasn't his fault but mine; he was an imposing figure who had a no-nonsense attitude in his face and stance. But he treated me as I imagined fathers would with any young man dating their daughters. He might have been less cordial had he known Tumpy and I were in love and already committed to each other.

I wanted to buy Tumpy a really expensive Christmas present but lacked money and ideas. I didn't want to give her a book, perfume, or box of handkerchiefs, which were so ordinary. So I asked Mama to suggest an appropriate gift within my price range, and she took me to Kempner's, where she so often shopped. We looked at simple, inexpensive costume jewelry, but decided a beautiful cosmetic kit by Charles of the Ritz would allow her to choose her own color of powder, eye shadow, and lipstick.

I decided, after reading lyric poetry in English class, to add the poem in Cavalier style I had written and dedicated to her:

If thou were but a fragile rose
I from a thorny bush had chose,
I'd press your petal lips to mine
And taste their nectar, sweet, sublime.

If thou were but a weeping willow
Whose limp limbs sway in the wind's billow,
I'd bury my face in thy leafy hair
And breathe thy dewy freshness there.

Ah, but where's the need for fairy dreams
Which clearly cannot be,
When all of Nature's gentle schemes
Are satisfied in thee.

The war in Europe and the Pacific, though abstract for us in the States, was fully imagined by me listening to the radio and reading the newspapers. I sympathized with real soldiers caught in the violence of real events we saw in newsreels rather than war movies, like Wake Island or Bataan, starring "heroic" warrior actors like Brian Donlevy and Robert Taylor. After my classmate, cherub-faced R. J. Prickett, died, the prospect of my dying in combat seemed more likely. R. J. left Jaycee and joined the Merchant Marines at the end of the fall term, only to die when the ship on which he served as a junior officer was torpedoed in the Atlantic. Then, within weeks of R. J.'s death, the word *mortality* was even more clearly defined for me when another classmate, tall, raw-boned George Calder, was missing after the aircraft carrier he served on sank in the Pacific.

The prospect of my own death and the deaths of friends my age, whose lives were yet unfulfilled, was painful. I realized how protected and insensitive to the suffering and passing of others of any age I had been. When I heard about the deaths of older relatives, many of whom I had never met or seldom saw, I felt no direct emotional ties. But when boys I palled around with were killed, I felt the deepest compassion for them and their families and friends. I could only hope my vicarious suffering and fear of the worst would be an advantage, mentally and emotionally, when I was finally drafted. In the meantime, I attempted Scarlett O'Hara's procrastination: "I'll think about that tomorrow."

After Battlecriers and Delta Kappa wooed us so warmly and persistently throughout the fall semester, Tumpy and I had succumbed during the holiday break and become pledges. I'm not sure what Tumpy wore as an identifying symbol as a pledge, but Delta Kappa required us to wear beanies, little skull caps of alternating red and yellow triangles with tiny bills. I didn't mind wearing what I called "a gentile yarmulke," though I felt childish with it on my head and wearied of keeping track of it after removing it in classes.

The Delta Kappa initiation ceremony was more juvenile, though, than the pledge beanies. The ceremony took place late at night in someone's home, maybe Harvey Walthall's on the east side of town. Harvey's father owned the liquor store at the bottom of the hill the Hilltop nightclub stood on, and his mother often spent evenings with his father at the store, so they wouldn't have interrupted the initiation ceremony.

Harvey's house, like those darkened on Halloween to scare little kids, had few lights on, so the members performed their silly initiation pranks in dim lights and shadows. Behind the pledge master's commands, records were playing weird, frightening background music as he threatened us pledges in a harsh voice, warning us to submit without protest to the silly tortures and insipid questions we underwent. His assistants challenged us to commit infantile acts and drink nauseating, nasty substances, dripping it on our faces and hands. Since the liquids were administered in the dark, we had no idea what was dripping off our faces or sliding down our throats. Thank goodness we weren't asked to chew tobacco or push anything along the sidewalk with our noses. Two more susceptible pledges became nauseated and doused initiation team members with real vomit. Thus I became a member of Delta Kappa fraternity.

The "busyness" of my social life and theatrical responsibilities diverted me from my courses in the fall, and I was lackadaisical about tending assignments while deep down increasingly anxious about my draft board status.

Still, I was on the dean's scholarship honor roll again and wrote a letter thanking the sponsors of the Lamar Porter Scholarship for their financial support. Then, without wholly believing it, I warned them of the possibility of my being drafted and not completing the second year of their award.

In the spring semester of 1943, I took the second half of the same academic subjects: commerce (typing), English, zoology, and Spanish. Mrs. Gladys Kunz Brown, my new English teacher, vividly contrasted with Miss Yarnell in physique and pedagogy. Mrs. Brown, a tall, angular woman with prominent hip bones, walked in a slow, rolling gait, much like a sailor on a ship's deck at sea. Middle-aged, she had naturally brown skin, thick brown hair, and large eyes, nose, and mouth, and almost always had either a smile or bemused expression on her face.

In the study of literature, Mrs. Brown tailored our outside reading to our special individual needs and wishes. The only novel we read in common, Thomas Hardy's *The Return of the Native*, was extremely long and taxing to read—each of the six books composing the novel had multiple chapters, and the book was over four hundred pages long. Mrs. Brown, attempting to inspire in us a fascination that matched hers, dwelled upon Hardy's long descriptions of Egdon Heath and the annual ritual of fire building. I read a synopsis of *Return* in the equivalent of Cliffs Notes a friend had and pretended to have read the book on Mrs. Brown's essay exam; I knew a lot about the book but nothing of the book's text.

Of all her literary assignments, my favorites were poems in *Chief Modern Poets of England and America*, especially the works of British poets Alfred Noyes, James Stephens, Siegfried Sassoon, and John Masefield; and Americans Vachel Lindsay, Carl Sandburg, Robert Frost, and Kenneth Fearing, all of which lent themselves to dramatic oral readings.

In the composition portion of her course, she introduced S. I. Hayakawa's *Language in Action*, a basic study of semantics—a completely eye-opening approach to language for me. One of Mrs. Brown's writing assignments challenged us to compose an essay about "What makes a dog a dog?" introducing the difficulties of precise linguistic definition at even the simplest level.

There were no euphemisms in the draft board's notification of my first physical examination for the armed services that arrived in the mail on January 19, 1943. Three days later, on January 22 at 7:30 p.m., I reported to the Arkansas Medical School Clinic in City Park for a preliminary exam that would check me for "only obvious physical defects," with an assurance that the exam would not determine acceptance or rejection by the armed forces. The doctor's quick, perfunctory exam of my body could only confirm I was alive and kicking, with all the proper moving parts.

Though only a token exam, it frightened Mama into assuming they would take me immediately. Trying to forestall that possibility, she phoned her first cousin, H. T. "Will" Terry, chairman of Local Draft Board B, and asked for a delay. He assured her that I, like all registrants of my age and classification, would not be called for a full examination until the spring term ended. I considered that a proper and fair response. Why should I be excluded from the draft?

Alert to the military news, like a birddog to quail, I read a War Department notice on the bulletin board outside the dean's office in February about an army-navy pre-induction qualifying examination for 17- and 18-year-old male students at the high school in March. I didn't consider the exam seriously until my good friends and classmates, Boykin Pyles and Herbie Cunningham, decided to take the test and persuaded me to join them. Since the exam concentrated on sciences and math, I was afraid I wouldn't do well. And, indeed, my lack of scientific information and mathematical skill and the narrow time limits on sections of the test left me struggling through several parts. I completed the exam questions convinced that I had failed.

On campus, Mrs. McD produced two more plays in the spring semester, the one-act *The Flattering Word* by George Kelly, and the three-act *Time for Romance* by Alice Gerstenberg, with an all-woman cast.

To complete the season, members of Delta Psi Omega produced *George and Margaret*, by Gerald Savory, so that Blaine Nicholson, who had already received his draft call, would have one more chance to perform before reporting for active duty. We increased the number of rehearsals and presented the play sooner.

The life of a suburban family is disrupted when they learn that two old friends, George and Margaret, are coming to visit, and everyone is thrown into a tizzy, struggling to prepare. One of three brothers in the family chooses that inopportune moment to announce his plans to marry the household's maid. Then the cook organizes a kitchen strike. But things finally settle down, and the household is ready to entertain the esteemed guests—but they never show up. Tumpy's role as Gladys, the maid, was very small, but mine as Malcolm was very large. The only thing that mattered to us, though, was being together at rehearsals.

As the character Malcolm, I had a chance to develop my standard British accent since the family was upper-middle-class English. Since Malcolm was a middle-aged man, I had a chance to use suits and shoes from my father's wardrobe, which helped me develop the character, although my dad certainly wasn't addlepated and forgetful like the father in the play. Showing a man of middle age without resorting to the usual amateur vocal and physical clichés was a real challenge.

The play was set in the center of the auditorium with the audience seated around the stage in "penthouse style," a first at Jaycee. The name had been adopted from the Penthouse Players at the University of Washington. Performing "in-the-round" introduced us to an exciting new approach for the cast and audience. The style demanded that the director find ways to open the action up and balance the action so that all sides of the arena audience could see the performers. The actors had to find ways to relate to other actors while maintaining concentration despite being surrounded by the audience, and the audience had to remain focused on the action of the play rather than other audience members.

We performed on Thursday, March 4, 1943, and Blaine Nicholson reported for army duty the following Monday. The *Chatter* reviewer observed:

> GEORGE AND MARGARET ... was a decided hit. It was
> a good weekend for dramatic enthusiasts. It is reviewed
> elsewhere in the Chatter, by Eugene Bowden, but another
> column of praise is not too much. The play was a good
> one and the Delta Psi Omega did it complete justice. That
> is rather a sweeping statements [sic], but it is deserved,
> especially in view of the fact that the play was given ahead
> of schedule and the penthouse arrangement is probably
> a new one to the JAYCEERS.

My last Jaycee theater effort, on Friday evening, April 16, 1943, included three one-act plays and the Witches' scene from *Macbeth*.

The *Chatter* reported:

> Climaxing the evening's entertainment was the act one
> witches scene from Macbeth, by William Shakespeare,
> which was enthusiastically applauded. The weird dance
> and mysterious incantations of the black robed witches

around the steaming pot created a dramatic effect …
heightened by the subtle lighting, lightning flashes,
and mood music. Cleveland Harrison directed this
artistically executed sequence, and turned in his usual
fine performance as Macbeth.

The plays performed on Friday evenings began between 8:00 and 8:15 p.m. with no admission charge. Mrs. McDermott permitted no curtain calls: "I'm just childish enough to want my dead men to remain dead, my hurt victims to remain hurt, and my unconscious men to stay 'out cold.'" Silly attitude, for make-believe.

After my Delta Kappa initiation and pre-induction test, I tried to put the military service out of my mind by involving myself in the fraternity's social activities as chairman of the decorating committee and in the Delta Kappa Quartet. Our quartet first appeared at dances and club meetings, and then we received invitations to sing at more events, like the Battlecriers spring dance, the May Queen Festival, and the Donaghey Founders Day celebration. So we scheduled frequent rehearsals, keeping Earl Nichols (baritone), Harvey Walthall (bass), Boykin Pyles (second tenor), and me (first tenor) together most of the time.

My Delta Kappa brothers were extremely fond of Tumpy. To honor her and our relationship, she was elected "Sweetheart of Delta Kappa" and presented a dozen American Beauty roses at the next dance sponsored by the Battlecriers. I wrote new words to the melody of the fraternity's song, "Sweetheart of Delta Kappa":

Deep in my memory's a girl,
A sweetheart dear,
Friend of old Delta Kappa for always.
As the years all unfurl
I see pictured clear—
Sweetest lady of old college days.
Friendships and sweet sentimental sweethearts, I see,
Arbors of memories that flower for me,
But the sweetest of all, as I always recall,
Is the sweetheart of dear Delta Kappa.

In the first week of the merry month that followed, the May Queen and her maids ruled the May Day Festival in the open area among the trees at the front of the campus. The festival followed the pattern of a traditional English "Maying," usually held in June in Britain because of the good weather. In the weeks preceding Jaycee's celebration, students chose popular Mary Trieschmann as May Queen and her sophomore maids, Betty Lou Pipkin and Sarah Louise Steed, and freshmen maids, Betty Jean Schmuck and Billie Louise Wilson.

On the festival day, a procession of girls bearing an ivy chain, intertwined with fresh flowers, formed parallel lines with the garlands for the queen and her maids to walk between on the way to her throne. Once crowned with a garland of flowers, she pronounced the law for the day, sitting on a throne with her court beside her on the college's front porch. From the side of the building, a bevy of girls in pastel dresses entered to perform a Maypole dance. The pole, standing in the middle of the lawn, had colored ribbons attached at the top, dangling down the sides. The dancers, forming a circle around the pole, each took hold of the loose end of a ribbon, circling and weaving the ribbons in a multi-colored braid covering the surface of the pole. Then the dancers in reverse direction unwound the ribbons from around the pole. And that was the dance!

Following the Maypole dance, the all-male cast of *Saint George and the Dragon*, the ancient mummers play directed by Miss Elizabeth Harden, appeared from every direction and rambled into the playing area like the cast of the play *Pyramus and Thisbe* in *A Midsummer Night's Dream*. The play was not really about St. George slaying the dragon but focused on the farcical operation Old Doctor Ball (Bob Halley) performed with a saw, hammer, and pliers to extract the dragon's innards seeking to cure him. Operating on the patient's stomach, the Old Doctor removed shoes, ties, fruits, and a long string of sausages. The operation was performed in the presence of King Alfred (John Hodges) and his Queen (Grover Hughes). I played the effeminate Prince William reciting doggerel poems, and Boykin was Merry Andrew, a twittering imbecile. The actors had a ball regardless of what the audience around us felt about the silliness.

Soon after, we celebrated the annual Donaghey Day, honoring the late Governor George W. Donaghey and his wife, who contributed the Donaghey and Wallace Buildings on Main Street as financial support for the college. Mrs. Donaghey was present for the special assembly on campus. Jean Jones, president of the student council, welcomed Mrs. Donaghey, and Tumpy, representing the freshman class, presented a bouquet of roses to her on behalf of the college. Then followed a music and speech program directed by Mr. Adams and Mrs. McDermott.

Another big social event was the Sophomore Prom sponsored by the faculty on May 19, with the graduating class as guests of the college. The Jaycee custom was for freshman girls to buy their own tickets to the prom and the formal dinner at the Hotel Frederica. A program dance followed with Harris Owens and his orchestra at the Jaycee gym from nine to midnight. Tumpy and I were there in our best bib and tuck, dancing the night away.

In the middle of May, I found a War Department letter in our mailbox and put off opening it, fearing failure on the army-navy test taken in February. Curiosity got the better of me, though; as it turned out, I passed the army-navy exam but now had to choose either the army or navy college program. I picked the Army Specialized Training Program (ASTP V-12) rather than the navy because I couldn't swim. If I had based my decision on the uniform, the navy would have won hands down. While I waited for some signal from ASTP or the draft board, my pals Boykin and Herbie received orders from the navy to report to the University of Oklahoma at Norman at the end of the spring term.

As the college year neared its end, I joined other theater students in a minor contribution to the war effort in a radio play written by Dick Upton, *Hints for Hitler.* We presented the play over Radio Station KGHI on the YMCA's regular weekly program with a cast of Tumpy and me, Bob Halley, John Larson, Billie Louise Wilson, and John Hodges.

Finally, the familiar greetings from the draft board arrived on July 5, ordering me to report two weeks later, on July 21, at the front of the Boyle Building. Our group of potential inductees gathered there as ordered, and the sergeant in charge led us up Capitol Avenue to Broadway and turned left, taking us three blocks more to a building at Eighth and Broadway, a former automobile dealership where we would spend the better part of the day naked, parading under the examining eyes and hands of a procession of bored physicians who pounded, poked, and pummeled each of us. I was judged to be underweight with low blood pressure but classified A-1.

We put our clothes back on and waited several hours until an officer came into the room, demanded our attention, ordered us on our feet, and administered the army's oath of allegiance. He announced that we were in the inactive reserve until we reported for duty at the front of the Boyle

Building on the morning of August 11, 1943. I wondered how we would ever find our way into the army if the Boyle Building wasn't there.

To encourage our compliance, he said, "You're in the army now!" and cited Articles of War number fifty-eight (desertion) and sixty-one (absent without leave).

Without summer school or a job, and no family or employee obligations, my main task was advertising to sell my balloon-tired, chrome-fender Western Flyer bicycle that I had tended since junior high school. A young boy came the day the ad appeared in the *Gazette* and paid the same price for the bike that my folks had at the Western Auto Store five years before.

I visited my old haunts, saying farewell to my few as-yet-undrafted buddies who kidded me that ASTP stood for "All Set To Party," saw Tumpy every day I could, and reassured my tearful little Mama, who spoke as if her two boys were as good as dead already, as if she would soon replace the silver stars on the white silken banner in the front living room window, signifying loved ones in uniform, with gold ones for two who gave their lives.

Unlike older married men sworn into the army at the same time I was, I had neither family nor work obligations to fulfill. But I did share a regret similar to the one they must have felt leaving their wives. I realized more fully that, as much as I loved my parents, the most wrenching separation was leaving Tumpy. With our secret plan to marry when and if I returned, we remained arm in arm as much as possible until the fateful day.

The week before I reported for active duty at Camp Robinson, Tumpy and I picked up our Trojan yearbooks in the college gymnasium at the biggest Jaycee social event of the summer. Gathered in the hot gym, without fans or air conditioning, we all drank cold Cokes pulled from washtubs full of ice, and signed each other's yearbooks with conventional clichés—sweet, sentimental, or mocking. Many boys who were my classmates were already in some branch of the armed forces and were there saying farewell like me. But our conversations and yearbook inscriptions seldom referred to those who were already gone or about to go. Our teachers, older and more experienced, seemed to understand the significance of goodbyes in wartime as they wished us good luck in the service.

Though unremarked, a palpable sadness, a counterpoint to Glenn Miller's music in the background, touched all of us in the gym. For as we traded yearbooks and inscribed remarks, I realized the melancholy contrast between our laughter and playful gestures and the poignancy of girls and boys leaving each other for another college or military service. Parting from safe havens of home, college, and loved ones made my throat ache much as it did when I ate ice cream too quickly as a kid.

I felt emotions signing yearbooks I never had before and had no words to describe them if I tried. Too young and naive growing up in the midst of the Depression, I never felt fears and threats of physical or economic harm, since my parents protected me from hardships as best they could. Until this fateful summer at the end of my freshman college year, I never said goodbye to someone without knowing where they or I were going, but always with the secure feeling we would meet again.

The three weeks of inactive reserve had slipped by far too quickly. On the sweltering morning of August 11, I kissed my parents goodbye on the front porch and walked out the lopsided gate at 322 Spring Street, where we had lived since 1935. Looking back from a block away at the corner of Fourth and Center Street, I saw my tearful Mama and stoical Daddy watching and waving. I walked away more quickly daring not to turn again to wave, fearing I would cry.

After passing Harley-Davidson's motorcycles across from Rebsamen Ford's garage for second-hand cars, I turned at the corner of Louisiana where the Kansas City Steak House, Union National Bank, and Arkansas Power and Light sat cattycornered from each other, and hastened to Capitol Avenue, where I skipped past Franke's Cafeteria and crossed the alley to the Boyle Building. Merely three and a half blocks from home, I was already an incalculable distance from my family, Tumpy, and civilian life.

Standing beside the alley with the other draftees were Clyde Brockett, Bill Sims, Tommy Snodgrass, and Newton Shuffield, four familiar faces from high school and Junior College, along with thirty-two strangers. I counted them all! The fellows I knew exchanged quiet hellos and waited, conversing in the soft morning sunlight.

In the midst of the roaring traffic, an old olive-drab army bus lumbered up, and the bus door struggled opened. A sergeant leaped off, and, after answering his roll call, we all boarded the bus, and I took a seat by a window. The old bus, starting reluctantly, chugged onto Main Street and turned north.

Moving slowly up Main, the bus passed the National Shirt Shop, the empty Exchange Bank Building, Kempner's, Haverty's, the Royal Theater, Kress Five and Ten Cent Store, Blass Department Store, Hegarty Drugs, Food Palace, Baumans Men's Store, Triangle Cafe, Allsopp & Chapple,

Steins, Kenny's Shoe Store, the Roxy Theater, Western Union, People's Bank, the New Theater, and Snodgrass and Bracy's Drugstore—all part of my growing up in Little Rock.

The bus stopped for the traffic signal at the Markham Street intersection, waiting for the light to turn green. I gazed out the window at the Ben McGehee Hotel, on the northwest corner beside the Main Street Bridge, and its tall, dark, thin silhouette became in my mind the exclamation mark punctuating my FAREWELL!

As the light changed and the bus mounted the bridge and crossed the Arkansas River bound for Camp Robinson, I hummed and sang, under my breath, a stanza from the ancient Baptist hymn, "Blest Be the Tie that Binds":

When we asunder part,
It gives us inward pain;
But we shall still be joined in heart,
And hope to meet again.

Afterword

EDUCATIONAL THEATER was my life's work. For forty-five years, I studied and taught English, speech, and theater arts at colleges and universities in Ohio, Arkansas, Kansas, and Alabama—lecturing, acting, directing, administering, and writing. When I retired as Professor Emeritus of Theatre in 1991, after twenty-one years as head professor at Auburn University, the Alabama Conference of Theater and Speech gave me the Theater Hall of Fame Award "for distinguished contributions and enduring dedication as a past pioneer in Alabama Theater."

Yet, in this memoir, I chose to recall my Depression-era childhood rather than my professional career, searching for an answer to how an ordinary boy, in a small-town family far from America's artistic centers, could become obsessed with the theater arts.

My conclusion: I was born a player, since I invented substitute worlds, imagined other versions of reality, and fabricated personalities other than my own from earliest childhood. I created theater without a stage or script, made up stories and imitated other persons—the preliminaries to an adult calling. My father and mother silently tolerated my theatrical ambitions, so I owe my career to them; for if we invent ourselves through the eyes of others, the nonjudgmental eyes of my parents were my good fortune. Furthermore, my happy childhood, youth, and career prove that one need not suffer physical or mental abuse in personal life to develop a creative spirit and achieve success in the arts, as many memoirists' lives suggest.

Photos

1 *Cleveland and his mother.*

2 *Cleveland's father and their dog, Kate.*

3 *Marian (Tumpy) Gammill.*

4 *Cleveland's ID for summer job at the U.S. Engineers' Office.*

5 *Big Daddy and Grandma Harrison.*

6 *Tumpy Gammill as she was when Cleveland left for the army.*

7 *Heinie Loesch's nieces, Cleveland, and Jim MacFarlane.*

8 *Buster in Warren.*

9 *Cleveland in front of Little Rock Junior College.*

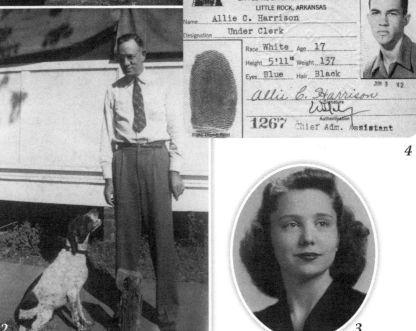

Index

D

Dad's Oatmeal Cookies, 124
Daniels, Vivian, 315
David, Leland, 26
Davis, Aubrey, 83
Davis, Governor Jeff, 28
Dawson's Drugstore, 115
Dean, Dizzy, 85, 190
Delta Kappa, 338, 346, 357, 361
Delta Sigma, 293
Denver, Colorado, 95, 98, 102-4
Denver Museum of Natural History, 102
Deroux, Evelyn, 58
Detroit Electric Car, 177
Dollarway highway, 53
Donaghey Building, 28, 108
Donaghey Day, 362-63
Donaghey, Governor George W., 146

E

East Side Journal, 105
East Side Junior High, 18
Elliott, Clayton, 245
Elliott family, 90-91, 106-7

F

Federal Theater Project, 218
Ferguson, Maynard, 184-85
Flood of 1927, 19-20
Flowers family, 122, 138-41
Food Palace, 252, 292
Fort Smith, Arkansas, 96
Franke's Cafeteria, 30
Franklin, Benjamin, 214
French, W. Clarence, 270, 310
Fryer, Ada Bess, 223-24
Fulmer, Dr. Silas, 110, 147
Furniture Row, 87
Fussell, Reba, 26

G

Galloway College for Girls, 42, 172
Gammill family, 354-55
Gammill, Marian "Tumpy," 300, 330, 345
Garland, Augustus Hill, house, 90
Geis, Clarence, 299
Glasgow's Confectionary, 60
Goff, Norris, 74
Goforth, Mary, 210, 233-34

Gold, Ernest J., 342-43
Gone with the Wind, 292
Goode, William, 159, 190-91
Green, Alma, 32-33, 68, 192
Griffey, Annie G., 169
Griffin, Lois, 242-44
Griffithville, Arkansas, 71
Guggenheim Fund, 29

H

Hall, James Norman, 244
Hall, R. C., 210
Halley, Bob, 177-79, 250-51, 362-63
Harrington, Janette, 296
Harris, Alberta, 314, 329
Harrison, James David, 137, 257-62
Hart, Joe, 243, 270, 278, 304-5
Hart, William S., 111
Hazen, Arkansas, 66, 99
Hegarty's Drugstore, 109, 148
Hemans, Señora, 341-42
Hemphill, Mrs. John, 58
Hendon, Russell and Liz, 62-65, 84-85
Henry, Orville, 317-18, 351
Hermitage Highway, Warren, 50, 54
Herring, Homer and Maymie, 71
Hill, Essie, 297
Hilltop Night Club, 346, 357
Hogue, Harris, 267
Holland, Claude, 222, 232
Honea family:
    Albert LaFayette, 66
    Benjamin Franklin, 14, 66
    Charles, 66, 257, 318
    Elizabeth McCuin, 66
    Floy Estelle, 66
    Naomi Abington, 257
    Ralph and David, 256-57
    Walker and Oma, 112
    Willie Cleveland, 35, 66
Honea Mercantile Company, 32, 66, 159
Hooper, Sanford, 146
Hoover, Herbert, 39, 82
Horn, LeRoy, 209-10, 222, 233
Hotel Marion, 24

I

Imperial Laundry, 94-95
Ish, Dr. Jefferson G., 91